ENGLISH MEN AND MANNERS IN THE EIGHTEENTH CENTURY

Queen Charlotte and her favourite Pug

Reproduced from 'The Wellesley Silhouettes' after the painting on glass by Walter Jorden

ENGLISH MEN AND MANNERS IN THE EIGHTEENTH CENTURY

An

Illustrated Narrative by

A. S. TURBERVILLE

A GALAXY BOOK

NEW YORK · OXFORD UNIVERSITY PRESS

TO MY

FATHER AND MOTHER

First published, 1926; second edition,
with revisions, corrections, and additions, 1929.

First published as a Galaxy Book, 1957
Third printing, 1964

PREFACE

I OWE to my former colleague Miss M. O. Davis the suggestion that I should write an introduction to the eighteenth century as it is reflected in the lives of some of the principal figures of the period, and although in execution the book has turned out to be larger than in prospect, the aim is still no more ambitious than to give a sketch of the age. The political narrative ends with the year 1783, as the administrations of the Younger Pitt and the Revolutionary and Napoleonic Wars belong to a different epoch.

If the present volume awakens sufficient interest to induce readers to make the acquaintance of some of the books suggested for further reading, it will have amply fulfilled its modest purpose. In a work of this nature the illustrations form an integral part of the design; they are as important as the letter-press. I wish to express my sense of deep indebtedness to Mr. John Johnson, Printer to the University, for the unremitting zeal of his collaboration in this essential part of the enterprise. I wish also to thank my Father and my friend Mr. Albert Charles of Friars' School, Bangor, for help in reading the proofs.

A. S. T.

PREFACE TO THE SECOND EDITION

I AM much indebted to reviewers and others who have made helpful criticisms and suggestions for the improvement of this book. A more detailed Bibliography at the end of the volume has been substituted for the original suggestions for Further Reading at the ends of the chapters. The chapter on the Artists has been recast so as to give more space to Architecture and Sculpture and to include Water-colour. Some minor alterations and a number of corrections have also been made.

A. S. T.

CONTENTS

LIST OF ILLUSTRATIONS

Paris Cher Morji's Frolaria

An eighteenth-century Coffee House

Douce Portfolio W., 1, 2, No. 203.

I

INTRODUCTORY

THE period of English History of which this book treats
is sometimes known as the Classical or Augustan Age. This
designation refers especially to the character of its literature, to
its adoption of classical models for its own style of expression ;
but it will bear a wider signification. An attempt will be made
in the following pages to look at this period from the biographical
point of view, by taking several outstanding groups of statesmen
and politicians and certain other characteristic types. But in
order to appreciate the representative character of these men
let us first of all consider what are the outstanding features of
the eighteenth century, and how far the general description of it
as Classical is warranted.

We must first note that every age in developing its own distinctive genius is to a certain extent in reaction against its predecessor.
Such is the explanation of the literary school which dominates the
first part of the period—the school of Pope. Its work was
extraordinarily chaste in expression and highly polished ; it was

also notably devoid of enthusiasm. This was because it thoroughly disliked and disapproved of the florid, extravagant language and forced involved ideas and conceits which had marred some of that so-called late Elizabethan literature which is really Jacobean. The Classical school condemned that style as unnatural and in bad taste, and demanded greater restraint, correctness, and purity of diction. It made literature ' gentlemanly ', and it appealed to a small educated class composed of London society and of men of letters themselves, those Wits who frequented the Coffee Houses, which became so popular at the opening of the century, and which performed the function, nowadays exercised by the literary journal, of criticizing the current poetry, drama, and other writings of the day. Rather formal, rigid, and dogmatic were the canons of criticism thus laid down ; for, though found in greater critics such as Johnson, the modern conception of estimating a work of art with reference to the distinctive equipment, taste, and outlook of its own generation did not really win its way until the days of Coleridge and Hazlitt, which come after our period. Now, the inevitable consequence of literature's being addressed to an exclusive class, and being written in accordance with rather unbending ' classical ' rules of correctness was that, while this school of letters originated in a wish to get back to nature and simplicity, we nowadays are apt to find it distinctly unnatural and very far from simple, so that the epithet we most commonly apply to it is ' artificial '.

Matthew Arnold once declared that Dryden and Pope were classics, not of our poetry, but of our prose ; and unquestionably many people feel that even the poetry of the eighteenth century is rather prosaic. Its versification is brilliant and wonderfully finished, but in its matter we find more of wit than of fancy, of cleverness than of inspiration. Ecstasy would have been considered barbaric and the cult of Nature highly ' unnatural '. Not only the average eighteenth-century squire, but the average eighteenth-century poet had no enthusiasm for ' noble, wild prospects ' of mountain and torrent. The type of scenery which appealed to Gray, Goldsmith, and Cowper was quiet,

gentle, and pastoral. In Macpherson's *Ossian*, in the poetry of
Thomson there is the sign of the approach of the Romantic
Movement, which reached its culmination in Wordsworth, Keats,
and Shelley, and in Blake there is a mysticism as great as that of
Coleridge. That is to say, there is a quite clearly defined develop-
ment between 1700 and 1780 from the 'classical' to the 'romantic'.
But for the most part the former is much more in evidence.

Pope with his friend Sir Samuel Garth, the physician and occasional poet, in
Button's coffee house. From a drawing by Hogarth

For the most part also the period is richer in prose than in poetry.
It is, indeed, one of the greatest periods in English prose, including
as it does the names of Defoe, Swift, Steele, Addison, Fielding,
Johnson, Hume, Burke, Gibbon. Some of these writers may
seem stilted and pompous, but it must be a dull ear indeed that
cannot appreciate the grandeur of their diction, the majestic
rhythm of their periods. While the Queen Anne writers are as
a rule simpler and more homely in expression than their successors,
the general inspiration of our eighteenth-century prose was
Latin ; it abounds in Latin words and constructions.

If the writers derived their style from classical models, so also did the orators. Eighteenth-century oratory is as great as its prose literature. English eloquence reached its greatest height in the speeches of Chatham and Burke ; and on only a slightly lower plane were those of Bolingbroke, Hardwicke, Sheridan, Fox, and Erskine.

Sometimes, as in Bolingbroke and occasionally in Johnson, the sonorous language seems to garb thought which is somewhat threadbare ; but ordinarily manner and matter are in keeping ; power of expression is accompanied by force of argument. Here we have one of the finest characteristics of the century. It is a reasonable age. If it is lacking in enthusiasm, it is dispassionate. There were of course sects and ideas outside the limits of its toleration, as has been the case in every age ; but in comparison with any other, and very markedly indeed in comparison with the two preceding centuries, the eighteenth century was an eminently tolerant age. Englishmen were still suspicious of Roman Catholics—painful experience of the later Stuart *régime* had made them so—but even of them they were not actively oppressive, and the whole temper of the age in matters of religious belief was open-minded and conciliatory. The most powerful school in the Church of England was what is called latitudinarian, and its great members, like Burnet, Tillotson, Stillingfleet, Hoadly, Warburton, Conyers Middleton, invariably addressed themselves to reason, never to passion. Broad-mindedness was their common characteristic. Sometimes they were by no means orthodox themselves. There are instances of prosecutions of unorthodox writers for blasphemy, but the striking thing is the amount of sceptical writing on matters of faith, the prevalence of religious controversy, which is academic, not envenomed. A very undogmatic deism was popular, subscription to the large-hearted, comprehensive conception of Pope's Universal Prayer :

> Father of all, in every age,
>   In every clime adored,
> By Saint, by Savage, and by Sage,
>   Jehovah, Jove, or Lord.

At the Bear-Garden in Hockley in the Hole, near Clarken-well-Green.

THefe are to give Notice to all *Gentlemen* and *Game-fters*, that this prefent *Monday*, there will be a Match fought by Four Dogs, two of *Weftminfter* againft two of *Eaftcheap*, at the Bull, for a Guinea. Five Let goes out of Hand, faireft and fartheft in wins all.

And a *Mad Bull* let loofe to be baited, with fireworks all over him, and Dogs after him.

With other Variety of Bull Baiting and Bear Baiting: Being a general day of Sport by all the Old Gamefters.

Beginning at Three a Clock.

The Gentlemen are defired to come betimes, becaufe the Sport will be long.

Vivat Regina.

'*Brutal were its popular sports of bear-baiting, bull-baiting, and cock-fighting*'

Harl. 5946. No. 25

The religious life of the eighteenth century—particularly in the Church of England—has often been condemned as cold, listless, and barren. There is a good deal of truth in the charge. Religion that is unemotional is apt to be phlegmatic. But this is only a half-truth. The teaching of comprehensiveness and brotherly love among sects of differing doctrinal views is a great religious achievement. And the coldness and lifelessness that undoubtedly did exist in the Church of England produced its reaction—in the mysticism of William Law and the evangelicalism of the Wesleys and Whitefield. The eighteenth century contains both—Burnet and Law, Wake and John Wesley.

Another charge which is frequently brought against the eighteenth century is that it was extremely coarse in mind and manners. No one will deny the marked coarseness of the drama, usually known as Restoration drama, though some of its most notable productions, plays by Congreve, Vanbrugh, Farquhar, and Cibber, appeared after 1700. Coarseness is an obvious feature of the novel, whose development is one of the marked features of the literary history of the century, in the fictions of Defoe, Laurence Sterne, Fielding, Smollett. It is a coarseness of fibre as well as a mere coarseness of language ; but it is only right to add that the hard cynicism, so apparent in Restoration comedy, is not a characteristic of the period as a whole. Together with this literary phenomenon goes a certain brutality of manners, which from the pages of the novelist we should infer to have actually existed, and the reality of which is confirmed by the picture which we get in contemporary memoirs, not solely of the court circle. The escapades of the Mohocks and the dissolute Medmenham Brotherhood are the notorious extreme in the upper classes, while the lower classes too often allowed themselves to be made sodden and brutalized by the drinking of spirits, especially gin, which became so prevalent in the early decades of the century.

Brutal were the great prize-fights which were popular in the later years of the century, the classic period of the ' ring ', the public fencing-matches common under Anne and George I having fallen out of favour ; brutal were its popular sports of bear-baiting, bull-baiting, and cock-fighting; brutal were the punishments of its penal code, beyond those of other countries generally supposed to be much less progressive; and notoriously eighteenth-century England was distinguished by the violence of its criminal class. Smollett declared in reference to the year 1730, ' thieves and robbers were now become more desperate and savage than they had ever appeared since mankind were civilized '. There are no more famous criminals in our history than the highwaymen, Jonathan Wild,[1] Dick Turpin, Jack

---

The fame day, at noon, the Seffions ended at the Old Baily, when the 2 following perfons [*drew blanks, and*] received fentence of death, viz. John Turner, for breaking into the apartments of Mrs. Turner, who was an inmate of his father's, near Queenhithe, and ftealing from thence 1 guinea, 5 l. in filver, and feveral wearing apparel ; and Anne Palmer, alias Hinks, for ftealing 8 l. in money, and goods to the value of 38 s, the property of Mr. Sam. Ruffel. *C* Five were burnt in the hand, and 30 were caft for tranfportation *P* Seven were burnt in the hand, and about 20 ordered for tranfportation. *D P*. Eight were burnt in the hand. *C*.

Crime and its reward. An illustration of the severity of the penal code, on which see also Chapter X. From ' The Grub-street Journal' of 21 October 1731

Sheppard, and their maritime contemporaries, the pirates, England, Teach, and Roberts.

Let us remember the other side of the picture, without which an estimate of the period must be misleading—the crusade of Steele and Addison in the *Tatler* and *Spectator* to refine the public taste ; the popularity of Young's *Night Thoughts*, with its perhaps somewhat lachrymose and obvious moralizings, but certainly very excellent tendency ; the appeal of the somewhat similar not very deep morality of Dr. Johnson's *Rambler*, which is, however, stronger by reason of its sound manly sense and hatred of shams. If the earlier drama of the period was coarse, there

---

[1] Although he never himself went upon the road, Wild obtained such an influence among highwaymen as a receiver of their stolen goods that he has been termed the ' Director-General of the united forces of highwaymen, house-breakers, footpads, pickpockets, and private thieves '.

was a Jeremy Collier to denounce it, and a distinct new school to follow of a very different type—that of Goldsmith and Sheridan. The novels of Richardson, ponderous and wearisome as they may appear to us, made the most pious sentimentalism as popular as the grossest realism. Indeed, the devotees of *Clarissa Harlowe* were more numerous than those of *Tom Jones* and *Roderick Random*.

Again, against the violence of the law-breakers we place the current sense of the majesty of the law ; the fact of the extraordinary ascendancy exercised, not only over the judicature, but over the politics and general life of the time, by such great lawyers as Somers, Hardwicke, Camden, and Mansfield ; the immense influence and authority of Sir William Blackstone's *Commentaries*.

When we think of social evils let us remember also attempts at social amelioration—the social legislation of the Pelhams, and still more the work of individual humanitarians, the great outburst of philanthropic effort which was ushered in by the evangelical movement.

Yet again, when we are reminded of the coarse-grained insensibility of the eighteenth century, let us also bear in mind its considerable artistic achievement and artistic interests—the great popularity of Handel and the Italian opera ; the canvases of Hogarth, Reynolds, Gainsborough ; the acting of Betterton, Garrick, and Siddons and the revival of Shakespeare [1] ; the noble architecture of Wren and his successors, counterbalancing the ugly and ponderous sculpture of the period ; the simple beauty of domestic architecture and decoration, the names of Adam, Chippendale, and Sheraton. Let us remember also that this period, incontestably one of intellectual dormancy in the universities and of inattention to the needs of education till near its close when a revival began, was yet adorned by the names of Richard Bentley and other great classical scholars, such literary critics as Johnson, Steevens, and Malone on Shakespeare, and

---

[1] It has to be admitted that some of the manifestations of the reawakened interest in Shakespeare, such for example as the ' adaptations ' of Colley Cibber, were singularly atrocious.

Tyrwhitt, the founder of Chaucerian scholarship, and such antiquarian collectors as Hans Sloane and Thomas Hearne.

If we turn to the purely political record of the century, we may perhaps think first of all of the control exercised by the great landowners—especially the Whig families between 1714 and 1760 —and reflect that this was an oligarchical system, the predominance of a narrow caste. This system is associated with parliamentary corruption, the organized manipulation of a House of Commons' majority by means of places and pensions and other kinds of bribery. There is much in this that must offend modern democratic sentiment, much that appears sordid and debased. But let us at the same time remember that the great Whig oligarchs included men of very brilliant gifts and that their system was not unpopular ; also, that the methods of running a party machine, though less obvious and unblushing, are not essentially so different to-day as they may appear to be from those pursued by Sir Robert Walpole. Let us also remember that the campaign for parliamentary reform starts in this period with the proposals of Chatham and the Duke of Richmond and the propaganda of Wilkes, Horne Tooke, and Major Cartwright. Moreover, even in its unreformed state, the political system of Great Britain was greatly in advance of the systems of most continental countries. The Whigs were genuinely and very justly proud of the 'glorious Revolution' of 1688 and of the constitution. With all its manifold and glaring defects the party system was a popular system and a healthy one, and the great eulogy pronounced upon it by Burke was justified because it at least ensured popular government.[1] And the conception of the sacredness of individual rights and rights of property, the genuine enthusiasm for the idea of political liberty was fine and robust. The value of these great possessions—party government and personal freedom—was only made plainer to Englishmen by the dangerous attack made upon them by George III, while foreign observers like Montesquieu and Voltaire were lost in admiration of the English system.

There was sterling patriotism in the eighteenth century. There was to be sure something of the 'one Englishman equal

---

[1] In *Thoughts on the Cause of the Present Discontents.* See *infra*, pp. 276-7.

to three Frenchmen' spirit fostered by the great victories of
Marlborough ; but it was something more than mere boastful-
ness, it was sincere, and it was quite free of the fustian of much
of the imperialist jargon of a later epoch. The fortunes of war
during the period were chequered indeed, but the brilliant
achievements of the Seven Years' War under the masterful
inspiration of Pitt were legitimate cause for pride. In Wolfe
at all events a soldier of genius appeared, and if no Nelson or
Jervis was produced, yet in men like Anson, Hawke, and Boscawen the essential qualities of the fighter and the seaman were
manifest. Canada and India were added to the British Empire ;
Clive and Warren Hastings, progenitors of many great proconsuls, laboured to establish ideas of English civilization and
English government among natives. The obviously outstanding
fact of the colonial history of the eighteenth century is of course
the disastrous American War and the loss of the thirteen colonies ;
but even here good was to come out of evil, and we were to
learn by our tragic experience what are the true principles of
colonial government, the true foundations of lasting amity
between parent and daughter states. With colonial expansion
there went economic growth. This epoch of the development of
the Bank of England, of great trading companies, of the remarkable mechanical inventions in the spheres of agriculture and
of the iron, spinning, and weaving industries, of the enunciation
of free trade principles by Price and Adam Smith, was clearly
one of first-rate importance in the history of English commerce.
It is a very mistaken view which regards such achievements as
these as humdrum. That the country was in process of becoming
a nation of shopkeepers was not a thing to be deplored. Diffusion
of prosperity, with a rise in the standard of living and of comfort,
is a very good thing, not (as is sometimes with a curious per-
versity suggested) something to be a little ashamed of—unless,
indeed, it engenders decadence and effeminacy. But there was
certainly no effeminacy in the 'coarse' eighteenth century.

It was not a heroic age, as a whole, though (as we shall see) it
is marked by many heroic incidents ; but the classic virtues of
restraint and balance, of maintaining a mean by compromise

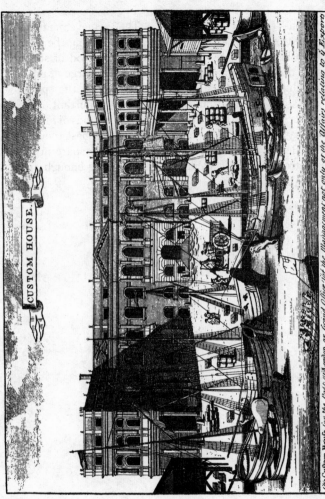

CUSTOM HOUSE.

The Custom House *for the Port of London, or Grand Office for the Management not only of the Affairs relating to the Exports and Imports of this Opulent City; but of the Customs throughout England, according to the Regulation of Parliament. It was built by K. Charles the 2ᵈ Anno 1668, at the Expence of about 10,000 Pounds, the former House being consumed by the Fire of London. It is a large and graceful Building, fronting the Water-side, very Commodious as well for the Commissioners and the several Officers and Clerks above Stairs, the Ware houses underneath, and the Cranes for Landing and Loading the Merch^ts Goods.*
&c.

The London Custom House at the beginning of the eighteenth century

From ' Several Prospects of the most noted Public Buildings in and about the City of London'

or conciliation—these it did possess. The achievements of religious toleration and of an ordered liberty are among the most honourable in humanity's record. This was no period of storm and stress, of the clash of passionate ideals, of the surge of great national or religious emotions. But, if less exciting, the epochs of quiet and solid accomplishment are no less important. We must remember finally that even the more placid periods of human history are only comparatively peaceful, that at the best they are fitful and restless ; there was strife enough and to spare in the eighty years treated in this volume, and issues big enough and difficult enough.

II

OUTLINE OF EVENTS

§ i. *1702–14*

WHILE the scheme of this book involves the substitution of treatment by subject for a purely chronological narrative, something in the nature of a chronological summary is desirable by way of preface, if the interrelation of the different aspects of the period is to be appreciated and the significance of its fundamental political issues understood. While it is true that we get most value out of the study of history when we begin to dissect and analyse its happenings, making separate investigation of those phenomena which belong to the sphere of economics, social conditions, literature, law, and so on; on the other hand there is such a thing as the pageant, the march, the drama, of events. The historian may arrange his facts according to all sorts of plans for convenience of exposition and in all sorts of order, but he will not be able to expound them aright unless he is first thoroughly familiar with the order which is theirs inherently, the order which they have in time, in the movement of human progress. The significance of an event depends upon many things, but above all it depends upon its date.

At the opening of the eighteenth century England had but recently entered upon a new phase in her history, which introduced new currents in her domestic affairs and also in her relations with other powers. By the Revolution of 1688–9 she had deposed James II and had deflected the strict order of the succession into the nearest *Protestant* line, in substituting for James his sister Mary and her husband William of Orange. The constitutional significance of the event was that the nation had decisively rejected the theory of sovereignty based on hereditary divine right, and had started upon a new era of limited monarchy and parliamentary government. The change was a most significant one in the purely internal history of England, but so it was also in the general history of Europe, because of its bearings upon the foreign situation. It is not too much to say that the future destiny, not only of England, but of Europe, depended upon the relations of England and Holland at this epoch. When the Dutch had revolted in the sixteenth century against Philip II of Spain, they and the subjects of Queen Elizabeth had been united as co-religionists in defiance of the might of the great catholic power—the greatest power in the world at that time—of Spain. There was similarity in the fortunes of the two peoples in the middle of the seventeenth century in the coincidence that in England the parliamentary party overthrew the Stuarts and established a Commonwealth, while in Holland the republicans under John de Witt abolished the ascendancy of the house of Orange, which was connected with that of the Stuarts by the marriage of Mary, the sister of the future Charles II, to William II of Orange in 1641, a connexion strengthened later on by a second marriage, that of the younger Mary to her cousin William III of Orange. There was similarity, again, in the maritime instincts of the two peoples and in their commercial and colonial enterprises. But that similarity bred rivalry, which ripened into war. There were three Dutch wars, one in the days of Cromwell, the others under Charles II. There was another still more important difference. Whereas Charles II stooped to accept Louis XIV's bribes by the secret Treaty of Dover in 1670, thus making England subservient to France, Holland stood out as the centre of resistance to the overweening ambitions of Louis, and as the leader of her resistance there figured William III of the now restored house of Orange. What was at issue, therefore, while the pig-headed James II was

THE Gazette of *Sept.* 24. 96. says, That three *English East-India* Ships were taken care of by Rere-Admiral *Benbow* : That several Associations were presented. Of *Sept.* 28. 96. Gives a Proclamation for sitting of the Parliament, on the 20 of *October* next, and an Order for receiving clipp'd Money and Plate at the Mints, at 5 s. 8d, the Ounce, and for coining Gold at the Proprietors Charge; and says that the Contract of Marriage, between the Duke of *Burgundy*, and the Princess of *Piedmont*, was signed by the said Princess; and she was thereupon treated with the Title of Dutchess of *Burgundy* · That the Neutrality for *Italy* not being excepted, the Duke of *Savoy* went to command the *French* Army, and the Mareschal *de Catinat* entred the *Spanish* Teritories, and advanced to *Satirana*, where the Duke of *Savoy* arrived; the 17th the Allies also march'd from Place to Place, to observe the Ennemy: That the King of *Spain* has labour'd with a Double Tertian, and his Fit on the 11th was attended with contiued sleeping, which made his Physitians apprehend great Danger, but after his Majesty receiv'd the Sacrament, he grew better, and the next Day he took Physick, and receiv'd great Benefit; and since that took the Tincture of the Jesuite's Powder, with very good Success · That on the 16th his Catholick Majesty miss'd his Fit and passed it almost without any Feavour, with such favourable Symptoms, that they have Reason to hope that he will have no more returns of it, and that he is in a good Way of recovery : That the Queen continues very Weak. Letters from *Piedmont* say, the *French* invested *Valence* the 17th, and would open the Trenches the 20th : That the Parliament of *Scotland* have settle the Funds for raising the Supply of 1440000 Pounds *Scots*; and an Act was brought in for Security of the Kingdom, for signing the Association by all in publick Trust : That an Association from *Ireland* has been presented.

Showing with what anxiety the Country watched every detail of the health of the King of Spain (p. 16). From Houghton's 'Collection' of 2 October 1696

antagonizing public opinion in England by his favouritism to Romanists and his prosecution of the Seven Bishops, was not merely whether he would retain the throne, but whether the country was or was not to be ranged under William of Orange in his great crusade against the ascendancy of France.

William undoubtedly valued his new position as King of England mainly because it enabled him to enlist that country's financial, military, and naval resources in his crusade. The nation was not whole-heartedly with him, because it viewed the conflict from an insular point of view. It fought because Louis XIV had embraced the cause of the deposed King and sought to restore him by force of arms. What it had in view was the security of the new constitutional *régime* and the immunity of the country from invasion, not the restoration of the balance of power in Europe and the humiliation of Louis. When the war was brought to a close in 1697 by the Treaty of Ryswick, Parliament was eager to reduce the standing army to the minimum. William was disgusted ; indeed, he contemplated leaving England altogether and returning to Holland. He realized, as the English people did not, that the peace was likely to prove of the briefest. The tranquillity of Europe was threatened by the problem of the Spanish succession. The reigning King of Spain, Charles II, was the last of his house in the male line. Through the female line there were three possible claimants—the French Dauphin, the Archduke Charles of Austria, and the Electoral Prince of Bavaria. An attempt on the part of either the French or the Austrian claimant to secure the whole Spanish inheritance for himself, which included not only Spain, but Sicily, the Milanese and the Spanish Indies, would certainly provoke a war. William endeavoured by negotiation with Louis to avoid this by arranging a division of the Spanish dominions between the three claimants. An agreement was come to in the first Partition Treaty of 1698. Then the Electoral Prince died, and the work had to be done afresh. The second Partition Treaty of 1699 divided the Spanish Empire between the two remaining claimants. When these negotiations were made public, English feeling was on the whole very hostile.

What business had we to arrange the parcelling out of an empire which did not belong to us ? The Spaniards were naturally infuriated ; they were determined that their empire should remain intact ; and in the end Charles II, on his death-bed, left a will which, entirely ignoring the Partition Treaties, left the entire inheritance to Philip, Duke of Anjou, the Dauphin's second son. Louis probably had honestly intended to abide by the treaties when he negotiated them, but he was unable to resist the new temptation afforded by the will and acknowledged his grandson as King of Spain. There should henceforth be no Pyrenees. Louis' action did not immediately give rise to a renewal of hostilities, but it made it almost inevitable sooner or later. When Louis went out of his way, on the death of James II in September 1701, to recognize his son as King of England, he succeeded in arousing resentment in England, where his conduct in connexion with the Spanish succession question had created no great feeling. Before his death William III had the satisfaction of seeing the English people staunchly united once more in hostility to his arch-enemy.

The interest of the reign of Queen Anne is divided between our participation in the War of the Spanish Succession, on the one hand, and, on the other, the lively and at times embittered warfare of parties at home. Complete national support was at first accorded to the war, but as it continued year after year, marked indeed with many brilliant successes, but barren of decisive result, fervour tended to cool. Throughout there was a difference of view between Whig and Tory as to the proper nature and extent of our participation in the struggle. The Whigs favoured the full commitment of all our resources and our engaging in the continental campaigns, while the Tories urged the limitation of our activities, their confinement to the sea, our natural element. At the same time the Tories accused their political opponents of being lukewarm in seeking peace, because their great bankers, who largely financed the war, profited by its continuance.

The struggle was fought out in several theatres, on the sea, in Italy, on the Rhine, in the Netherlands, and in Spain. It was in the Netherlands that our principal military effort was made, under Marlborough, whose problem was to break through or to turn the great barrier of fortresses protecting the north-eastern frontier of France and so to menace Paris. There was one brilliant interlude in 1704 when he made his famous march up the Rhine and saved Vienna from a converging French attack by the great victory of Blenheim. Scarcely less splendid were his chief successes in the Netherlands—the triumphs of Ramillies and Oudenarde, the capture of Lille. But baulked over and over again by the obstinate objections of our cautious Dutch allies, he was thwarted of his ultimate object until in 1711 he seemed at last on the threshold of success ; and then owing to the ministerial crisis in England he was relieved of his command.

At first our military effort in Spain prospered. Gibraltar was captured in 1704, Barcelona in the year following ; Madrid was occupied and the Archduke Charles proclaimed there. Then the fortunes of war completely changed. Apart from the important capture in 1708 of the island of Minorca—esteemed by contemporaries a great deal more important than that of Gibraltar—there were no further successes, but two severe defeats, one at Almanza in 1707, by which the whole of Spain passed into the hands of Philip with the exception of Catalonia, and Brihuega in 1710, which entirely ruined the allies' cause in the Peninsula. The ill-success of the campaign in Spain itself was particularly unfortunate, seeing that the control of Spain was one of the most essential issues of the war. Negotiations for peace which took place in 1709 and 1710 (at Gertruydenberg) were shipwrecked on this vital question. Refusing to recognize the obstinate facts of the military situation in the Peninsula, which their signal but indecisive achievements in other quarters did not counterbalance, the allies made the preposterous demand that Louis should co-operate in driving his own grandson out of Spain. Louis preferred rather to fight to the last gasp than accept such ignominy.

The Whigs were responsible for the failure of the negotiations in 1709 and 1710 ; when peace *pourparlers* were resumed, a Tory ministry was in office. The two most important dates in

The raising of ye Siege of Gibraltar, & Destroying Monsr. Ponti's Squadron.
By Sir John Leake, March 20. 1705.

Shortly after its capture by Rooke Gibraltar was besieged by a mixed French and Spanish army, and by a French squadron
under Admiral de Pointis. Leake surprised and defeated part of this squadron, and the siege was abandoned

the history of parties under Anne are 1708 and 1710. Prior to 1708 the ministry was a composite one under Godolphin and Marlborough, who then ranked as a Tory. The Queen's pre-dilections were strongly in favour of the Tories. She is best known by her devotion to Sarah, the termagant Duchess of Marlborough, and afterwards to Mrs. Masham, and she is usually thought of as a colourless woman very patient under provocation. She had more strength of character, more sagacity, and more policy than she is generally credited with having. Her chief characteristic was devotion to the interests of the Church of England, and it was mainly because the Tories were essentially the Church party that she favoured them. But as the war went on, the Whigs, more zealous for its vigorous prosecu-tion, became increasingly powerful, and skilfully led by a quin-tet of very expert managers, the so-called Junto—Wharton, Orford, Halifax, Somers, and Sunderland—they eventually succeeded in forcing some of their members upon the Government, until it became in 1708 a largely Whig body including Orford, Wharton, Sunderland, and a very distinguished Whig lawyer, Cowper, as Lord Chancellor.

By far the greatest event in the domestic history of this earlier period of the reign was the legislative union with Scotland (1707). It was indeed one of the greatest achievements of British states-manship. Although the Scots had accepted William III and Mary as their rulers in 1689, relations between the two kingdoms were strained during their reigns, mainly owing to commercial jealousies, and there was no certainty that Scotland would necessarily accept the succession of the Electress Sophia of Hanover, whom the English Parliament by the Act of Settlement of 1701 designated as successor to the Princess Anne on the death of her last surviving child. Preliminary negotiations for a genuine union between the two countries at the opening of the reign of Anne broke down over financial difficulties. In chagrin the Scottish Parliament in 1703 proceeded to pass a so-called Act of Security, which reserved to it the right of refusing recogni-tion to the successor chosen by the other kingdom unless such arrangements were made as would give to Scotland guarantees as regards her religion, her trade, and the preservation of her distinctive law and customs. The English Parliament passed a retaliatory measure designed to show that Scotland was not

---

THE Dominion from which came moſt Ships to *London* in the Year 1694, under a hundred, was *Scotland*; and from thence came 66. How! what no more from ſo near an *Allie*; 212 from little *Holland*, and but 66 from great *Scotland*; it's like Siſters, we envy one anothers Proſperity, and wiſh well to any body rather than to each other: Sixty ſix! Methinks it ſounds like the Mark of the Beaſt; and like Beaſts we are; *Homo homini Lupus.*

Some will ſay they are *Poor*, and will eat up our *Fat* ; but what reaſon is there to think they will e're carry it to their own Country, we encourage the Coming of the *French*, moſt of which I preſume have been as poor as they ; but will not *Preferments, profitable Employments*, and a *warmer Air* bring their *Nobility* and *Gentry* more ſouthward ? and will not their Children born here be *Engliſh* ? came we not all originally from abroad ? Yea, but they will enjoy an equal Liberty with us in our *Plantations*; Much good may it do them, ſo long as they go there to work, and to help keep under a far greater Number of *Blacks* than now ; will not all the Cuſtoms, Exciſe and Taxes be brought to the King's *Exchequer* ? and will not the Poſts, Coaches and other Entercourſes be far larger : One might write a Book of the Advantages, and I ſtrongly perſuade my ſelf It might be done, could the Matter about Precedency of the Nobles be adiuſted, which I'll hope to ſee, and the old Verſes uſed in time of King *James* the firſt, revived.

One only Nation now are we,
And ſo let us for ever be.

A protest against commercial jealousy of the Scots. From a Leading Article in Houghton's ' Collection' of 27 Dec. 1695

---

in a position to act independently of England, to the effect that failing a satisfactory settlement of the succession question by the Scottish Parliament by 1705, after that date all Scotsmen in England, not domiciled or in the forces, would be seized and regarded as aliens, and that no Scottish cattle, sheep, linen, or wool would be allowed into England. As Scotland was dependent upon her English trade, there could be no answer to this measure, and the Scots agreed to negotiate for a complete union of the two kingdoms, not merely one of the crowns as heretofore. At first, however, they pressed for a federal system, which would allow them to retain their existing Parliament. The English commissioners insisted on a legislative union. Despite the previous atmosphere of hostility, the new negotiations were carried through with a statesmanlike absence of friction and

The Sacheverell impeachment. Satire on the Low Church Party. Cromwell rides in the coach; the postilion is Hoadly, Bishop of Bangor

recrimination, their success being pre-eminently due to the Duke of Queensberry on the Scots' side and Lord Somers, though he was not a member of the Government, on the English side.

The terms of the settlement established a common Parliament at Westminster, with forty-five Scottish representatives in the House of Commons, sixteen representative peers in the Lords. Complete freedom of trade with England and her colonies was granted to the Scots; and although at first the Union was not popular with them, the commercial prosperity which presently ensued as a direct consequence of the Union led to a change of view in the northern kingdom, and rendered the new system a complete and signal success.

The party triumph of the Whigs was shortlived. Before the

end of 1709 Godolphin had made the fatal decision to have
Dr. Henry Sacheverell impeached. This high-church cleric had
made himself notorious by sermons in which he had maintained
that the Church of England was in danger owing to the toleration
given to Dissenters, and had advocated the doctrine of non-
resistance to constituted authority, in a way that involved a
condemnation of the Revolution of 1688/9. Incidentally in one
sermon preached at St. Paul's he had applied an opprobrious

*The Sacheverell impeachment. Satire on the High Church Party. The Pretender
rides in the coach; the postilion is Sacheverell*

epithet to Godolphin, which rankled so deeply that against
wiser advice that minister decided to take drastic measures
against the doctor. These only gave immense publicity and the
halo of martyrdom to a man who, though of little account
himself, yet represented a point of view shared by a considerable
section of the community. Sacheverell became a hero with the
London populace, and the strength of unreasoning fanaticism
was evinced by the crowd's acclamations of the Queen—'We
hope your Majesty is for High Church and Dr. Sacheverell'—
by a number of attacks on Dissenters' meeting-houses and the
triumphal procession of the doctor, when after a purely nominal
sentence he journeyed from London to take possession of a new
living in Shropshire.

The Queen, perceiving in these demonstrations the sign both of her own personal popularity and of a revulsion of feeling against the Whigs, was emboldened to rid herself of her Whig advisers and to form a new administration, in which the two leading figures were Harley and St. John, subsequently ennobled as Earl of Oxford and Viscount Bolingbroke respectively. At the outset of a mixed party complexion, the new ministry became entirely Tory. Its great preoccupation was the securing of peace. In the summer of 1711 the British troops were withdrawn from Spain and Portugal, and at the same time private negotiations were commenced at Paris, with the Duke of Shrewsbury and Matthew Prior the poet as the English intermediaries. These preliminaries were much more important than the formal negotiations which opened at Utrecht on the 29th January 1712, by which date the Government had already decided to come to terms with the French and enforce them upon their allies, whether they liked them or not. In pursuance of this previous secret understanding with the enemy, the Duke of Ormonde, who had been given the command in the Netherlands in succession to Marlborough, was instructed not to engage in any siege or take part in any offensive movement against the French. Our troops were thus completely immobilized, our Dutch allies abandoned, the French commander Villars informed that he had only the Dutch troops to fear, the British contingent would do nothing.

While these negotiations were in progress the ministry had been meeting with considerable difficulties in Parliament, where the Whigs raised their battle-cry, ' No peace without Spain ', by which they meant no peace which allowed Philip to retain the Spanish throne. The opposition being particularly formidable in the Upper House, the ministers took the, at that time, unprecedented step of persuading the Queen to create twelve new peers for the express purpose of securing a majority for the Government's peace policy in the Lords. This measure and the so-called ' restraining orders ' to Ormonde, the Whigs in the next reign seized upon as two wicked acts meriting impeachment. The Opposition assailed the actual terms of the peace with whole-hearted venom, although our gains by the Treaty—or rather

By this means they can fill the Plantations with *Blacks* and have Stock enough to furnish the *Spaniard*, which at this time make Overtures to them, and to shew what a Trade it might be, take the following Account.

The *Spaniards* treated with the Royal *African Company* of *England* for 5000 whole Pieces of *India* the Year for 7 Years to be delivered at some of the Islands.

But to make this good, the Company were to ship from *Africa* 7 or 8000 Pieces, out of which the *Spaniards* were to chuse 5000 whole Pieces, and the Company to dispose of the rest.

A whole Piece of *India* was according to the Ages of the *Negroes*, Male or Female. Those between 15 and 45 or 36, were a whole Piece; between 4 and 8, were 2 for 1; between 8 and 15, or above 45 or 35, were 3 for 2, and those under 4, were cast in with the Mother.

Now considering the Allowances, there were to be ship'd from *Africa* yearly about 10000 Persons in 7 Years 70000.

The *Spaniards* not being in good Credit, negotiated this by *Augustino Lomelino* and other *Genoeses* Bankers at *Madrid*, in and about 1664, and transferr'd it to *Signor Ferini* at *Amsterdam*; But the *Dutch* War in 1665 broke all off.

This I have from a Gentleman who had the Perusal of a Book of the Letters and Negotiations of the Treaty.

Such a Trade as this made by an Act of Parliament for 99 Years certain, wou'd much improve all our Western Plantations. and by degrees perhaps find as good Mines in *Carolina* as in *Potosi*; 'twou'd encrease Seamen and Ships of Strength for our Use at home, and encourage Growths and Manufactures here greatl , 'twill bring us in Gold apace to make Guineas with, and the Goods from the Plantations will fetch us in Silver, besides the Silver is gotten for the *Blacks*: And this is what I verily believe might have been already done, had not our Misunderstandings hinder'd in; and I do think I shall never meet with the Man that can and will fairly gainsay it. But perhaps this is not best for us: For if *Jessuron* shou'd wax fat, he won'd kick till Maker: Therefore God thinks fit to let us be divided, which will keep us poor, and perhaps more humble.

The lucrative nature of the traffic in African negroes with the Spanish colonies of America. Extract from a Leading Article in Houghton's 'Collection' (14 Feb. 1695/6), which advocates an expansion of the trade

Treaties—of Utrecht were very considerable. If Philip was not driven from the throne of Spain, he abandoned his claims to the French crown, while the French princes of the blood renounced any claim they might ever have to the crown of Spain, so that the horrid spectre of a union of the two Bourbon monarchies in a single person was laid. The Asiento agreement was made between Great Britain and Spain, which gave us a share in the very lucrative slave-trade between Africa and Spanish America and the privilege of sending one ship a year to trade with the Spanish colonies. Gibraltar and Minorca we retained. France agreed to dismantle the fortress of Dunkirk by destroying canals, &c., so as to render the port suitable only for commercial purposes, and ceded to us Hudson's Bay territory, Acadia, St. Kitts, and Newfoundland (save for certain fishing rights on the coast). The Government also negotiated a commercial treaty with France, which went far towards establishing freedom of trade between the two countries. The considered judgement of posterity on this series of treaties is that they represent a signal advance in the history of our maritime trade, the growth of our colonial empire, the development of our naval control over the Mediterranean.

As we shall see, the Whigs, not content with attacking the Ministry for its peace settlement, accused it of Jacobite intrigue, bruited it about that now Oxford, at another time Bolingbroke, was scheming for the restoration of the Pretender. The internal history of the Tory party is doubtful and obscure; certainly there were personal differences and divisions of opinion, culminating in a complete breach between Oxford and Bolingbroke. What that rupture betokened can only be conjectured, for Queen Anne died almost immediately afterwards. If there were plots on foot for tampering with the Protestant succession, they had no time to mature, and George I was proclaimed without opposition.

Medal celebrating the arrival of George I in England, 18 Sept. 1714. The King, as Neptune, approaching the coast

§ ii. *1714–27*

The new king was already on good terms with the Whigs, who had been at pains to ingratiate themselves with him and the late Electress Sophia at Hanover, and he was disposed to look askance upon the Tories as at any rate *suspect* of Jacobite tendencies. Such an attitude was encouraged by a memorial which Lord Cowper, who presented it, termed an impartial history of parties, but in which it was clearly represented that the security of the Hanoverian dynasty depended upon a close understanding between the new king and the Whigs. Thus it came to pass that the constitutional era inaugurated by the Revolution, which, popular only in the opposition to absolutism and in the ultimate consequences it presaged, had so far in effect meant the supremacy of an aristocracy, came to mean something narrower still—the predominance of a Whig aristocracy, the *régime* which Disraeli described as 'the Venetian oligarchy of the Whigs'.

The first leading ministers of the new reign were Sunderland, Townshend, Walpole, and Stanhope, who had for a time commanded our forces in Spain in the late war, a scholar and statesman as well as a soldier, regarded by many foreigners as the

most distinguished of living Englishmen. This combination did
not last long, Townshend and Walpole soon leaving it ; nor
did the subsequent Stanhope-Sunderland alliance, for this was
struck down in the financial panic which resulted from the
bursting of the famous ' South Sea Bubble ' in the winter of
1720. This calamity led to the return to office of Townshend
and Walpole, the latter as First Lord of the Treasury. With
them were associated William Pulteney and Lord Carteret.

The opening years of the reign of George I had naturally been
uneasy. There were at the outset apprehensions of serious
trouble, and a number of local disturbances occurred, especially
in the Midlands, where there were instances of crowds shouting
for James III and of Dissenters' places of worship being attacked,
which seemed to prove that fears of graver discord were not
groundless. The principle of an obsolete law was revived,
whereby any assembly of twelve persons or more, being ordered
by a magistrate to disperse and failing to do so, became thereby
guilty of a felony and could be forcibly apprehended even to the
extent of shedding of blood. This law, still in force, is known
as the Riot Act. One other special measure in view of the
dangerous state of the country after the Jacobite rising of 1715
was taken in the following year. A general election was due
under the existing system of triennial parliaments the following
year. The Ministry considered that a general election in existing
circumstances would be hazardous—at all events to their own
party. They therefore introduced a bill, which duly became
law, extending the life of the present parliament and of future
parliaments to seven years. It is an interesting constitutional
question whether members elected by their constituencies to
sit for three years had any right, without consulting the country
on the matter, to decide to sit for a longer period. The important
fact is that they did it, and that there does not exist in the constitution any means which could have prevented them from doing
that or anything else they might have chosen to do ; in other
words there is no legal limitation to the sovereignty of Parliament.
The Septennial Act remained in force till the inauguration of
a quinquennial system by the Parliament Act of 1911.

The apprehended Jacobite rising took place in 1715. Coming so soon after the King's accession it might well have proved serious ; that it did not was due partly to the dilatoriness and want of energy of the Earl of Mar, who led the very considerable Jacobite forces in Scotland, partly to the lack of co-ordination between his movement and that of Forster and Lord Derwentwater in Lancashire ; most of all to the fact of our being at

---

Yesterday there was a General Court of the South-Sea Company, when each Proprietor was examined, whether he had a 1000 l. stock, before he was suffered to go in : Sir John Eyles opened the Court, by offering a method to discharge part of their bond debts, which was, to annihilate 6 ⅓ per cent. of the principal ; but after several debates it was put to the vote and rejected. —— A Gentleman made a proposal, that a Committee of the Proprietors might be chosen to inspect the accounts ; and the previous Question, whether this proposal should be put to the vote, was carry'd in the negative. —— Another proposal was made to discharge the bond debts, by reducing an half per cent. of the interest ; which was also rejected. —— There were likewise many disputes relating to their trade ; some were for carrying it on, others for dropping it, and others for farming both the Assiento and annual Trade, but they could not come to any resolution ; so they agreed to leave it to the Directors, to consider of some method to put their affairs under a better regulation ; and adjourned the Court till to-morrow se'nnight. *D P.*

Report of a meeting of South Sea Company Proprietors. From ' The Grub-street Journal ' of 23 March 1731

---

peace with France, which prevented the Pretender's receiving foreign assistance. The Old Pretender, who landed in Scotland after Mar's failure to break through the very much smaller force led by the Duke of Argyll at Sheriffmuir had spelt failure for his cause, proved a very spiritless leader. None of the vital factors of success were present in the Jacobite effort.

The foreign relations of Great Britain during the reign of George I are somewhat complicated, but the main facts can be followed without difficulty. The best guarantee for the maintenance of the Hanoverian succession was a policy of peace with

other Powers.   Ministers sought to follow this policy, but despite
the strain of the prolonged War of the Spanish Succession the
general situation in Europe was far from quiet, and it was not
easy to steer clear of dangerous complications.   The relations
between the two Bourbon monarchies were all-important.   Circumstances which served to estrange them were very welcome
to British ministers ; and these arose when, upon the death of
the old King Louis XIV in September 1715, France entered upon
a long period of minority rule with the Duke of Orleans as Regent.
The little Louis XV, aged five, was extremely delicate.   The next
heir by blood was Philip of Spain ; his claim being debarred by
the Treaty of Utrecht, the next heir under that dispensation was
the Regent.   There was little love lost between the two, therefore ;
and Orleans, in whose interests it was to maintain the Utrecht
settlement, gravitated towards Great Britain.   A definite treaty
between the two countries was negotiated by the Abbé Dubois.
In February 1716 the Dutch joined in this alliance.   The danger
to European peace came, not from France, but from Spain,
whose policy was directed—in rather different directions—by
two exceedingly ambitious persons, the Queen, Elizabeth Farnese,
and the chief minister, Cardinal Alberoni.   While the Queen
thought of Spain mainly as a Mediterranean power and the
minister thought of it mainly as an oceanic power, both were
united in their determination to develop its navy, revive its
prestige, and in particular to recover territories in Italy, once
Spanish, now Austrian.   With a view to persuading Spain to
keep the peace, Stanhope in 1718 devised an extension of the
existing Triple Alliance into a Quadruple Alliance by the inclusion of Austria ; but when it became apparent that Spain was
determined on attacking Sicily, the British Government dispatched a fleet under Admiral Sir George Byng to insist upon
the maintenance of peace.   On arrival in Sicilian waters, Byng
discovered that the Spaniards had already occupied a considerable part of the island.   He proposed an armistice, which was
refused.   Byng then attacked the Spanish fleet off Cape Passaro,
and destroyed the greater part of it.   Thus the British Navy
scotched the Spanish schemes, though we were not technically at

war with Spain. War followed three months later, and Byng was rewarded for his services by being made Viscount Torrington.

Alberoni sought revenge by planning a new Jacobite enterprise against England. His first attempt, arranged in conjunction with Russia and Sweden, was frustrated by the death of the King of Sweden, the great warrior, Charles XII. The second scheme, in which Alberoni provided a fleet to convey an expedition under Ormonde, now an avowed Jacobite, to effect a landing in England, was also ruined—by the violence of a gale; the few Spaniards who landed being captured at Glensheil. After this last disaster, Alberoni was dismissed from office in December 1719.

A new series of dangerous entanglements started in 1725 when the young Louis XV, who had been engaged to the Spanish infanta, suddenly repudiated her and married the daughter of Stanislaus, ex-King of Poland. Infuriated by this indignity, Spain took the extraordinary course of allying herself with Austria. Exasperated with France, she was also disgusted at Great Britain's refusal to return Gibraltar, which in an unguarded moment in 1721 Stanhope had suggested as a possibility. As it happened, relations between Great Britain and Austria were at this time rather strained owing to the competition our East India Company was meeting with from a so-called Ostend Company, which the Emperor had established for the benefit of his subjects in the Austrian Netherlands. The Emperor agreed by the Treaty of Vienna to assist Spain in the recovery of Gibraltar and in promoting a new Jacobite descent upon England. This danger was parried by Townshend's negotiation of the Treaty of Hanover between Great Britain, France, and Prussia. A desultory war of little intrinsic interest followed, brought to an end by the Treaty of Seville of 1729 between Great Britain and Spain, followed in its turn by a second Treaty of Vienna, by which the Emperor agreed to terms, which included the dissolution of the Ostend Company.

Kaleidoscopic as had been the changes in the diplomatic situation since the accession of George I, the one combination of Powers which had been most feared and which seemed on the

face of it the most natural—one between France and Spain—
had for a variety of reasons not materialized. That combination
came into existence in 1733, when it was cemented by a secret
treaty known as the First Bourbon Family Compact. The main
object of that understanding was reciprocal aid against Austria,
but the possibility of French assistance to Spain for the recovery
of Gibraltar and Minorca and for an assault upon British commerce was also contemplated in the treaty. Inasmuch as Elizabeth Farnese was still the dominant force in Spanish affairs and
her ambitions were still centred upon Italy, while Cardinal
Fleury, the French negotiator of the agreement, was by no
means anti-British in his personal sympathies and was, like
Walpole, a peace minister, the Compact did not immediately
threaten Great Britain. Nevertheless there was a sinister element
in the secret treaty which boded no good to Great Britain and
which in the end did bring trouble.

The Royal Family, 1732. Medal struck by order of the King for distribution to foreign princes and others whom he wished to honour

§ iii. *1727–60*

When George II succeeded his father in 1727, it had not been anticipated that he would retain Walpole in office. Notoriously, he had been at daggers drawn with his father and had included his father's advisers in his dislike. But George II, though inferior to his predecessor, had plenty of common sense and sagacity; moreover, he allowed himself to be guided by that very remarkable woman and statesman, Caroline of Anspach, and between her and Walpole there existed throughout a very firm friendship and sympathy. The only serious difficulty which Walpole found in dealing with the new king lay in the latter's anxiety for his electoral dominions in Hanover and his desire for martial glory, both of which motives inclined him to take sides in Continental disputes. In 1733 a European war broke out, which was no concern whatever of Great Britain. Yet Walpole had much ado to keep out of it because of the King's desire to take part on the side of the Emperor. This was the War of the Polish Succession, in which France intervened on behalf of the claim to that throne of Louis XV's father-in-law, supported by Spain, who saw in these circumstances an opportunity of attacking Austrian territories in Italy, since Austria was ranged with Russia against Stanislaus. While successful in avoiding this entanglement, Walpole failed to keep the peace when our existing differences with Spain over the retention of Minorca and Gibraltar and her demand for compensation for the destruction of her ships at Cape Passaro were aggravated by serious disputes between British merchants and Spanish guard-ships in American waters over the interpretation of the trading privileges accorded to us by the treaties of 1713. Our merchants were undoubtedly exceeding the limits of those privileges ; the Spanish *guarda costas* were also undoubtedly guilty of barbarity in exercising their pretended right of search. In the end Walpole had to yield to popular clamour, and war broke out in 1739.

Walpole did not shine as a war minister, and the naval operations in this war against Spain after a promising opening proved exceedingly unsatisfactory. No man ever succeeded in war whose heart was full of forebodings and whose will was not resolute for victory. Such a man was Walpole, with his gloomy prophecy (soon verified), ' They now ring the bells, they will soon wring their hands.' The ill-success of the war forced his resignation in January 1742. His great work had been accomplished in the sphere of domestic politics, wherein his career for the last twenty years had been the history of England. Its significance will be considered in the chapter on Walpole.

When the Spanish war was but young, a new disturbance arose on the Continent, threatening far more serious trouble than any event so far since 1714. This was the death of the Emperor Charles VI, who left no male heir. By a so-called Pragmatic Sanction he had left all the great Habsburg territories in Austria, Hungary, Italy undivided to his daughter, Maria Theresa. Realizing the dangers and difficulties of a female succession to this great empire, he had secured the guarantee of the Pragmatic Sanction from the chief European Powers. But when the Emperor died they did not all prove true to their bond. Frederic the Great of Prussia, coveting the rich Austrian province of Silesia, seized the opportunity and marched into the province, considerately offering Maria Theresa the chance of voluntarily ceding it to him if she did not like to see him forcibly take it. Thus commenced the War of the Austrian Succession, in which

France, Bavaria, and Spain were soon ranged against Maria
Theresa. For a time Great Britain, while continuing her private
quarrel with Spain, remained neutral in the larger struggle, only
supplying Maria Theresa with subsidies ; but when Lord Carteret
succeeded Walpole in the direction of her foreign affairs, she joined
in as a principal, and George II had the satisfaction of taking
part in the military operations, fighting bravely at Dettingen,
the last battle in which an English king was a combatant.

*Goat Island, off Loch Nanuagh, under which tradition says Prince Charlie
sheltered during the night before he landed in Moidart*

Dettingen, though blunderingly conducted, was an undeniable
victory, but the next important engagement in which the British
forces were engaged, that of Fontenoy, in which the Duke of
Cumberland showed himself no match for the great French commander, Marshal Saxe, was an unequivocal defeat. This was in
May 1745. In the following July Prince Charles Edward Stuart
landed in Moidart, on the west coast of Scotland, on his heroic
adventure. The previous year the French had planned a very
formidable invasion in the Jacobite cause, which was to be

directed by Saxe himself, but the vigilance of the British fleet in the Channel under Sir John Norris had led to the abandonment of the scheme. Now the Young Pretender landed without any foreign army at his back. The British Government was not prepared to meet the danger, but at first made light of what certainly seemed on the face of it to be a foolhardy and desperate enterprise. Carteret, now Earl Granville, assured the King that it was of no consequence, and when any minister proposed any emergency measure, George merely cried, ' Pho ! don't talk to me of that stuff.' But the rebellion proved to be no jesting matter. The Prince, with a small army of clansmen who had joined him in the western Highlands, slipped past the force sent to intercept him under Sir John Cope and occupied Perth, at Colt Brig encountered some dragoons under Colonel Gardiner, the fine soldier immortalized in Scott's *Waverley*, scattered them in flight, and entered Edinburgh. Cope hurriedly brought his men south by sea from Aberdeen to Dunbar and gave battle to the terrible Highlanders at Prestonpans. In six minutes the furious charge of those Highlanders had swept Cope's army off the field in disgraceful rout.

The Jacobite army, by this time some 5,000 strong, now proceeded to invade England. As an English army under the veteran Marshal Wade barred the eastern route at Newcastle, they took the western road through Carlisle, over Shap Fell to Manchester. The Prince had strong hopes of support from Sir Watkyn Williams Wynne and other Jacobites of North Wales, but these failed to give practical help and the support forthcoming in England on the Prince's line of march was negligible. At last aroused to a sense of the danger of the situation, the Government had transhipped Cumberland's army from the Netherlands, and the Duke now lay in the Midlands. Trained bands were being organized at Finchley to defend London's northern heights. Wade at Newcastle was in a position to sever the Jacobite communications with Scotland. But the invaders managed to slip past Cumberland as they had before slipped past Cope. With no regular force remaining between it and the rebels, London was seized with panic on learning on the

A New *SONG*,
By Mr Rann one of his *Ma-*
jeſtys Forreſters at *Windſer.*
Tune King Georges March,

FROM London to ſcotland
    with ſpeed the Duke did flye
All for to face the Rebels
    or make them for to fly,
But when he came to ſterling
    no Rebels there could find,
Their Magazine blew up
    and their Cannon leaſt behind,
Then ſcotland did Rejoice,
    O that the Youth was come,
The Glory of the Nation
    King George's Youngeſt Son,
    Reſolved like a briton
to conquer or to Dye,
He march'd to Abordeen
    but before him they did fly.
He croſs'd the River Spey
    a battle did Enſue,
But few were left alive
    Rebellion to purſue,
Then Britons all rejoice
    O that the Youth is come,
The Glory of the Nation
    King Georges Youngeſt ſon.
    Now Peace and Plenty
amongeſt us all will Reign,
In ſpite of a Pretender, Dupe
    to France and Spain,
French ſoupes we do diſpiſe
    it ſuiteth not our blood,
Brown bear and good roſt beef
    is holſome britiſh food,
Then britons all Rejoice
    O that the Youth is come,
The Deliverer of his Country
    King George's Youngeſt Son.

A BROADSIDE OF '46

6th December, long known as 'Black Friday', that the Prince was no farther off than Derby.   But the Pretender never approached any nearer to the capital.   Alarmed by the threat to their rear from Wade and Cumberland, disappointed by the apathy of the English, Prince Charles's chief followers unanimously counselled retreat.   The enterprise was from the first essentially a gambler's escapade ;   only a gambler's reckless audacity to the end could have crowned it with success.   When once the retreat from Derby was sounded, eventual defeat was a certainty.   The Jacobite army gained a last success at Falkirk Muir, but met its death-blow on Culloden Moor on the 16th April 1746.

The era of the War of the Austrian Succession was the era of the Pelhams and Carteret (or Granville), whose brilliant gifts greatly impressed his contemporaries, who notoriously despised domestic politics, delighted in the business of wars and alliances, and devoted his efforts to the creation of a great combination to resist France.   As alone among ministers Carteret always had an eye to the interests of Hanover, George II was devoted to him ;   but as his policy was expensive and by no means successful, his colleagues rebelled against it, and the Pelham brothers succeeded in turning him out.   Their efforts at conducting the war after he had gone were no happier than his had been.   They were in power at the time of Fontenoy and the disasters of 'forty-five'.   There were certainly isolated successes, the most notable being the capture of the fortress of Louisbourg on the island of Cape Breton, which commands the mouth of the St. Lawrence, but in the main the war continued to go badly, the British forces sustaining two severe defeats at the hands of Saxe, one near Liége in October 1746, the other at Lauffeld in July 1747.   Since the fall of Granville Newcastle had displayed just as bellicose a spirit as that statesman had ever done.   When that ministerial crisis had taken place, ' We must not,' he had naïvely remarked, ' because we seem to be in, forget all we said to keep Lord Granville out.'   But the Pelhams had proved unable to devise anything different.   In the beginning of 1748 Newcastle was constrained to admit the desirability of making peace.   ' We were beat ', said Bolingbroke, ' on every spot where my Lord Marlborough had conquered.' The peace came in April at Aix-la-Chapelle. Nothing was said about the right of search, the original cause of quarrel with Spain ; the *asiento* was renewed for another four years, but by a subsequent Treaty of Madrid (1750) was surrendered for a money payment ; Madras, which the French had taken from us in India, was exchanged for Louisbourg. On the Continent Frederic the Great retained Silesia, but otherwise Maria Theresa's position was intact.

While the attention of contemporaries was fixed mainly on the course of events on the European continent, in the eyes of posterity the most significant events during the period of the War of the Austrian Succession took place in India and North America, where the future destinies of those two vast countries were at stake in the warfare between French and British. In the brief interval of uneasy peace between the Treaty of Aix-la-Chapelle and the outbreak of the Seven Years' War in 1756, though the home governments were not at war, the English colonists along the Atlantic littoral strove with the French settlers of Canada and Louisiana, disputing in particular the control of the Ohio valley, where George Washington first comes into prominence as a loyalist, attempting to capture the important French position commanding the Ohio basin, Fort Duquesne. In India the two rival East India Companies utilized the quarrels of native princes in the Deccan and the Carnatic to push their own political as well as their commercial interests, the French at first playing the game with the greater success owing to the genius of Dupleix, who first realized the great opportunities for the expansion of a European power afforded by Indian conditions, but the balance being reversed after 1751 by the efforts of Saunders, the Governor of Madras, of Colonel Stringer Lawrence, who has been called ' the father of the Indian army ', the first notable bearer of a name illustrious in the history of British India, and of Robert Clive, the young office clerk in the service of the Company, who, leaving his desk, proved himself a greater than Dupleix, a wonderful soldier and administrator, the founder of our Indian Empire.

Between 1748 and 1756 a change in the grouping of the

European powers took place so complete that it is known as the Diplomatic Revolution. While the steps by which it was brought about are somewhat complicated, the essential causes of the change are simple enough. The most significant feature of the existing European situation was the emergence of Prussia under Frederic the Great as a great power. Austria's anxiety about her possessions in Italy, which had involved hostility to

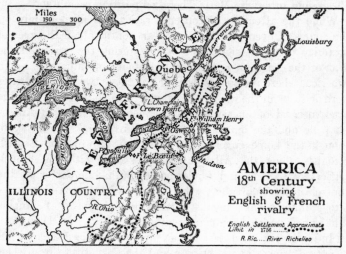

AMERICA
18th Century
showing
English & French
rivalry

English Settlement Approximate Limit in 1756 ......
R. Ric. .... River Richelieu

Spain, was now completely subordinated to her resentment at the loss of Silesia. In these circumstances the great Austrian minister Kaunitz recommended that a new orientation should be given to Habsburg policy. For the crushing of Prussia the most useful alliance would be with France. The trouble was to persuade France that such an alliance was in her interests, when as a matter of fact it was not. It was contrary to all her traditions, and her animosity being still directed mainly against Great Britain, an understanding with Prussia was for her more advantageous, because Hanover was peculiarly vulnerable to Prussian attack. But when George II, in his anxiety for his beloved electorate, sought assurances for its protection from Kaunitz, that minister, having no desire for any engagement with Great Britain, whose assistance in the later stages of the late war had not been regarded as satisfactory by Maria Theresa, refused to give any assurances. Rebuffed at Vienna, George approached Berlin, and an agreement was come to by the Convention of Westminster (16th January 1756). On the 1st May Kaunitz achieved a brilliant diplomatic success in the Treaty of Versailles concluded between Austria and France, which gave Austria what she wanted, and from which France (given any clear-sighted view of her real interests) had nothing to gain.

The interest of the Seven Years' War is twofold. On the Continent we witness the heroic, and in the end the successful, efforts of the King of Prussia, in the face of tremendous odds—France, Austria, Russia, Sweden, and minor German states being arrayed against him—to save his kingdom from destruction and partition among his foes ; on the seas we watch the predominance of British naval power ; in Canada and India the further extension of the British Empire, mainly at the expense of France. Over all our efforts the presiding genius of the war is Pitt, imperatively summoned by the united voice of the British people to come to the helm, when our initial failures had overwhelmed Newcastle in consternation—Pitt, so superbly and, as events proved so rightly, confident of his ability to drive the ship of state triumphantly through the storm.

*+ Born & Educated in this Country I glory
in the Name of Britain; & the peculiar happiness
of my Life, will ever consist, in promoting the
Welfare of a people whose Loyalty & warm
affection to me, I consider; as the greatest &
most permanent Security of my Throne.*

§ iv.   *1760–83*

In the midst of the war died George II. In the place of a
sovereign who had been grossly irregular in his private life,
essentially a foreigner, not at all kingly in action or appearance,
there came to the throne a young man of impeccable virtues,
glorying in the name of Britain, determined to be every inch a
king. Taking a most high-minded and conscientious view of
the obligations of his high office, essentially courageous, indefatigable in the carrying out of his duties, an excellent man of business,
with the best interests of the nation at heart and with not a little
understanding of many of its needs, George III is yet in considerable measure responsible for the most calamitous blunders of his
lifetime—the assaults upon constitutional liberty associated with
the name of Wilkes, the breach with the American colonies,
and the refusal of Catholic emancipation to Ireland. The
generation of liberal enthusiasts, who were inspired by the
French Revolution, came to regard him as the very archetype
of reaction. Byron in *The Vision of Judgment* could write :

> A better farmer ne'er brush'd dew from lawn,
>   A worse king never left a realm undone !

And again :

> He ever warr'd with freedom and the free :
>   Nations as men, home subjects, foreign foes,
> So that they utter'd the word ' Liberty ! '
>   Found George the Third their first opponent. Whose
> History was ever stain'd as his will be
>   With national and individual woes ?

[1] By permission of the Trustees of the British Museum.

George III's first ambition was to free the Crown from the dictation of the over-mighty subject, both from the people's idol, Pitt, and from the great Whig oligarchs who had ruled the country for nearly fifty years. In the second place he aimed at personally directing national policy, and this meant an attack upon the principles of cabinet government as they had been evolved during the last two reigns. Not a Prime Minister, but the King, should direct the counsels of the realm ; ministers should be his ministers, responsible solely for their own respective departments, not conjointly for a party programme. It should be for the King to gather the various strands of policy together into a single whole.

As the first agent of this plan George III had the assistance of Lord Bute, who, at first acting solely as a power behind the scenes, enjoyed a brief and embarrassed period of office, and then passed into obscurity, his usefulness at an end. Anxious for peace, so that he might achieve the purpose on which his heart was set, the King wanted a glorious peace, one which would ensure the monarchy prestige. In the meantime Pitt was needed, much as George disliked him. While negotiations for peace were being carried on with small success between France and Great Britain, ministers got wind of a second Family Compact between France and Spain and the likelihood of Spain joining in the war. Pitt advised that, having this knowledge, ministers should take the initiative and declare war on Spain. His colleagues were opposed to such aggressive action, and Pitt resigned. The Spaniards duly entered the war, as he had seen they inevitably would ; nevertheless our operations continued to be successful up to the last moment of hostilities, culminating in our conquest of Manila and Havana, two of the most valuable Spanish possessions. This was exchanged for the much less valuable Florida in the peace negotiations which were concluded at Paris, of which the preliminaries were signed in November 1762. This treaty was criticized, as that of Utrecht had been, as less profitable than our great victories warranted. Certainly Bute and the Duke of Bedford, our plenipotentiary at Paris, showed the utmost willingness to make concessions, and the alienation of Frederic the Great was gratuitous and inept ; yet a treaty which gave us Canada, Florida, and Senegal in West Africa, is a notable landmark in British imperial development.

Following shortly after the resignation of Pitt had come the dismissal of Newcastle, the chief living representative of the great Whig families, and with him had been dismissed a number of his friends. The Duke's influence had been largely due to his control, during his long period in office, of the great resources of the Treasury in money and patronage. These resources were now transferred to the direct management of the Crown, and having these sinews of war at his disposal George III proceeded to create a party of his own, who came to be known specifically as ' the King's friends ', and who could be implicitly relied upon to vote to order on all occasions. Peace had been obtained, Pitt and Newcastle had been ousted, the parliamentary henchmen were secured. So opens a period notorious for the various phases of the Wilkes case, the breach with the American colonies and their eventual severance from the mother country.

It was during the Bute administration in 1762 that John Wilkes, assisted by the satirical poet Charles Churchill, started his scurrilous newspaper *The North Briton*, which first became famous for the violence of its attacks upon the favourite and all his compatriots. In May 1763 a new ministry came into office, its outstanding member being George Grenville. At the proroga-tion of Parliament the King had made the customary speech from the throne. In No. 45 of his paper, published on 23rd April, Wilkes had severely criticized the passages in the speech relating to the Peace of Paris and especially a reference to what the King of Prussia had gained from the treaty. Wilkes bluntly declared that the King had given ' the sanction of his sacred name to the most odious measures and to the most unjustifiable public declarations from a throne ever renowned for truth, honour, and unsullied virtue '. Speeches from the throne in Parliament are always regarded as the declarations of the ministers ; but it was characteristic of George III to regard this criticism as an accusation of falsehood and as being therefore a gross personal libel. He insisted on the prosecution of the

The Distressed Statesman.

Pitt as seen by the cartoonist at the time of his dismissal in 1757

author, and the new ministers were nothing loath to acquiesce. As the article was anonymous the Government issued a ' general

JOHN WILKES
Caricature by James Sayers

warrant, mentioning no specific names, for the apprehension of " the authors, printers, and publishers " of the *North Briton* ', and under this warrant Wilkes was arrested, together with forty-eight other persons, who were suspected, some of them quite wrongly, to have been concerned in the issuing of No. 45. Wilkes stigmatized the general warrant as illegal and ' a ridiculous warrant against the whole English people ', and he also claimed his release as a member of Parliament, whose privilege exempted him from arrest save for ' treason, felony, or breach of the peace ', libel being none of these. Lord Chief Justice Pratt, afterwards Lord Camden, upheld this plea, as he also did that of several of the forty-eight other victims, who demanded not only release but damages on the ground that general warrants were illegal.

The scene now shifts to the House of Commons. By a majority of 273 to 111, it voted that No. 45 was ' a false, scandalous, and seditious libel ', and ordered that it should be burnt by the common hangman ; by 258 to 133 it decided that Parliamentary privilege did not extend to libel. Both these resolutions were of serious consequence. By the first the House pronounced an opinion on a case pending in the courts before

THE
NORTH BRITON.

NUMBER I.

To be continued every SATURDAY. Price Two Pence Halfpenny.

SEJANUS, WOLSEY, hurt not honeſt FLEURY,
But well may put ſome Stateſmen in a fury.

POPE.

SATURDAY, JUNE the 5th, 1762.

HE liberty of the preſs is the birth-right of a BRITON, and has by the wiſeſt men in all ages been thought the firmeſt bulwark of the liberties of this country. It has ever been the ter-ror of bad miniſters, whoſe dark and dangerous deſigns, or whoſe weakneſs, inability, or du-plicity, have been detected and ſhewn to the public in too ſtrong colours for them long to bear up againſt the ge-neral odium. No wonder then that ſuch various and infinite arts have been employed, at one time entirely to ſuppreſs it, at another to take off the force and blunt the edge of this moſt ſacred weapon, left for the defence of truth and liberty. A wicked and corrupt adminiſtration muſt ever dread this

A   appeal

judgement had been given. As regards the second, the determination to reduce the special exemptions of members of Parliament was in itself salutary—members of Parliament enjoyed far too many special privileges—but as it had an obvious personal reference to Wilkes, it was objectionable because it was vindictive.

The House summoned Wilkes to appear before it; instead, having been seriously wounded in a duel, he retired to France. The House thereupon expelled him. During his absence from the country his trial for libel came on, he was found guilty, and, because of his non-appearance to answer the charge, was exiled. But this was not the end of the career of John Wilkes. Already he had made history by awakening popular sympathy as a deeply injured man and by drawing attention to the chasm that was now opening wide between Parliament and people. The House of Commons, when controlled by the great Whig houses, had been more in touch with popular opinion than it was now when filled with the ' King's friends '. In 1768 Wilkes, despite his outlawry, was back in England; he stood as parliamentary candidate for Middlesex and was triumphantly elected, his supporters going to the polls with the battle-cry, ' Wilkes and liberty '. The champion was then committed to the King's Bench prison as an outlaw; crowds gathered round the prison demanding his release, and there was a series of street disturbances, one producing bloodshed. The House of Commons refused to have Wilkes, and resolved that he be expelled. The Middlesex electors chose him again. The House of Commons retorted by voting that as he had been expelled already, he was incapable of being elected during the present Parliament. Here it went beyond its rights. While the House could expel whom it pleased, it was an arbitrary act to declare any one *incapable* of sitting. Wilkes was promptly returned again. A writ was now issued for an entirely new election, and a certain Colonel Luttrell contested the seat with Wilkes, who was returned by a four to one majority. The House of Commons now declared that Colonel Luttrell had been elected. This was a flagrantly unconstitutional proceeding; it defied the whole elective system, the whole representative principle to which the House of Commons owed its very existence. So monstrous a decision gravely impaired the authority and the prestige of the most illustrious representative chamber in the world.

Yet, indirectly, good came out of evil in more than one way. The determination of disputed elections was an undoubted right of the House of Commons. Hitherto no attempt had ever been made to treat these cases impartially on their merits ; the rival parties had regarded them simply as trials of voting strength. Grenville had disapproved of the recent proceedings of the Commons, and in 1770 he introduced a bill which became law, transferring the right of deciding disputed elections from the whole House to a committee of fifteen, thirteen chosen by ballot, two nominated by the rival candidates, all fifteen being sworn to impartiality. In the second place, the Wilkes case served to advertise the deficiencies of a representative assembly whose merits had become so much a matter of faith as to pass unquestioned. Criticism was provoked, and from this period we trace the development of a campaign for parliamentary reform which, despite many setbacks, culminated in the passing of the great Reform Act of 1832.

George Grenville is best known as the statesman who set on foot the march of events which led to the loss of the American colonies. It has been said that he was the first minister who took the trouble to read the American dispatches, and that this was the ultimate source of the mischief. Certainly he was a very conscientious, punctilious, business-like man, cursed with a pedantic and unimaginative mind. To him the course he took seemed eminently just and reasonable, and so, viewed from a purely legal standpoint, it was. With the removal of French rivalry in North America the English colonists had gained immensely from the triumph of British arms in the Seven Years' War. It seemed only fair that they should contribute something to the upkeep of the small army of 10,000 men deemed necessary to defend them against the possibility of an attempt by France to recover her lost possessions and against the ever-present menace of the Indians, one of whose chieftains, Pontiac, was a formidable foe. Accordingly, Grenville in 1764 laid before

Parliament the celebrated Stamp Act, which imposed a tax in the shape of stamps, which were to be affixed to all legal documents in America.

Before introducing this measure, which Parliament accepted with very little demur indeed, Grenville had consulted the colonial agents in England, including Benjamin Franklin, who had proposed as an alternative that the provincial assemblies of the different colonies should be asked to contribute. The difficulty was that it was impossible to say beforehand what these assemblies would be willing to give, or even if they would be willing to give at all, and there was no prospect of uniformity, because the colonies were very disunited, there being little in common in respect to origin, traditions, or essential character between the Virginian planter, the staunch descendant of the Puritan Fathers in New England, the Dutchman of New York, the Quaker or German of Pennsylvania, the Swede of Delaware, the Catholic of Maryland, the Moravian of Georgia, the Huguenot merchant of Charleston. Grenville tolerantly, and, as the event proved, unwisely, gave the colonists a year to consider the matter before the Stamp Act was enforced, and that delay gave ample opportunity for a vehement opposition to leap into flame, fanned by such men as Samuel Adams in Massachusetts and Patrick Henry in Virginia, who raised the cry : ' No taxation without representation.'

They made a distinction between internal and external taxation. The latter, the regulation of colonial trade by customs duties, they admitted ; the former not. There was really no difference in principle. If Parliament could legislate for the colonists and regulate their trade, it could also impose ordinary taxes. The impolicy of the Stamp Act lay in its being an innovation, which sharply raised a difficult imperial problem before public opinion on either side of the Atlantic had even grasped that there was such a problem. The significance of the transformation of a haphazard collection of trading stations into a series of politically-conscious communities had not been appreciated ; it was not realized that the whole question of the relations between the mother country and her colonies needed

careful reviewing in the light of American development. That
no crisis had arisen before was partly due to the good-humoured
laxity or indifference of most British Governments and to the

GEORGE GRENVILLE
From the painting by William Hoare

fact that the mercantile code was not in itself oppressive. If
the colonist could export his goods only in British or colonial
ships, and some of them only to Great Britain, the British
subject at home was forced to purchase certain articles only
from the colonies. Besides, Great Britain had winked at a very
serious evasion of the code in the shape of extensive smuggling.

Shortly before the Stamp Act was introduced the colonists had already been made restive because Bute's Administration had started upon a determined attempt to suppress this illegal traffic. The opinion of the average Englishman on the whole matter at this stage, so far as can be ascertained, probably was that the colonists were ungrateful, endeavouring to evade both their recognized legal obligations and their unrecognized moral obligations ; that the Stamp Act was so slight a burden that only ill-will and wrong-headedness could explain the violent opposition to it ; that to give way at this juncture on so vital an issue as the sovereignty of Parliament would be merely to court more serious trouble later on. The Grenville Administration decided to ignore the American opposition and put the Stamp Act into operation ; the colonists refused to use the stamps and began a vigorous boycott of British goods, which hit British traders severely.

In July 1765 the King against his will had to accept a new Ministry of Whigs led by the Marquess of Rockingham. In the following March this Government repealed the Stamp Act, accompanying the repeal, however, with a Declaratory Act, which affirmed the right of Parliament to tax the colonies, although its exercise was waived in this particular instance. Rockingham's Administration was very shortlived, being succeeded in August by a very heterogeneous Ministry under Pitt (now Lord Chatham), who soon became too ill to attend to his duties, so that the leadership devolved upon the Duke of Grafton. The most conspicuous member of the Government was Charles Townshend, brilliant and irresponsible. The situation in America had not improved since the repeal of the Stamp Act ; by some it had been interpreted as a sign of weakness and an encouragement to make new demands. In Boston the revenue laws were defied, revenue officers molested, and the Governor felt that he had only a ' shadow of authority '. In these circumstances opinion in Great Britain once more hardened against the colonists, and when Townshend decided to impose new duties on paper, paints, glass, and tea in America, the proceeds to go to the cost of American administration and defence, he had general support. This was an *external* tax, and the colonists admitted the legality

Quaker traditions in America. A Quaker meeting, early in the nineteenth century, under the tree in Flushing, Long Island, beneath which George Fox once preached

of such taxes ; on the other hand, it was being imposed not to regulate trade but to raise revenue. There followed more exasperation in America, and the home Government, vacillating between ideas of conciliation and repression, withdrew all the obnoxious duties save the one on tea.

LORD NORTH
Caricature by James Sayers

But in January 1770 Lord North came into office, more completely the King's servant than any previous head of a Government had been, and from that date feeling hardened on both sides, as the result of a series of unfortunate incidents—the so-called 'Boston' massacre of the 5th March 1770, an affray between soldiers and mob, for which the latter were entirely to blame; the burning in Boston Harbour on the 16th December 1773 of three tea-ships and the throwing of their cargoes into the sea ; the publication by Franklin of the Whately correspondence, consisting of private letters of Hutchinson, the Governor of Massachusetts, in which he freely expressed his opinions of the troublesome Bostonians. These opinions gave great offence in America ; their publication by Franklin at least equal umbrage in England. Measures of repression came in 1774—the closing of the port of Boston, the revision of the Massachusetts charter

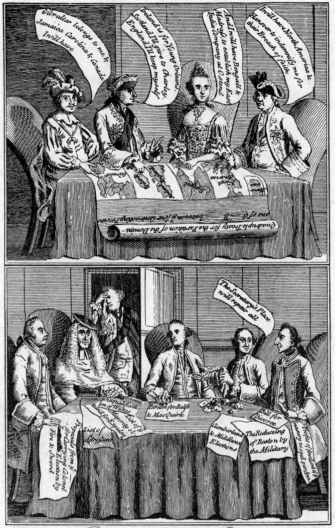

What is doing at Home.

A caricature of 1769 in the spirit of Junius. The upper picture shows Charles III of Spain, Louis XV, Maria Theresa, and Frederic the Great discussing the dismemberment of the British Empire; the lower picture depicts the Cabinet engrossed in its malpractices at home. The figures at table are the Duke of Bedford, Lord Mansfield, Lord Rochford, Lord Weymouth (the two Secretaries of State) and the Duke of Grafton. The King looks in at the proceedings of his ministers in sorrow and dismay.

Balfe and McQuirk were members of a rowdy mob of supporters of the Government's candidate at an election at Brentford, who made an assault upon a certain Dr. Clark, as the result of which he died. They were condemned to death for murder, but were subsequently pardoned by the King. From 'The Political Register' for May 1769

so as to give much more power to the Governor. Almost equally resented by the rabidly Protestant New Englanders was the passing in this same year of the Quebec Act, a very statesman-like measure which allowed the French Canadians the free exercise of their native laws, customs, and religion.

Opposition to the home Government had by this time evoked in America the idea of co-operation as it had never been evoked before, and in September 1774 there assembled at Philadelphia a ' continental congress ', representing all thirteen colonies with the exception of Georgia. The driving force of the most ardent spirits in that assembly was already in favour of independence, though the loyalists in America were still strong, especially in the south. A complete breach was not yet inevitable ; Burke and Chatham strove hard for conciliation. At the last even North put forward a compromise ; but by that time it was too late. On the 19th April 1775 the first shots in the American War of Independence were fired in a skirmish at Lexington.

The war falls naturally into two periods—the first, when it was fought solely on the continent of America and against the revolted colonists, up to March 1778 ; the second, when France and Spain participated, up to 1783. The Government anticipated little difficulty in suppressing the revolt, and through over-confidence failed in a difficult, but by no means impossible, task. Too much reliance was placed on the help of the loyalists ; the impracticable attempt was made to direct strategy from White-hall ; appeals from generals on the spot for necessary reinforcements were not answered. The initial movements of the British forces were singularly lacking in decision ; and the colonial levies gained unexpected successes so encouraging to them that on the 4th July 1776 the Declaration of Independence was adopted by all the colonies. Then things began to go badly for the Americans. An ill-equipped expedition sent against Canada, owing to the energy of the Canadian governor, Sir Guy Carleton, had proved a fiasco ;[1] General Howe forced Washington to abandon New York, next year defeated him at Brandywine Creek, and took the chief of American cities in those days,

[1] The French Canadians preferred the English Government which had given them the Quebec Act to the Colonists who had declaimed against it.

View of Boston about 1720

Philadelphia. Then followed a complete reversal of fortune. An expedition of General Burgoyne, operating from Canada, in what was intended as a great concerted movement with Clinton, starting from New York, and Howe, advancing up the Hudson river, met with complete disaster at Saratoga, where the whole force was compelled to surrender on the 17th October 1777. This event was decisive, not because it was in itself by any means an irretrievable calamity, but because it was so signal a success on the part of the American colonists that France no longer hesitated to espouse their cause, being shortly afterwards followed by Spain, so that the American War of Independence was transformed into a world war, in which Great Britain's energies had to be so largely devoted to the needs of self-defence against the Bourbon powers that she was unable to concentrate upon the suppression of the American revolt.

Before long our ships were engaged in the Atlantic, the Mediterranean, and the Indian Ocean, and our armies were fighting in Europe, America, and India. In 1780 Holland was added to the list of our adversaries, and the same year in resistance to our exercise of the right of search for contraband in neutral vessels, Austria, Prussia, Russia, Sweden, and Denmark joined in the so-called ' Armed Neutrality of the North '—an armed neutrality which, had the war continued much longer, might easily have developed into an armed hostility, so that we should have been at war with most of Europe, without a single ally to help us. Between 1780 and 1783 we were fighting for our very existence as a maritime and imperial power. In the Mediterranean Spain sought to wrest from us our two great naval stations, subjected Gibraltar to a prolonged siege, and succeeded in recapturing Minorca. In India Hyder Ali, the famous Sultan of Mysore, swept into the Carnatic, having in the words of Burke,

resolved, in the gloomy recesses of a mind capacious of such things, to leave the whole Carnatic an everlasting monument of vengeance. . . . Then ensued a scene of woe, the like of which no eye had seen, no heart conceived, and which no tongue can adequately tell. . . . A storm of universal fire blasted every field, consumed every house, destroyed every temple. The miserable inhabitants flying from their flaming villages in part were slaughtered ; others, without regard to sex, to age, to the respect of rank, or sacredness of function, fathers torn from children, husbands from wives, enveloped in a whirlwind of cavalry, and amidst the goading spears of drivers, and the trampling of pursuing horses, were swept into captivity, in an unknown and hostile land.

Hyder Ali's army owed its training to 400 French officers, and he was assisted by a French fleet under the brilliant Admiral

HYDER ALI

Suffren, who proved more than a match for the British commander, Hughes, and succeeded in securing two valuable naval stations for the French in Indian waters, Trincomalee, in Ceylon, and Cuddalore near Fort St. David. In the end the situation was saved by the resolution of the great Governor-General, Warren Hastings, the stubbornness of Hughes, who never gave in to his more skilful adversary on the high seas, and the military genius of Eyre Coote, who heavily defeated Hyder at Porto Novo (July 1781). On the American continent French volunteers under Lafayette afforded moral rather than material assistance to the colonists.

In all the theatres of war the decisive factor was command of the sea; and the conduct of British naval operations in these years left much to be desired. Owing to neglect and jobbery, the condition of our ships of war had been allowed to deteriorate, and although the human material in the crews was as good as before and we had many able commanders, the true principles of naval strategy, as they had been understood and exemplified in the Seven Years' War, were forgotten. Instead of closely blockading the enemy squadrons in their European harbours, we spent our time chasing them from one quarter of the globe to another. Our position in the West Indies was frequently in peril, the French under D'Estaing, De Guichen, or De Grasse maintaining a constant threat. The success or failure of our troops in America depended ultimately on the situation in those waters and on the American seaboard. Since 1778 our efforts in America had been mainly confined to an attempt to retain the southern colonies, and Cornwallis had achieved considerable success, first in the Carolinas, then in Virginia. Unhappily his troops there and the other British army under Clinton at New York, separated by hostile forces, had no means of communication save by sea. At a critical moment, in September 1781, when Cornwallis found himself attacked by greatly superior forces at Yorktown and urgently needed reinforcements from Clinton, the British lost command of the sea, and the fall of Yorktown resulted on the 19th October. The last hope of success against the Americans therewith perished. Next year the French made a great attempt to drive our fleets from the West Indies and to capture Jamaica. This was foiled, first by the skill of Admiral Sir Samuel Hood, second by Rodney's brilliant victory at the Saints (12th April 1782), which not only saved Jamaica, but (more important) re-established British naval prestige. Such was British grit and determination that in 1782 the position was distinctly better than in the previous year; France and Spain, alike near bankruptcy, recognized that their adversary could not be forced to her knees, and a peace by negotiation became possible. It was signed at Versailles on the 3rd September 1783. By it we acknowledged the independence of the United

States, surrendered Florida and Minorca to Spain, some conquests to France, but kept our possessions on the whole intact. Nevertheless the treaty was interpreted by other countries as proving that

Paper-money ('continental currency') issued by Congress 1779

Coins issued by Congress 1793

Great Britain had sunk heavily from her proud position twenty years earlier. She had lost all the American colonies, on which her trade and her prestige had so largely depended.

The American revolution had rendered critical an important

problem much nearer at home. The manifold grievances of
Ireland in the eighteenth century had caused many of her sons
to regard the cause of the colonists with keen sympathy.
Ireland's troubles were religious, commercial, agrarian, and
political. Three-quarters of her population was Roman Catholic ;
yet much the greater part of the land was owned by Protestants.
In Roman Catholic families inherited land was divided equally
among the children ; in Protestant families it passed by primo-
geniture. Hence all the great estates were in Protestant hands.
Roman Catholics were forbidden to acquire land by purchase,
and there was an iniquitous arrangement whereby a Roman
Catholic by turning Protestant could disinherit his brothers.
Again, education was virtually unobtainable by Roman Catholics.
Of the Protestant landlords the greater number were English or
Scottish—the most important belonged to the close fraternity of
the peerage. They rarely visited their Irish estates, which were
managed by agents, who were able to exact extortionate rack-
rents from the Roman Catholic tenantry, owing to the fact that
practically the only Irish industry was agriculture, as the result
of the deliberate policy of British governments of protecting
British traders and manufacturers against all possibility of Irish
competition. Only the linen manufacture was sanctioned.
Direct trade between Ireland and the colonies was prohibited.
In short, Ireland was governed solely in the interests of Great
Britain and of the Protestant minority in Ireland, who, owing
to the disqualification of all Roman Catholics, monopolized
political influence and had the Dublin Parliament entirely to
themselves. That legislature was kept in leading strings by the
provisions of Poynings' laws (1494), which required that all bills
brought before it must have the approval of the British and
Irish Privy Councils. This ancient stipulation had been reinforced
by an enactment—a so-called Declaratory Act—of 1719, which
transferred the right of hearing Irish appeals from the Irish to
the British House of Lords, and which affirmed the competence
of the Parliament at Westminster to legislate for Ireland over the
head of its own assembly.

Prior to the accession of George III eighteenth-century Ireland had been pretty quiet apart from the agitation over Wood's Ha'pence in 1724. In 1761 there started the excesses of the so-called Whiteboys in Leinster and Munster, masked marauders whose agrarian outrages had little political significance, being

The Great Parliament of Ireland, elected 1790

simply evidence of land-hunger. Much more important is the commencement about this time of a movement in the Irish Parliament for an enlargement of its powers. The duration of an Irish Parliament was the lifetime of the sovereign : the Irish opposition pressed for a Septennial Act. Their first success was achieved in 1768, when they secured the passing of an Octennial Act. They also aimed at obtaining a Habeas Corpus Act, an annual Mutiny Act, and an Act giving security of tenure to the judges during good behaviour—all three being safeguards which Great Britain regarded as veritable corner-stones of her liberties, but which she deemed unnecessary for Ireland. Another object with the Irish reformers was the enactment of a measure against absenteeism on the part of landlords. In all these aims they at first failed. But after the outbreak of the American troubles they met with much greater success, when—as it so happened—they had as their leaders two of the greatest patriots and orators in Irish history—Henry Flood and Henry Grattan. It is note-worthy that while the battle, being mainly a parliamentary one, was fought by Protestants, great sympathy was shown with Roman Catholic claims, and Grattan held that the removal of Catholic disabilities was a necessary concomitant of the political emancipation of Ireland.

Under Grattan the reformers became more ambitious. They aimed at entirely freeing both Irish trade and the Irish legislature from the shackles which fettered them. Lord North's govern-ment was willing to go a long way towards meeting Grattan on the commercial question, but a liberal measure introduced with this object into the British Parliament in 1778 was shipwrecked owing to the frenzied resistance of English and Scottish traders. But the strategic position of the Irish opposition grew stronger as the menace of the war became more serious. The entrance of France and Spain into the conflict meant that Ireland had to be denuded of her usual garrisons. To protect their own shores against the possibility of French invasion, of which they were genuinely afraid, the Irish banded themselves into loyal volunteer associations. The movement spread rapidly and the Volunteers soon numbered many thousands and constituted a force which could not be ignored. Conscious of their new power, the Irish threatened a boycott of British goods if their commercial demands were not granted. Resistance was no longer possible, and by Acts of 1779 and 1780 the Government allowed to Ireland practically complete commercial freedom—both as regards foreign and colonial trade. Grattan now pressed for the abroga-tion of Poynings' laws. On the 19th April 1780 he brought forward a memorable resolution—which was ominously termed

The House of Commons in 1793

' a declaration of independence '—to the effect that, while Great Britain and Ireland were indissolubly united under the one crown, none save her own legislature had any right to make laws for Ireland. The Volunteer movement continued to expand, and in February 1782 there was a great congress of the Ulster Volunteers at Dungannon, which made a solemn pronouncement in favour of the two great causes of legislative independence and liberty of conscience. The British Government, faced with difficulties and dangers on all sides, was in no position to make a stand against the powerfully organized Irish demand for a free Dublin Parliament. The lord-lieutenant, Lord Carlisle, advised Lord North that it should be conceded. North had resigned before the advice could be acted upon, but the next ministry accepted the situation and the edifice of Poynings' laws and the Declaratory Act was demolished. For a brief period of under twenty years there existed a completely independent Irish legislature. The circumstances which induced Pitt to adopt a diametrically opposed policy, ending in the legislative union of 1801, belong to a different story.

Up till the fall of Yorktown Lord North's government, despite the earlier failures of the war, owing to royal support both in the closet and in Parliament, remained stable. Though it is often thought of as reactionary, this period saw two notable reforms —1st, the Regulating Act (June 1773), which brought the management of the political, as distinct from the commercial, activities of the East India Company within the purview of the Secretary of State, and united the three presidencies of Madras, Bombay, and Calcutta under the control of a governor-general; 2nd, Sir George Savile's Catholic Relief Act of 1778, which exempted English Catholics from certain of their disabilities. The Government's proposal to bring in a similar Bill for Scotland provoked the Lord George Gordon No Popery riots, familiarized by Dickens's *Barnaby Rudge*. When North, greatly to the King's chagrin, insisted on resigning in 1781, a second Rockingham Ministry came into office, its two ablest members being Charles James Fox and Lord Shelburne, Chatham's most distinguished successor. These two acted as joint Secretaries of

Westminster Hall and the old Houses of Parliament, from St. Stephen's Yard

From an engraving in the British Museum

State. They were utterly opposed to one another, and when in July 1782 Rockingham died and Shelburne became First Lord of the Treasury in his place, Fox not merely refused to continue in the ministry, but went into active opposition as the ally of Lord North—a transaction which shocked the not very sensitive political proprieties of that day as a very outrageous proceeding. Shelburne was driven out and his two triumphant enemies formed a coalition ministry. The King was enraged beyond measure ; he hated Fox and regarded this action on the part of his old henchman North, whom he had not forgiven for what he regarded as his desertion in 1781, as a gross betrayal. He was ready to seize any opportunity for getting rid of the pair. It came speedily in the shape of a new Government of India Bill, which aimed at placing that Government in the hands of seven commissioners, who should have full control over policy, administration, and the appointment to offices. The Opposition represented that these commissioners would become all-powerful, not only in India but in Great Britain, where, with the great wealth at their disposal, they would be able to manage Parliament. The King was easily persuaded that the royal power itself would be seriously menaced. The Bill passed the Commons by a large majority, but the King took the arbitrary step of informing the peers that he would esteem any one who voted for it in their House as his enemy ; whereupon the Lords threw out the Bill. George joyfully seized this opportunity, and on the 19th December 1783 entrusted the seals of office to William Pitt the younger, who thus became Prime Minister at the age of twenty-four.

With this event we are on the threshold of a new era. The boy, who was thus suddenly placed at the head of the Government, though leading only a small minority in the House of Commons, with all the talent of the House as well as the force of numbers arrayed against him, not only triumphed over Fox and North, but triumphed over the King, by re-establishing the authority of the Prime Minister and securing cabinet solidarity as it had never existed before. He was tackling the problem of parliamentary reform, and by his economic policy had already shown himself to be a great finance minister, when the tempest of the

French Revolution suddenly arose and changed the whole course of history. Europe was engulfed in mightier wars even than that which the genius of his father had directed. With none of his father's innate aptitude for war to help him in the tremendous task with which he was now confronted, the son faced its ardours and dangers with a heart just as dauntless. Under the intrepid leadership of this ' pilot who weathered the storm ', the country of Jervis and Nelson had already abundantly proved before his death in the year of Trafalgar that she was no decadent but still

strong in will
To strive, to seek, to find, and not to yield.

After Moreau le Jeune

Fashionable head-dresses of 1780

III

THE SOCIAL SCENE

§ i. *Fiction and Memoirs*

THERE are many different aids to any one who wishes to imbibe the atmosphere of the eighteenth century. Some will best appreciate the period by studying its costume; others by contemplating Adam doorways, Chippendale chairs, Sheraton sideboards, or Wedgwood ware; some by turning over the cartoons of Hogarth or admiring the portraiture of the century; while others will most readily understand it in its characteristic literature—in the poetry of Pope, in Boswell's picture of the Johnson circle, in the philosophic treatises of Berkeley and Hume, or the great history of Gibbon. But for those to whom atmosphere means specifically social atmosphere the best guides are the fiction of the century and its memoirs. Perhaps one should add descriptive poetry, for there is not a little social history to be learnt from such poems as Goldsmith's *The Deserted Village*, Cowper's *The Task*, and Crabbe's *The Village, The Parish Register*, and *The Borough*. The eighteenth-century novel, as a whole, is essentially a novel of manners. Sterne stands in a class by himself; the fantastic romanticism, popularized by Horace Walpole's *The Castle of Otranto* and cultivated by Anne Radcliffe, belongs to an entirely different *genre*. But the novels of Defoe, Smollett, Fielding, and Fanny Burney, and in a lesser degree of Richardson, are distinctively studies of contemporary life. From this source something can be obtained of the utmost value, which the historian is unable to provide—a living picture of the average man as a real live individual. The small company of persons who in each age succeed by reason of their achievements in entering the charmed circle of those whom history remembers, in so doing cease to be typical. Ordinary men and women do not achieve such immortality; consequently, in so far as the historian deals with them at all, it is apt to be perforce in a series of generalities. But the novelist seizes upon the ordinary man and woman and presents them as vital personalities, and so can make the whole class which they represent real to us. Thus in Squire Western Fielding presents us to the typical squire; in Tom Bowling and Commodore Trunnion Smollett delineates the typical seaman; in the Vicar of Wakefield Goldsmith gives us the best type of country parson; and in the Branghtons Fanny Burney introduces us to the typical vulgar aspirants to gentility.

FANNY BURNEY
Charles Turner's mezzotint after the painting by E. Burney

The Branghtons are characters in the first and the liveliest of Miss Burney's novels, *Evelina*, than which there is perhaps no more faithful or attractive guide to contemporary society. Here we are shown all sorts of types, the vulgar world of Madame Duval, Mr. Smith and the Branghtons, the distinguished nobleman in Lord Orville, the fine gentleman in Sir Clement Willoughby, the fop in Mr. Lovel. Here again we are introduced to the thrills of London, its sights and its shows, to the opera, to the tea-room at the new Pantheon in Oxford Street, to the balls at the Long Room in Hampstead, to the excitement of the fireworks at Vauxhall and of the rough jollifications of Ranelagh.

But while eighteenth-century life may seem to be reincarnated in the pages of a single vivid novel such as *Evelina*, the scholar will betake himself, for an insight into many of its most interesting phases, to the memoirs, private diaries, and correspondence in which the period is extraordinarily rich—to what Lord Hervey, Lord Chesterfield, Horace Walpole, Fanny Burney, Lady Mary Wortley Montagu, Gibbon, George Selwyn, Bubb Dodington, Nathaniel Wraxall, and others have to tell us about themselves, their friends, and their surroundings. We shall not indeed derive even from such variegated authorities as these a complete picture of eighteenth-century society; they all belong to a brilliant and rather exclusive sphere and can tell us little of middle and lower class existence. Let us, however, with such guides as these take a few glimpses at their social group; and then go to the lives of other humbler folk, who did not leave their own records behind them, for a summary view of other classes.

§ ii. *The Court*

First let us glance at the Court. Here the memoirs of Lord Hervey may be our guide. We must remember the character of our showman. Deficient in moral principle, his outlook on men and affairs was cynical and ill-natured. He was foppish and effeminate, and he had obviously a keen relish for scandal. Such a man was likely to have enemies. Hervey had many; one of them was vitriolic in his hatred—Pope, who made one of the most venomous attacks in our literature on him in the character of Sporus. Another wit—it is uncertain which—declared that this world consists of 'men, women, and Herveys'. Some readers may be antagonized by the author's mordant tone; some will be wearied by his extreme fondness for antithesis; but he admittedly presents us with a most vivid and dramatic picture of the court of George II, the King and the Queen and their great minister, Sir Robert Walpole. The delineation of the royal family is unforgettable. George II, when Prince of Wales, had been at daggers drawn with his father; similarly the new King hated his eldest son, Frederic. In this detestation the mother joined with equal thoroughness, cursing the day he was born. The mother was the remarkable Caroline of Anspach, through whose unwavering support Walpole retained his influence with the King. Caroline ruled her husband, as the minister was acute enough to realize, but it took real penetration to appreciate this, for the Queen was a long-suffering woman. Devoted as

THE DESIGNS here and on pp. 83 and 103 reproduce calling-cards in the Italian fashion of the end of the century.

George was to her in his inmost heart, it never even occurred to him to be faithful to her. Caroline buried her pride and submitted to the mistresses. When the King during one of his Hanoverian visits fell in love with a certain Madame Walmoden, the Queen even humiliated herself so far as to write, at the King's request, to the Walmoden[1] to come over to England. Although she thus tactfully and unobtrusively guided him in affairs of state policy and constantly deferred to his wishes in private matters, George latterly became so perverse in temper that she could scarcely make a single remark uncontradicted or do a single action unreproved. What with the faithlessness of the father, and the parents' and the son's mutual animosity, it was a most unhappy family. Frederic for the greater part of his life as Prince of Wales tenanted Leicester House, as his father had done before him, and maintained the tradition of that establishment as a centre of social gaiety, wit, and fashion in contrast with the more sombre character of St. James's Palace. Here assembled politicians who were out of humour or out of favour with the court, so that there was a regular Leicester House party always ' agin the Government '.

Incidents, trivial in themselves, as narrated by Hervey, give a vivid impression of the atmosphere prevailing at St. James's. During one of the King's customary absences in Hanover, the Queen seized the opportunity to substitute some good for some very bad pictures in the great drawing-room at Kensington Palace. George notoriously knew nothing whatever about pictures and cared less, but the mere fact of alterations of any sort being made in his absence and without his leave put him into a thoroughly bad temper. He insisted on the return of all the original paintings, including a particularly unattractive ' gigantic fat Venus '. While Lord Hervey was informing the Queen of her husband's commands on the subject of the pictures, George himself entered, still very irritable, ' snubbed the Queen, who was drinking chocolate, for being always stuffing ; the Princess Emily for not hearing him ; the Princess Caroline for being grown fat ; the Duke [of Cumberland] for standing awk-

[1] Created Countess of Yarmouth in 1740.

wardly ; Lord Hervey for not knowing what relation the Prince of Sulzbach was to the Elector Palatine ; and then carried the Queen to walk and be snubbed in the garden '. Whenever he came back from his frequent Hanoverian visits, he had nothing but abuse for the land of his adoption.

No English or even French cook could dress a dinner ; no English confectioner set out a dessert ; no English player could act ; no English coachman could drive, or English jockey ride ; nor were any English horses fit to be drove or fit to be ridden ; no Englishman knew how to come into a room, nor any Englishman how to dress himself ; nor were there any diversions in England, public or private ; nor any man or woman in England whose conversation was to be borne—the one, as he said, talking of nothing but their dull politics, and the other of nothing but their dull clothes.

When, later on, Queen Caroline lay on her death-bed heroically uncomplaining though in agony, tortured no less by the physicians' drastic and useless remedies than by the malady itself, the King was all anxious solicitude, for ever pronouncing eulogies upon her, saying she was ' the best wife, the best mother, the best friend, and the best woman that ever was born ', belauding her wisdom, her charm, and her *utility*. ' And yet,' observes Lord Hervey, ' so unaccountable were the sudden sallies of his temper, and so little was he able or willing to command them, that in the midst of all this flow of tenderness he hardly ever went into her room that he did not, even in this moving situation, snub her for something or other she said or did. When her constant uneasiness made her shift her posture every minute he would say to her, " How the devil should you sleep, when you will never lie still a moment ? You want to rest, and the doctors tell you nothing can do you so much good, yet you are always moving about. Nobody can sleep in that manner, and that is always your way : you never take the proper care to get what you want, and then you wonder you have it not ".' Hervey notes that his majesty's solicitude for his wife was mixed at this time with a great deal of self-laudation. ' He never talked of her . . . being a good wife without giving strong hints of his deserving a good one, and being at least as good a husband.'

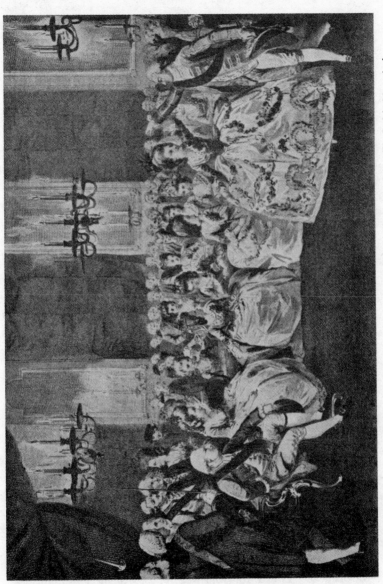

A View of the Ball at St. James's on the King's Birthday, June 4, 1782. Engraved for 'The Lady's Magazine'

What sort of husband he was she knew only too well. She urged him to marry again. ' Non, non,' he exclaimed through his tears, ' j'aurai des maîtresses.' ' Ah, mon Dieu,' answered the Queen, ' cela n'empêche pas.' Thackeray says of Hervey's description of these scenes, that its ' grotesque horror . . . surpasses all satire : the dreadful humour of the scene is more terrible than Swift's blackest pages, or Fielding's fiercest irony '.

The court life of George III was very different. The grandson of George II, he had been brought up by the Princess of Wales, Frederic's widow, in great seclusion and with jealous care, under the tutorship of Lord Waldegrave and other less able preceptors. The Princess was anxious that he should avoid the companionship of young men of his own age for fear of contamination. Thus it came about, as the Princess herself confided to Bubb Dodington, that he was ' shy and backward ; not a wild, dissipated boy, but good-natured and cheerful, with a serious cast upon the whole '. He was genuinely religious, exceedingly abstemious in all his habits, and entirely decorous in his mode of life. He fell in love, just before his accession, with a girl of fifteen, the lovely Sarah Lennox, daughter of the Duke of Richmond and sister-in-law of Henry Fox, the first Lord Holland. ' Her beauty ', writes Fox, ' is not easily described, otherwise than by saying she had the finest complexion, most beautiful hair, and the prettiest person that ever was seen, with a sprightly and fine air, a very pretty mouth and remarkably fine teeth, and excess of bloom in her cheeks.' But, he concludes, essentially her loveliness consisted in ' a peculiarity of countenance, that made her at the same time different from and prettier than any other girl I ever saw '. Fox was no doubt very anxious that the King should make a match of it, and for a time it seemed he would. Meeting Lady Sarah's greatest friend, Lady Susan Strangeways, the King inquired whether the coronation would not be a finer sight if there were a Queen, then went on to say that he had had a great many ' applications from abroad, but would rather have one at home ; did she not think her friend fittest ? ' But the infatuation was allowed to die ; the voices of prudence, Lord Bute (who was opposed to the Fox influence)

Lady Sarah Lennox (aged 17) at a window of Holland House. Below are Lady Susan Strangeways (aged 19) and Charles James Fox (aged 13). From the mezzotint by James Watson after the painting by Sir Joshua Reynolds

and the Princess of Wales, were allowed to prevail, and after all George III did marry some one from abroad, while Lady Susan—as her first husband—married plain Mr., afterwards Sir Charles Bunbury, a notable patron of the turf.

Another glimpse of George III's court at a later period we get from the vivid pages of Fanny Burney's Diary. The future Madame D'Arblay (1752–1840) was the daughter of Dr. Burney, a pupil of the great Dr. Arne, and himself the most indefatigable and the most popular and respected music-teacher in London, a friend of Johnson, Garrick, and the Thrales. Miss Burney's descriptions of that coterie are an indispensable supplement to Boswell, for she has a wonderful fund of lively anecdote. From an early age Fanny had been addicted to writing, and at the age of sixteen

SYMPTOMS of DEEP-THINKING.

SIR CHARLES BUNBURY, the sportsman
Caricature by Gillray

she had, obedient to her step-mother, who considered that she was wasting her time in such an occupation, made a bonfire of a work of fiction. But to this same occupation Fanny returned, and at the age of twenty-six achieved the great triumph of successful authorship ; the merits of *Evelina* were on every tongue. The approval of Dr. Johnson made her dance an impromptu jig out of sheer exhilaration. Her success caused much chagrin to the third-rate dramatist, Richard Cumberland, who figures in Sheridan's *The Critic* as Sir Fretful Plagiary, for he could endure no one's literary success but his own. Miss Burney followed up *Evelina* with *Cecilia, Camilla,* and *The Wanderer,* less spontaneous and enjoyable than her first venture, the last two being distinctly inferior in quality to their predecessors. Authorship, which was not only successful but virtuous, brought the little lady into the cognizance of the court, and four years after the appearance of *Cecilia* the Queen decided to take

FRYING SPRATS,

Ah 'tisn't a pair was never seen,' Vide Royal Supper

TOASTING MUFFINS,

'So justly formed to meet by nature' Vide Royal Breakfast

Gillray's caricature upon George III's alleged parsimony

Miss Burney into her household as one of her dressers. It was a dull, monotonous life for one who had been accustomed to the exhilaration of Johnson's circle. She had to get up every morning at 6, go into the Queen's apartments at 7.30 to help her to dress, after which she was free to spend the rest of the morning writing or walking, returning to her duties before 1 o'clock and not being again free as a rule till 3. She had dinner at 5, followed by coffee ; supper at 11. Some time between that and midnight her last summons came to attend on the Queen, when she went to bed. Not an arduous day, except that the hours for sleep were short, but dull between 5 and 8, 9 and 11, and exceedingly tiresome, for during those periods Fanny Burney was at the mercy of her colleague, a very heavy, peevish German lady of the name of Schwellenberg, who was crotchety, haughty, and

A CONNOISSEUR examining a COOPER.

Gillray's caricature of George III, who is examining a miniature of Oliver Cromwell. A political gibe at the despotic tendencies of the King

ignorant, termed the works which were dear to Miss Burney's heart ' stuff ', and found amusement only in the croaking of two pet frogs, whose voices harmonized with her own raucous and barbarous jargon. No wonder that Miss Burney was glad to exchange the amenities of a royal palace for the attractions of M. D'Arblay, who made her his wife.

The World of Fashion

§ iii. *The World of Fashion*

While the inner life of George III's court was both dull and
decorous, there were some sorry rakes and profligates among
those who filled the household offices—for example, the Earl of
March and Lord Sandwich. Nothing is as a rule easier than to
exaggerate the delinquencies of the fashionable world. It lives
in the limelight ; it has the means and the leisure for dissipation,
and the doings of its rakes and its ladies of doubtful reputation
will invariably receive more than a fair share of attention, so
that there is always a danger of confusing the normal with the
exceptional. Whilst making this proviso, one must add that the
nobility at the close of the seventeenth century and the opening
of the eighteenth included rather a high percentage of rakes—
men like Thomas, Lord Wharton and his son, Philip, the first
duke, the riotous Lord Mohun, best known now because
he figures in *Esmond*, the eccentric Charles Mordaunt, Earl of
Peterborough, Bolingbroke, and many others. It is probably
true that on the whole there was a distinctly better moral tone
in the days of Anne than in those of Charles II, less vice and less
open defiance of the laws of decency and restraint. On the
other hand there was certainly an increase of brutality and
coarseness. In 1712 there was formed an atrocious club of

young bloods, known as the Mohocks, whose practice it was to sally forth at night into the streets, drunk and armed with naked swords, to molest harmless wayfarers and inflict atrocious outrages upon them. In the reign of George III among a certain set libertinism was as bad as it had been in Restoration days. Sir Francis Dashwood, afterwards Lord le Despenser, founded a profligate society called the Medmenham Brotherhood, of which Sandwich and Wilkes were outstanding members. The Earl of March, afterwards Duke of Queensberry, lived into the nineteenth century and was notorious in his extreme old age as 'old Q', because he shocked a none too fastidious generation by continuing a mode of life which had been habitual in his own set in his younger days.

Lord Sandwich paying attention to a flower-girl.
Caricature by Gillray

Drinking and gaming were the prevalent vices of the eighteenth century. Hard drinking among the upper classes sensibly decreased during the century, but that only means that at the beginning the practice was almost incredibly bad. Oxford, Bolingbroke, Carteret, Walpole were all heavy drinkers. 'They tell me', George III once said to Lord Chancellor Northington, 'that you love a glass of wine.' The reply was, 'Those who have informed your Majesty have done me great injustice; they should have said a bottle'. And although Northington spoke of *one* bottle, he probably meant *two*. The eighteenth century boasted its two-bottle men, who were accustomed to consume that amount of wine at a single sitting. At the end of the previous century, owing to the prohibition of French imports, the headier wines of Portugal began to displace the lighter French clarets; and this tendency was strengthened by the Methuen Treaty of

The ravages of strong drink.   Caricature by Gillray

1703 with Portugal, which admitted her wines into England at a specially low rate. Port drinking spread the ravages of gout, which is the characteristic malady of the eighteenth century. Its numerous victims succeeded in persuading themselves that its tortures, however unpleasant, were rather beneficial to general health than otherwise. George III with sturdy common sense refused to believe in the validity of this comforting reflection. In truth there can be no doubt of the devastating results of the prevalent hard drinking on most constitutions; many men, as the result of their intemperance, were quite worn out and elderly before they reached fifty; some showed visible signs of decay at the age

It may be some sort of Amusement to present our Readers with the following List of Officers established in the most notorious Gaming-houses.

1. A *Commissioner*, always a Proprietor, who looks in of a Night, and the Week's Accompt is audited by him and two others of the Proprietors. 2. A *Director*, who superintends the Room. 3. An *Operator*, who deals the Cards at a cheating Game called *Faro*. 4. Two *Crowpees*, who watch the Cards, and gather the Money for the Bank. 5. Two *Puffs*, who have Money given 'em to decoy others to play. 6. A *Clerk*, who is a Check upon the Puffs, to see that they sink none of the Money that is given them to play with. 7. A *Squib*, is a Puff of a lower Rank, who serves at half Salary, while he is Learning to deal. 8. A *Flasher*, to swear how often the Bank has been stript. 9. A *Dunner*, who goes about to recover Money lost at Play. 10. A *Waiter*, to fill out Wine, Snuff-candles, and attend in the Gaming-room. 11. An *Attorney*, a *Newgate* Solicitor. 12. A *Captain*, who is to fight a Gentleman that is peevish for losing his Money. 13. An *Usher*, who lights Gentlemen up and down Stairs, and gives the Word to the Porter. 14. A *Porter*, who is generally a Soldier of the Foot Guards. 15. An *Orderly Man*, who walks up and down the outside of the Door, to give Notice to the Porter, and alarm the House, at the Approach of the Constables. 17. A *Runner*, who is to get intelligence of the Justices Meeting. 17. *Linkboys*, *Coachmen*, *Chairmen*, *Drawers*, or *others*, who bring the first intelligence of the Justices Meetings, or of the Constables being out, at half a Guinea Reward. 18. *Common-bail*, *Affidavitmen*, *Ruffians*, *Bravoes*, *Assassins*, cum multis aliis.

The Loss of the FARO BANK; or The Rook's Pigeon'd. "When Greek meets Greek then comes the tug of war!"

The KNAVE wins all.

MODERN HOSPITALITY, or A Friendly Party in High Life.

Gillray's satire upon the gambling craze. Caricatures of 1792 and 1797

of thirty. The middle classes did not indulge in port, and the tendency among them to substitute the drinking of wine for ale probably aided sobriety. Such at any rate was the opinion of Dr. Johnson, who tells us that in his early days ' all the decent people in Lichfield got drunk every night, and were not the worse thought of '. That was in the ale-drinking days. French visitors to England in the 'sixties ascribe the ' melancholy ' which they professed to discover in the people to their drinking not French wines, but home-made concoctions, compounded of sloes, blackberries, or cherries with the juice of turnips, slightly fermented and sometimes sold as port wine in London taverns.

From the reign of Anne till the beginning of the nineteenth century gambling was a national disease among the leisured classes of both sexes. Games of skill and games of chance, horse-racing, lotteries, and commercial speculations—all made an irresistible appeal. While the men spent most of the day, and sometimes of the night also, round the card-tables at the fashionable clubs of Almack's, White's, and Boodle's, the ladies occupied themselves in similar fashion in their own drawing-rooms. Thousands of pounds would be won or lost at a single sitting. It is recorded that Charles James Fox would occasionally sit for nigh twenty-four hours at play, losing £500 an hour. Before he was twenty-five he had squandered £140,000, mostly at cards. He played whist and piquet very well, but it was the element of chance that really attracted him, and it was in such a purely gambling game as the popular ' faro ' that he lost most of his money. Men would take wagers on anything—that X would not be made a vice-admiral by such and such a date, that Y would be found wearing a certain suit on a particular occasion, that Z would, although seriously ill, be still surviving on the first of next month, and so forth.

Less exalted than the fashionable clubs were the more numerous ordinary coffee-houses, where tea, coffee and chocolate could be drunk, picquet and basset played, where the best of political and literary conversation was to be had, and where mine host could retail the latest gossip of the town and introduce his clients to samples of the latest fashion in coiffure and the latest craze in

The Representation of the Drawing of the STATE-LOTTERY at Guild hall. 1751.

The zest for speculation was encouraged by the existence of State-Lotteries, which were particularly
popular early in the eighteenth century. They were not abandoned till 1823

No. 7 in 222   LOTTERY
Anno 1778.

*The Bearer of this Ticket will be intitled to such
Beneficial Chance as shall belong thereto in the LOTTERY to be
drawn in pursuance of an ACT made in the Eighteenth Year of
His Majesty's Reign.*

A Lottery Ticket of 1778. Reproduced by the courtesy of the Editor of 'The Connoisseur'

1736. Jernegan's lottery. J. was a goldsmith and banker in Russell St., Covent Garden. He made
a curious silver cistern to be disposed of by lottery. The price of entry was five or six shillings, and
each entrant received one of these silver medals valued at 3s. The medal induced many people to buy,
so that about 30,000 were struck. Queen Caroline appears on both sides (on one as Minerva), because
she encouraged the lottery sale

walking-sticks. The coffee-houses, which were at the zenith of their popularity in the reign of Anne, speedily became identified

---

WHEREAS other *Coffee-Houses*, and other *Pub-lick Houses*, take of their Customers 8 s. for a Quart of Arrack, and 6 s. for a Quart of Rum or Brandy made into *Punch*, so that it is now become the settled Price though-out the Town, and seldom less than a Bowl of 1 s. 6 d. is to be had: Therefore, for the better accommodating all Gentle-men, that are Lovers of *Punch*,

This is to give Notice,

That I have opened on Ludgate-hill, the *London-Coffee-House* and *Punch-House*, (Two *Punch-Bowls* on Iron Pedestals before my Door,)

Where the finest and best old Batavia Arrack, Jamaica Rum, and French Brandy, are made into *Punch*, with the finest Ingredients, viz.

A Quart of Arrack made into *Punch* for 6 s. and so in Pro-portion to the smallest quantity, which is half a Quartern for four Pence Half-penny.

A Quart of Rum or Brandy made into *Punch* for 4 s. and so in Proportion to the smallest Quantity, which is half a Quartern for 3 d. And Gentlemen may have it as soon made, as a Gill of Wine can be drawn, with the best of Eating, Attendance, and Accommodation.

This Undertaking has occasion'd many, whose *Interest* it is to possess Gentlemen with such an Opinion, that the Liquors by me used are not good The Publick is hereby assured, that I buy my Goods on the Keys, and at the best Hand, with Ready Money, and am at this Time provided with as well-chosen Brandies, Rum and Arrack, as any in Town, and will at all times procure the best that is imported. But what may convince Gentlemen of the Truth hereof, is, (not only by the Encouragement I meet with) that the Sherbet is always brought by itself, and the Brandy, Rum, or Arrack in the Measure, so there can be no Imposition, either in Quantity or Quality; for the Proof whereof I appeal to all Gentlemen who have done me the Honour to call at my House.

James Ashley.

A Coffee-House advertisement
From ' The Grub-street Journal' of 16 March 1731

---

with particular professions and with the different political parties. Addison in the first number of the *Spectator* wrote : ' There is no place of general resort wherein I do not often make my appear-ance : sometimes I am seen thrusting my head into a round of politicians at Will's, and listening with great attention to the narratives that are made in those little circular audiences; sometimes I smoke a pipe at Child's,[1] and while I seem attentive to

---

𝔓𝔲𝔟𝔩𝔦𝔠𝔨 𝔑𝔬𝔱𝔦𝔠𝔢 𝔦𝔰 𝔥𝔢𝔯𝔢𝔟𝔶 𝔤𝔦𝔳𝔢𝔫,

[*For the Information of all* GENTLEMEN *and* LADIES]

THAT *Charles Lyon, Grecian,* Maker of the JERU-SALEM WASHBALLS, otherwise called GRECIAN WASH-BALLS, so universally esteem'd by all the Quality, who, for many Years, have made use of no other, being removed from Ironmonger-Lane, where he had carried on his Business about 40 years, to the House of *Edward Hubbard,* over against Serjeant's-Inn, Chancery-Lane, where they may at any Time be furnished therewith, by sending a Letter to the said *Edward Hubbard,* who has, for ten Years past, assisted Mr *Lyon* in making them, being the only Person intrusted with the true Method of preparing them, and to whom alone the Receipt will be communicated upon the Decease of the said Mr. *Lyon.*

N B. At the following Places is sold an incomparable Tooth-Powder, which makes the Teeth as white as Ivory, and preserves them from Rotting or Decaying. It effectually cures the Scurvy in the Gums   Price one Shilling each Box.

Also a delicate LIP-SALVE, that cures any rough and chopp'd Lips, and makes them of a fine lively red, Price one Shilling each Pot, viz Cocoa-Tree Chocolate-House, Pall-Mall; Will's Coffee-House, Scotland-Yard.   Charing-Cross; Guildhall Coffee-House, by Guildhall; Sword-Blade Coffee-House, Birchin-Lane ; and the East-India Coffee-House, Leadenhall-Street

An advertisement of soap illustrating the use of the Coffee-House as an emporium.
From ' The Grub-street Journal' of 25 Nov. 1731

---

nothing but the potman, overhear the conversation of every table in the room. I appear on Sunday nights at St James's coffee-house, and sometimes join the little committee of politics in the inner room, as one who comes to hear & improve. My face is likewise very well known at the Grecian and the Cocoa Tree. . . . I have been taken for a merchant upon the exchange for above these ten Years, and sometimes pass for a Jew in the assembly of stock-jobbers at Jonathan's.'

[1] The favourite resort of the clergy.

Among the characteristic amusements of eighteenth-century London were masquerades and ridottos or assembly dances, such as took place in the Pantheon in Oxford Street, which was opened in 1770. Other favourite places of amusement were Ranelagh and Vauxhall. The chief attraction of the former was its Rotunda, where to the accompaniment of an orchestra a fashionable throng used to parade on the promenade or take refreshments in the side boxes. Vauxhall Gardens, usually approached by the Thames, still the most important highway and the greatest glory of London, were entered from a dark alley, whose meanness was in strong contrast to the gardens themselves, with their great trees festooned with coloured lights, with their imitation Greek temples and statuary, their little alcoves set with supper-tables, the central quadrangle, called the Grove, with its large pavilion, a glorified concert-hall and restaurant, the Grand Walk, the Cross Walk, and the Lovers' Walk, dark with the shade of interlacing trees, a favourite haunt, apparently not so much of peaceful lovers as of young rakes on the look-out for opportunities of horse-play.

In exploring the idle diversions of the period we can have no more efficient companion than George Selwyn (1719–91), prince of the wits of his day. We must take the brilliance of the witticisms mainly on trust ; few of them have come down to us, and those that have survived have mostly lost their savour. One of his best *bon-mots* was with reference to the execution of a namesake of Charles Fox's at Tyburn. Fox asked him if he had attended the execution. ' No, Charles,' Selwyn replied, ' I make a point of never attending rehearsals ! ' In any case his was not a great wit, being of the type which consists in playing upon words, not the rapier play of a powerful mind. Selwyn was a member of Parliament, but he was never known to do anything there but sleep and record his vote in accordance with instructions. He also held certain offices under government, but they were complete sinecures. He held, for example, the post of Registrar to the Court of Chancery in Barbados, though he never even visited that island. At the age of twenty-five he was elected a member of White's, and henceforth that club became

The Inside View of the Rotunda in Ranelagh Gardens, with the Company at Breakfast.— Vüe de la Compagnie a Dejeuner dans la Rotonde au Medierre des Jardins de Ranelagh

27

The Rotunda in Ranelagh Gardens. From an engraving in the British Museum

his daily resort and his chief occupation in life. His manner of existence is thus described by a friend. He gets up at nine, puts on a gorgeous dressing-gown, plays idly with his dog till twelve, then crawls down to White's, where he spends five hours at the card-table, then sleeps till supper-time, after which, filled with good claret, he is carried in a sedan chair to home and bed.

'*The Smoaking Club*', *a satire on club-life by Bunbury, about 1780*

Rule 4 (hanging on the wall) : ' Any member who puffs designedly in the face of another to be fin'd sixpence or be puff'd at in return by the whole company '

His chief peculiarity was a fondness for looking at corpses and attending executions ; his chief virtue was a genuine fondness for children, though he never had any of his own. He had only one real love affair—at the age of sixty when he fell in love with Mie Mie Fagnani, afterwards Marchioness of Hertford, aged ten, to whom he lost his heart, and whom he adopted.

The careers of such wits as Selwyn and of the beaux of his day suggest complete emptiness. They seem to live a life of pure dissipation, to spend all their money and their thought on gambling and fine clothes, which were in any case exceedingly expensive. We hear of men wearing dresses on special occasions which cost as much as 500 guineas, and a waistcoat alone might

A satire on the earlier and later sympathies of Charles James Fox

cost upwards of fifty guineas. The greatest extravagants were the young men, known as Macaronis, who in the 'sixties and 'seventies wore masses of artificial hair with very small hats and clothes fitting very close to the figure, and carried huge walking-sticks with long tassels. It is true that later in the century both men's and women's dresses became simpler,

A perruquier's shop

ALL Sorts of Perukes, curiouſly made, after the beſt Manner, viz. Tye Wigs, Clergymens Bobs, and Long Bobs, with a handſome Feather Crown in the manner of a Tye-Crown, after the neweſt Faſhion, and never yet made uſe of in Canterbury. Alſo Bag-Wigs, Spenſers, Tuck-up Wigs, and Naturals, all drawn with a handſome Topee done in ſuch a manner as ſcarcely to be perceived from one's own Hair.

All made of the beſt of Hair, by WILLIAM HILLES, at the Roſe in St. George's, Canterbury. Where may be had fine Bottle Pale Beer at 6 d. per Bottle, drank in the Houſe, or 5 s. per Dozen delivered out of the Houſe, the Bottles to be exchanged or paid for at the Delivery.

A perruquier's advertisement. From ' The Kentish Post, or Canterbury News-letter ', 9 May–12 May 1739.

Fox, who had been very dandified in his early days, introducing after 1789 a new style of negligence in demonstration of his sympathy with the democratic doctrines of the French revolu-

The Macaroni Card Players

tionaries. A petition to the King from the peruke-makers in 1765, in which they complained of the growing habit of gentlemen wearing their own hair instead of a wig, is an indication of a change in fashion. Notwithstanding the clear tendency towards greater simplicity in the late decades of the century, for most of the period the dress of men of fashion was costly and elaborate, and their etiquette accorded with their costume. Their mincing gait, formal bows, grandiloquent expressions of courtesy, would now appear ridiculous. In so far as eighteenth-century manners were really courtly and expressive of genuine feeling, they had something in them that an off-hand and unceremonious age may reflect upon with profit ; but only too often eighteenth-century ceremony was merely foppish and superficial, and some of its habits at table and in the drawing-room would nowadays appear indescribably boorish. When a gentleman came into the presence of ladies drunk, and bedecked his conversation with foul oaths, the depth of his bow did not indicate any true politeness. Too often the beau and man of fashion lightly concealed under a thin veneer of polish the heart of a scoundrel, and the prevalence of the abduction motive in the fiction of the period is no mere accident.

We must bear in mind that men who appeared to waste their time in mere frivolity or worse were not necessarily fools or idlers. Bolingbroke in certain of his moods had all the semblance of a debauchee ; but he was also a brilliant writer, orator, and politician. Chesterfield, the cynicism of whose *Letters to his Son* has become a byword, who seems to lay such stress upon the superficialities of behaviour, was not the intolerable dandified hypocrite suggested by Dickens's caricature of him as Sir John Chester in *Barnaby Rudge*, but a man of wide reading and artistic taste, and a wise statesman into the bargain, as he showed when he was Lord-Lieutenant of Ireland. Even Sandwich, the apparently worthless libertine, of whom Gray wrote a pithy and scathing character-sketch in *The Candidate*, was a most assiduous and hard-working secretary of state. Charles Fox was not simply a gambler and a spendthrift ; he was a man of genius, a great debater and orator, a great party leader, and incidentally

W. Hogarth del.   J. I. fe.

Mary & Ann Hogarth

from the old Frock-shop the corner of the Long Walk, facing the Cloysters, Removed to y.ᵉ Kings Arms joyning to y.ᵉ Little Britain-gate, near Long Walk. Sells y.ᵉ best & most Fashionable Ready Made Frocks, sutes of Fustian, Ticken & Holland, stript Dimmity & Flanel Wastcoats, blue & canvas Frocks, & bluecoat Boys Dr.ᵃ. Likewise Fustians, Tickens, Hollands, white stript Dimitys. white & stript Flanels in y.ᵉ piece, by Wholesale or Retale, at Reasonable Rates.

Dresses and Dress materials. The shop-bill which Hogarth engraved for his sisters about 1725

a man of the widest culture. His friend Topham Beauclerk
called at his lodgings one morning after he had had a particularly
disastrous night's play. Beauclerk expected, Wraxall tells us,
' to behold a frantic gamester stretched upon the floor, bewailing
his misfortunes, or plunged in silent despair '. Instead he found
him reading Herodotus. ' What would you have me do ? '
exclaimed Fox. ' I have lost my last shilling ! ' Wraxall com-
ments : ' With so little effort did he pass from profligate dissipation to researches of taste or literature.' Fox not only knew his
classics thoroughly, but had read widely in the literatures of
France and Italy, where like so many of his contemporaries he
had travelled considerably. The education provided by the
English public schools may not have been wide, but within its
limits it was certainly thorough. The custom of decorating
parliamentary speeches with classical quotations was no mere
affectation. Another saving grace with Fox, as with many other
men of fashion, was that with his love of the gaming table
and the stuffy inside atmosphere of Almack's and White's went
a genuine love of the countryside, of hunting and outdoor
sports. It is worth noting that the fourth Duke of Bedford
was an ardent devotee of the game of cricket, which was just
beginning to come into vogue in the middle of the century.

A Hint to the Ladies to take Care of their HEADS.

Plumage head-dresses of extravagant dimensions were fashionable between 1776 and 1783. From a satiric caricature in the British Museum

LEARNING.

The Design of Learning, is either to render a Man an agreeable Companion to himself, and teach him to support Solitude with Pleasure; or, if he is not born to an Estate, to supply that Defect, and furnish him with the Means of getting one.

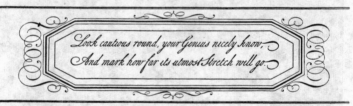

Look cautious round, your Genius nicely know,
And mark how far its utmost Stretch will go.

Nobility, Riches, State, and Supremacy can procure us a customary Respect, & make us the Idols of an unthinking Croud; but Knowledge and Learning alone recommend us to the Love of those in a superior Class, who admire more the Merits of our Understanding, than the Advantages of our Birth & Fortune.

Samuel Vaux scrip.

From 'Bickham's Universal Penman', 1741

§ iv. *The Litterati*

It is possible to distinguish broadly between two different types of temperament in the eighteenth century, just as between two different types of countenance, as a glance at any collection of portraits of the century will prove. These may be differentiated as the robust and boorish type on the one hand, the thin and quizzical on the other. A large proportion of the distinguished men of the time had heavy corpulent figures, fat cheeks, and double chins. As Thackeray says, ' Swift was fat ; Addison was fat ; Gay and Thomson were preposterously fat ; all that fuddling and punch-drinking, that club and coffee-house boosing, shortened the lives and enlarged the waistcoats of men of that age.' Men of the other type had neither the inclination nor the necessary digestive powers to consume great quantities of fat beef and gallons of port wine, and they despised the crude and animal pleasures which appealed to their more full-blooded neighbours. Such were Lord Hervey, who dieted himself with extreme severity and ate practically no meat at all, and Horace Walpole, who drank nothing stronger than iced water. Such men, less hearty, more fastidious and more critical than the majority, turned a detached and rather sardonic regard and a mordant wit upon the doings of their fellow men both in private and public life. In his memoirs and his letters Horace Walpole (1717–97) gives us a most vivid picture of contemporary politics and society, all the more arresting because though he was *in* the world he describes he was not *of* it. He was not popular in his own day, and many critics, notably Macaulay in after days, have been bitter against him. He undoubtedly saw people's bad points much more readily than their good ones, and he quarrelled with everybody. But it has been said with truth that when you find a specially illuminating passage in a secondary authority on the history of the period, trace it to its source and the chances are you will come upon Horace Walpole.[1] He liked to get some little distance away from the great world—to his house at Twickenham — and there discuss it with his cronies, in his ironical way and with great wealth of anecdote. This house of his, Strawberry Hill, was a remarkable place—a queer mixture of original cottage with strange 'Gothic' additions. Inside it was a museum,

Horace Walpole, fourth Earl of Orford
From a drawing by Sir Thomas Lawrence, P.R.A.

full of paintings, statuary, collections of coins, bas-reliefs, enamels, miniatures, and other curios. For Walpole was essentially a connoisseur, with a great love of Italian art in particular, to whose advocacy the English craze for things Italian in the latter part of the century was largely due. Another treasured possession at Strawberry Hill was a private printing-press, which produced several of its owner's works and some of Gray's poetry.

Although Walpole was exceptional in the originality of some of his artistic views and in the extent of his collecting, in his

Leslie Stephen on Horace Walpole in *Hours in a Library*.

interest in foreign art he was typical of a fairly large class. The
English aristocracy of the eighteenth century were to a consider-

*Horace Walpole's Gothic dwelling at Strawberry Hill and a specimen
of his Gothic furniture, both drawn by himself*

able extent cosmopolitan. They regarded Continental travel as
an integral part of education. They studied art and letters in

France and Italy, brought back with them certain foreign influ-
ences into England, and also helped to disseminate a good deal
of English influ-
ence abroad, par-
ticularly in France,
where the interest
taken in English
thought and insti-
tutions by Voltaire
and Montesquieu is
a matter of com-
mon knowledge.

D. Chodowiecki del.   D. Berger Sculpsit 1784.

Scene in the Mitre Inn, Oxford, 1784
From the Second German Edition of Moritz's Travels

Gibbon owed
much to the Conti-
nent. Pondering
on the Coliseum he
conceived his great
design of writing
the history of the
decline and fall of
the Roman Em-
pire; at Lausanne
he lived so long
that he came to
speak French as
his native tongue,
so that, by his con-
fession, it took
some years' service
in the militia during
the Seven Years'
War to make him
into an Englishman. A man of immense erudition, Gibbon owed
nothing to his academic career. Upon the University of Oxford
he, together with such other distinguished alumni as Adam Smith
and John Wesley, poured the utmost derision. The under-
graduates were not taught; while ' from the toil of reading, or

thinking, or writing, the fellows had absolved their conscience '.
' Their conversation stagnated in a round of college business, Tory
politics, personal anecdotes, and private scandal: their dull and deep
potations excused the brisk intemperance of youth.' According
to Chesterfield, the conditions at his own University of Cambridge
were no better. But the inadequacy of the two great English

'A Chemical Laboratory'. Engraved for ' The Universal Magazine', 1747

seats of learning at this period[1] must not cause us to forget the
great scholars who added lustre to those institutions even in
these decadent days—Isaac Newton, identified with Cambridge
through so much of his long life; Edmund Halley, Savilian
Professor of Astronomy at the beginning of the century, best
known for his discovery of the comet which bears his name, but
also noteworthy for his researches into the subjects of meteoro-
logy, the action of the trade winds, the variations of the com-
pass; Richard Bentley, Master of Trinity College, Cambridge,

[1] There was a great improvement in both Universities towards the end
of the century.

one of the greatest classical scholars of all time. The Scottish
universities were graced with several very illustrious names.
Some of the most learned men of the century were Scots : David
Hume, one of the most original and one of the most influential
of modern philosophers and a brilliant historian ; William Robertson, noteworthy for his application of methods of scientific

---

Publiſhed by the Royal Society.

PHiloſophical Tranſactions; giving ſome account
of the preſent *Undertakings*, *Studies* and *Labours* of the *Ingenious* in many conſiderable parts
of the *World*. The Eighteenth Volume : for the
Months of *November* and *December*, 1694.
Numb. 214.

The CONTENTS

1. **A** *Paper aſſerting ſome* Mathematical Inventions *to their
true Authors, by Dr.* David Gregory, Aſtr. Prof. Sa-
vil. II. *Monſ.* Caſſini's *Tables for the Eclipſes of the Firſt* Satel-
lite *of* Jupiter, *reduc'd to the* Julian *Stile, and Meridian of* London *by Mr.* Edm. Halley, S. R. S. III. *A Paper about* Magne-
tiſm, &c. *by Mr.* J. C. IV. *Of a Lamb ſuckled by a Weather
Sheep : From Mr.* Tho. Kirk, S. R. S. V. *A Second Letter concerning the ſame.* VI. *An Account of Books.* 1. *Reflections upon*
Ancient and Modern Learning, *by* W. Wotton, B. D. R.S.S.
2. Horti Malabarici. Pars Undecima, Duodecima & Ultima,
with Remarks thereon, by T. R. M. D. S. R. S.

A Royal Society Advertisement in Houghton's ' Collection' of 15 Feb. 1694/5
Note an early work by Edmund Halley. He had been assistant-secretary to the
Royal Society and the editor of its Transactions from 1685 to 1693

---

research to his history of the Emperor Charles V ; Adam Smith,
successively Professor of Logic and of Moral Philosophy at
Glasgow, most famous as an epoch-making economist, but owing
his pre-eminence in that sphere in no small measure to the
extraordinary range of his general and especially his historical
learning. To these names should be added that of John Hunter,
a great biologist and something of a geologist, but deserving of
remembrance because he strove to apply scientific and experi-
mental methods to Surgery and Medicine.

§ v. *The Blue-stockings*

Men of great learning are always exceptional in their day,
whatever that day may be ; yet any sketch of the society of
a particular epoch would be lacking in verisimilitude which among
the activities of the nation made no mention of its men of letters
and of science. Some mention should also be made of the learned
women of the period, for it is in the eighteenth century that the
phrase ' blue-stocking ' first appears [1] and that ' blue-stocking '
societies first came into existence. The heroines of eighteenth-
century fiction are not learned. They may be charming and
sprightly, but they are as a rule very much given to tears and to
fainting-fits ; they are the natural prey of the other sex ; they
have few thoughts but of matrimony and amusement. When
they grow older they become excellent housewives and mothers,
entirely satisfied with the narrow horizon of their own household
affairs. The Vicar of Wakefield chose a wife ' for such qualities
as would wear well '. She ' could read any English book without
much spelling ; but for pickling, preserving, and cookery, none
could excel her '. Lord Chesterfield declared that he had never
known a woman of ' solid reasoning, good sense . . . or one who
reasoned or acted consequentially for twenty-four hours together '.
A man of sense trifled, played with, humoured, and flattered

[1] The name seems to be derived from the grey or blue worsted stockings
which Benjamin Stillingfleet, the impecunious grandson of the famous
Edward Stillingfleet, Bishop of Worcester in the days of William, used to
wear, instead of the correct black silk, when he attended Mrs. Elizabeth
Montagu's salons, of which he was a *habitué*.

women as he would a forward child ; but would never consult
or trust them in serious matters, though he would often make
them believe he did. Lord Lyttelton wrote :

> Make not too dangerous wit a vain pretence,
> But wisely rest content with modest sense ;
> For wit like wine intoxicates the brain,
> Too strong for feeble women to sustain.

Yet the century produced women of very notable power and
intellect—such, for example, as Sarah Jennings, who, if she knew
nothing of books, knew men ;[1] Mrs. Howard, afterwards Lady
Suffolk, not only the confidante of George II, but the friend
and correspondent of Pope, Swift, Arbuthnot, Gay, Peterborough,
Bolingbroke, Chesterfield, and many others ; Selina Countess of
Huntingdon, Mrs. Siddons, Fanny Burney, Mrs. Thrale, Lady
Mary Wortley Montagu, Mrs. Elizabeth Montagu, Mrs. Vesey,
Mrs. Delany, Mrs. Chapone, Hannah More, and right at the end
Mary Wollstonecraft, who published her *Rights of Women* in
1793. The lasting significance of the last few names is that their
owners stood for the principle that women ought to be liberally
educated and that they had a right of entry into the intellectual
world, that they were not mere ornaments for the drawing-room
and ball-room, intended only for men's diversion, but fit to
converse on an equality with them, to talk as Johnson and
Reynolds understood talking, not merely the tittle-tattle of the
tea-table.

Amid the numerous brilliant letters of the century none are
more famous than those of Lady Mary Wortley Montagu (1689–
1761), hard, clever, vivid, incisive. The eldest daughter of the
first Duke of Kingston and a distant relative of both Pepys and
Evelyn, she was from her earliest years an omnivorous reader,
not only of romances but of more serious kinds of literature.
Her father arranged a suitable match for her, but on the eve of
the wedding she eloped with Mr. Edward Wortley Montagu. In
1716 he was appointed ambassador at Constantinople, his wife
accompanying him thither. At Adrianople Lady Mary was

---

[1] ' Books ! prithee, don't talk to me about books. The only books
I know are men and cards.'

LADY MARY WORTLEY MONTAGU

Painted by Jonathan Richardson

struck by the common Turkish practice of inoculation as a safeguard against small-pox ; she had her own son inoculated, and
on her return home did her utmost to introduce the practice into
England, where small-pox was still regarded as an inevitable
scourge.[1] It is noteworthy that Caroline of Anspach, then
Princess of Wales, at once supported the system and had two
of her own children inoculated. But it had to struggle hard
before the first small-pox hospital was opened in 1746 and before
the physicians generally accepted it in 1754. Public opinion
took still longer to win. But the credit for the initiation of the
first serious attempt to deal with the small-pox evil belongs to
Lady Mary. When she and her husband settled down in England
after their temporary sojourn in Turkey they took a house at
Twickenham near to Pope, who conceived an infatuation for
Lady Mary. He seems to have received a sharp rebuff ; at any
rate there was a quarrel ; lines of a very opprobrious nature in
the *Dunciad* and elsewhere seem to be clearly written against
Lady Mary, and she retaliated in like kind. The last part of her
life was spent abroad, in Italy and Switzerland. It was rather
miserable. She had ceased to care for her husband, though she
had not actually quarrelled with him. He spent his solitary
existence at Shorncliffe, living the life of a miser except that he
indulged one extravagant habit, that of drinking tokay. His
wife appears to have developed into a slovenly, slatternly woman
in personal appearance, but her letters continued to be as keen
and humorous as ever.

[1] Small-pox was the most terrible scourge of eighteenth-century England,
but society was ill-guarded against any infectious disease. Excessive
drinking—particularly of gin—was bound to have an injurious effect upon
the public health, and the favourite remedy of the contemporary physician
for all maladies, that of bleeding his patient, while no doubt serviceable
in certain cases, more often lowered the resisting powers of the constitution
in its fight against the prevailing epidemics, which were influenza, measles,
and whooping-cough. There was little or no idea of keeping infected persons
in isolation. The Rev. J. Woodforde (of whom more in another place)
having what appears to have been measles or scarlet fever, the only
instructions his doctor gave him were to keep warm and encourage the
rash. He saw just as much company as usual during the illness. See
The Diary of a Country Parson, vol. I (ed. J. Beresford), p. 87.

FROM my Correspondent in *Devonshire*, I have this following Account: (*Viz*) We have a terrible *Feaver*, It began about *Michaelmass* last, at the East End of a Valley that borders on *Somersetsh.* and reach'd Westward beyond *Crediton* ; in which are these Towns : *Samford-Perenel*, *Halberton*, *Collumpton*, *Bradninch.*, *Silverton*, *Tharverton*, *Crediton-Bow*. So far I hear the *Feaver* is gone Westward ; but it moves like a great Shower, having some Droppings before and behind it, but its main Body is violent : For about two Months it has been very terrible in *Collumpton*, where now it abates, and is most terrible in *Silverton* and *Tharvertön*, tho' several have been sick of it, and some died there all this Spring.

Since this Hot Weather, 'tis got into *Exeter* ; where several are dead that I knew to be strong healthy Men. Before this Hot Weather they would lie 10 or 14 Days before they died ; but now many lie not above 3 or 4 Days.

Some have Spots, some have none ; such as have Spots, are observed not to relapse ; such as have none, have been taken a second some a third time after they have been very well, as they thought.

It appears to be very infectious ; so that now the Sick have few Visiters but those that have been so.

Most of them are taken with an extraordinary Deafness, that a Trumpet or Hunting-Horn does not affect them : These, at first were thought to be dying when this Deafness seiz'd them, People not knowing their Defect of Hearing, and so let them lie, looking for their Departure ; but now they present things to their Sight, which the Sick do accept or refuse ; and this way they come to take in some Refreshment.

The *Small Pox* goes with it, but not mortal, but where the *Feaver* and that meets in one.

The ravages of small-pox and of epidemic fever (perhaps influenza). Paragraph from Houghton's 'Collection' for 5 July 1695

ONe that is very well quallified to wait upon a Gentleman, or to be Clerk to a Brewer or Woodmonger, desires some such Employment.

He lookes gracefully, has had the Small-Pox, can give security for his Fidelity, and can be well recommended.

To have had the small-pox is a qualification often urged in advertisements of the period. This is from Houghton's 'Collection' for 1 March 1694/5

Mrs. Elizabeth Montagu (1720–1800) was not a brilliant woman as Lady Mary was, and her letters, much admired at one time, are seldom read nowadays. But she had a great contemporary reputation, and she has a certain permanent importance in history. She and her friends and less important rivals Mrs. Vesey and Mrs. Boscawen first established the *salon* in London after

MRS. ELIZABETH MONTAGU
After Sir J. Reynolds

the manner of the contemporary and more brilliant French *salons* of Madame du Deffand and Mademoiselle de Lespinasse. Mrs. Montagu achieved some literary reputation among men of letters by her *Essay on Shakespeare*; but it was her power of conversation, a power of repartee, which seems to have disconcerted even Dr. Johnson (who after a time ceased to like her), and her lavish hospitality, which attracted to her celebrated Chinese drawing-room in Hill Street, and afterwards to a great mansion she had built for herself in Portman Square, the *élite* among writers, scholars, politicians, &c. Here came Dr. Johnson, Mrs. Thrale, the Burneys, Burke, Reynolds, Pulteney, Chesterfield, Lyttelton, Wilberforce. Hannah More celebrated Mrs. Montagu's triumphs in these lines :

> Long was society o'er-run
> By whist, that desolating Hun ;
> Long did quadrille despotic sit,
> That vandal of colloquial wit ;
> And conversation's setting light
> Lay half-obscured in Gothic night ;

At length the mental shades decline,
Colloquial wit begins to shine ;
Genius prevails, and conversation
Emerges into *reformation*.
The vanquish'd triple crown to you
Boscawen sage, bright Montagu,
Divided fell ; your cares in haste
Rescued the ravag'd realms of taste.

As Wraxall notes, the *salons* of Mrs. Montagu and Mrs. Vesey
never rivalled those of Madame du Deffand, Madame Geoffrin,
and Mademoiselle de Lespinasse because London was not the
intellectual capital of Great Britain in the same way that Paris
was of France ; Hume, Adam Smith, Robertson seldom came
south of Tweed ; Gibbon and Goldsmith were never of the circle ;
others among the *élite* did not permanently reside in London ;
whereas in France ' every person distinguished by talents, with
few exceptions, commonly resided altogether in Paris, and visits
to the *salons* were for them part of the routine of existence '.
As Wraxall also remarks, the English were too much addicted
' to clubs composed exclusively of men, to be capable of relishing
a mixed society, when researches of taste and literature constitute
the basis and the central point of union '. That criticism constitutes Mrs. Montagu's chief right to fame. In the age of
Almack's and White's it was a notable achievement to have
created the *salon* of Hill Street.

Tunbridge Wells and its outskirts about 1700

An eighteenth-century ticket of Sydney Gardens Theatre in Bath

§ vi. *The Watering-places*

Whilst the world of politics, of fashion, and of letters was centred in London, one of the most distinctive features of eighteenth-century social life is the gaiety of the watering-places, which had first become fashionable when Charles II, determined to amuse himself all the year round and not wishing to stay in London during the summer, must needs establish the life of fashion in the provinces. Epsom and Tunbridge Wells were earlier in the field, but in the eighteenth century Bath outstripped them both. Later on, owing to George III's patronage of it, Cheltenham became a serious rival, but Bath retained pride of place. These spas were visited by the ailing for the purpose of drinking or sometimes bathing in their medicinal waters for the benefit of gout, corpulence, indigestion, and other prevalent ailments ; but the great majority of *habitués*, though they might drink the waters for form's sake, came to these resorts purely for pleasure.

The story of how the fashionable life of Bath, the establishment of a routine and of a whole code of etiquette, were created by a penniless adventurer makes one of the curious romances of the eighteenth century. Richard Nash (1674–1762), born at Swansea of uncertain parentage, went up to Oxford and either voluntarily decamped or was sent down without taking his degree. He then went into the army and dressed the part to perfection, but finding the other duties of the military profession somewhat irksome, he abandoned army life as he had already abandoned the academic sphere. He next decided to study for the bar and entered the Middle Temple, where he was again distinguished by the magnificence of his apparel. He was notoriously destitute of regular income, and some of his acquaintance, at a loss to know where the money he spent so lavishly could come from, even suspected him of being a highwayman. The real explanation was that he was one of those few mortals who have been able to make gambling almost consistently profitable. He is also said to have made money by taking high wagers to perform the wildest pranks—riding naked on a cow through a certain village, standing clad only in a blanket at the great west doors of York Minster when the congregation was leaving on Sunday morning. Bent on finding new victims at the card table in pastures new, Nash first appeared at Bath in 1705. Three years earlier Queen Anne, by paying a visit, had drawn the attention of the fashionable world to its springs ; but in 1705 the city had none of the amenities of a watering-place except for the water. There was no accommodation ; the only decent building in the place was the abbey ; lodgings were mean, and like the streets, very dirty ; there was no ball-room ; the sedan chairmen were extraordinarily rude and boorish. Since the Queen's visit a certain Captain Webster, apparently also like Nash a professional gambler, had done something to arrange dances in the Town Hall, but he does not seem to have done more than this in organizing a round of pleasure for the place. There was no etiquette ; it would seem indeed that the ordinary rules of politeness were scarcely observed. Men smoked at the dances in the Town Hall, and they danced in their heavy boots. They habitually wore swords, and brawling and duels were frequent. Under such conditions Bath would never have become a popular pleasure resort. A policy was needed for the development of the town, which the municipality had done nothing to provide. The needy adventurer saw his opportunity in Bath's opportunity. By his ease and charm of manner, his genuine social gift, his complete self-assurance, Nash succeeded completely where many an abler man would have failed completely.

Though not really a talented man, he had a gift for organization. He first started a good band ; then he secured a house to serve as a temporary assembly-room ; by 1706 his prestige had

King's bath pump	113°			
Hot bath pump	114			
Cross bath pump	108			
King's bath *	99 97 100	coolest part		
	101 99 103	hottest part		
Queen's bath *	97 95 98	coolest part		
	98 96 99	warmest		
The pump in the bath	113			
Cross bath	89	coolest part		
	90	warmest part		
Cross bath pump	107			
Hot bath	96	coolest part		
	97	warmest part		

The pump in the hot bath 113

Pump in the Market-place, Bath	54
Springs on Claverton, and at late Mr. Allen's	47
Springs on Lansdown	45
St. James's spring water	43
Old well house, Bristol	67
New well, ditto	76

The temperature of the above springs taken in November, and December last 1765, by Farenheit's scale (Bird's Thermometer).

* Taken at three different days.

From Vol. 57, 'Transactions of the Royal Society'

Bath, Oct. 31. This morning, between 10 and 11, a duel was fought with pistols in Harrison's Walks, between Mr. Bazil Prise of this City, Merchant, 2d son of Will. Prise, Esq; formerly Knight of the shire for the County of Hereford, and one Mr. Charles Jones, late a Fellow of New College in Oxford, who about 5 years since quitted his Fellowship, and came down here with 200 l. and won upwards of 4000 l. but his good fortune not continuing, was reduced to the stage The night before, Mr. Prise and he were at a Billiard Table, and agreed to play a game for half a crown, which Mr. Prise won, and demanded his money; but Jones said he would owe him half a crown; whereupon Mr. Prise growing angry, kicked him down stairs. Jones went out of the house, and wrote him a challenge. Mr. Prise discharged his pistol first, but missed him; when Jones, as 'tis said, went up to him, and shot him under the right pap, so that he never spoke afterwards, but expired in about 10 minutes. Jones made his escape immediately: the Coroner's inquest brought in their verdict Wilful Murder, the challenge being found in Mr. Prise's pocket. *D J.*

Gaming and duelling in Bath. From 'The Grub-street Journal' of 11 Nov. 1731

become such that he was able to raise £18,000 for the improvement of the roads round Bath. Anything which helped to ease the journey to the city was immensely to its advantage. It took not less than two and more often three days to reach Bath from London by stage-coach even in the middle of the century. The Pump Room was rebuilt, a theatre and proper Assembly Rooms were built. In the meantime Nash had arranged a daily programme of occupations for the visitors to the town and had drawn up a code of manners, which was put up in the Pump Room. Some of these regulations seem so rudimentary and childish that they are eloquent of the lack of common politeness that must have been prevalent in Bath before Nash came there. Thus Rule 6 runs : ' That gentlemen crowding before the ladies at the ball show ill-manners, and that none do so for the future— except such as respect nobody but themselves.' Rule 7 : ' That no gentleman or lady take it ill that another dances before them —except such as have no pretence to dance at all.' The Master of Ceremonies, King of Bath as he was styled, fast became a despot, whom none of its denizens or visitors, however exalted in rank, dared to disobey. Nash's methods of asserting his authority and maintaining discipline were sometimes very brusque and summary. Thus, upon one occasion, hearing a young gallant at the baths address a lady in terms which he regarded as indecorous, he tossed him, clothes and all, into the bath itself. This incident led to a duel, which only served to increase the King of Bath's prestige. On another occasion he found the charming Katherine Hyde, Duchess of Queensberry, at a dance wearing the white apron which ladies habitually wore as part of their morning apparel. This was against his regulations ; Nash tore it off and threw it to the back of the room. A uniform standard of costume and etiquette he insisted upon, from a duchess just as much as from a country squire's unsophisticated daughter. Duelling he suppressed ; upon the exorbitant lodging-house keepers and the surly chairmen he imposed his authority. He immensely relished the parade of royalty ; clad with extraordinary richness, possessing a marvellous chariot, fine horses, gorgeously apparelled footmen, surrounded at his levée with admirers and sycophants,

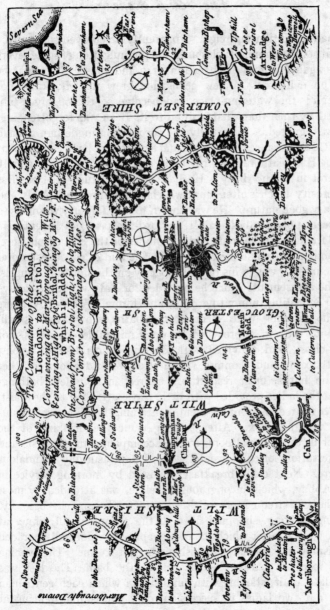

Part of an eighteenth-century road-map; London to Bristol and Bath

he had a scintillating reign. Apparently he enjoyed some of the profits of the gaming-tables until the promulgation of some severe laws against games of chance in 1740 and 1745. After that he fell on evil days ; a new generation grew up who knew not Joseph ; the watering-place had become so thoroughly established by then that what it owed to its Beau was forgotten, and he was ignored. Eventually the corporation made him a small monthly allowance. Forgotten and embittered, he lived to a great age. His death revived his fame and he was given a stately funeral in Bath Abbey. He had certain virtues—the careless generosity which is often found with lavish natures such as his, and an easy good nature. He was known to give fatherly warnings to innocent young ladies against the card-sharpers and adventurers who frequented the routs and assemblies of the city of pleasure. Although himself so little above a rogue and of the laxest moral principles, he was in his official capacity on the side of the angels.

The amusements which he provided for Bath would nowadays seem incredibly uninviting, dull, and formal. The early hours of the morning were spent at the baths, which were small, open to the air, approached by dark miserable entrances, not over-clean, and provided with dressing-rooms like dungeons, both steamy and clammy. Both sexes walked about together in the baths, most respectably attired in complete bathing-suits, the ladies provided with little trays, attached to the waist, which floated in front of them, containing handkerchief, snuff-box, and puff-box. After bathing came the drinking of the water in the Pump Room, to the accompaniment of music and conversation, often it would seem of a pleasurably scandalous nature. Next came breakfast, followed by morning service in the Abbey, which, incongruous to relate, was attended by most of the gay frequenters of Bath punctually and irreligiously. Riding, driving, shopping filled in the afternoon till dinner at three o'clock, after which the fashionable crowd formally paraded to display its sartorial embellishments till tea-time. The evening was spent at cards, the theatre, or the ball. The last was a sedate affair, starting with minuets, in which each gentleman took out two ladies in succession, only one couple dancing at

The Pump Room, &c. From 'Bath, illustrated by a Series of Views, from the Drawings of John Claude Nattes, 1806'

a time and the company following one another in rigid order of precedence. Country dances came next—the whole accompanied by the rather pensive notes of a somewhat thin and reedy orchestra. Such entertainments do not sound exciting to the twentieth century, but evidently the gaieties of Bath were sufficient for their own day and generation. All the great people of the time and many smaller fry flocked to its gates—representatives of the most various walks in life—statesmen, courtiers, soldiers, men of letters, judges, bankers, merchants, actors, musicians, dancers, dealers in all sorts of wares. Amid this variegated throng were to be found some who belonged to an utterly different world, Puritans in a Vanity Fair, the Countess of Huntingdon and her *protégés*, John and Charles Wesley and Whitefield. In Bath she built a Methodist chapel, and she insisted on taking such men as Chesterfield, Bolingbroke, Chatham, and Horace Walpole to hear the greatest preachers of the age discourse either in her chapel or her drawing-room. Nash fell foul of John Wesley and tried to stop his preaching on the ground that it frightened people out of their wits. So at least he had heard, he told Wesley, ' by common report '. ' Common report ', retorted Wesley, ' is not enough to go by. Is not your name Nash ? I dare not judge of *you* by common report.' In the eyes of the Methodists preaching the Gospel in Bath was, to quote Charles Wesley, ' attacking Satan at his head-quarters '. Doubtless there were a great many worthless, corrupt, and evil persons among the frequenters of the city. From Smollett's references to it—and Bath figures prominently in his novels— one would suppose that people of that type predominated. But this is a reflection less upon Bath than upon Smollett. There were all sorts, as well as all conditions, among the city's visitors. If Smollett found nothing but evil, Jane Austen not so many years later found little worse than a light-hearted frivolity, such as one expects in any place which caters for people on holiday. There were naturally some who disliked Bath. Horace Walpole did so ' exceedingly ', and wrote : ' They may say what they will, but it does one ten times more good to leave Bath than to go to it.'

Among the resorts which sprang into popular favour later in

COMFORTS of BATH.

Comforts of Bath. From a print after Rowlandson, 1798, in the Collection of Mr. Dyson Perrins

the century were one or two seaside places—notably Scarborough
and Weymouth.   In 1750 a certain Dr. Russell published a book
proclaiming the health-giving properties of salt-water, and with
remarkable rapidity sea-bathing leapt into favour.   Smollett
takes Mr. Bramble's party to Scarborough in *Humphry Clinker*,
and when Sheridan adapted Vanbrugh's play *The Relapse* he

A CALM.

The increasing popularity of the Seaside.   Caricature by Gillray

transferred the scene of action from London to that watering-
place, and entitled his version *A Trip to Scarborough*.   Cowper
sang with reference to the new craze :

> Your prudent grandmamas, ye modern belles,
> Content with Bristol, Bath, and Tunbridge Wells,
> When health required it, would consent to roam,
> Else more attached to pleasures found at home ;
> But now alike, gay widow, virgin, wife,
> Ingenious to diversify dull life,
> In coaches, chaises, caravans and hoys,
> Fly to the coast for daily, nightly joys,
> And all, impatient of dry land, agree
> With one consent to rush into the sea.

Fashionable Dresses in the Rooms at Weymouth
1774.

Engraved for ‘ The Lady's Magazine

George III on the Esplanade at Weymouth. Caricature by Gilray

A city merchant's bill, engraved by Hogarth

§ vii. *The Middle Classes*

The history of the development of the watering-places in the eighteenth century is a matter, not merely of curious interest, but of genuine importance. The original frequenters of these places belonged almost exclusively to the aristocracy, who looked down with ill-mannered contempt upon humbler visitors. But the powerful general attraction of the spas was not to be denied, and visitors flocked in who came from the squirearchy and the unobtrusive middle classes, which Thackeray so charmingly delineated in the Lambert family in *The Virginians*. These shared with the aristocracy the same pump-rooms, the same baths, the same assembly-rooms ; and under the *régime* of Nash and other Masters of Ceremonies, all, to whatever class they belonged, had to conform to the same rules of conduct. This helped to break down class barriers, to moderate the haughtiness of the aristocracy, and to soften the rusticity of their social inferiors. Such men as Sir Roger de Coverley and Squire Western lived on their own rural estates, seldom went beyond their immediate county town, and only very occasionally visited the metropolis. But increasingly as the century advanced and travelling became more rapid and more comfortable, this provincialism was corrected, and the country gentlemen and their families mixed with the greater world of London and other centres of fashion ; and so, in process of time, the rural boorish-ness of the squirearchy, of which Western is a typical example, was mitigated, and their horizon came to be widened beyond their interests in the trencher-board, the hunting-field, and prize pigs. Yet even so the great virtue and value of the English squire continued to be in his interest in his pigs, in his land, in his tenants, in his own locality. His influence was on the whole a healthy one, because it was redolent of the soil and the open air.

While their activities and mode of life do not bulk as largely in the popular imagination as those of more leisured classes, a picture of the social scene in the eighteenth century would be incomplete and out of perspective if nothing was said of the denizens of the city, the great financiers and merchants, who played so influential a part in the national economy and whose business interests had so much effect on the national policy. One or two commanding figures may be taken by way of illustra-tion. Sir John Barnard (1685–1764) was an exceedingly pros-perous wine merchant. For many years he was M.P. for the City of London and an alderman ; he was once Lord Mayor, and he came to be styled ' the father of the City '. He took a prominent part in opposing Walpole's excise scheme, was the author in 1737 of a plan for reducing the National Debt, and was a genuine philanthropist, in particular seeking to improve the lot of poor debtors. He aimed at the suppression of mendicancy, the improvement of the London police, and the discouragement of the theatre, which he regarded as a dangerous source of social corruption. On any matter of finance and commerce, it was noted, Walpole always wanted to know what Barnard thought of it.

A better-known London merchant of the century was Pitt's great friend and confidant, William Beckford (1709–70), the father of the author of *Vathek*. Like Barnard, he too was an alderman and M.P. for the City, besides being twice Lord Mayor. Born in Jamaica, he made his money as a West Indian merchant. Although his own personal tastes were simple, he had a palatial residence in

A DESCRIPTION *of the* DESERT *of his Majesty's Table at* Guildhall, Nov. 9, 1761.

THE desert was composed in a triumphal chariot, Neptune, the god of the sea, with his queen Amphytrite, attended by tritons and sea nymphs, adorned with triumphal arches, palm trees, and other emblematical figures. The palm trees were about four feet eight inches high, and the porticos two feet; the figures thirteen inches, and the pyramids eighteen inches. The length of the desert was twelve feet long by seven wide. The whole was most superb and exceeding grand, and did honour to the gentlemen employed in the execution of.

The following are the TOTALS OF THE SEVERAL BILLS *which we have taken the Liberty to range in a different manner from that published by the Committee, which it is presumed were set down as they were ordered for Payment.*

		l.	s.	d.
Cooks, Wareham, Oswald, Angel, Horton, and Birch,		1600	0	0
Confectioners, Kuhff,		212	1	0
Wilder	-	121	4	0
Scott		91	14	0
—Kuhff, Wilder, and Scott joint.		174	9	0
Fruiterers, Barber and Shuttleworth		100	0	0
Butter, Dent and Forster		190	0	0
Baker, Dixon	-	8	10	0
Brewer, Mrs. Stephens		8	8	0
Pewterers, Ellis and Cleve		264	3	0
Plate, Ballance of exchanging the city plate for new		57	17	0
Use of other plate	-	20	0	0
China, Cotterell		30	11	0
Vere	—	18	12	0
Wine, Mrs. Allan		178	12	0
Brown and Righton		48	5	0
Magnus	—	175	8	0
Standert, Hock		116	8	0
Coffee and Tea, Gripton		56	10	0
Wax-lights, Baughan		31	0	0
Garrard		30	12	0
Jones		30	12	0
Denny for lighting them		20	0	0
Musick, The band under Mr. Stanley		105	0	0
For erecting an organ		10	0	0
City music		13	3	0
Artillery Company		20	0	0

ARTIFICERS BILLS for fitting up the hall, erecting the kitchen, temporary porch, &c.

		l.	s.	d.
Clerk of the Works. Mr. Dance		65	4	6
Bricklayer, Mr. Wix		147	16	0
Carpenter, Mr. Read	—	876	6	0
Glazier, Mrs. Harrington		15	16	0
Mason, Mr. Easton		6	4	0
Painter, Mr. Pope and son		27	18	0
Plumber, Mess. Willis & Machell		63	12	0
Smith, Mess. Alexander & Shrimpton		300	11	0
Papier Machée, Mr. Bromwich		70	14	0
Ribbans, Mr. Mason & Whitworth		7	3	0
Upholsterers, Mess. Chesson, Woodrooffe and Saunders		469	9	0
Woollen-Drapers, Mess. Burton & son		258	5	0
Piston & son		74	13	0
Stationary, Mr. Walkden		6	15	0
Engraving and making Tickets, &c. Mr. Gardner		23	13	0
Printing, Mr. Charles Rivington		3	3	0
June, 1762.				

	l.	s.	d.
For entertaining the gentlemen pensioners, yeomen of the guard, horse and grenadier guards, coaches, horses, and servants, attendant on the king and royal family, in the neighbourhood of Guildhall, in all 729 persons, at the Paul's-Head tavern, including the dinner for the band of music	47	13	0
Bear-inn, in Basing-hall-street	42	15	0
Bell-inn, Wood-street	12	10	0
Blossoms-inn, Laurence Lane	34	5	5
Castle-inn in Wood-street	29	5	0
Swan with two Necks, Lad-lane	20	15	0

Gratuities, &c.

	l.	s.	d.
Town clerk, sir James Hodges as clerk to the committee	157	10	0
Clerk to the town cl. William Rex	15	15	0
Town clerk's domestic servants	5	5	0
The chamberlain's clerks	5	5	0
The chamberlain's domestic servants	5	5	0
The remembrancer, P. Roberts, esq;	63	0	0
The hall keeper, including his bill of disbursements	126	0	0
—— his man Andrew Boson	10	10	0
Sword bearer's claim	5	0	0
Sen. attor. of the mayor's court his cl.	2	0	0
Serjeants of the chamber	4	10	0
Yeomen of the chamber	4	0	0
Six marshal's men	1	10	0
Six necessary women	6	6	0
Thomas Deane attending the committee on Nov. 9	1	1	0
City marshal, including his bill for constables, watchmen, &c. during the fitting up of Guildhall, as well as on the 9th of November	100	0	0
His majesty's cook, D. Philpot, esq;	10	10	0

Expences incurred by the committee.

	l.	s.	d.
For coffee and tea at their several meetings, before and since the entertainment, to Richard Gripton	37	13	0
	6898	5	4

It was ordered that the said report be entered in the journal of the court, and the following motion being made was unanimously agreed to.

" That the thanks of this court be, and are hereby given to the committee appointed to conduct the entertainment of their majesties and the royal family, at Guildhall, on lord mayor's day last, for their constant and spirited attention, in that service, to the honour of the crown, and the dignity of this city.

U u THE

Wiltshire, and the city banquets he gave during his terms of office as Lord Mayor were reckoned the most lavish known since the reign of Henry VIII. He was a great supporter of Wilkes and a fearless defender of the principles of constitutional liberty. He is famous for having once, upon an occasion when George III had returned an unfavourable answer to a petition formally

---

AT *Waltham-Cross* in *Hertfordshire*, Twelve Mile from *London*, is the half part of a very pretty House to be Let; 'tis next the Road, with Rails and Trees before it; it stands clean, and has a good prospect over the Marshes to *Epping-Forest*, and other parts of *Essex*: There is *Orchard, Garden, Pasture,* and all other *Necessaries* for a Country Dwelling. A great many Coaches and other Carriages go every Day by the Door to and from *London*: And to my own Knowledge, the Houskeepers are very civil, and as genteel as can reasonably be expected from Country Folks. *Enquire there for* George Storey.

'*As genteel as can reasonably be expected from Country Folks.*' *The town view of the Countryman; advertisement from Houghton's 'Collection' for 25 May 1694*

---

presented to him by Beckford as leader of a deputation, made an impromptu speech so bluntly outspoken that it caused the King to redden with anger and produced consternation among all its hearers.

Among the notable financiers of the century the most distinguished was Sir Francis Baring (1736–1810), the founder of the fortunes of the great banking firm which bears his name. His father had emigrated from Germany and set up a cloth manufactory at Larkbear in Devonshire. Francis, the third son, showed in his early days that he was a remarkable mathematician, and in particular a lightning calculator. He carried on the Larkbear business on a much larger scale than during his father's lifetime, then became a proprietor in the East India Company, a dealer in funds and shares, and a magnate on the Stock Exchange. Lord Shelburne described him as the prince of merchants, and ministers of the Crown and politicians generally were accustomed to go to him for advice in questions of trade, especially those affecting India.

The demoralizing influence of the Indian Nabob's wealth. Gillray's caricature shows the King and Queen and dignitaries of Church and State scrambling for rupees; 1788

The volume of our Indian trade and the prosperity of our East India Company increased by leaps and bounds, as our hold upon India became more and more extensive. Indian merchants became so wealthy as to enter into serious rivalry with the landed aristocracy in the political influence which control of the purse-strings always gave in the eighteenth century. It was noticed by contemporaries that great as parliamentary corruption had been before, it seriously increased in the 'sixties and 'seventies, when the Indian merchants made their way into what may be justly termed the electioneering market.

In 1767 Chesterfield, on the look-out for a seat for his son, found that the price of a seat, which he had estimated at £2,500, had been forced by the new competition up to £4,000 or £5,000. Lord Clive was able to return as many as five members in his interest. So much money was forthcoming that one borough—Sudbury—shamelessly put itself up to auction. We find Chatham, Burke, and Horace Walpole lamenting this influx of wealth, and taking the gravest view of the moral consequence of a luxury which, according to Voltaire, was so corrupting that England was fast becoming decadent. In 1770 Chatham declared :

For some years past there has been an influx of wealth into this country which has been attended with many fatal consequences, because it has not been the regular, natural product of labour and industry. The riches of Asia have been poured in upon us, and have brought with them not only Asiatic luxury, but, I fear, Asiatic principles of government. Without connections, without any natural interest in the soil, the importers of foreign gold have forced their way into Parliament by such a torrent of private corruption as no private hereditary fortune can resist.

Advertisement of a manufacturer of agricultural implements. End of century

§ viii. *The Farmers*

The influx of great wealth was not the only, or indeed by any means the most important, factor disturbing the even tenor of English society at the time when Chatham spoke. New economic forces were coming into operation which were shortly to produce an entirely new era in our social history. Great Britain up to now had been a thinly populated country, of a singularly simple economic and social structure. It was small, placid, comfortable, untroubled by problems. A very different country, in outward appearance, in density of population, in social organization and political outlook was to be evolved from those immense economic changes which we are accustomed to designate as the Industrial Revolution. In agriculture a great development took place, intimately connected with the enclosure movement, which was especially rapid after 1760. Enclosures were not a new phenomenon, as every student of the sixteenth century knows, but they were now made on a larger scale than ever before. The movement involved two distinct processes—first, the development of waste lands, of hitherto uncultivated heath and common ; second, the absorption by the large landowner of those open fields wherein from time immemorial the village small-holders had been wont to till their little strips of arable. In the eighteenth century great tracts of England were converted from a countryside of small holdings into one of large farms. Some of the latter were created by prosperous agriculturists who had so thriven as to be able to buy up other land in the neighbourhood of their original holdings ; others were purchased by men who had made money in the shop and the counting-house. In whatever way the process took place, the small farmer and cottager lost considerably and tended to degenerate into the status of farm-labourer on the lands of the wealthier and more prosperous owners. It is this state of things which Goldsmith laments in his picture of the ' deserted ' Auburn.

> One only master grasps the whole domain,
> And half a tillage stints thy smiling plain.

It is estimated that at the end of the seventeenth century there were about 180,000 small freeholders or yeomen in England—the famous backbone of the country through so much of its history ; before the Great Reform Bill they had practically disappeared.

The ordinary villager was not in any two minds as to the merits or demerits of the enclosure movement. In his eyes it appeared as an unmitigated evil. Great were the rejoicings in the countryside affected on the rare occasions when an enclosure bill was rejected by Parliament. During the first half of the century, when the greater part of the soil of England was still in the hands of the small proprietor, while the lot of yeoman and labourer had been hard enough, it had been distinctly better

Open fields and strip cultivation still surviving to-day at Epworth in Lincolnshire

than that of any other rural population, with the possible exception of the Dutch, and there had been general contentment. But with the rapid advance of the enclosure movement under George III, not only were the small farmers being forced out of existence, but the labourers were finding their lot grow harder and harder.[1] As the century went on, food prices greatly increased, and the wages did not rise in anything like the same degree. When a man had possessed his own cow and some poultry, he had had means of subsistence even if he could not make much of a livelihood out of his little holding. The wholesome food that the farm-yard provides tended to drop out of the dietary of the land-worker. Bacon became very dear, and meat at times was unobtainable by the rural labourer. In years of bad harvest the cost of bread rose beyond the means of the poor, and in such seasons attacks were made on bakers' shops, attacks which

	l.	s.	d.
1000 Bullocks, at 6l. a-piece	6000	00	00
6000 Sheep, at 12s. a-piece	3600	00	00
2000 Calves at 1l. 4s. a-piece	2400	00	00
3000 Lambs, at 8s. a-piece, for six months	1200	00	30
1500 Hogs in pork and bacon, at 20s. a-piece for six months	1500	00	00
2000 Pigs, at 2s. 6d. a-piece	250	00	00
1500 Turkies, at 3s. 6d. a-piece for six months	175	00	00
1000 Geese at 2s. 6d. a-piece for six months	125	00	00
2000 Capons, at 1s. 8d. a-piece	166	13	02
3000 Pullets, at 1s. 2d. a-piece	175	00	00
500 Dozen of chickens at 9s. per dozen	156	05	00
4300 Ducks at 9d. a-piece	161	05	00
1500 Do. of rabbits, at 7s. per doz. for 8 months	525	00	00
2000 Doz. of pigeons at 2s. per doz. for 8 months	200	00	00

Before the rise in prices. Figures from ' The London Magazine' of 1750

were construed by the ruling classes as an ugly symptom of a spirit of lawlessness in the proletariat. Arthur Young praised the frugality of the small farmer in England. It was mistaken praise, for this was a frugality, not voluntarily chosen, but enforced by necessity—it betokened a low standard of living.

Pauperism was beginning to increase to an alarming extent towards the end of our period. The ordinary eighteenth-century

[1] This, the generally accepted view of the significance of the enclosure movement, has been criticized by Mr. E. Davies (see list of authorities *infra*), who believes that the small owners had almost disappeared *before* 1780; there was actually an increase in their numbers between 1780 and 1802.

TABLE of the Assize and Price of STANDARD WHEATEN BREAD,

In TWO PARTS. —— According to an ACT passed in the 13th Year of GEORGE III.

Nº I. Price of a Bushel of Wheat, and Baking.	Penny oz. dr.	Twopence lb. oz. dr.	Sixpence lb. oz. dr.	Twelve Pence lb. oz. dr.	Eighteen Pence lbs oz. dr.	Nº I. Price of a Bushel of Wheat and Baking.	Quartern Loaf s. d.	Half Pk. Loaf s. d.	Peck Loaf s. d.
s. d.						s. d.			
2 9	25 4	3 2 9	9 7 11	18 15 5	28 7 0	2 9	0 2¼	0 5¼	0 11
3 0	23 3	2 14 5	8 11 0	17 6 1	26 1 1	3 0	0 3	0 6	1 0
3 3	21 6	2 10 12	8 0 5	16 0 11	24 1 0	3 3	0 3¼	0 6½	1 1
3 6	19 14	2 7 12	7 7 13	14 14 5	22 5 8	3 6	0 3½	0 7	1 2
3 9	18 9	2 5 1	6 15 4	13 14 7	20 13 11	3 9	0 3¾	0 7½	1 3
4 0	17 6	2 2 12	6 9 9	13 0 9	19 8 13	4 0	0 4	0 8	1 4
4 3	16 6	2 0 11	6 2 2	12 4 4	18 6 7	4 3	0 4¼	0 8½	1 5
4 6	15 7	1 14 4	5 12 11	11 9 6	17 6 1	4 6	0 4½	0 9	1 6
4 9	14 10	1 13 4	5 7 13	10 15 10	16 7 7	4 9	0 4¾	0 9½	1 7
5 0	13 14	1 11 13	5 3 7	10 6 13	15 10 4	5 0	0 5	0 10	1 8
5 3	13 4	1 10 8	4 15 7	9 14 14	14 14 5	5 3	0 5¼	0 10½	1 9
5 6	12 10	1 9 4	4 11 13	9 7 11	14 3 8	5 6	0 5½	0 11	1 10
5 9	12 1	1 8 3	4 8 9	9 1 1	13 9 10	5 9	0 5¾	0 11½	1 11
6 0	11 9	1 7 3	4 5 8	8 11 1	13 0 9	6 0	0 6	1 0	2 0
6 3	11 2	1 6 4	4 2 12	8 5 8	12 8 3	6 3	0 6¼	1 0½	2 1
6 6	10 ?	1 5 6	4 0 3	8 0 5	12 0 8	6 6	0 6½	1 1	2 2
6 9	10 5	1 4 10	3 13 13	7 11 9	11 9 6	6 9	0 6¾	1 1½	2 3
7 0	9 15	1 3 14	3 11 9	7 7 3	11 2 12	7 0	0 7	1 2	2 4
7 3	9 9	1 3 3	3 9 8	7 3 1	10 12 9	7 3	0 7¼	1 2½	2 5
7 6	9 4	1 2 9	3 7 10	6 15 0	10 6 13	7 6	0 7½	1 3	2 6
7 9	9 0	1 1 15	3 5 13	6 11 10	10 1 7	7 9	0 7¾	1 3½	2 7
8 0	8 11	1 1 6	3 4 2	6 8 4	9 12 7	8 0	0 8	1 4	2 8
8 3	8 7	1 0 14	3 2 9	6 5 2	9 7 11	8 3	0 8¼	1 4½	2 9
8 6	8 3	1 0 6	3 1 1	6 2 2	9 3 3	8 6	0 8½	1 5	2 10
8 9	7 15	0 15 14	2 15 11	5 15 5	8 15 0	8 9	0 8¾	1 5½	2 11
9 0	7 12	0 15 7	2 14 5	5 12 11	8 11 0	9 0	0 9	1 6	3 0
9 3	7 8	0 15 0	2 13 1	5 10 3	8 7 4	9 3	0 9¼	1 6½	3 1
9 6	7 5	0 14 10	2 11 14	5 7 13	8 3 11	9 6	0 9½	1 7	3 2
9 9	7 2	0 14 4	2 10 12	5 5 9	8 0 5	9 9	0 9¾	1 7½	3 3
10 0	6 15	0 13 14	2 9 7	5 3 7	7 13 2	10 0	0 10	1 8	3 4
10 3	6 13	0 13 9	2 8 11	5 1 9	7 10 1	10 3	0 10¼	1 8½	3 5
10 6	6 10	0 13 4	2 7 12	4 15 7	7 7 3	10 6	0 10½	1 9	3 6
10 9	6 7	0 12 15	2 6 14	4 13 10	7 4 6	10 9	0 10¾	1 9½	3 7

An EXPLANATION of the preceding TABLE.

PART the FIRST, or the ASSIZE-TABLE, contains, in Column No. I. the Price of the Bushel of Wheat, Winchester Measure, from 2s. 9d. to 10s. 9d. the Bushel, the Allowance of the Magistrates to the Baker for Baking included:— And in Column No. II. are the Weights of the several Loaves. So that at whatever Price of the Bushel of Wheat with the Allowance, the Magistrates shall set the Assize, the same Price of Wheat is to be found in Column No. I. and even therewith in Column No. II. will be found the Weights of the several Loaves.

Note, That the same Weight of Standard Wheaten assized Bread as costs Seven-pence, of Wheaten assized Bread will cost Eight-pence, and of Houshold assized Bread Six-pence: Or, Seven Standard assized Loaves will weigh Eight Wheaten assized Loaves, or Six Houshold assized Loaves of the same Price, as near as may be.

PART the SECOND, or the PRICE TABLE, contains, in Column No. I. the Price of the Bushel of Wheat, Winchester Measure, from 2s. 9d. to 10s. 9d. the Bushel, the Allowance of the Magistrates to the Baker for Baking included: And in Column No. II. are the Prices of the Peck, Half-Peck, and Quartern Loaves.

Note, That the Standard Wheaten Peck-Loaf is always to weigh 17 lb. 6 oz. Averdupois, and the Half-Peck and Quartern Boaves in proportion; and when the said Peck-Loaf is sold for Fourteen-pence, the Wheaten Peck-Loaf is to be sold for Sixteen-pence, and the Houshold Peck-Loaf is to be sold for Twelve-pence, and always as near as may be in the same proportion. No Half-Quartern Loaves are to be made.

Note, That this Table is framed for Bread to be made of the whole Produce of the Wheat, except the Bran or Hull thereof only; the said Produce to weigh three-fourths of the Wheat whereof it is made.

This Table should be preserved in every Family, as it at once points out the Weight and Price of Bread in proportion to the Price of Wheat.

The rise in prices. Regulations for the price of bread

point of view was that apart from sickness and old age there was no other cause of poverty but idleness. In 1723 the Act had been passed which established a workhouse in every parish or parish union, and, in consequence of the application of the workhouse test, the national expenditure on poor-relief had fallen from well over £800,000 in 1700 to under £700,000 by 1750. But a change of opinion began soon after George III's accession, and the severity of the system was much mitigated, until in 1782 the so-called Gilbert's (permissive) Act made it possible for magistrates, if they chose, to restore outdoor relief for the able-bodied and to supplement wages out of the rates. When in 1795 the workhouse test was abolished and the Berkshire magistrates adopted a mischievous plan of supplementing the wages of the poor out of the rates in proportion to the size of their families and in accordance with the price of the loaf, a plan which was speedily adopted all over the country, there started that orgy of poor-law extravagance which provoked the strong reaction typified by the rigid Poor Law Reform Act of 1834. At the opening of the nineteenth century 28 per cent. of the population was in receipt of relief, and the burden of the rates upon the small farmer was insupportable. He no longer had any motive to pay a decent wage, and economy in his wage-bill became the obvious way in which to recoup himself. These developments belong to later history, but already before the close of our period the effects of enclosure had intensified the problem of pauperism.

The enclosure movement meant the depopulation of many a countryside. There were instances of villages being reduced to the squire's house and the parsonage. Goldsmith, in depicting the desolation of ' sweet Auburn ' may have had in his mind's eye scenes of eviction which he had witnessed in Ireland rather than any sudden rural catastrophe which he had known in England, for the depopulation of the English village was a gradual process, not so violent as Goldsmith's poem suggests. Nevertheless the facts of the enclosure movement are sufficient to justify in its general outlines the picture drawn in the later passages of *The Deserted Village*. Again, while we have to bear in mind that Crabbe was of a melancholy, not to say morbid, temperament, that he tended to dwell upon the gloomy side of things in general, and that in writing *The Village* he was in revolt against the conventional bucolic descriptions of nature still characteristic of the pastoral poetry of the day, still it is certainly the case that the sombre tones of Crabbe's delineation had their counterpart in the actual conditions of many an English countryside.

The most deplorable feature of the social situation was not the privations of the rural labourers, but the disappearance of a class, that of the yeoman farmer. It is this that Goldsmith most deplores.

> Ill fares the land, to hastening ills a prey,
> Where wealth accumulates, and men decay ;
> Princes and lords may flourish, or may fade :
> A breath can make them, as a breath has made ;
> But a bold peasantry, their country's pride,
> When once destroyed, can never be supplied.

Many migrated to the towns ; others, remaining, submitted to the loss of their small holdings and of their independence, to a drop in the social scale. Such acquiescence too often meant a moral reverse, the loss of something more valuable than land—hope, courage, initiative, even self-respect. By such a failure in moral stamina the whole country was made the poorer. ' A man ', Arthur Young once wisely said, ' will love his country the better for a pig.' Or as he put it elsewhere in words which have become famous : ' For whom are they to be sober ? For whom are they to save ? For the parish ? If I am diligent, shall I have leave to build a cottage ? If I am sober, shall I have land for a cow ? If I am frugal, shall I have an acre of potatoes ? You offer no motives ; you have nothing but a parish officer and a workhouse !—Bring me another pot—.'

From the point of view of agricultural efficiency, leaving out of consideration social consequences—the change was in the main beneficial. Arthur Young, the great agricultural enthusiast and apostle of the new movement at the end of the century, showed how infinitely superior the large English farm was to the small holding of the French peasant.[1]   Though in later years he lamented the disappearance of the yeomen, he considered that the crops in the open fields were often beneath contempt.   Only the wealthy farmer had capital sufficient for large development ; only he could afford the cost of bringing into subjection to the plough tracts of the waste land of England, computed in 1727 to have constituted half the country.   Between 1700 and 1760 there was little agricultural improvement ; after 1760 the process was rapid.   It was from that date approximately that there started the phenomenal expansion of the population which is the dominant fact in modern social history.   The total population of England and Wales in 1700 was about five and a half millions, considerably less than that of greater London to-day.   In 1750 it was rather under six and a half millions.   That is to say, the rate of increase in the first half-century was about 18 per cent. In 1801 the population had risen to 9,187,176 ; so that the rate of increase in the second half of the century was 52 per cent. This was a stupendous phenomenon.   Up till 1760 England had been a corn-exporting country ; by the end of the century she could no longer supply the needs of her own population.   Had it not been that the sheer necessity of this unparalleled situation acted as a powerful incentive to agricultural improvement, the country would have been quite unable to support the new millions.

Since, as we have seen, big-scale farming necessitated capital, the representative farmers of the eighteenth century were wealthy men, often members of the aristocracy.   There was no keener farmer than George III himself, justly known as 'Farmer George'.   Some of the most notable names are those of peers— Lord Townshend, the fifth Duke of Bedford, the Duke of Grafton, and Lord Rockingham.   'Turnip Townshend' is famous for the good work he did for English agriculture.   His nickname does not mean that he was the first to go in for the extensive

[1] Young was not successful as a practical farmer, but he was an earnest student of the new methods, and his records of his travels in Great Britain and France reveal a most vivid and inquiring mind and an encyclopaedic knowledge of agriculture and rural conditions.

cultivation of turnips ; its meaning is that he developed what is known as the ' Norfolk system ', or ' four crops rotation ', in which turnips were included. Under the open-field system it had been the invariable custom to leave the soil fallow for one year in every three or at most four, so as not to exhaust it. Townshend saw that land need not lie entirely unproductive at

---

The challenge given by Mr. COKE of Norfolk, at the late sheep-shearing at *Woburne*, to the Leicestershire breeders, with a view to ascertain the comparative excellence of the *new Leicestershire*, and the *South-Down* breed of sheep, was not, as has been falsely stated, in all the papers, refused by the latter. On the contrary, the Leicestershire breeders told Mr. COKE, that if he would reduce his proposition to writing, so that it might be clearly understood, and all possibility of evasion avoided, they would willingly stake *five hundred guineas* on the superiority of their own breed. This Mr. COKE declined, and in a manner that evidently shewed he was convinced that the superior excellence of the *South-Down sheep* was not to be supported.

Rivalry in stock breeding. A newspaper cutting of the 'nineties

---

any time, so long as turnips and grasses were alternated with cereals. Another notable farmer was Mr. Coke, of Holkham, afterwards Earl of Leicester, who took over the management of his estates in 1776. Having at that time no practical knowledge of agriculture, he got together the most efficient farmers on his land and learnt all that they could teach him. He soon became a very keen and progressive agriculturist. Before he started, his district of Norfolk produced nothing but an inferior crop of rye. Coke fertilized the poor and sandy soil by a liberal use of lime, marl, and manure, and so transformed the countryside from a rye-producing to a wheat-producing district. At the same time he increased and improved his live stock, and he erected model farm buildings and workers' cottages.

One of the early pioneers in scientific farming was Jethro Tull (1674–1741), a man of a mechanical turn of mind, who invented a so-called drill, an implement for sowing seeds in the requisite quantity and at the requisite depth. He was a great believer in sowing, not broadcast but in rows, not thickly but thinly, since he found by experiment that this produced the richest crops. He

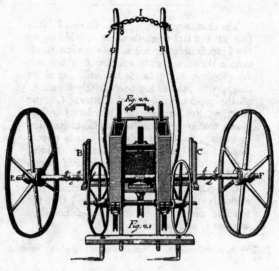

Jethro Tull's Wheat Drill

found it possible by this method, even without the use of manure, to grow wheat crops, increasing in richness, on the same piece of soil for thirteen years in succession. Tull did not make a financial success of farming, and he died quite unrecognized.

Much better known than Tull was Robert Bakewell (1725–95), whose attention was devoted chiefly to stock-breeding, with a view principally to the meat-market. His new Leicestershire sheep were very profitable animals, being small of bone, compact of frame, fat in the joints. Bakewell was a remarkable figure, tall, heavily built, broad shouldered. He was extremely methodical, his daily routine never varying, though he often entertained nobility and sometimes even royalty in his kitchen, so wide-spread was his fame. Round the hall of his farm-house were the skeletons of his most celebrated animals, and he also had, hung on the walls, joints of meat preserved in pickle, illustrating the points he was most intent upon in his stock-breeding, small-ness of bone, richness of fat, &c.

ROBERT BAKEWELL

MR. BAKEWELL—THE BREEDER.

This justly celebrated, because *really useful*, member of society, died last Thursday. He has long been declining in health—he was very ill when Mr. MONK surveyed Leicestershire last year, for the Board of Agriculture. From his report, we have the following anecdotes of the Dishley œconomy :

" On viewing the hospitable mansion of Mr. BAKEWELL, I was highly gratified by viewing the sheep, &c. Every thing at Dishley is conducted with the greatest order and regularity, and, I may add, with every politeness and attention a stranger can wish for. The sheep are shewn one by one, in a place built for the purpose. They are brought in at one door ; and after you have satisfied your curiosity, they are returned back by another door, and then another is brought in ; and I soon observed, that they brought them regularly better and better, so that the best came last. On my asking the reason of this, I was informed, if they had brought the last first, the great superiority would have made the others much worse than they really were. This too I found was the reason that they never shew their rams after they are engaged, it being natural to human nature to covet that which it cannot possess.

" To shew the difference of judgment in respect to the value of cattle, Mr. BAKEWELL informed me, that some years since he used to attend Loughborough Tup-market, where he had a ram which he let for Twenty-five Guineas. Soon after the agreement, another Farmer wanted to purchase this ram, and Mr. BAKEWELL (in joke) asked him twenty-five shillings for it. The Farmer offered eighteen ; and at last they parted for two shillings !

Mr. MONK gives us another anecdote which shews the value of Mr. BAKEWELL's breed. Mr. BAKEWELL had let a bull to a Gentleman for fifty guineas for the season. The Gentleman dying in the interim, and the Executors not knowing any thing of this transaction, sold the bull by auction with the rest of the cattle. When the season was over, Mr. BAKEWELL sent for his bull ; and, after investigating the matter, found, to his great surprise, that the bull had been sold to a butcher for about eight pounds, who had killed it, and sold it for two-pence half-penny per pound. Mr. BAKEWELL, in course, applied to the Executors for the value, which was fifty guineas for the season (the stipulated agreement) and 200 guineas for the bull. The Executors refused payment, thinking that, as the bull was sold by public auction before a great number of Farmers, and many of them thought to be men of judgment, for only eight pounds, it was an imposition. Mr. BAKEWELL was, therefore, obliged to bring an action for the amount ; and People appearing as witnesses on the trial who were acquainted with this Breed, and making oath, that Mr. BAKEWELL had not over-valued his bull, a verdict was given in Mr. BAKEWELL's favour to the full amount with costs of suit.

SALE OF CATTLE.

The sale of the capital stock of bulls and cows, the property of the late Mr. Robert Fowler, commenced on Tuesday last, at Little Rollright, in the county of Oxford ; and it was supposed that five thousand persons attended, and many of them from distant counties. We have been favoured with the following particulars :

A bull, called Garrick, five years old, sold for 205gs.

A ditto, called Sultan, two years old, for 210gs.

A ditto, Washington, two years old, for 205gs.

A ditto, ————, one year old, for 150gs.

A ditto, ————, one year old, for 180gs.

Two ditto, ————, one year old each, for 200gs.

A cow, Brindled Beauty, in calf, for 260gs.

A ditto, Washington's mother, in calf, 185gs.

A ditto, Garrick's sister, in calf, 115gs.

A ditto, Long-horned Nancy, in calf, 105gs.

A ditto, Young Nell, 120gs.

A ditto, Spotted Nancy, 80gs.

A ditto, red, 73gs.

A heifer, black, three years old, 135gs.

A ditto, Young Brindled Beauty, two years old, 63gs.

A ditto, Nell's White Back, two years old, 85gs.

A calf, three or four months old, 30gs.

The amount of the first day's sale was 3,427l. 4s.

EXTRACTS FROM NEWSPAPERS

Above is a newspaper cutting of April 1791 illustrating the development of pedigree stock (partly from Bakewell's strain) in Oxfordshire. Two of Mr. Robert Fowler's long-horns are shown on the facing page, photographed from the paintings which still hang at Little Rollright.

On the left is an obituary notice of Robert Bakewell, who died in 1795.

Robert Fowler's bull 'Garrick'

Robert Fowler's 'Old Nell'

From the paintings in the possession of Mrs. Williams of Little Rollright Manor

A picture showing the earliest stage in the transformation of a rural district into a centre of industrial life. Coalbrookdale in 1758

Hargreaves's spinning-jenny

§ ix. *The Manufacturers*

Side by side with the agricultural improvements of the century went those remarkable discoveries and mechanical inventions, which by making mass production of manufactures possible, transformed industrial Britain. Such were the spinning-jenny of Hargreaves, which enabled a single spinner to spin as many as a hundred threads at once ; Arkwright's water-frame, a spinning-machine worked by water-power ; Crompton's mule, a combination of these two inventions which spun a finer yarn and made possible the manufacture of muslins. As the result of these improvements in the manufacture of cotton, the production of cotton-yarn began to outstrip the capacity of the weavers to make use of it. This fact was in 1784 brought to the notice of a clergyman named Edmund Cartwright, who had no personal experience either of trade or machinery ; yet such was his newly awakened interest that he set himself to invent a machine for rapid weaving, and the result was his power-loom. The motive power used both for Crompton's and Cartwright's machines was water : when steam was substituted for water manufacture on an enormously increased scale became possible. Newcomen had in 1705 made a steam-engine for the purpose of pumping water out of mines ; far more important was the much more elaborate engine of James Watt, patented in 1768, first used for cotton manufacture at Papplewick, near Nottingham, in 1785.

The great iron industry was going through a similar revolution to that in the textile trades in the same period. The problem of the effective smelting of iron had been solved by Abraham Darby's invention of coke in 1735, by the Cranages' reverberatory furnace of 1766, which made it possible to use untreated coal for smelting, and by the production of an effective blast by means of water-power, first used at the well-known Carron Ironworks near Larbert in Stirlingshire. The association of big ironworks and steelworks—the latter only in their infancy before 1780—with the great coalfields of northern England, South Wales, &c., was the first step towards the creation of the typical black countries of the nineteenth century.

So far as communications are concerned, the Industrial Revolution did not bring much improvement before the dawn of the nineteenth century. Roads remained as a rule deplorable, and travelling upon them was a slow, wearisome and uncomfortable process. Even the turnpike roads—maintained from tolls levied by special turnpike trusts, which were created in hundreds during this century, but whose efforts were not co-ordinated—were seldom in a decent state of repair. The tolls were so unpopular that there were serious turnpike riots, notably in the 'twenties and 'thirties, in which toll gates were demolished. Even the best highways were apt to be deep in mud after comparatively light rains, so that coaches sometimes became almost inextricably buried in the mire, while so uneven was the surface, so enormous were the ruts, that vehicles were frequently overturned. In winter the conditions became so dreadful that coach journeys usually took three times as long as in summer and the only really efficient mode of travel was on horseback. The turnpike roads did not extend into the north of England. In 1740 the traveller from London to Scotland found no turnpike beyond Grantham. Twenty years later the roads north of Manchester on the west, of Newcastle on the east, were still little more than narrow causeways, suitable only for pack-horses. No wonder the

London-Edinburgh coach in the mid-century ran only once a month and took between a fortnight and three weeks on the

---

IN the time of King *Charles* the Second, Sir *John Robinson* being Lieutenant of the *Tower*, uſed to go hunt often into *Epping-Foreſt*, but the Ways without *White-Chappell* were very bad and troubleſome to him, upon which he was reſolved to have them mended, either by Indictment or other Way : Upon this (as I have been informed) were laid croſs the Ways, Trees, Earth, and then Gravel, and Ditches were made, which made it good for the preſent; and to keep it ſo every Year, in the middle is laid a high Row of large Gravel, which is forc'd in, and keeps that Part higheſt to throw off the Water, and the Dirt is preſs'd or caſt into the Ditches, which are every Year cleanſed, and thus it's likely to laſt for ever. Indeed by reaſon of it's being a *Flat*, in the Winter 'tis pochy, but it's generally without Holes and even

Sir *Chriſtopher Wren*, the King's Surveyer General told me, that when he came firſt into his Place, he found the Way by the Privy Garden, between the 2 Gates at *White-hall*, to be extreme bad, and it had baffled all his Predeceſſors by means of being and ill Earth ; upon this he dug it down (I think) 2 Feet, and there pitch'd and ramm'd it well : upon that he threw what came out, and pitch'd it again ſubſtantially, and it remains firm to this Day, only muſt be mended what the Coaches wear out.

To add to my Propoſal of mending the High-ways, and the Hiſtory how ſome have been mended, I muſt tell you that one Dr *Harvey* (the Inventour of the *Harvey-Apple*, Maſter of *Trinity Hall* in *Cambridge*) about 60 Years ſince, left an Eſtate to mend the Roads *verſus Londinum* (towards *London*) and 'tis as well mended as any in *England* to *Fulmer*, 6 Miles. *Vide Fuller's Hiſtory of Cambridge.*

The badness of the roads in and near London at the end of the 17th century. From Houghton's ' Collection', 17 April 1696

---

journey. The events of the '45 revealed the inadequacy of the road system if only from a strategic point of view, and a good deal more road construction and repair were undertaken after that date. But the improvement, though considerable, left a vast amount to be desired, and Arthur Young in his descriptions of his tours in England has praise for four roads only—for all the others nothing but contempt and execration.

For the poor traveller the ordinary conveyance was the stage wagon, ponderously slow and horribly uncomfortable. But the stage coach, in which his wealthier neighbour journeyed, was little preferable, since, until near the end of the century, it had no springs. After 1780 there was notable progress in carriage design. But the biggest advance in the history of road transport in the century came in 1784 with the introduction of special fast mail coaches which easily outdistanced even the most up-to-date *diligence*. Hitherto the best passenger services had covered the ground twice as fast as the mails, which had been conveyed by post-boys in the slower, more old-fashioned vehicles or even on horse-back. The next improvements in road communications belong to the nineteenth century—they are the achievement of Macadam and Telford. More significant than road developments, so far as the eighteenth century is concerned, was the building of canals.

Among the most curious and interesting figures connected with the industrial expansion of the later eighteenth century were James Brindley (1716–72) and his patron the Duke of Bridgewater, who were jointly responsible for the building of the canal named after the Duke between Manchester and his coal-pits at Worsley. Brindley, the son of a small Derbyshire farmer, a very rough customer, had started life as apprentice to a wheelwright, who formed a very poor opinion of him as a worker. The boy's heart was in mechanical things. For a time he was employed by Josiah Wedgwood, at that time a potter in quite a small way. Incidentally he gave his attention to the problem of pumping mines and of improving Newcomen's engine. Then the young Duke of Bridgewater took Brindley into his service at a salary of 3s. 6d. a day, and the canal was started. Brindley had no knowledge of civil engineering, yet such was his enthusiasm, practical capacity, and inventive genius, that the canal was a brilliant success. Seven miles in length, it was opened in less than two years from the commencement of the work; its practical utility was proved when the price of coal in Manchester

Whereas the Stage-Coaches that are driven between *London* and *Norwich*, have for several Years last past, been so ill perform'd, that the Passengers travelling therein, have been very much *Incommoded*, and the Journeying by the said Coaches rendred very *Irksome* and *Burdensome*. And, notwithstanding great Complaints have been made thereof, to the Masters of the said Stage, yet have they refus'd and neglected to remedy the same. And forasmuch as no single Person, or five or six in Company would venture to set up a *New Stage*; it was therefore thought reasonable and necessary, that a more considerable Number should joyn together, and by a *Joynt Stock* set up a new and more convenient Stage, for the better Accommodation of themselves and all others that have occasion to travel upon that Road; which accordingly is done by the Subscription of above 200 Persons. And it is by the Subscribers agreed, That what Profit shall be made of the Moneys employed in the said Stock, above 10 *l. per Cent. per Annum* shall be applyed to Charitable *Uses*. And several of the Subscribers have agreed to give the whole Profit of their Shares to the Poor; and it is not doubted, but many more will follow their Examples. By which means not only all Persons Travelling, will be much better accommodated, but a considerable Summ of Money may be brought in for the Relief of the Necessitous. It is therefore hoped, That all Persons who have occasion to Travel upon that Road, will give all due Encouragement to so *Generous*, *Necessary*, and *Charitable* an Undertaking.

This New Stage sets out from the Four *Swans* in *Bishopsgate-street* in *London*, and from the *King's Head* in the Market-Place in *Norwich*, upon *Mondays, Wednesdays* and *Fridays*. 158.

I Hear there goes to, and comes from *Norwich*, a Coach every *Wednesday*; both which perform the Stage in One Day, which is above 90 Miles.

Rival advertisements for the London-Norwich coaching service at the end of the 17th century. From Houghton's 'Collection' of 21 June and 9 August 1695

IF any sober Family of 3 or 4 and some tolerable Substance, will look after a large House, about 20 Miles from *London*; he shall have an Apartment *gratis*, with a Dairy, pretty large Kitchen, Gardens and Orchards new planted. There will be a great many Herbs for distillation : There are 2 good Market-Towns a Mile on each Hand, to which Post comes 3 times a Week, and Carriers as often, and Coach to and fro every Day.

The relative frequency of the stage coach and the mail at the end of the 17th century. Advertisement from Houghton's 'Collection', 28 August 1696

promptly fell by 50 per cent. Brindley was next engaged on a Liverpool-Manchester Canal, which was opened in 1773, the year after his death. He had contemplated the construction of a Grand Trunk Canal, joining together the Trent, Severn, and Mersey. The Duke of Bridgewater had been thought a madman because of his intense concentration on his original scheme and the poverty-stricken mode of life he adopted in order to save every penny for the enterprise; but already before Brindley's death the advantages of canals in relieving the bad and congested roads and so cheapening transport were so obvious that their construction had become very popular. Brindley remained throughout his life quite illiterate. He never acquired any scientific knowledge, and he never made use of either drawings or mathematical calculations. When he had a knotty problem to solve his specific was to go to bed and remain there, possibly for two or three days, with his mind concentrated on the puzzle till he found a solution.

As an illustration of how the new Britain of industrialism was rapidly springing up, the career of John Wilkinson of Bersham, near Wrexham, is interesting and typical. John inherited the Bersham ironworks from his father. He was a friend of Watt, and it was at Bersham that the cylinders for Watt's steam-engines were first made. Believing firmly in the new motive power, Wilkinson soon dispensed with the old waterwheels. He produced all sorts of iron commodities—pipes, cylinders, rollers, pistons, wheels, and many of the cannon used in the Peninsular War. His trade expanding, he set up other foundries in Staffordshire and Shropshire. He had other interests. He sank a coal-mine at Brymbo, and near the same place he purchased a number of farms and enclosed a considerable acreage of waste. By the tilling and manuring methods of the new husbandry he had soon triumphed over the obstacles of rough ground and thin soil, and was producing excellent wheat. Here we have iron-master and farmer all in one! [1]

Side by side with the collieries and the ironworks rose those

[1] See *John Wilkinson and the Old Bersham Iron Works*, by A. N. Palmer (published by the Honourable Society of Cymmrodorion).

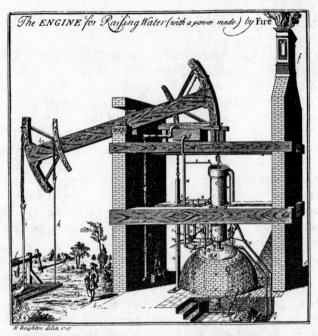

The ENGINE *for* Raiſing Water *(with a power made) by* Fire

H Beighton delin 1717

*From the earliest known engraving (1717) of Newcomen's steam-engine.
Newcomen (1663–1729) improved upon a patent by Thomas Savery for raising
water from mines by the use of steam-power*

*The Duke of Bridgewater's Navigation across the Irwell. 'The Oxford
Magazine', 1777*

busy hives of the textile trades, the factories. Hitherto the spinning-wheel and the hand-loom had been part of the cottage furniture, and manufacture had been domestic. While the men worked in the fields, their women-folk spun or wove at home. But the advent of machinery changed all this. In order to be near the coal-pits, the sources of steam-power, the cotton trade became localized in Lancashire ; the woollen trade migrated from East Anglia into Yorkshire. Into the buildings where the machinery was housed trooped the workers, no longer their own masters, but ' hands ' employed by the capitalist who owned the factory and its plant. So came into existence the rigid division between Labour and Capital. Great Britain was in process of becoming the workshop of the world.

In the new factories the labour was supplied by emigrants, who were attracted to the towns from the decaying villages. But to quite a large extent it was provided by workhouse children. In the earlier decades of the century the great majority of the babies born in these institutions died, the community having no use for them. But the extension of large-scale industry suggested a use for the offspring of the pauper, and Hanway's Act of 1767 allowed workhouse children to be boarded out, to the considerable diminution of the rate of infantile mortality and to the considerable enrichment of employers of labour in the new manufacturing areas. There was indeed nothing new in the employment of young children in industry. Defoe, describing the domestic spinning and weaving of the cottages early in the century, noted with approval that ' scarce anything above four years old, but its hands were sufficient for its own support '. The novelty lay in the increase in the supply of juvenile labour.

No doubt the hours which parents caused their children to remain at work even in the period of purely domestic manufacture would appear to us heartless and scandalous. The parents were not forced to send their children into the factories, and a certain measure of the responsibility for the conditions which prevailed in them is theirs ; the employer was not entirely to blame. But wages being low, when there were many mouths to feed, the economic argument in favour of having as many

The Revolution in Iron

'*An Iron Work, for casting of Cannon; and a Boring Mill. Taken from the Madeley side of the River Severn, Shropshire*', 1788

CORRECT STATEMENTS,

Shewing the Wages, Deductions, and nett or clear amount of a Weaver's weekly labour.

Statement First.— For 6-4ths Cambrics, 60 Reeds. Suppose a man weaves a Warp of this description, in five weeks, and receives from the master 8s. per cut, this will amount to one pound twelve shillings.

	s. d.		s. d
His weekly receipt will be for weaving one fifth of the Warp 6 4¼		His weekly expences will be	
		Rent, (*if paid*) ...	1 9
		Fire	1 0
		Sizing Warp.........	0 3
		Looming do..........	0 3
		Size or Sowen for do	0 3
		Soft Soap, Tallow and Oil.....	0 2
		Candles.................	0 4
		Soap for family washing	0 4
			4 4

This leaves him 2s. 0¼d. to support himself, wife, and children during seven days!

Statement second.— For a journeyman weaving the same kind of work :—

	s. d.		s. d.
His weekly receipt as above, is......6 4¼		His weekly deductions are for loom room, &c. one-fourth, or........	1 7
		Sizing warp........	0 3
		Looming do.	0 3
		Candles	0 4
		Lodging, cooking, and washing......	1 6
			3 11

This leaves him 2s. 5¼d. per week, for meat, drink, and clothing!

Statement third.— For ⅞ths cambrics, 44 reeds.— Suppose an *aged man* weave a cut per week of this description, and his wife wind his picking :—

	s. d.	*Weekly deduction, &c.*	s. d.
Their weekly receipts for weaving and winding 4 0		Rent	1 9
		Fire	0 10
		Sizing warp...... ..	0 3
		Looming do.	0 3
		Size, or sowen for do.	0 3
		Candles	0 4
		Soft soap, tallow, and oil.........	0 2
		Ditto for family washing	0 2
			4 0

Low wages at the end of the eighteenth and the beginning of the nineteenth century. Paragraph from ' The Liverpool Mercury' of 1816

wage-earners as possible in the family was wellnigh irresistible, and women betook themselves with their children into any employment available, upon the only sort of terms offered. What made the factories so terrible was not the fact of the long hours itself, but the rigour of an impersonal system, the remorselessness of machinery which never stopped and which seemed to demand from poor human beings an activity as tireless as its own. Small children therefore worked their twelve or fifteen or even eighteen hours in the day, rising in the early hours, kept

Children in a rope factory. An eighteenth-century engraving

till late in the evening at their task, which might not in itself be in any way exacting, till they almost dropped with fatigue and were only kept awake by the foreman's cane or strap.

The factories were not the only scene of the children's toil. Quite early in the century children of twelve were being employed in the coal-mines, where the conditions were peculiarly degraded, and to which the attention of the legislator or the philanthropist had never been attracted until John Wesley thought of preaching his gospel even to the collier. In the mines, dirty, half-naked, away from the sunlight and the pure air which were essential for their healthy growth, youngsters were occupied in the monotonous occupation of opening and shutting the pit-doors. Early in the century also, it is worth noting, there started the practice— peculiar to England—of using small boys to clean chimneys.

Even to the most unsensitive urchin the task of wriggling himself up through long narrow flues was terrifying, and, at any rate to begin with, until the skin had become hardened, it was exceedingly painful. We are apt to associate all these abuses of child labour, which inspired Mrs. Browning's poem *The Cry of the Children* and which led to the passing of the Factory Acts of 1833 to 1854, specifically with the early nineteenth century, but they had all fastened upon the country long before that century was born.

The same is true of slum conditions in the manufacturing towns. The new towns shot up like mushrooms, with all the evils of underground cellars, ugly tenements, narrow streets and courts, ugliness and grime, without architectural plan, hygienic forethought, or civic ideal. The State of England Question was not discovered by the national conscience till the eighteen-forties ; it was being rapidly created in the seventeen-seventies and eighties. The new teeming town life was not ennobled by any tradition of local patriotism ; was not kept sweet by allowing some open spaces to remain to ventilate the squalid streets ; was not enlightened by an organized philanthropy. The conception of national education, for example, had not been grasped at all in England, which was many years behind despotic Prussia and other arbitrarily governed Continental countries in this respect. Except for the well-to-do there was no education obtainable save in charity schools and Sunday-schools ; and although the latter existed before his day, the beginning of the Sunday-school movement is rightly associated with the name of Raikes of Gloucester, the Sunday-school union not being started till 1785.[1]

[1] Conditions at the great public schools in this period were very rough. Discipline was harsh ; yet the boys were apt to be turbulent. The Etonians more than once broke out in open rebellion, and the Riot Act had on one occasion in 1770 to be read at Winchester. The course of study consisted of little but the classics—it must be added that these were taught with great thoroughness—the staffing was inadequate, and there were no organized games. Good work was done by those very efficient nonconformist academies which the Tories tried to suppress by the Schism Act of 1714, and many sound Anglicans owed their schooling to these establishments. The Church of England charity schools, established under the auspices of the S.P.C.K. in 1699, aimed at teaching the children

The younger Pitt, speaking in 1794, described the inhabitants of the manufacturing towns as 'ignorant and profligate', but there was little attempt to make them otherwise. That population of helots remained outside the pale of the eighteenth-century polity. In rural England aristocracy and peasantry were in touch with one another in a common fellowship of the soil; but

---

ONE whom I hvve known feueral Yeats, and have great Reafon to believe very well underftands Mathematicks, and particularly how to teach them. He would willingly teach them to Males or Females in *Englifh* or *Latin*, at home or abroad, at convenient Hours in the Evening. He lives in *London*, and I can tell further.

ABout 40 Miles from *London* is a *Schoolmafter* has had fuch Succefs with Boys, as there are almoft 40 Minifters and Schoolmafters that were his Scholars. His Wife alfo teaches Girls *Lace-making, Plain Work, Raifing Pafte, Sauces,* and *Cookery* to the Degree of Exactnefs. His Price is 10 or 11 *l.* the Year, with a *Pair of Sheets* and *Spoon* to be returned if defired. *Coaches* and other Conveniencies pafs every Day within half a Mile of the Houfe; and 'tis but an eafie Days Journey to or from *London*.

Schoolmasters' advertisements in Houghton's 'Collection' for 25 December 1696

---

between those who had a stake in the country and the bondmen of the towns there was no such sense of community. When Selina, Countess of Huntingdon, wrote to the Duchess of Buckingham about the Wesleyans, her grace replied: 'I thank your Ladyship for the information concerning the Methodist preachers;

of the poor, between the ages of 7 and 12, reading, writing, arithmetic, and the catechism. The movement spread over all England and most of Wales. There were nearly 1,400 charity schools in England and Wales in 1727, but the original impetus seems to have spent itself by that date. A certain number of private academies existed for the benefit of the lower middle classes, aiming principally at providing some elementary occupational training in the shape of commercial arithmetic and other subjects useful for a clerk's career. In girls' schools writing, English, simple arithmetic, needlework, drawing and dancing formed the average curriculum; but in the more *élite* music, French, and Italian were sometimes added—the Italian being simply an adjunct to singing.

ADVERTISEMENTS.

I shall go the Round of Publishing. I. Physicians and Chyrurgeons. II. Lawyers and Attorneys. III. Schools, and Woodmongers. IV Coaches and Carriers, and such like; and then Physicians, and so round again if desired: And if any would see the Lists not here, 'tis but booking One, Two, or Three Numbers back, and they may have their desire. And any in England, if it be reputable for me, may be thus inserted.

WOODMONGER.

MR Worster, as Crow-nest.
Mr. Pettit, at Hartshorn Brew-house.
Mr Twin, at Iron-gate.
Mr Inwood, and Belchor, near Dyers-Hall.
Mr. Hatch, at Cole-harbour.
Mr. Marlot, at Still-yard.
Mr. Speed, at Dowgate.
Mr. Throtwell.
Mr. Lupton.
Mrs. Butterfield, at Three Cranes.
Mr. Lilly.
Mr. Jackson, at Queenhith.
Mr. Millard, at
Mr. Vere, at Baynard-Castle.
Mr. Scarle.
Mr. Kempe.
Mr. Blackham, at St. Mary Overies Dock.
Mr. Ferrys.

SCHOOLS.

BOARDING.

MRs. Dyer, Greenwich.
Mrs. Freeman, Hackney.
Mrs. Beckford, Hackney.
Mrs. Smith, Hackney.
Mrs. Adiman, Mile-end.
Mrs. Palfryman, Bednal-green.
Mrs. Prieft, Chelsey.
Mrs. Hazard, Kensington.

DANCING.

MR. Barker, Lea'sbury
Mr. Holt, St. Bartholomew lane.
Mr. Hughes, Cornhil.
Mr. Couch, Stocks-market.
Mr. Ecclesfield, Pater-noster-row.

FENCING.

MR. Waichind, Outropers-Office.
Mr Forster, Leadenhall-street
Captain Crisp, Walbrook.

FRENCH.

MR. Maliard, Wheeler-street Greenwich.

GRAMMAR.

DR Udal, Enfield.
Mr. Tolley, Kensington.
Mr. Day, chelsea.
Mr. Ogilvy, Coleman-stret.
Dr Busby's Westminster.
Dr. Gale, St. Paul's
Mr. Shortrug, Merchant-Taylors.
Mr. Young, Greenwich.
Mr. Turner, Losham.
Mr. Bayford, Chestnunt.
Mr. Chaddock, Totenham.
Mr Haines, Bednal-green.

MATHEMATICAL.

MR Williams, Cornhill.
Mr. Colion, Goodman's-Fields.
Mr. Coley, Baldwin's-Garden.
Mr. Salt, Broad-Street.
Mr Hindmarsh, Armitage.
Mr Newton, Wapping.
Mr. Linton, Ratcliff-cross.
Mr. White, near Tiverton.

WRITING.

MR Smith, Christ's-Hospital.
Mr Orpheus, Poultrey.
Mr. Chalmer, St. James's.
Mr. Shrowsbridge, Whitechappel.
Mr Marshal, Spittle-fields.
Mr. Lane, Houndsditch.
Mr. Higgins, Pudpot-lane.
Mr. Clifton, Bloomsbury
Mr Aires, St. Paul's Church-yard.

A list of eighteenth-century schools, including those which were purely commercial

From Houghton's 'Collection', 29 June 1694

their doctrines are most repulsive and strongly tinctured with impertinence and disrespect towards their superiors, in perpetually endeavouring to level all ranks and do away with all distinctions. It is monstrous to be told you have a heart as sinful as the common wretches that crawl on the earth. This is highly offensive and insulting, and I cannot but wonder that your Ladyship should relish any sentiments so much at variance with high rank and good-breeding.' The chasm between ' high rank and good-breeding ' and ' the common wretches that crawl on the earth ' is one of the tragic features of the eighteenth century.

O RARE TURPIN.

AS I was riding over Hunslow Moor,
There I saw a lawyer riding before,
And I asked him if he was not afraid.
To meet bold Turpin that mischievous blade.
CHORUS.—I asked him if he was not afraid,
To meet bold Turpin that mischievous blade.
Says Turpin to the lawyer and for to be cute,
My money I have hid all in my boot,
Says the lawyer to Turpin they mine can't find,
For I have hid mine in the cape of my coat behind.
I rode till I came to a powder mill,
Where Turpin bid the lawyer for to stand still
For the cape of your coat it must come off,
For my horse is in want of a new saddle cloth.
Now Turpin robbed the lawyer of all his store,
When that's gone he knows where to get more,
And the very next town that you go in,
Tell them you was robb'd by the bold Turpin.
Now Turpin is caught, and tried and cast,
And for a game cock must die at last,
One hundred pounds when he did die,
He left Jack Ketch for a legacy.

A Broadside in the collection of Sir Charles Firth

A VVitty arch Boy that is apt to play by the way when he goes of Errands, would be disposed to a Captain or Master of a Ship, if any wants such,

WHEREAS Nathan Whittlow, Apprentice at Siddington Smithy, in Cheshire, hath run away from his Master at the said Smithy: He is about 18 Years of Age, and a little pitted with the Small-pox, and had on when he went off, a Brown Coat, Leather Waistcoat, a Pair of Tann'd Leather Breeches, a Linen Cap, and a new Hat.
Whoever will inform Thomas Cooper at the said Smithy, of the above Person, shall be handsomely rewarded for the same.

*The raw material. The upper advertisement from Houghton's ' Collection ' of 26 July 1695;
the lower from ' Adams's Weekly Courant ' of 4 September 1753*

§ x.   *Men of the Highway and the Sea*

Already before the end of the century the Industrial Revolution was presenting the problem of its attendant evils. As the result of the enclosure movement and low wages, many rural labourers were reduced to destitution, and the question of poor relief became acute. The wave of humanitarian feeling which swept over the country after 1770 led to the virtual abolition of the ' workhouse test ' in 1782. In the earlier decades of the century a very simple and rigorous view had been taken of unemployment—the same that had prompted the Elizabethan Poor Law, viz. that unemployment was due to idleness, and that a whipping was the best remedy. It is a mistake to suppose that the earlier eighteenth century, with its small population and simple social structure, had no problem of pauperism. It also had its ' unclassed ', its ' submerged tenth '; but just as the Government regarded these as criminals and treated them with corresponding severity, so their activities very often were criminal. In eighteenth-century literature the criminal bulks largely, and deeds of violence are common.

The highwayman was the characteristic criminal of the century. It is notorious how unsafe was every lonely spot on the high road, even those so close to the metropolis as Blackheath,

Hounslow Heath, and Finchley Common. Travellers used to congregate at certain places in the environs at stated hours in order to make the journey into the capital in company. 'One is forced to travel,' wrote Horace Walpole in 1751, 'even at noon, as if one were going to battle.' Thirty years later he was finding it difficult to induce friends to dine with him at Strawberry Hill, so infested were the roads near Twickenham. In Richmond the marauders did not wait even till sundown to start robbing. The streets of London itself were very insecure till Fielding's suggestion in 1753 of the famous Bow Street Runners, a force of picked men, introduced a distinct improvement. Even so, robberies with violence continued to be rife in London streets. The audacity of London shop-lifters, both male and female, was also notorious. Such men as Charles Speckman and Hardy Vaux made a handsome livelihood by this means for several years—the former for fifteen—before they were finally caught and punished.

Comparable to the highwaymen who infested the roads were the desperate smugglers and pirates who prowled upon the pathways of the sea, and who were particularly active in the years immediately following the Treaty of Utrecht. One of the most celebrated of English navigators, William Dampier, began his life at sea as a buccaneer with the great pirate captain, Davis, and even when this literary hydrographer was given command of a King's ship, the old Adam remained in him and he was court martialled for ill-treating his officers. It was on one of his later voyages that Alexander Selkirk was marooned on the island of Juan Fernandez, to be rescued after years of solitude by Dampier on his last voyage. The most celebrated of the eighteenth-century pirates were Roberts, England, and Thatch or Blackbeard. Thatch's famous beard was extravagant in length and breadth, twisted with ribbons in small tails, and during action it was lighted up with matches secured under his hat, so that he became 'such a figure that imagination cannot form an idea of a fury from hell to look more frightful'. Of such desperadoes and their deeds the eighteenth century loved to read in Captain Charles Johnson's *History of the Pyrates*, just as they rejoiced in Captain

BATH GUARDIAN SOCIETY,

For the Profecution of FELONS, FORGERS, RE-CEIVERS of STOLEN-GOODS, &c. and to de-fray the Expences of Advertifements, Hand-Bills, and Rewards; all of which are paid out of the Public Stock, raifed annually at Five Shillings each Member refiding in the City of Bath; and Two Shillings and Sixpence additional for fuch as re-fide in the Out Part of the Parish of Walcot, the Parish of Bathwick, and Lyncombe and Widcombe.

THIS Society has been eftablifhed upon its prefent Plan Fourteen Years, and a great number of Offenders, who had robbed or defrauded the Members of this Society have been *apprehended, profecuted,* and *brought to juftice ;*—many of whom. would probably have efcaped the punifhment due to their crimes, and conti-nued much longer a peft to the Community, thro' the dread of the heavy expences that muft ever be incurred in carrying on Profecutions, fituated, as we are, at fo confiderable a diftance from every place where the Aſſizes or Seſſions of the Coun-ty are ufually holden.

    The Committee of this Society do therefore invite their Fellow-Citizens, and the neighbour-ing Inhabitants, to join in this laudable Under-taking, the good effects of which have been fen-fibly felt by the Public, not only in the Punifh-ment of Offenders ; but, it is prefumed, in the Prevention of Crimes.

The state of public insecurity gave birth to subscription societies for the legal protection of members. Second half of the eighteenth century. Newspaper cutting of the nineties

John Sheppard

Jack Sheppard in prison. Engraved in mezzotint by G. White after a drawing by Sir J. Thornhill

Alexander Smith's *Lives of Highwaymen, The Newgate Calendar*, and the story of Rob Roy in *The Highland Rogue*, and that of the fictitious Macheath in *The Beggar's Opera*.

Violence and brutality were characteristic of the sea in those days alike aboard the pirate vessel, the slaver, or the peaceful

WILLIAM DAMPIER, Capt. R.N.
From the portrait by Thomas Murray in the National Portrait Gallery

merchantman. Often the trading ship was converted into the privateer, and the merchant skipper, such as Captain Fortunatus Wright, who had a brilliantly successful career in the Mediterranean in the Seven Years' War, proved as bold and resourceful in action as any naval officer. The sea-captains presented to us by contemporary writers, both of fact and fiction, are apt to be unmannerly, like Captain Mirvan in *Evelina*. Fielding, in his *Journal of a Voyage to Lisbon*, notes the ill-effects of autocratic power on the sea-captains of the day, which made them regard themselves as ' entirely free from all those rules of decency and civility, which direct and restrain the members of a society on shore '. But at the same time the picture of his own skipper on

Thatch ('Blackbeard the Pirate') *Captain Bartholomew Roberts*
From Johnson's 'Lyves of the Pyrates'

that pathetic voyage to Portugal is singularly attractive. Captain Richard Veal, crude and often hectoring, was full of native good humour; cherished a delightfully naïve belief in witchcraft when unfavourable winds persisted; was very tender-hearted, devoted to his pet kittens, carrying ' his fondness even to inanimate objects . . . in his demonstration of love and tenderness towards his boats and ship ', acting ' the part of a father to his sailors ', looking after their ailments and never allowing

' any the least work of supererogation to go unrewarded by a glass of gin ', though a sober man himself and of a simple piety, conducting prayers ' with more devout force and address, than they are commonly read by a country curate '.

The sea was a hard calling; the condition of the vessels insanitary, so that scurvy, dysentery, and a terribly high rate of mortality were regarded as the inevitable incidents of every long voyage. A great English seaman, Captain James Cook (1728–79), first discovered the virtues of lime-juice as a remedy for scurvy, and marvellously reduced the ravages of the disease in his ships. Among all the great figures of the Georgian era none is finer or more attractive than that of the discoverer of Australia. He is heroic always, as he pilots his vessel through the dangerous and uncharted waters between the shores of New South Wales and the outer reefs, as he picks his way amid the Antarctic ice in quest of the fabled Southern Continent, as he searches for the north-eastern passage between Kamchatka and Alaska through Bering Strait. Her seamen, more often absent from her shores than present in her midst, were ever the most indispensable supporters of England's solid fabric. They were the land's very life-blood—in the eighteenth century a wild, uncouth lot, seeming as Fielding said, to ' think themselves entirely discharged from the common bands of humanity ', and seeming ' to glory in the language and behaviour of savages '. But later on he remarks that though on land ' there is nothing more idle or dissolute; in their own element there are no persons near the level of their degree, who live in the constant practice of half so many good qualities '. Perfect masters of their business, always alert, regardless of fatigue and hazard, they submit to ' every difficulty which attacks their calling with cheerfulness, and no less virtues than patience and fortitude are exercised by them every day of their lives '. It was in men of a coarse but powerful fibre that much of the greatness of Georgian England lay; it was upon their staunchness that the existence of society's elegances and refinements, its pleasures and its culture, alike depended.

An eighteenth-century impression of the South Seas, from the Atlas to 'Cook's Third Voyage'. A drawing by the artist to the Expedition.

1708. Medal struck for distribution among the partisans of the exiled family in 1708. The inscriptions are an adaptation of 'Render therefore unto Caesar the things that are Caesar's'

IV

WHIGS AND TORIES IN QUEEN ANNE'S DAY

HALIFAX, SOMERS—OXFORD, BOLINGBROKE

THE party system was still in its childhood in Queen Anne's reign, and it is not even easy to state what exactly the two great contending parties stood for. It is roughly correct to say that the Whigs maintained the principles of limited monarchy and parliamentary government embodied in the Revolution settlement of 1689, religious toleration, the interests of the banking and commercial magnates; while the Tories supported royal prerogative, High Church doctrine, and the interests of the squirearchy. Such a broad generalization must be qualified by the reminder that there were plenty of Whig squires; that there were Whigs who betrayed the cause of toleration of the Dissenters and Tories who aided that cause; that there were Tories who had helped to bring about the Revolution settlement and Whigs who did not remain true to it. There is one distinction between the parties during this reign that is not so much in need of qualification—the Whigs were more thoroughgoing supporters of the war with France than their rivals, and in particular were more in favour of the land campaigns in Flanders and Spain than the Tories, who would have liked to see operations confined to the sea. It was for this reason that Marlborough

CHARLES SPENCER—Third Earl of Sunderland

From the portrait by Jonathan Richardson belonging to the Earl Spencer, K.G.

and Godolphin, themselves Tory in sympathy, came to lean more and more on the Whigs, who thus became increasingly influential in the government until they actually controlled it. That control was exercised and organized by a coterie of five, who are known as the Junto—Wharton, Orford, Sunderland, Halifax, and Somers. Of these the first three were men of talent, the other two were men of genius.

The least distinguished yet possibly the most useful to his party was Thomas, Lord Wharton, the son of a very strict Presbyterian, who became perhaps the most dissolute of all the dissolute rakes at the court of Charles II, a brilliant swordsman and a frequent duellist. The Tories hated him. Swift called him ' the most universal villain I ever knew ', and a lampoon writer assailed him as

> A monster, whom no vice can bigger swell,
> Abhor'd by Heaven and long since due to Hell.

On the other hand, we find him described as ' one of the completest gentlemen in England, hath a very clear understanding, and manly expressions, with abundance of wit '. To the Whigs he was ' honest Tom ', because of his bluff directness and jovial *bonhomie*. He was the author of the famous doggerel verses, ' Lillibullero ', with which it was claimed he had whistled James II off the English throne. ' Perhaps ', said Bishop Burnet, ' never had so slight a thing so great an effect '. His friends delighted in him, his enemies feared him because of his sledge-hammer methods in debate. His attacks were merciless, unscrupulous, and scurrilous, so that Bolingbroke termed him ' the scavenger of his party '. But even more useful than his coarse and fluent aptness in debate was his rare skill in electioneering. In many counties his influence was supreme ; he was willing to spend thousands in bribery, and the task appealed strongly to his type of mind, his rough affability and downrightness standing him in good stead on his electioneering expeditions.

Also of an essentially coarse type was Edward Russell, Earl of Orford—a bad-tempered, insolent and, above all, self-seeking

THE EARL OF HALIFAX
From the portrait by Sir Godfrey Kneller in the National Portrait Gallery

THE EARL OF ORFORD
Engraved by George Vertue after Thomas Gibson's painting

man. Ambitious for office, when he got it (as he often did), he proved himself irritable, perverse, and impracticable. He early adopted the sea as a calling, and he is popularly known as the victor of the battle of Barfleur or Cape La Hogue, fought on the 19th May 1692. He had a great superiority of force over the French, who should have been, and were not, annihilated. The subsequent naval history of the reign shows William III realizing, as his expert advisers did not, the strategic significance of the Mediterranean and insisting on Russell wintering at Cadiz and that admiral dolorously protesting against the unbearable hardships of remaining at sea at all in winter. Suspicion of Jacobitism was thrown upon him at the time of the Fenwick plot and, whether he was implicated in that or not, there can be little doubt of his having had Jacobite dealings at one time or another. Particularly after the conclusion of peace at Ryswick he was a very discontented man. In the reign of Anne, though note-worthy as a party manager, he held office only for a short while at the head of the Admiralty. A man of real ability and a genuine seaman, brave to effrontery, he was essentially mean and false of spirit, a degenerate scion of the great house of Russell with its tradition of public service, devoting his career to making public capital out of the new *régime* introduced in 1689.

Charles Spencer, Earl of Sunderland, we shall meet again as a colleague of Walpole. The son of the tortuous and underhand first earl, whose ambiguous career is one of the most curious studies of the reigns of Charles II and James II, he was as outspoken and violent as his father was subtle and secretive. Not merely a Whig, he avowed himself a republican and was fond of expressing the hope that he would live to see the day when there would not be a peer left in England. He had been a precocious and disagreeable child ; as a man his studied insolence made him sometimes as embarrassing to his friends as he was invariably offensive to Queen Anne. Indeed, so much did she abhor the boorish republican that whenever he holds office we know that Whig influence must be indeed invincible. Yet partly because he was a son-in-law of the Churchills, partly because of his genuine intellectual gifts, this disagreeable and restlessly ambitious man was invaluable to the Whigs and gained the highest office in the reign of George I.

We breathe a purer atmosphere when we turn to Charles Montagu, Earl of Halifax, though he also was vainglorious and ambitious. But there was nothing ignoble about Montagu, and he used his undoubted genius for his country's welfare. Educated at Westminster School under the great Dr. Busby and at Trinity College, Cambridge, he was destined for the Church. But at the university his interests took another trend, for he studied under Sir Isaac Newton, of whom he became a lifelong friend, and developed a strong taste for mathematics and philosophy. He also dabbled in verse, none of it in the least inspired; but he collaborated with Matthew Prior in a noteworthy parody of Dryden's *The Hind and the Panther*, entitled *The Country Mouse and the City Mouse*.

MATTHEW PRIOR

On the accession of William III Montagu entered the House of Commons, his first important speech being on a bill for allowing prisoners on trial for treason the assistance of counsel, when he adroitly used a momentary lapse of memory to clinch his argument in favour of the measure. If he from mere nervousness broke down in a friendly assembly, how helpless must be a man, unpractised in public speaking, called upon to combat the ablest advocates in the realm, his faculties paralysed by the knowledge that failure meant the gallows!

Montagu early proved himself a financier of quite exceptional ability and insight, and in 1694 he became Chancellor of the Exchequer. To him is due the establishment of the National Debt and of the Bank of England, while together with Somers, Isaac Newton, and John Locke he was responsible for the reform

The Bank of England. The original building

of the very debased coinage current at the time. These achievements not only vastly improved English credit and facilitated the financing of the war, but they also had far-reaching consequences in developing our commerce and making London the great money-market of the world. It is not too much to say that all the most important economic accomplishment of the reign of William III is directly connected with the name of Montagu.

He had had a great influence in the House of Commons, but latterly this tended to wane owing to a rather boastful pride and ostentation which were the unfortunate products of a

career of uninterrupted success. In 1700 he entered the House of Lords as Baron Halifax. There he found himself, together with Portland, Somers, and Orford, impeached by the Tory majority then predominant in the Commons. In addition to the general charge of complicity in the Partition Treaties brought against all four, particular articles were exhibited against each, the counts against Halifax being of embezzlement and nepotism. The House of Peers rallied to the support of the ex-ministers and the articles of impeachment were dismissed.

The growth of the Bank of England

Above, a £100 Exchequer Note of 1709. Below, one of the first £1 notes which were issued in the financial crisis of 1797. Reproduced by the courtesy of the editor of 'The Connoisseur'

Halifax was an acquisition to the Upper House owing to his natural gifts, knowledge of business, and skill in debate. His methods were sprightlier and less formal than were at that time usual in that somewhat solemn assembly ; it was complained of him and Wharton that they ' brought up a familiar style with them from the House of Commons, that has been too much practised in the House of Lords ever since, where everything formerly was managed with great decency and good manners '. He was a great source of strength to the Whig Opposition in the Lords both at the opening of the reign of Queen Anne and in the final period of Tory domination. In the former period he took an active part in defeating the various Tory measures brought forward for the suppression of the practice of occasional conformity, whereby Protestant Dissenters desirous of entering the public service evaded the provisions of the Test Act. In the latter period he took one of the leading parts in the great onslaught of the Whig peers on the whole policy of the Tory administration, especially on the disgraceful ' restraining orders ' to Ormonde, on the Treaty of Utrecht, particularly its commercial clauses and the supposed danger to the Hanoverian succession from the proximity of the Pretender to the English shores, and indeed from the whole policy of the ministry. But Halifax's principal achievement during the reign of Anne was his work between 1706 and 1708 on the commission which arranged that great triumph of statesmanship, the legislative union with Scotland.

On the accession of George I, Halifax was rewarded for his services to the house of Hanover by an earldom, the garter, and the First Lordship of the Treasury ; but he enjoyed these honours only a short time, for he died in May 1715.

It is necessary to add something about Halifax as a patron and man of letters. Though he figures in Johnson's *Lives of the Poets*, his right of admission into that circle is of the flimsiest. But although Swift, with a bitterness which betrays personal pique, declared that his encouragements of learning ' were only good words and dinners ', as a matter of fact, as a patron he gave substantial help to Congreve, Addison, and Prior, and

View *of the* HOUSE *of* COMMONS, *from*
the River Thames

holding that ' a lamp that gives so much light must not be left without oil ', he obtained the post of Master of the Mint for Newton. Even a much wealthier Maecenas than Halifax could not have ministered to the wants of all who sought his favours. ' He was ', said Pope, ' fed with dedications '. Halifax became President of the Royal Society, and in 1706 he took important steps for the adequate housing of the public records, which lay in a bad state of confusion in the Tower, and also of the valuable collection of manuscripts left to the nation by Sir John Cotton, now in the British Museum.

Greater than Halifax, indeed pronounced by Macaulay to have been in most respects the greatest man of his age, was Lord Somers. Born of good but comparatively humble parents, John Somers was educated at Trinity College, Oxford. He showed himself a pronounced Whig in a pamphlet published at the time of the Exclusion Bill, by which the Whigs in the reign of Charles II had sought to exclude the future James II, then Duke of York, from the succession to the throne on the ground of his Romanism, and through his friendship with the fascinating Charles Talbot, Duke of Shrewsbury, he was later introduced to the inner circle of the party. He made his mark when in 1688 he was selected as junior counsel for the seven bishops. To have had even a small part in securing their acquittal was a short cut to fame and popularity. In the Convention Parliament, which met during the interregnum occasioned by James II's flight out of England when William of Orange in the role of the Protestant deliverer of the country reached London, he sat for Worcester, and the vexed constitutional questions at issue gave a fine opportunity for the exercise of his great legal gifts, while his republished Exclusion Bill pamphlet had considerable influence outside the Convention. His advocacy of the principle involved had not a little to do with the adoption by the House of Commons of the view that James II's flight from the kingdom was equivalent to abdication. Subsequently the Declaration of Rights was drawn up by a committee under Somers's direction, so that no one had a more intimate connexion with the legal framework of the Revolution.

His advancement after the proclamation of William and Mary was very rapid. From the first he won William's confidence. He at once became Solicitor-General; in 1692 Attorney; next year Lord Keeper of the Great Seal, and in 1697 Lord Chancellor, with the title of Baron Somers of Evesham. To him is due the credit of having advised the discontinuance of the licensing laws, i.e. the establishment of freedom of the press— one of the outstanding reforms of the reign. During these years Somers was remarkably well liked both as lawyer and statesman by both parties—an unusual distinction in days of acrimonious party strife; but in the troubled period which followed the conclusion of peace in 1698 there came a great change in this respect. He does not appear to have approved of the Partition Treaties; nevertheless he duly affixed the Great Seal to them, and the

JOHN, LORD SOMERS.
From J. Smith's engraving after the painting by Jonathan Richardson

upshot was his impeachment in company with the three other Whig lords. His enemies had another convenient handle against him in the fact that he had been partly responsible for the sending out of the notorious Captain Kidd to suppress piracy, and Kidd had instead turned pirate himself, either voluntarily or under pressure of a mutinous crew. By a large majority the Commons agreed to an address to the King that Somers be removed from his service, and to this William thought it wisest to agree. Bishop Burnet was aghast at so great a minister being

removed 'without a shadow of complaint against him', failing
to recognize (as perhaps no contemporary could be expected to
recognize) that it was not a question of merit but of responsibility of ministers to Parliament that was involved; the House
of Commons' majority, rightly or wrongly, had no confidence in
Somers.

Queen Anne did not love him either, and for the first six years
of her reign he was out of office. But there was nothing small-
minded or mean-spirited about his conduct, for he gave his full
support to the foreign policy of the government. At the same
time he strongly opposed the Occasional Conformity Bills in
which the Tories delighted, and with great force espoused the
cause of Ashby *v.* White and of the Aylesbury men in the very
important constitutional causes involved.[1] In 1706 he introduced
a most necessary measure which aimed at diminishing the vexa-
tious charges and pettifogging delays in the law courts. Vested
interests robbed the bill of some of its effectiveness, but a valuable
reform was nevertheless effected. In 1708, Marlborough and
Godolphin having entered into a thorough-going alliance with
the Whigs, Somers became Lord President of the Council. The

---

[1] The essential facts in a complicated case are that Matthew Ashby,
a native of Aylesbury, was refused his claim to vote for that borough in
the general election of 1702. He thereupon brought an action for damages
against the mayor, William White. Judgement was given against him in
the Court of Queen's Bench, on the ground that the determining of all
election disputes was the sole right of the House of Commons and that the
law courts were not entitled to deal with such cases. Ashby then appealed
to the House of Lords, which, taking his view that a vote was equivalent
to a piece of property, declared that 'the property of Englishmen' could
not be subjected 'to the arbitrary votes of the House of Commons'.
The House of Commons regarded the Lords' action in championing Ashby's
cause as an intolerable interference with their privileges, and a serious
quarrel between the Houses ensued, which was still further exacerbated
when five other Aylesbury men, whose votes had also been refused,
encouraged by the Lords' action, proceeded at the end of 1704 to follow
Ashby's example and to claim damages. The Commons promptly had them
arrested and imprisoned for breach of the privileges of their House. No
settlement of the question at issue was arrived at, but when Parliament
was prorogued in March 1705 the prisoners were released, the Commons
having no power to extend their imprisonment beyond the expiration of
the session.

Whig triumph was brief owing to the indiscreet prosecution of Sacheverell, against the impolicy of which Somers had protested.

With the Tories in office Somers, like the other members of the Junto, was a powerful opponent of the government, being particularly interested in the question of the prosecution of the war in Spain, which he considered ought to be pressed until Philip of France was driven out of the Peninsula. There is one instance of purely factious conduct during this period of opposition which is very discreditable to Somers. When some discontented Scots peers moved for the repeal of the Scottish Union which he and Halifax had played so large and honourable a part in securing, he with the remainder of the Junto gave the motion his support, with the result that it was very nearly carried.

George I would certainly have made Somers one of his ministers, but his health broke down utterly, and in 1716 he died of apoplexy at the age of sixty-six.

Such in the briefest outline was the career of this remarkable man, whom even Swift, who usually hated Whigs with great gusto, was constrained to praise. Burnet's description of him is of a wise and strong man. ' He was very learned in his own profession, with a great deal of learning in other professions, in divinity, philosophy, and history. He had a great capacity for business, with an extraordinary temper ; for he was fair and gentle, perhaps to a fault, so that he had all the patience and softness, as well as the justice and equity becoming a great magistrate.'

By common consent one of the greatest of Lord Chancellors, he was the first of the remarkable succession of lawyer-statesmen who played so influential a part in the eighteenth century. He owed his predominance to his width of view. He was no merely pedantic lawyer, but one who delighted in general principles and who united to legal knowledge many other intellectual interests—literature, philology, and art. He was a generous friend of Locke, Newton, and Addison, though he made no parade of his generosity. He was ostentatious in nothing. Devoid of avarice and selfish ambition, he was the moral and intellectual leader of the Whigs. 'All the traditional accounts of him,' says Horace Walpole, ' the historians of the last age and its best authors represent him as the most incorrupt lawyer and the honestest statesman, as a master orator, a genius of the finest taste, and as a patriot of the noblest and most extensive views ; as a man who dispensed blessings by his life and planned them for posterity.'

Such was the greatest member of the Junto. The word itself means ' faction ', and we have seen that even Somers could be guilty of pure factiousness, as in the discreditable support of the motion for the repeal of the Union. On the other hand, the Junto certainly accomplished a good work. On the whole they stood for the principles of personal liberty and religious toleration ; they were instrumental in securing the Hanoverian succession ; and they were very closely associated with two of the great constitutional triumphs of our history, the Revolution of 1688 and the Act of Union of 1708.

Who, now, were the Tory leaders in the reign of Queen Anne ? Marlborough and Godolphin are often spoken of as moderate Tories, and possibly that is the best description of them ; but the latter seems to have had little in the nature of a party creed, and Marlborough's domineering duchess was so entirely a Whig, the duke was so much forced by political exigencies during his great campaigns to lean upon Whig support, and after 1711 he so closely associated himself with the opposition to the Tory administration, that it would not be wrong to class him with the Whigs. There were other magnates whose party allegiance was doubtful. There was for example the stiff and ridiculous Somerset, ' the proud duke ', who for a time acted with Harley, was then given the cold shoulder by him, and who acted with Argyll and Shrewsbury in the crisis at the Queen's death. It is of the ' proud duke ' that the story is told that his young second wife once tapped him lightly with her fan. ' Madam !' her husband exclaimed in tones of icy dignity, ' my first wife was a Percy, and she never did such a thing.' Then there was the Duke of Shrewsbury, that most handsome, polished, attractive 'King of Hearts', William III's favourite, ever shirking responsibility, anxious to avoid political life, undoubtedly a Whig during the reign of William III, but quite definitely voting with the Tories at the Sacheverell trial and subsequently on more than one occasion.

The Tories were a mixed combination. There were some scarcely distinguishable from Whigs; at the other extreme there were undoubted Jacobites, like the famous Atterbury, Bishop of Rochester, a High Church cleric and an inveterate conspirator, who was certainly a Jacobite plotter after the accession of George I. The Duke of Ormonde may also have been already a Jacobite. He was a most attractive figure, popular with all parties, brave, chivalrous, the *beau idéal* of the soldier in outward appearance at all events, and, according to Prince Eugène, ' the finest cavalier and

SIDNEY, EARL OF GODOLPHIN.
J. Smith's engraving after the painting by Sir Godfrey Kneller

most complete gentleman that England bred, being the glory of that nation, of so noble spirit that he would sacrifice all for his Church and Sovereign '.

The old-fashioned courtly type of Tory was well represented by the Queen's uncle, the Earl of Rochester, who at the opening of the reign had much influence. Another intense zealot for the Church of England—the most determined enemy of the practice of occasional conformity—was Daniel Finch, Earl of Nottingham, a very tall dark man, looking like a foreigner, of a very grave and melancholy mien for which he was nicknamed ' Don

Dismallo '. Then there was the very high-minded, indefatigable member for the University of Oxford, always intensely concerned for the welfare of the Church, Mr. Bromley. He became Speaker of the House of Commons in 1710, having failed to obtain that office in 1705 owing to his publication of a journal of the Grand Tour, which he had made in common with most men of fashion of his day. He had visited Rome, had an audience of the Pope and kissed his slipper—so his Protestantism was called in question. We may mention the Duke of Buckinghamshire, thus described by a contemporary : ' He is a nobleman of learning, and good natural parts, but of no principles. Violent for the high-church, yet seldom goes to it. Very proud, insolent, and covetous, and takes all advantages. In paying his debts, unwilling ; and is neither esteemed nor beloved.' There was the moderate Harcourt, who became Attorney-General in 1707, Lord Keeper in 1710, and subsequently Lord Chancellor, who as the chief Tory lawyer in the Upper House had to stand up to Somers. There was Matthew Prior, the poet and diplomatist, who helped to negotiate peace with France for the Tory administration. There was another diplomatist, one of our plenipotentiaries at Utrecht, Thomas Wentworth, Earl of Strafford. Strafford was not an outstanding man, but one is happy to know him if only because of his mother, whose letters to him are a constant source of delight. Neither mother nor son could spell. Lady Wentworth spells Italian sometimes Etalyon, sometimes Etallian; equipage, ekopadg; promising, prommisseing; Wales, Wails ; citizens, sittissons ; torture, torter ; guests, gess ; opera, operer ; superfluity, suparflewety. Her great anxiety is to get her son married to an heiress, and she is constantly offering match-making suggestions. But she is most genuinely affectionate. Thus she closes one letter : ' I cannot help wishing myself in cogneto with You, who is the Darling of my soul, and the delight of my eys, and dearer to me than any words can expres, neither is it possible for me to tell you, how much I am, my dearest dear, your moste infenit affectionate mother.'

But the two outstanding Tory figures of the reign are Robert

ROBERT HARLEY, FIRST EARL OF OXFORD
From the portrait by Sir Godfrey Kneller in the National Portrait Gallery

Harley, Earl of Oxford, and Henry St. John, Viscount Boling-broke. They form such clearly contrasted types, and their friendship and later rivalry had so dramatic a bearing on the course of history, that few periods are more interesting than that of their joint administration.

Robert Harley was by parentage and education a Dissenter, but, although he was always regarded as a protector of the Non-conformists, he very soon after entering political life identified himself with the Tories and the High Anglican interest. Two qualifications distinguished him—one was a very close acquain-tance with all the forms and routine of parliamentary business, the other a gift of conciliation, so that despite his close associa-tion with High Churchmen and Tories he succeeded in remaining on good terms with Dissenters and Whigs. In the reign of William III he distinguished himself as the mover of the Triennial Bill of 1694, as the foremost agent in the establishment of the Land Bank, which was designed as a counterblast to the Bank of England for the benefit of the landed interest as against the commercial interest, but which proved a dismal disappointment, and as the author of the motion for the very drastic reduction of the forces after the conclusion of the Treaty of Ryswick. In 1701 he became Speaker of the House of Commons.

In 1704 Harley became a privy councillor and one of the two Secretaries of State, though he did not give up the Speakership till next year. He strenuously supported the House of Commons as against the Peers in the famous case of Ashby *v.* White, maintaining that in all election disputes the sole determination rested with the Lower House. While the ministry of Godolphin became more and more Whiggish, particularly after the beginning of 1708, when the high Tories Buckinghamshire, Rochester, Nottingham were dismissed, Harley for the time being remained. But considerable suspicion was aroused by the discovery of the treasonable Jacobite correspondence of one of his clerks, a man called William Gregg. No evidence was discovered to incriminate Harley, but it was proved that he had been criminally negligent in the management of his office, allowing the most highly con-fidential documents to be accessible to junior clerks. As a matter of fact Harley, at this period at all events, was loyal enough to the Protestant succession[1]; he was not loyal to Godolphin and Marlborough. Indeed, he had for some time been turning his energies to the task of supplanting the Duchess of Marlborough in the Queen's favour by means of the graces of Abigail Hill, who was his cousin. He sought by these means to instil into the Queen the idea that her beloved Church of England was endangered by the policy of the Whigs, and could only be adequately safeguarded by the admission of the Tories into office. Realizing the duplicity of their colleague, the Whig leaders secured the dismissal of Harley in 1708. But the High Church enthusiasm engendered by the Sacheverell impeachment routed the Whigs. Moreover, the influence of Abigail Hill, now Mrs. Masham, which had steadily increased since 1708, had made an irreparable breach in the Whig stronghold at court, and Harley in 1710 took easy possession.

He was the head of the new administration, and with a strong Tory phalanx behind him and the force of popular fanaticism still very powerful, he seemed to be starting out on a most prosperous career. But events were soon to prove that although a most skilful parliamentarian and a good party leader, he was deficient in the higher qualities of the statesman, and that in the endeavour to weld together the different elements in the Tory party, where his forte might have been supposed clearly to lie, he failed lamentably. For what manner of man essentially was this Robert Harley? A genuine lover of letters, perhaps the first statesman who, deliberately studying public opinion, realized the value of the press as a political organ, the patron of Swift and Defoe, most amiable in address, in private life most virtuous; he was, on the other hand, very vain, consumed by an exaggerated sense of his own importance, a man who rejoiced in all manner of petty secrecies and superfluous intrigues, who had an eye for detail but not for strategy; and he was strangely indolent, casual, and careless. He did not even take the trouble to retain the favour of Lady Masham, the 'dirty chambermaid', whom, in the words of a Whig ballad, the Queen 'made a minister of state'. He succeeded in offending the Queen herself. Latterly

[1] He took a prominent part in carrying the Act of Settlement of 1701.

she complained 'that he neglected all business ; that he was seldom to be understood ; that when he did explain himself, she could not rely on the truth of what he said ; that he never came to her at the time she appointed ; that he often came drunk ; lastly, to crown all, he behaved himself to her with bad manners, indecency, and disrespect'. His efforts to keep together his disunited followers led to his pleasing neither extreme. Some thought him too subservient to Hanover ; others saw in him a Jacobite.

H. S . L . B.
NIL ADMIRARI.

Henry St. John, Viscount Bolingbroke, without his wig. An engraving of 1753

The man who brought about Harley's downfall was, curiously enough, his chief and ablest coadjutor, Henry St. John. St. John was a man of great ability. It is universally agreed that he was very brilliant and very dissipated ; and there agreement ends and controversy begins. Was he a mere superficial *poseur* or was he a great and original statesman and philosopher ? He certainly possessed all the charm and all the foibles of the fine gentleman. Swift speaks of his uniting ' wit, capacity, beauty, quickness of apprehension and an excellent taste '. He particularly admired Petronius and Alcibiades and aspired to be like them ; he aimed at combining the man of pleasure and the man of business. He had an obvious fascination. He was quite exceptionally handsome ; he had a manner of open-hearted *camaraderie* ; he had a great command of language in speech and on paper. He was probably the greatest orator and he was certainly one of the most distinguished writers of his day. He united winsomeness and the faculty of command. He had great ambition, belief in his star, a determined will for the realization of his schemes for himself and his party. Prince Eugène speaks of him as ' the bull-dog of the party ', and as ' a bold and daring spirit '. He was too bold, too daring for Harley.

By the time of Queen Anne's accession St. John had become well known as a speaker and a debauchee, but had not as yet made a great mark in politics. But in the new reign he came to the forefront as a protagonist of the High Church party, a zealot against occasional con- formity. He was notori- ously a free-thinker, and no one imagined that his attitude was due to religious conviction. He was merely playing a party game, attacking one of the powerful battalions in the hostile

Henry St. John, Viscount Bolingbroke, with his wig. From the painting by T. Murphy

political array. The Whigs could not cast stones. Their motives were not sincerely religious either ; and when later they found they could win over the invaluable support of the high church Tory Nottingham by accepting his measure against occasional conformity, they abandoned the cause of religious toleration with alacrity. In 1704 St. John became Secretary at War, and he seems to have been thoroughly efficient in that office ; at all events his administration gave great satisfaction to Marlborough. In 1708, together with his friend Harley, with whom he had always been identified, he resigned, and he for a time retired into private life and studied history. Then came the Whig *débâcle* in 1710, and St. John came into office with Harley, being appointed Secretary of State.

The first desire of the new ministry was peace. Herein they had the support of at any rate a very large proportion of the population, who were heartily tired of the protracted war in spite of Marlborough's superb victories. It was known to some that the Whigs had had opportunities of arranging peace on excellent terms, but had refrained from taking them. Pending a peace settlement the Tories, in pursuance of their avowed policy throughout the reign, being in office, sought to alter the nature of our participation in the war. They had always maintained that we should have confined our operations mainly, if not exclusively, to the sea, and left the continental campaign to our allies. St. John accordingly planned a naval expedition to Canada, which proved a complete failure. But the negotiation of peace was his main preoccupation ; and he was carrying on secret conversations with the French, through an unofficial intermediary, the Abbé Gaultier. Later, the Duke of Shrewsbury and Matthew Prior, the poet, were sent to Paris to discuss definite preliminaries of peace. Thus a separate understanding was arranged with France before the Dutch were consulted at all ; indeed a settlement had practically been agreed to at Paris before the ostensible peace negotiations were started at Utrecht, and special commercial privileges for England had been bargained for, which our Dutch allies subsequently complained were prejudicial to them. Indeed, there is much to be said for the view that we treated the French as if they were our allies, the Dutch as if they were our enemies. The Whigs, especially in the House of Lords, where they were strong, made a natural and determined attack upon the Government's peace policy, in particular insisting that no peace should be signed which left Philip of Anjou on the Spanish throne. In order to make sure of the acceptance of their policy, the ministry persuaded the Queen to create twelve new Tory peers to give them a bare majority in the Upper House—an unprecedented proceeding which was denounced by the opposition as an unconstitutional use of the royal prerogative. They also dismissed Marlborough, whom they superseded in the command of the British forces in Flanders by the Duke of Ormonde. When, before the peace parleys at Utrecht had actually been concluded, they sent the famous 'restraining orders' to Ormonde, forbidding him to co-operate in any offensive operations with our allies, thereby on St. John's own admission saving the French army from destruction, they certainly laid themselves open to the charge of infamy.

In the meantime all was not well inside the Tory camp. As early as February 1711, according to Harley, his subordinate 'began listing a party, and set up for governing the house'. St. John was certainly jealous and discontented. A French refugee attempted his assassination, but actually wounded Harley. Instead of being thankful at his own escape, he was aggrieved at the sympathy extended to Harley; he felt that it ought to have gone to him. When Harley was promoted Earl of Oxford, instead of feeling flattered to be left leader of the House of Commons and by the knowledge that he had been deliberately left there in order to pilot the peace settlement safely through troubled quarters, he was again angry at not being at once elevated to the peerage. When he was promoted to the Upper House, the fact that he was made Viscount, and not Earl of, Bolingbroke was again a grievance. He complained that he ' was dragged into the House of Lords in such a manner, as to make my promotion a punishment, not a reward'. The version given by Oxford, now Lord Treasurer, is, ' Nothing could appease a restless, ambitious man'.

But there was more in the quarrel between the two men than mere personal pique. There was a wide divergence of policy. As time went on the attack on the government carried on by the opposition in Parliament and in the press became more and more formidable. They attacked the peace settlement from many points of view—the abandonment of our allies, the Catalans; the ' restraining orders'; the commercial treaty, which as a matter of fact was a good one on free trade principles. Above all, they asserted that the Protestant succession was in danger. Both in England and, perhaps more important, in Hanover they industriously bruited it abroad that the administration were aiming at a Jacobite restoration. They dinned this into the ears of the aged Electress and insisted that her son should be brought over into England to take his seat in the Lords as Duke of Cambridge. It was a very natural game for the opposition to play, and a very effective one, whatever its basis in truth.

What in these circumstances ought the Tories to do? Go on conciliating, was Oxford's answer. He was merely a looker-on, exclaimed Bolingbroke impatiently. 'The sum of all his policy had been to amuse the Whigs, the Tories, and the Jacobites, as long as he could. . . . When it became impossible to amuse mankind any longer, he appeared plainly at the end of his line.' Bolingbroke's answer to the problem was a very different one. It was not conciliatory; it was bold. It was to strengthen the Tory party on its traditional basis of loyalty to the Church and the Prerogative; to purge out all the lukewarm semi-Whig elements, the Hanoverian Tories or 'whimsicals' led by Sir Thomas Hanmer—'those odd animals', the Jacobite Lockhart terms them.

Did this policy involve the design of a Jacobite restoration on the death of Queen Anne?

A Whig ballad put it:

> 'Tis now no dispute between Tory and Whig;
> But whether a Popish successor or no.

The evidence is very conflicting. There are Jacobite papers incriminating both Oxford and Bolingbroke. Certainly both were in correspondence with Jacobites; but then so were many of the Whig leaders. They all wanted to be on the safe side. It is possible to argue either that Bolingbroke, knowing himself to be (as he indeed was) in very bad odour at Hanover, definitely worked for a restoration of the Pretender; or, that, realizing that the Pretender's refusal to abandon his Roman Catholicism made the design of his restoration impracticable, he aimed at making the hold of a thoroughly organized Tory party on the country so powerful that the first Hanoverian ruler would find that party indispensable. The question will probably always be one for conjecture at best. Some apologists for Bolingbroke, however, fall into the error of treating it as unthinkable that he could ever have contemplated the idea of a Jacobite restoration, as if there were something very nefarious in the idea. There was nothing necessarily nefarious in it. There would have been nothing wicked in upsetting the Act of Settlement or deciding after all rather to have the Stuarts back than to welcome the unromantic Germans of Hanover, if the country as a whole could have been persuaded to favour that plan. The Hanoverians were unknown and singularly unattractive. Had the Pretender been willing to renounce his Romanism might he not easily have proved the more popular sovereign ? We may at least take it for certain that Bolingbroke seriously considered the possibility of a restoration, and take it as probable that he decided on a strong policy of organizing a Tory party on High Church, loyalist, patriotic, national lines, making sure of that at any rate and then waiting for circumstance to point out the best use of this powerful weapon, once it had been well forged and sharpened.

The last few months of the reign of the Queen, dark with intrigue and suspicion, have an intensely dramatic and exciting quality. Civil war seemed by no means inconceivable. The Jacobites were convinced that Bolingbroke was working for them ; in March 1714 Halifax wrote : 'Unless the Queen or the Pretender die soon, you may look upon the succession as lost.' Important positions in Scotland and Ireland, military governorships and the command of regiment after regiment were being given to high Tories and suspected Jacobites. Berwick, at the Pretender's court, claimed that he had part in the business, was inciting Ormonde and his party to secure the removal of Oxford. Lady Masham also was determined upon his removal. In these circumstances Bolingbroke's right-hand man in the Commons, Sir William Windham, introduced the persecuting Schism Bill, aimed at the destruction of the Dissenters' schools. It was noted that Oxford was very lukewarm in support of it. The crisis came on the night of the 27th July, when Oxford resigned his Lord Treasurer's staff, and a stormy cabinet meeting took place, leaving Bolingbroke in command of the situation and the Queen violently agitated. On the 1st August she died. The time that Bolingbroke needed for the carrying out of his scheme of policy, whatever it was, had been denied him. ' What a world is this,' he wrote, ' and how has Fortune bantered us ! ' The Queen's last act had been the appointment of Shrewsbury as Treasurer at the instance of the two Opposition peers, Somerset and Argyll, it is said at a Cabinet meeting but probably in the Privy Council ; the Bolingbroke administration had not even come into existence.

The fall of Oxford and the failure of Bolingbroke meant the disruption of the Tory party. The Whigs succeeded in thoroughly ingratiating themselves with the new sovereign ; indeed, George I landed in the country, already fully persuaded that every Tory was suspect of Jacobitism. The Whigs, therefore, came into power and remained there for practically fifty years. It soon became clear that the triumphant party were likely to impeach the late Tory ministers. Oxford elected to stand his ground ; Bolingbroke, on the other hand, fled in disguise to France, and shortly afterwards became Secretary of State to the Pretender.

Oxford's trial was a most protracted affair. He was confined for nearly two years in the Tower ; but in August 1717, when the animosities of 1714 had considerably died down, he was acquitted. Bolingbroke had meanwhile become thoroughly disgusted with the bungling impracticable schemes of the Pretender's court ; had protested in vain against the attempted rising of 1715, which he knew was foredoomed to failure ; and was anxious only to return to England. His efforts to gain his rehabilitation were successful ; he was pardoned in 1723, and allowed to come back to the country, though not to take his seat in the House of Lords.

Once returned he took a leading part, as we shall see in the next chapter, in organizing the powerful opposition in the press to Walpole. He also produced his chief literary works, most notably *A Dissertation on Parties* and *The Idea of a Patriot King*. ' Who now reads Bolingbroke ? ' Burke once exclaimed. If he was little read in Burke's day, he is read scarcely at all in ours. His brilliant periods soon pall ; his philosophy may glitter, but it

A Hue and cry after the Lord B—k

OR

Young *Perkin* glad to see his Friends.

WHen guilty Consciences do Knaves accuse,
What cunning Shifts and Stratagems they use,
To 'scape the Punishment of those good Laws,
Which only will support a *Righteous* Cause.
In *Britain* we had once a Ministry,
Endu'd with *Justice*, *Truth* and *Loyalty*,
But after it was chang'd a Pack of Knaves
To Bribery and Ambition wholly Slaves;
Their Native Country wou'd for Intrest sell,
And wou'd against their Sovereign George rebell,
To bring a base *Pretender* to the Crown,
And *Popish Rascal* to surround the Throne,
Had *B*—and *H*—, with their Crew,
Succeeded in those Practices they knew,
Would be obnoxious to our British State,
Which (Heaven be Prais'd) is now most Fortunate,
In the Enjoyment of a Glorious King,
Who does the greatest *Blessings* with him bring,
In him, and his most royal Off-spring too,
Our Blessing will eternally renew,
But yet we're sorry that those Enemies,
Who wou'd our Right and Liberties surprize;
Do *Justice* 'scape; for *B*—is fled -
To save, but more the Pity, that base Head,
Which plotted to bring *Perkin* to a Realm
Which *Laws* prohibited to sit at *Helm*.
But now let's see how *Perkin* will maintain
His *Lordship* for his Service in a *Reign*.
When he with others study to invaid
Our Properties, and spoil our *British* Trade,
Now could an *Hue and Cry* but fetch him Home,
That he might here have his deserved Doom-
With *Joy* good Subjects wou'd behold his Fate,
Who sought the *Ruin* of both *Church* and *State*,
But ah! his *Lordship* now has took a Dance
Last Sunday went from *Dover* into *France*;
And without doubt will Travel to *Lorrain*,
As dreading *Catch* if he comes back again.

London; Printed in the year 1715.

A Broadside of 1715 attacking Bolingbroke

gives the impression of superficiality all the time. There is plenty of evidence of a first-rate brain ; none of a sincere and genuine nature. Yet it has been maintained that his influence on the oratory, philosophy, and political ideas of the eighteenth century was very great, and this is true. If Burke reacted against him, he was in the first instance inspired by him. His facile deism so transparently reflected the religious outlook of the intelligent upper classes that it was often imitated, and it had its effect upon Gibbon. Pope reproduced the chief philosophic ideas of Bolingbroke in his *Essay on Man*. But more important were his ideas on the science of politics ; his attack not only on the existing Whig system, but on the party system as a whole ; his conception of the rule of the ' patriot King ', the national sovereign, overriding all parties, because representing more truly than any party combination the wishes and the interests of his whole people. These ideas were re-echoed in the Tory Democracy of Disraeli, who acknowledged his indebtedness to Bolingbroke. Long before the days of Disraeli the ideals of Bolingbroke had already exerted a remarkable effect upon the course of English history. George III had been well nurtured in these doctrines ; he was resolved to realize the conception of the Patriot King. In his endeavour to secure his own personal rule George broke up the great Whig system and incidentally restored the Tory party. Thus was Bolingbroke indirectly the recreator of the Tory party in the eighteenth century, its inspiration in the nineteenth.

Walpole's family seat at Houghton

V

WALPOLE AND THE OPPOSITION

THERE are few more familiar figures in English history than
that of Sir Robert Walpole ; like *Hamlet*, his life is so full of
quotations. Every one remembers certain well-worn tags, things
he said or is supposed to have said, things that his contemporaries
said about him. The worst of people who are best known through
familiar phrases is that they are apt to appear like waxwork dolls
jerking their limbs automatically to order, and very little like
real live human beings. So it sometimes seems to be with
Walpole. Let us therefore try to get a glimpse at the man, as
far as possible without reference to the somewhat too hackneyed
quotations.

Walpole was born in 1676, the fifth of the nineteen children of
a Norfolk squire of good family. He belonged essentially to
the provincial squirearchy, and he never lost his Norfolk accent.
He had all the spirit of the dweller in the country—something
homely, jovial, and practical. His father took a keen interest in

the farming of his estate, and when (by the death of his sole elder brother) Robert became the heir, the squire's ambition for his son was simply that he should follow in his footsteps. Robert had been at Eton and at Cambridge, but he was taken away from the university before taking his degree when his brother died. Yet although he was of the soil, and the life, and still more the sport, of the countryside attracted him, Walpole aimed at something more ambitious than the uneventful existence of an East Anglian squire, and on the death of his father at the early age of fifty, he entered Parliament for the borough of Castle Rising, which lay on his own property. This was in 1701.

Advancement came early. In 1705 he was a member of the Council of the Admiralty; in 1708 he was Secretary at War; next year he became in addition Treasurer of the Navy. In 1710 he was one of the managers for the House of Commons in the impeachment of Sacheverell. The prosecution of the doctor was also a vindication of the fundamental principles of the Revolution, with which the doctrine which he preached of absolute non-resistance to constituted authority was entirely incompatible. 'If', as Walpole argued, 'the doctrines advanced by Doctor Sacheverell are not criminal in the highest degree, it will follow that the necessary means used to bring about the Revolution were illegal, and consequently that the present establishment, and Protestant succession, founded upon that Revolution, are void and of no effect.'

When Harley came into power, his first design was to have a mixed ministry, and he tried to persuade several of the defeated party, Walpole in particular, that ' a Whig game was intended at bottom'. But Walpole refused to have anything to do with the suggestion that he should identify himself with the new administration. Fair words speedily gave place to direct enmity. The Tories opened their campaign with a grand assault on Godolphin's financial management during his ministry. Walpole took the chief part in defending the ex-minister, and gave a masterly parliamentary performance which greatly enhanced his own reputation. Such prominence did him no good at the time. In defending Godolphin he had marked himself out for

Sir R. Walpole sitting to Francis Hayman (1708–76)
From the painting by Hayman in the National Portrait Gallery

attack. The Tories charged him with notorious corruption, and succeeded in carrying a resolution that he should be expelled the House and committed to the Tower. The allegation of corruption was made in reference to a certain army contract for which Walpole as Secretary at War had been responsible. He had not made a penny for himself out of it, but he had arranged that a friend should profit. According to modern conceptions of political honour this could not be defended; but the standards of 1712 were much more lax in this respect than ours, and the pious horror expressed by the Tories at Walpole's expense did not mean that their standard of public duty was any higher than his. Whenever one ministry fell, it was customary for its successor, if of the opposite party, to indulge in an orgy of revenge by legal process. There was never very much difficulty in finding a suitable charge to bring forward. Walpole spent the remainder of the session in the Tower, and played no further part in the politics of Queen Anne's reign.

With the accession of George I and the sweeping victory of the Whigs, Walpole was inevitably selected for office. He first became Paymaster of the Forces, being promoted in April 1715 to the position of First Lord of the Treasury and Chancellor of the Exchequer. The leading minister in the new combination was Lord Townshend, Walpole's brother-in-law, and the two worked together for some time in close harmony, though they were men of very different temperaments, Townshend being as impatient and headstrong as the other was level-headed and circumspect. Four men easily over-topped all the others in this administration—these two with Sunderland and Stanhope. Sunderland we have already met. Stanhope was a man of finer mould—of high character, a genuine scholar, an accomplished soldier, and a true patriot. Sunderland was the only one among the ministers who had been a member of the Junto, and his restless ambition was no longer satisfied with the amount of power he enjoyed as one of a quartet. His propensity to intrigue soon found a way to gratify his ambition. He somehow or other succeeded in gaining the King's ear and in winning over the more scrupulous Stanhope, and Townshend was got rid of. He was followed into retirement by Walpole at the end of 1716.

Being now in opposition, Walpole opposed everything his two former colleagues did, whether it was good or bad, including the Mutiny Bill, which he knew to be necessary, and the motion to repeal the Schism Act, though he had vehemently and justly denounced that measure at the time of its introduction. But his most noteworthy achievement during this period was his attack on the Peerage Bill of 1719. The aim of its progenitors was the strengthening of the Upper House. The Lower had possibly been aggrandized and rendered more independent of the peers by the passage in 1716 of the Septennial Act. The Peerage Bill was, from one point of view, an answer to this Act, which had enhanced the authority of the chamber in which Walpole was easily the dominant personality. There

JAMES, EARL STANHOPE

Engraved by J. Simon after Sir Godfrey Kneller's painting

was another motive. Intense enmity existed between the King and the Prince of Wales. Because they had the confidence of his father the Prince cordially hated the ministers. Where would their influence be on his accession to the throne? They resolved to put an obstacle in his path in case he should endeavour, when he came to the throne, to raise up a counter-interest. They could not stereotype the House of Commons in their favour; the House of Lords they thought they could. They therefore drew up a scheme for rigidly limiting the future creation of peerages, and so making the House a permanent stronghold of their supporters. The idea appealed for obvious reasons to the great majority of the existing members of the peerage. The fewer the numbers of the lords, the greater must become their individual importance. The majority in the Commons disliked the scheme, but they at first felt powerless to oppose it. How could they, as Whigs, resist a restriction on the royal prerogative, especially when the sovereign voluntarily agreed to it ? Moreover, one of the chief counts in their indictment of Oxford had been his unconstitutional advice to Queen Anne to create twelve new peers in order to carry the approval of the Treaty of Utrecht through the Upper House. The present bill would render such a device impossible in future. How, therefore, could they with any consistency whatever resist so admirable an expedient ? The Whigs in opposition were therefore inclined to be despondent, until at a meeting at Devonshire House they were rallied by Walpole, who insisted on the imperative necessity of opposing the Bill, urging in particular its intense unpopularity with the squirearchy, whose hopes of admission into the coveted ranks of the peerage it effectively destroyed. Theirs was a point of view that Walpole, himself a member of their class, could thoroughly appreciate. He had his way, and in a masterly and most eloquent speech in the House of Commons he so successfully damaged the measure that it was rejected by the decisive majority of 269 to 177. The country was thereby saved from the establishment of a narrow oligarchy, from the degeneracy of the English nobility into a mere caste. This is by no means the least of Walpole's claims on the gratitude of posterity.

In 1720 the King and the Prince of Wales became reconciled, and the Whig schism came to an end. Townshend and Walpole rejoined administration, but in minor offices. The same year saw the passing of the famous South Sea Act, by which the South Sea Company, which had been incorporated in 1711, was to take over the management of the National Debt. The idea of the directors was that they would be able to induce the government's creditors, the fund-holders, to take shares in the company, that the profits of the company were going to be so large that it would

Playing cards satirizing the mania of speculation at the time of the South Sea Bubble

be possible actually to pay off the National Debt altogether. What actually happened is notorious. The anticipations of immense profits from South American trade were infinitely too optimistic. The scheme gave immense encouragement to all sorts of speculations in a stock-jobbing age, money being invested in the most ridiculous commercial enterprises. The tremendous run on the South Sea Company stock sent the purchase price of a £100 share from £130 up to £1,000, at which figure the holding could not possibly be profitable unless a dividend were paid far beyond the company's capacity to earn it. The inevitable collapse came quickly, and many thousand investors found themselves ruined. The cry rose for vengeance and also for some one to take the helm of the ship of state who was capable of rectifying the financial chaos which the crisis had produced. The one man for the situation seemed to be Walpole. Though by prudent dabbling in the shares he had himself made money out of the South Sea speculation, he had perceived the fallacies of the scheme and publicly criticized it, and he was in common knowledge the ablest financier among politicians of the day.

Accordingly Walpole returned to his old post as First Lord of the Treasury and Chancellor of the Exchequer, while Townshend once more became principal Secretary of State. Walpole remained in office for the next twenty-one years. As his work was financial—the reorganization of the South Sea Company and the re-establishment of national confidence—so his most successful work as a minister throughout his long ascendancy was really in finance. Walpole was remarkable in making the very first object of his policy the furtherance of the country's economic interests. Not territorial aggrandizement but peaceful commercial prosperity was what he cared about. The King's speech in 1721 laid particular emphasis upon the extension of commerce, and to that end commended the making ' the exportation of our own manufactures, and the importation of the commodities used in the manufacturing of them, as practicable and as easy as may be '. In other words the speech enunciated free trade doctrine ; and on free trade principles Walpole proceeded, herein following the example of the Tories Bolingbroke and Arthur

A Copy of the Paper drop'd in St. *JAMES's PARK*,

OR,

A Hue and Cry after a COACHMAN.

London, Jan. 5. 1725.

WHereas a Coachman, who for his unparallel'd and consummate Impudence has, for many Years past, gone by the Name of Brazen Face; about fifty Years of Age; full bodied; brown Complexion; five Feet ten Inches high, or thereabout; has lost a Tooth in the Forepart of his upper Jaw; dirty Hands; light finger'd, a heavy, clumsy, slouching, wadling Gate; an affected Toss with his Head; a supercillious, sneering, grining Look; of a malicious, vindictive, sanguinary Nature, a saucy, insulting, overbearing, imperious Behaviour in Prosperity; a Poor, low, wretched, mean, abject Spirit in Adversity; of a perfidious, impious, atheistical Principle; remarkably addicted to Lying; an ignorant, forward, positive unexperienced, headstrong, blundering Driver; despised, contemned, and hated by all his Master's faithful Servants, generally wears a Livery trim'd with a blue; garters below Knee; formerly serv'd a Widow Lady of the first Rank, till he was dismiss'd her Service for seling her Corn and Hay, for which he was committed, and lay several Months in Prison, and till her Death could not get into Service again, (but wander'd about in the Scorn and Contempt of every one that knew him) but upon her Demise procured himself to be chose Postillion, and afterwards Coachman, in the Service of his late Mistress's Successor, who was a perfect Stranger to all his scandalous, base, wicked and corrupt Practices; has plunged, bewilder'd and overset his present Master, imposed upon and deceiv'd his Mistress, and plunder'd, robb'd and strips the whole Family, which is exceeding numerous.

If any Person or Persons will seize and apprehend the said Coach-man, and bring him to the Axe and Block upon Tower-Hill, or the Gibbet & Halter in Tyburn Road, so that he may be brought to Justice, and dealt with as he deserves, such Person or Persons shall be nobly rewarded, and eminently distinguished by all the Family.

N. B. If the said Coachman is not apprehended by the 13th Instant, he shall be more particularly described, with his name commonly call'd his Christian Name and his Sir-Name at length.

London: Printed for *Tho. Davies* near St *Pauls*

Broadside of 1725 attacking Walpole, who had been thrown into the Tower in 1712 for alleged corruption; see p. 204

Moore in their commercial treaty with France. In the session of
1721 Walpole secured the removal of export duties on 106 articles,
of import duties on 38 articles of raw material. ' He found our
tariff the worst in the world,' it has been said; 'he left it the
best.' He was the predecessor of Pitt, Huskisson, and Peel
as a reformer of our tariff. Certainly the prosperity he aimed at
was abundantly secured. 'Walpole could make gold from
nothing,' declared George I. National credit was restored,
money became plentiful, the value of land went up, manufacturing towns throve and multiplied, the mercantile marine
considerably increased, the volume of trade both in imports and
exports expanded.

In spite of all this contemporaries were very far from satisfied
with the condition of affairs, and there was plenty of criticism
of what Walpole did and of what he failed to do as a finance
minister. Some of this was no doubt factious, but a good deal
of it was sincere. Some of the best economists of the day thought
that the country was in a parlous state, and contemplated the
future with the gravest apprehension. They regarded the
burden of taxation as crushing. Lord Hervey averred in 1735
that the country could not possibly ever raise beyond a million
more than it was then being called upon to pay. But it was
the National Debt that occasioned the greatest consternation.
Practically speaking, there had been no such thing before the
accession of William III ; at his death it stood at the figure of
16 millions ; in 1714 owing to the drain of the War of the Spanish
Succession it stood at 54 millions. Nowadays when the annual
revenue is many times that sum, it sounds paltry in the extreme ;
but it thoroughly alarmed contemporaries, and Walpole himself
considered that the country could not possibly stand a debt of
more than 100 millions. We have, of course, in considering these
figures to estimate them in comparison with the national income
in order to arrive at a calculation of the extent of the burden
involved. We have to remember that the population of England
and Wales in Walpole's day was only about six millions, considerably less than the population of greater London alone
to-day, and that what seems very small to a highly industrialized

GOODS *Imported to, and Exported from the* CUSTOM-HOUSE *of* London, *from the* 14th *of* May, *to the* 11th *of* June, 1692. *a Fourth Part whereof follows.*

Imported.	Imported.	Exported.
S Pice Cinam. *l.* 1175	Wine, *buts* 5, *pip.* 120	A Lom, *tons* 10, *l.* 150
Cloves, *l.* 3395	Alicant, *buts* 126, *hogsh.* 7	Apparel, *cert.* 4 *times*
Nutmegs, *l.* 2572	Canary, *pipes* 60	Aqua Fortis, *l* 6
Sprouter, *l.* 400	Florence, *chests* 43	Ashes, *bar.* 2
Steel, *c.* 70, *l.* 10	Portugal, *hogsh.* 22, *pip.* 115	Bed and Furniture, 1
Stones Dog, *lasts* 4	Rhen. *aumes* 607, *casks* 43	Beer, *tons* 20, *bar* 3
Grave, 4	*fats* 17, *pi.* 214	Bellows, 20
Marbles, 1048, *casks* 3	Span. *buts* 5, *casks* 6, *hamp.* 6	Bisket, *c.* 74
Blocks, 6	*hogsh.* 2, *jars* 3, *pipes* 108	Bodyes, *doz.* 2
Paving, 528	Wood Battins, 947	Books, *c.* 16, *l.* 223
Mill, 8	Beech, *quart.* 823	Boxes Dress. 13
Paving, 213	Brazoel, *c.* 17	Brass, *c.* 34, *l.* 519
Quern, *lasts* 7	Birch, *fath.* 206	Brushes, *doz.* 3 *cert.*
Rag, *ton* 15	Fir, *balks* 15675	Butter, *firk.* 200
Whet, 195600	Deals, 334622	Cabinet, 1
Succads, *l* 601	Masts, 132	Cage Bird, 6
Sugar Barbad. *casks* 170, *c.* 196.	Oars, 164	Calamancas, *l.* 16
Jamaica, *casks* 115	Sparrs, 5576	Candles, *doz.* 51
Nevis, *c* 415	Handspikes, 1184	Caps, 6
New-England, *casks* 154	Knees, 100	Monmouth, *doz.* 81
Prize, *chests* 105	Linboards, 842	Red, *doz.* 18, 1
Sumach, *c.* 472	Log, *ton* 50	Cards, *c.* 2
Tallow, *c.* 20	Oak Staves Barr. 36560	Chairs, 51
Tarras, *bar.* 233	Firk. 10700	Backs and Seats, *doz.* 10
Tape Incle, *doz.* 2100, *l.* 710	Hogsh. 11200	Chalk, *tons* 30
Teeth, *c.* 2	Pipe, 109700	Cheese, *c.* 1
Thimbles, 151000	Timber, *load* 4313	Clippings, *c.* 10
Thread Black and Brown *doz.* 56	Wainscoat, 2036	Clock Work, *c.* 2, *l.* 210
Bridges, *doz.* 479, *l.* 319	Rownd, *pi.* 3414	Cases, 2
Edging, *doz.* 60	Scale, *bund.* 1500	Watches, 12
Gold and Silver, *l.* 11	Scoops, 600	Cases, 5
Sisters, *l.* 14520	Spears, 2	Coach, 1
Whited Br. *doz.* 564	Wool Cott. *bags* 43, *c.* 3, *l.* 4900	Coals, *chald.* 34
Twine, *c.* 9	Goats, *bal.* 8	Collars Horse, 7
Twist, *doz.* 756	Polonia, *bags* 12	Copper, *c.* 10
Tiles Gally, *feet* 830	Woollen Caddaz, *doz.* 28	Copperas, *ton* 11, *c.* 301
Pan, 198500	Hose, *doz.* 146	Cordage, *l.* 140
Tobacco Bermud. *l.* 17550	Stuff mixt, *yards* 280	Corks, *gross* 588.
Virgin. *hogsh.* 18, *l.* 27600	Yarn Linnen, *fats* 26, *l.* 11100	Corn Flower, *quart.* 3
Tubs, *doz.* 10	Sail, *l.* 1500	Oatmeal, *bush.* 1
Vermilion, *l.* 96	Spinal, *l.* 570	Pease, *quart.* 6
Ware Brass, *certain*	Spruce, *c.* 22	Wheat, *quart.* 6, *bush.* 4
Earthen, *casks* 2	Twine, *l.* 400	Cowches, 9
Small, *cert.* 4 *times,* *fats* 2		Dornix, *l.* 240
Water Orange-flower, *gal.* 15		Drawers, *cert.*
Spaw, *bask.* 3		Chest 1
Sweet, *gall.* 11		Dresses, 19

Reproduced from statistics of English foreign trade at the time of the great commercial developments under William III. Houghton's 'Collection', 25 June 1692

society of over 45 millions with an immense world trade might well seem overpowering to a community of six millions before the advent of those gradual economic changes to which we give the name the Industrial Revolution. Nothing seemed in George I's day so desirable, nothing indeed so imperative, as the wiping out of the National Debt. And to this end Walpole established a sinking fund, set apart for the gradual redemption of the debt. To be effective the fund should have been treated as absolutely sacrosanct ; but in 1733 Walpole took half a million out of it to defray current expenses, and he continued to raid the fund in this way year after year, his object being to avoid increase of taxation. The consequence was that by the end of 1739 he had paid off a little more than eight millions only.

Walpole's economic policy is best known by his most ambitious plan, which unhappily miscarried—the Excise Scheme. The idea was not a novel one ; it was not Walpole's own ; indeed, the Dutch had been acting upon it for years with much advantage to themselves. Walpole's proposal of 1733 was a very limited one—it related only to two commodities, tobacco and wine, though it was of course understood that it would hereafter be extended to others. The plan was simply to substitute an excise for a customs duty. That is to say, the duty would not have to be paid upon the articles immediately after their landing in the country, but they were to be lodged in warehouses and duty paid only upon their release for home consumption ; so that if they were landed only for purpose of re-exportation, no duty would be paid at all. The advantages claimed for the proposal were that the tax would be more cheaply collected thereby ; that smuggling, which was rampant in those days, would be materially discouraged ; and that the country's carrying trade would be greatly benefited. London, so Walpole urged, would become a free port and ' the market of the world '. The fierce outcry with which the scheme was greeted was due to the vigour of the opposition, especially in the press, and the crass ignorance and credulity of the masses. They were ready to believe any evil of ' that plan of arbitrary power, that monster, the excise '. Somehow the scheme came in their eyes to be synonymous with

THE LONDON MERCHANTS TRIUMPHANT
(or Sturdy Beggars are Brave Fellows)
being a Sketch of the Rejoyceings
in the City &c. Occationd by the
Excize Bill being Postpond.

THE ROYAL EXCHANGE

Long, Long live the Glorious Two hundred and four:
And may we Such Senators have evermore.
Whom, Places nor Pensions, will ever perfuade
To give up our Juries, and Fetter our Trade,

Who Steadily Zealous, are always prepard,
To Maintain English Rights, & our Liberties guard
But a Curse on the Slaves, who Excises insist on,
May they daily be horse-ponded, pelted and piss on

A caricature exulting in the withdrawal of the Excise Scheme. 204 was the
largest vote recorded against Walpole's measure in the House of Commons

Medal struck in 1733 by the No-Excise faction. On the reverse flagon, glass,
and crossed tobacco pipes

slavery and wooden shoes. The opposition were assisted in their attack by the fact that an excise had first been levied in this country by the Parliamentary party during the Civil War, and Englishmen in Walpole's day were, as a rule, rather ashamed of the Civil War.

The picture of Walpole standing up to the vehement denunciations of his opponents in the House of Commons drew from George II praise of an unwonted enthusiasm. 'He is a brave fellow; he has more spirit than any man I ever knew.' But Walpole did not persist to the end; he withdrew the Tobacco Bill. This was typical of the man. His deference to public opinion is indeed one of his best-known traits. By some it has been attributed to cowardice, by others to inordinate love of power and unwillingness to abandon office. Before we attempt to analyse motives, let us take one or two other instances of this deference to public opinion. After the abandonment of the Excise Scheme the most notorious instance is the yielding to the popular clamour for war over the affair of Captain Jenkins's ear. Another case is the withdrawal of the patent which had been granted to an English ironmaster named Wood, for coining copper coins for Ireland, because the Irish vehemently protested on the ground that they had not been consulted in the matter. The ferment had been increased by the violent invective of Swift's *Drapier's Letters*. Walpole yielded to Swift. Yet another case is that of Captain Porteous, made familiar to us by Scott's *The Heart of Midlothian*. Porteous had fired upon an unruly crowd assembled in Edinburgh at the execution of a popular smuggler named Wilson. Because there had been some loss of life as the result of the firing, Porteous had been condemned to death. But he had been respited by the government, to the rage of the Edinburgh populace, who had taken the law into their own hands and lynched him. The government then introduced a punitive measure against the city of Edinburgh, among other penalties depriving it of its charter. To Scottish sentiment this measure seemed grossly unfair and great indignation was aroused. Walpole yielded to it. Just as he would not attempt to carry a tax at the price of blood, so he would not attempt to enforce any other measure at the expense of serious national discord. Believing in religious toleration as he undoubtedly did, he yet refused to offend tender Anglican susceptibilities by endeavouring to repeal the disabilities of Nonconformists.

In all this there is something suggestive of an easy-going slackness. That also may have been the impression conveyed by his unwillingness to prosecute writers in the press, as previous ministers had been accustomed to do, whenever they found themselves more violently assailed than usual. ' No government', Walpole claimed, ' ever punished so few libels, and no government ever had provocation to punish so many.' Again, was it from mere negligence that he refrained from reading the American dispatches and neglected the colonies, allowing them to do pretty well as they pleased ? When advised shortly after the failure of the Excise Scheme to impose a tax on America, he retorted, ' No, I have old England set against me, and do you think I will have the new England likewise ? ' One thing Walpole did do for the American colonies—he facilitated their trade by allowing the planters of Georgia and the Carolinas to send their rice, and the traders of the West Indian islands their sugar, direct to European ports and not indirectly *via* England, provided that they travelled in British ships. Heretofore the colonists had had to trade only with the mother country. Partly as the result of this measure of his, partly as the result of the policy of wholesome neglect, the colonies signally prospered in Walpole's day.

What is the true explanation of this respect for popular prejudice, this apparent indifference, so characteristic of Walpole ? We are not blinded nowadays by the fierce party animosities of his contemporaries ; and what seemed cowardice then we may be minded to term tact, which in a statesman is but another name for political wisdom. There are men who are distinguished by an intense devotion to abstract principle, which they follow consistently whatever the circumstances. Of such men prophets and martyrs are made. They are of a higher type than men like Walpole ; but they do not as a rule make successful statesmen. It is very common to find a successful statesman dubbed an opportunist as a term of reproach. If he has no principle at all the reproach is just ; but the capacity to make use of opportunity, to convert principle into action by the moulding of circumstance—that is a great gift. Statesmanship consists largely in getting things done without stirring up strife, because that is the most practical way of realizing an ideal. It is essentially a matter of compromise and conciliation. Walpole's greatness as a statesman largely lies in the fact that he acted on these lines.

But it may be objected : may not this sort of policy be simply a compound of weakness and inactivity ? Let us, then, consider what Walpole positively accomplished. We have seen that he unquestionably furthered the country's economic interests, making that the prime object of his policy. In the second place, he gave it peace ; and this was no small achievement. He was not the originator of this peace policy. The understanding with France had been contrived by the Tories ; it was simply maintained by the Whigs on their accession to power. Its advantages were obvious from the point of view of the security of the Hanoverian dynasty. The only real hope for Jacobitism lay in French support : consequently harmony between the French and British governments was the best protection against the designs of the Pretender. It was not so easy to maintain peace. The Treaty of Utrecht did not usher in a period of European quiet. Between 1711 and 1742 the international position in Europe was very much disturbed indeed. Neither Spain nor Austria was satisfied with the results of the late war ; in Austria there loomed ahead the problem of the future succession to the Habsburg throne, which the reigning Emperor Charles VI endeavoured to settle peaceably in favour of his daughter Maria Theresa by the Pragmatic Sanction, as events were to prove without success. The ambitions of Elizabeth Farnese, the ' termagant ' Queen of Spain, were a potent source of conflict. In France there was a party inimical to peace, although for the time the powerful influence of Cardinal Fleury was exerted in favour of its maintenance. There was the new and uncertain phenomenon of a strong and partially westernized Russia. There was a militant Prussia, shortly to be directed on paths of aggrandizement by the ambitious and unscrupulous Frederic the Great. Worst of all was the pervading cynicism of diplomacy and the arid maxims of the Balance of Power, a principle which is supposed to have guided statesmen in the eighteenth century and which did Europe no good.

From the point of view of British policy the chief difficulties were presented by the inevitable interest of the Georges in their Hanoverian possessions, which involved the country in continental affairs from which it might otherwise have steered clear. There was the added difficulty when George II came to the throne, that that monarch had decided martial inclinations. When in 1725, stung by the insult of Louis XV's repudiation of his betrothed, the Infanta, and his marriage with Marie, the daughter of Stanislaus, ex-King of Poland, Spain formed a most unexpected alliance with the Emperor by the Treaty of Vienna, a counter-blast was arranged by the Treaty of Hanover between Great Britain, France, and Prussia. But this was Townshend's work, and Walpole did not approve of it ; and in 1729 the diplomatic situation was reversed by Philip of Spain's abandonment of the Austrian alliance and his adherence to Great Britain and France by the Treaty of Seville. But Walpole was dissatisfied with this arrangement too ; he wanted to be on good terms with Austria as well, and in 1731 he succeeded in arranging an understanding with her by the second Treaty of Vienna, by which Great Britain became a guarantor of the Pragmatic Sanction. Scarcely had this satisfactory conclusion been reached when Europe was disturbed by the problem of the succession to the Polish throne, in which France, owing to the King's marriage, supported the candidature of Stanislaus, and Russia that of his opponent. The Polish war threatened to develop into a general European conflagration, in which George II thought his interest and duty as ruler of Hanover involved him. Not only the opposition but the majority of the Cabinet were eager for war, and it is a fine tribute to Walpole's tenacity of purpose, his dexterous diplomacy, and his skill in handling the situation at home that war was once again avoided.

But, notoriously, all Walpole's previous difficulties in the field of foreign policy were surpassed by those produced by the trading disputes with Spain which culminated in the War of Jenkins's Ear. At this distance of time it is easy for us to perceive how strong a case Spain had against us, that the stipulations of the Treaty of Utrecht were constantly being strained, evaded, or broken by British traders in Spanish-American waters, that most of their trade was illicit, and that the Spanish claim to right of search was abundantly justified. But public opinion, inflamed by the acts of an unscrupulous opposition, could only see in the right of search an intolerable insult, was maddened by tales of cruelties perpetrated by the crews of Spanish guardships on our seamen, and demanded the abandonment of the Spanish claim. When Walpole with infinite difficulty arranged an accommodation in the Convention of Pardo, the country would have none of it. His resistance to the popular demand for war was at last beaten down, and the hostilities which the great minister so much feared and hated broke out. He knew, as the public did not, of the existence of a Bourbon Family Compact which threatened to convert any war with Spain into a war with France as well. Walpole is sometimes blamed for his yielding to the popular insistence on war. But it is quite evident that it was beyond the power of Walpole or any other man to have prevented war.

If there was weakness in his attitude in 1739, it was not in failing to withstand the national demand, but in retaining office in a ministry pledged to a war in which he did not believe. No doubt he hoped that a favourable occasion might soon present itself for him to extricate the country from war. But even so he was much to blame according to modern standards, and the charge of over-fondness for the charms of office cannot reasonably be rebutted. On the other hand, here is not a case of a man following the weak and selfish rule of continuing in power by always obeying popular dictation ; it is a case of a strong man obtaining his position by right of ability, sticking to his work because he was supremely conscious of his own capacity, succeeding, despite the arts of a most effective opposition, in guiding public opinion along the paths he chose, succeeding because he knew with exactitude how far he could go, and where he must

Extract of the Narrative of Rob. Jenkins, *Master of the* Rebecca.—— We sailed from Jamaica, with sugar, &c. for London; but Ap. 9. near the Havanna, a Spanish Guarde Costa came up, rowing with 16 oars, and firing several shot, order'd our boat to be sent on board her; in which went the Mate, with our clearance from Jamaica. They detained our men, and sent the boat back full of armed men, who told Cap. Jenkins, that they were come to visit his ship for money, logwood, &c. the product of the Spanish settlements. The Capt answered, The King of Spain's Officers were wellcome; but that there was nothing on board, but what was the produce of Jamaica. Their number amounted to about 50 men: who broke open all her Hatches, lockers, and chests, but found nothing. Then their Lieutenant ordered Capt. Jenkins hands to be tied, and his Mates, and seized them to the fore-mast. Then they cut and violently beat a Mulatto boy: who confessing nothing, they put a rope about his neck, and another about the Captain's, which fastening together, they hoisted them up to the fore-yard: the boy slipt through the noose; and after a short space, they let the Capt. fall down amain on the deck, and asked him, if he would confess where his money was. He told them he had none; on which he was hoisted a second time, and swistly let down again, and gave them the same answer. In about half an hour, one of them search'd his pockets, took his silver buckles out of his shoes; and then he was hoisted up again, and kept hanging 'till he was quite strangled; after which they let him fall down the fore-hatch upon the casks, which bruised him very much; from whence he was dragged by the neck upon the deck, where he lay to appearance dead for near a quarter of an hour. When he recover'd, their Lieutenant, with pistols and a cutlass, went to him, crying, Confess or die he told him he had no more money than he shew'd him at first, being 4 guineas, 1 pistole, and 4 double doubloons; which being commanded, he gave him. No sooner had he done this, but the Lieut. took hold of his left ear, and with his cutlass slit it down; and another took hold of it and tore it off, but gave him the piece, bidding him carry it to his Majesty King George. His Mate and Boatswain were beat: the whole crew were stript of their cloaths, beds, &c. the Captain's own loss amounted to 112 l. They took away all his instruments of navigation, and all his candles. Being dismissed, the Capt. bore away for the Havannah: but those in the sloop stood after him, declaring that if he did not go immediately for the Gulph, they would set the ship on fire: and so rather than have a second visit from them, they recommended themselves to God; and after many great perils happily arrived in the Thames last friday. 4 Ev.

The story of Jenkins's Ear. From 'The Grub-street Journal' of 24 June 1731

not go. He maintained himself in office because he kept his finger always upon the national pulse.

Did he really engross power ? Was he really prime or even 'sole' minister, as the Opposition maintained in Sandys's famous motion for praying the King to dismiss Walpole from his counsels for ever ? The same motion was introduced on the same day, the 13th February 1741, by Carteret in the House of Lords. In both chambers the opposition were decisively beaten, but the administration suffered in popularity owing to the obloquy attending

1741. Revival of the agitation against Walpole, which finally drove him out of office

the King's action in arranging a treaty for the neutrality of his electorate in the war, and after the general election of 1741 the ministerial majority in more than one division was reduced to only three or four. Finally, on the 28th January 1742 the opposition gained a victory by one vote. On the 31st Walpole resigned ; on the 9th February he was created Earl of Orford. In July he was followed into the House of Peers by his old rival Pulteney, who had refrained from taking office in the new cabinet, in which the outstanding figure was Carteret. It is said that Orford greeted the new peer with the words, ' You and I are now two as insignificant men as any in England.' Despite his retirement many refused to believe that the ex-minister had become politically insignificant. ' All cry out ', wrote Horace Walpole, ' that he is still minister behind the curtain.' This is an exaggeration, but the idea that when he withdrew to his Norfolk home Orford faded into obscurity is at least equally wide of the mark. He continued to exert great influence at court, and when in 1744 there took place a serious breach in the ranks of the composite ministry between the Pelhams and Carteret (now Earl Granville), he was summoned by George II to London, and his advice in favour of the Pelhams was decisive in bringing about Granville's fall. This was the last important act of Orford's life, for he died on the 18th March 1745.

It is a common statement that Walpole was the first Prime Minister, while some language used about him would suggest that he both inaugurated the system and also brought it to its full development in all essentials. Indeed, it is with the history of the Cabinet that Walpole's name is most directly associated in most people's minds. There is a large measure of justification for this, but at the same time the significance of Walpole in this connexion can easily be misunderstood and exaggerated. In certain respects, it is true, Walpole's contribution to the

Struck in 1742 soon after Walpole had been driven from power by his political opponents and had been raised to the peerage by the King

development of the Cabinet System was unique. Without going into details it may be said at once that the fact of the first two Georges being primarily interested in Hanoverian affairs and not being present at Cabinet meetings was really epoch-making ; that the considerable period of peace at home and abroad during Walpole's administration was conducive to quiet constitutional progress ; that Walpole was a man who could not brook the existence of more than one will and purpose in his ministry. This does not necessarily mean that he was jealous of competitors or that he fully comprehended the advantages of complete unanimity in a ministerial policy. What it does really mean is that he was a man determined to be master in his own house. This is an important fact, of course. The predominance of a single forceful personality for a prolonged period undoubtedly involved a certain unity of policy, although we must not think of Walpole's ministers as always agreeing with him, or if they differed either at once resigning or else at once giving way.

Now for the necessary provisoes regarding Walpole's real position. He was not the first person to whom the title of Prime Minister was applied ; it had been applied to Harley. And although the name was not given him, Godolphin was quite clearly the prime, in the sense of the predominant, minister between 1702 and 1710. Again, while there were in the reign of Anne at least three distinct councils in which ministers might meet for consultation and transaction of public affairs, still a cabinet council was the most important of these and existed then as it did in Walpole's day. Walpole then was not an originator. Neither did he really develop the Cabinet System on modern lines. There was no conception in his day of joint ministerial responsibility, one of the most obvious characteristics of the modern Cabinet System. There was no conception of having a definite programme of policy to submit to the electors. There was no conception that the ministers must necessarily be chosen from the party which for the time being enjoys the confidence of the majority of the people. The people did not present Walpole to the King as their chosen leader ; the King presented Walpole to the people as his nominee. And Walpole, in the long run, owed his predominance, partly to his mastery over George I and his close understanding with that remarkable woman, Caroline of Anspach, who managed her husband, George II, partly to his manipulation of Parliament and the elections by an organized system of corruption, which he certainly did not originate and which continued unabated long after his day, but which he carried on with remarkable skill and equal success.

One is sometimes told that Walpole was indirectly the founder of an organized 'His Majesty's Opposition', because of the number of enemies he made. The opposition to him is certainly outstanding ; but we must not forget that there were organized oppositions under Pym and under Shaftesbury and under the Junto between 1710 and 1714. Still the opposition to Walpole was undoubtedly distinguished for its great energy and persistence,

for its use of the press, for the great influence exerted in particular by its periodical, *The Craftsman*, and for the heterogeneous
character of those elements united together through the genius
of Bolingbroke and by the one compelling motive of hatred of
Walpole and by none other. Here were gathered together the
unimpeachable Windham; the brilliant, the eloquent, but
unstable Pulteney; Carteret, the marvel of his age, the scholar,
the orator, whose self-appointed business it was to make kings
and emperors, imperious, intemperate, volatile; Chesterfield,
the wit, the cynical dilettante, yet fastidious connoisseur and able
administrator; Pitt, the ' boy patriot ', ' this terrible cornet of
horse '; Swift, Pope, Fielding, Gay, Thomson, and others of that
tribe of men of letters which Walpole despised, being a man of
no literary taste, though his speeches, as recorded, have the
literary touch; Sarah Jennings, as resolute as of old and full of
rancour against Sir Robert, and other great ladies of rank and
fashion, ambition and spleen. Seldom has there been a more
remarkable galaxy of talent and venom. In itself it was a most
eloquent tribute to Walpole's power.

Wherein did that power, after all, essentially lie? We have
seen that Walpole owed his position to the continuity of royal
favour, to a systematic corruption of Parliament and the
electorate; so that it must appear a paradox to say that he
was powerful ultimately because he was a great popular minister.
Yet such is indeed the truth. Walpole was able to rule because
he understood the English people, and because he was a typical
Englishman of his day and generation, only endowed with a touch
of genius. He was a very coarse man, both in mind and in
speech; though he could appreciate and openly acknowledge
disinterestedness when he saw it, he took a very low view of
human nature. His own character, in short, was low in many
respects. Yet much that appeals most strongly to the British
temper he possessed. He was a man of the soil, loving it; he
was open-hearted and companionable and honest, and he rode
hard to hounds; he had courage and firmness and self-reliance;
there was nothing petty or mean or malicious about him; and
he was direct and to the point in action and in speech and debate

—almost to homeliness. He was never pretentious or obscure. The English people could easily understand a personality built upon such simple and familiar lines. And he for his part, if he took no lofty view of it, yet understood something of human nature—and allowed for it. Lord Hervey observed with penetration that Walpole, 'understanding the fluctuation of human affairs, never built on certainty, and so instead of worrying about possible contingencies *always applied himself to the present occurrence*, studying and generally hitting upon the properest method to improve what was favourable, and the best expedient to extricate himself out of what was difficult '. It was said by his son, ' whatever was beyond common sense Sir Robert Walpole disregarded '. He was devoid of enthusiasms, sentiment, illusions ; but that common sense of which he was possessed was a rare commodity—a clear-sighted penetration into facts and a sane unbiased judgement of them. Finally, let it be said to his honour that he stamped upon his policy the hall-mark of much that is best in the eighteenth century—a conciliatory, tolerant temper, the lenient spirit of compromise which is the most stable security of peace.

VI

PELHAMS AND YORKES

THE period of the Pelham administration is not on the surface attractive ; it is often passed over as a barren interlude between the eras of two great statesmen, Walpole and the elder Pitt. The Pelham brothers, Thomas and Henry, seem unimportant, the one completely foolish, the other hopelessly commonplace. Yet the very fact of their being second-rate is interesting, seeing that they attained to the highest positions in the state.

The brothers were sons of Sir Thomas Pelham, a man of great influence in the county of Sussex, who was made a baron in 1706. The marriages of his various children connected the family with several noble houses and with some of the great Whig leaders, with the Churchills, Sunderland, Townshend, and Walpole ; and with Walpole the brothers decisively threw in their lot, the younger, Henry, who sat as M.P. for Sussex, being a defender of the Excise Scheme and a champion of the minister when Sandys's motion of condemnation was launched in the House of Commons. Having held several other offices, including that of Secretary at War, Henry in 1743 became Chancellor of the Exchequer and First Lord of the Treasury. This appointment was the signal for a violent struggle in the administration, in which Carteret was easily the outstanding personality. His predilection for playing a big part on the Continent had given him a commanding position at court, and in this, the year of Dettingen, he had converted Great Britain's participation in the War of the Austrian Succession from that of an auxiliary into that of a principal. This was more than public opinion in the country was prepared to support ; there was a feeling that we were becoming more deeply involved in continental affairs than was at all necessary or expedient, and the charge was brought against Carteret of subordinating British to Hanoverian interests. Of this view the Pelhams, herein aided by the fulminations of the youthful Pitt, became the avowed champions. They joined issue with Carteret, now Earl Granville, and secured his resignation in November 1744.

This did not mean the end of the war ; it only meant that it was henceforth badly conducted. Granville had been essentially a war minister ; Henry Pelham essentially was not. The year 1745 witnessed the Jacobite invasion, the defeat of Fontenoy, the loss of our base of operations at Ostend and of all Flanders to the French. Our Dutch allies became lukewarm after this and in 1747 the allies were badly beaten at Lauffeld, largely owing to Dutch inaction. Pelham was exceedingly anxious for a cessation of hostilities ; he had always taken a pessimistic view, ' had never any opinion of the success of the war, and was always preaching up peace '. That certainly is not the frame of mind which brings victories. The negotiations which resulted in the conclusion of the Treaty of Aix-la-Chapelle were difficult and complex, and were not helped by a serious lack of unanimity between Pelham and his brother, who ever since 1715 had been Duke of Newcastle-on-Tyne. While the former was anxious for a speedy settlement with France above everything else, the Duke (in this reflecting the King's point of view) was most of all anxious to remain on good terms with Vienna. In order to keep his hand on foreign policy and to be near the King, the Duke actually braved his horror of the North Sea, of which he was mortally afraid, and took the chief part in the negotiations at Aix-la-Chapelle. The fact that he *had* taken the chief part and deserved the whole of the credit for having secured the peace was not as apparent to his colleagues and the world in general as he thought it ought to be, and he was very much aggrieved at such ingratitude. He acknowledged himself to be ' horribly hurt ' ; declared he had done in three months what Townshend had not been able to do in three years. ' It may be vanity, but vain I am,' he concluded. Stung by incessant complaints, Henry at last wrote :

I must own to you freely I am tired of your complaining letters. . . . Letters of flattery, especially when they are called for, I can't write.'

THE DUKE OF NEWCASTLE, K.G.
From the painting by W. Hoare

The dispute between the two brothers was complicated by a disagreement regarding the political faction presided over by the Duke of Bedford,[1] whom Newcastle considered altogether too independent. When in 1751 the Bedfords were ousted, harmony was restored, and the peace of the Pelham household was undisturbed till Henry's death in 1754.

The domestic policy of the Pelham administration is not so humdrum as it is sometimes assumed to have been. As a matter of fact, although there was no coherent principle in it, it was in effect a reform policy, and there was much more legislative activity than one usually associates with the early Georgian period. One famous reform belonging to these years was not the

[1] Bedford, one of the most important of the great Whig peers, had a little coterie, of whom Lords Gower and Sandwich were the best-known members. The ' Bloomsbury gang ', as they were called after the Duke's London acres, were a very ignoble group, with the exception of their leader himself, who, if proud and aggressive, at any rate was not a time-server and held independent views.

work of the ministry, but of Chesterfield and the second Lord Macclesfield, a distinguished astronomer, viz. the rectification of the calendar. Another progressive piece of legislation was abortive, because public feeling became envenomed against it to such an extent that it became doubtful if the beneficiaries under the Act would be able to take advantage of its operation, and it was accordingly withdrawn. This was an enlightened measure for the naturalization of the Jews, and its adoption did credit to the Pelhams. But the opposition appealed to the lowest and most intolerant passions of the mob. It was wildly predicted that this more eligible Canaan, England, would be politically controlled by the Jews. More important was the so-called Tippling Act of 1751, which was intended as a cure for the terrible evil of the immoderate drinking of gin, which spread with extraordinary rapidity in the first half of the century owing to the cheapening of spirits. Between the date of the Revolution and 1750 the distilling of spirits increased twentyfold. Retailers hung out signs inviting people into their shops, with the inducement that they could be made drunk for a penny, dead drunk for twopence. Fielding, who was a very conscientious and efficient police magistrate as well as a novelist, attributed the very disquieting increase of crimes of violence in these days to the habit of gin drinking. The Tippling Act abolished distillers' licences and prohibited illegal distilling. Two years later another Act placed public-houses under efficient regulation.

The most celebrated of the reforms of this period was Lord Hardwicke's Marriage Act, which aimed a blow at clandestine and irregular marriages, and is in essentials the law regulating marriages to-day. Prior to this Act there was no civil law on the subject of marriage ; the consent of the parties alone was necessary, without consent of the parents or registration of any kind ; and any ordained priest could conduct a wedding at any time or place. A stamped licence was required by law, but failure to take out one did not invalidate the marriage contract, being regarded only as a fraud on the revenue. In these circumstances clergymen of questionable reputation living in or near the Fleet prison made a livelihood by wholesale weddings, the couples sometimes having met only a few hours before and often being under the influence of drink. Navy men, whenever their ships came in, were married by hundreds, generally when incapable. More respectable was the Rev. Alexander Keith, who at his chapel in Curzon Street is said to have married 6,000 couples a year. Hardwicke's Act provided that no marriage should be valid unless the banns had been proclaimed on three consecutive Sundays in the parish church or a special licence had been obtained, which could not be got in the case of minors without the consent of parents or guardians. Entirely reasonable and indeed necessary as its main principle was, the bill was most vehemently assailed. It was declared to be an attack upon the institution of matrimony itself ! In the Lords the Duke of Bedford denounced it as a measure beyond the powers of the legislature and contrary to the Gospel ! In the House of Commons the brilliant Charles Townshend could adduce it as a serious argument that it was unfair to debar younger sons from running off with heiresses. So effective was this speech that by it Townshend laid the foundations of the astonishing reputation he made in the House. Still more formidable was the bitter opposition of Henry Fox, the future Lord Holland, the father of Charles James Fox, who felt very keenly on the subject, having himself contracted a runaway marriage with a daughter of the second Duke of Richmond. As so often happens, it was the best acts of the administration that called forth the most violent opposition, the most acrimonious abuse.

Apart from the social reforms just mentioned, Pelham carried on the Walpole tradition, practised the same political corruption, was equally niggardly in his provision for the services ; but also was equally alive to the commercial needs of the country and to the practical blessings of peace. He was an able and economical financier. Altogether, it is true to say that he stood for the ideal of peace, retrenchment, and reform. On the other hand, he was obviously the inferior of Walpole, being entirely devoid of his genius, courage, and buoyancy of temper. Pelham was constitutionally timid and pessimistic, and essentially a mediocrity. But he belonged to a type of British statesman, of which

A Young Man about 25 Years of Age, in a very good Trade, and whose Father will make him worth 1000*l.* would willingly embrace a suitable Match. He has been brought up a Dissenter, with his Parents, and is a sober Man.

A Gentleman has enquired of me for a reputable Gentlewoman about 30 Years old, of good Breeding, Comliliness, Prudence and 5 or 600 *l.* in Money, Land or Joynture; Such One his friend would match with, tho' on the Square he deserves far more Fortune, which he minds less than his good Likeing.

Chester, Sep. 4. Last Tuesday was married at St. Bridget's Church, in this City, Mr. Robert Allen, an eminent Pawnbroker, aged 75, to Miss Catherine Powell, of about 17, youngest Daughter to Mr. Powell, formerly Peruke-maker, but since left off Business, all of said City, a young Lady of such sedate, womanly Carriage, as becomes one of three Times her Age, nothing of the giddy young Damsel appearing in either her Dress or Behaviour, which certainly was one of those captivating Charms, as well as her Beauty, (which is extensive) that enamour'd her ancient Lover with a Desire of joining Hymen's Knot, that he might pass the Remainder of his hoary Life with one so agreeable as she is, having surprising Wit, with Abundance of Eloquence, and in her is center'd, Virtue, Meekness, Humanity, and Decency, and other Qualifications, which will render the Marriage State very happy, and an handsome Fortune.

The same day, the Master of the Rolls committed a Clergyman to the Fleet, for marrying a young Gentleman, about 17, at Eaton school, and intitled to 1500*l.* per ann. to a servant maid; and at the same time committed the person who gave her in marriage. His Honour some days since had sent prisoner to the Fleet the person who pretended to be the youth's Guardian, and had given a bond to indemnify the Parson. *D. J.* ——— *By carrying on the trade of marrying in the* Flee, *this* Clergyman, *I suppose, will turn his punishment into* preserment.

The Marriage Market. The last passage aptly illustrates how the supply of the marrying clergy of the Fleet was maintained. Advertisements or paragraphs (read downwards) from Houghton's ' Collection' of 26 July and 20 September 1695, 'Adams's Weekly Courant' of 4 September 1753, and ' The Grub-street Journal' of 29 July 1731

A Fleet Marriage-certificate

Reproduced by the courtesy of the editor of 'The Connoisseur'

we have had a good many, who have been very useful to their country, because of their possession of safe and solid qualities. He stood for sanity and stability. When he died, it is recorded that George II lamented, ' Now I shall have no more peace.'

His death left the elder brother in sole control. On the whole the partnership of the two Pelhams had been very harmonious, and their close alliance had had the great tactical advantage that while the duke possessed the big fortune and the immense electioneering influence of the family, Henry, being in the Commons, was able to make use of this endowment to the very best advantage. Newcastle now became First Lord of the Treasury in his brother's place, but actually he was less powerful than before, because of the loss of his *alter ego* in the Lower House. Some one to lead the Commons there must be. The awkward thing was that, whereas the duke had been willing to share authority with his own brother, he was exceedingly reluctant to share it with anybody else. He first of all entered into negotiation with Fox, but he would not agree to Fox's conditions. He then pitched upon a mere cipher, Sir Thomas Robinson, a man devoid of all personality, with the result that the government's forces in the House of Commons were utterly routed by the powerful combination of Fox and Pitt, who easily pulverized Robinson. Newcastle capitulated and summoned Fox to his aid. He still had to face the deadly enmity of Pitt ; and then right in the opening stages of the Seven Years' War, in May 1756, came a terrible disaster in Byng's failure to relieve Minorca.

The unhappy duke was beside himself with consternation, and it is impossible to exonerate him from the charge of having sacrificed everything to saving his own reputation. In order to free the Admiralty from blame, it was necessary to fasten the whole of the responsibility for the failure on the unhappy admiral. Familiar is his anxiety to have Byng tried and hanged immediately. He was enraged that naval officers should have the temerity to lay the blame for naval mishaps on the civil authority. He overflowed with self-pity. No one had ever been so ill-used, and he simply could not bear it. In the end he retired, consoled with a new title, that of Duke of Newcastle-under-Lyne.

*A satire upon Newcastle's supposed responsibility for the Minorca disaster
and his promotion to a new dukedom*

From ' *A Political and Satirical History of the Years 1756, 1757, 1758, 1759, and 1760*

This ushered in Pitt's hour of triumph in November, when the nation's chosen leader was forced upon an unwilling Sovereign by the sheer weight of public opinion. At first a ministry was formed under the nominal leadership of the head of the great

Whig house of Cavendish, the Duke of Devonshire, but with Pitt as its driving force. This combination failed ; it is notorious how impossible Pitt found it to govern without the aid of the Duke of Newcastle. The people's champion could not command

George II, writing to the Duke of Newcastle on the formation of a Ministry in 1757, declares his own hostility to Pitt

the House of Commons, because the duke, not the English people, had control over the electoral machinery and the representative chamber. And so the famous bargain was struck. Pitt was to be free to direct the operations of war ; Newcastle was to manage Parliament. It was a queer partnership that ensued, but it was undoubtedly a most effective one. The 'great commoner' disapproved of the duke, because he typified the rule of the great Whig connexions, which he wished to break up. He undoubtedly bullied the duke in an insolent way, and the duke had to put up with such treatment.

But he resented it, and when the accession of George III

187

The Directing Post 1762

*From barren Lands by Famine led,
The scotchmen fly to us for bread*

The unpopularity of Bute. As Johnson put it, 'The noblest prospect which a Scotchman ever sees is the high road that leads him to England'

From ' A Political and Satirical History', &c.

brought Bute into prominence, Newcastle courted this new luminary and went over to his peace policy, treacherously abandoning his colleague. It was a sorry business; and it met with a just requital. The duke had completely misjudged the situation. He got rid of his too powerful colleague, it is true; but the fall of Pitt, far from leaving him in the ascendant, presaged his own fall. George III and Bute wanted to oust Pitt, but they also wanted to break up the whole Whig family system, which Newcastle represented. Indignity after indignity was showered upon him, so that even his anxiety to retain office was not proof against such humiliation and he in May 1762 tendered his resignation, hoping against hope it might not be accepted. His own fall was followed by a series of dismissals of noted Whigs from various dignities. Newcastle was bewildered ; he had not believed such barbarity possible in a civilized country.

For the space of just over a year (1765–6) Newcastle held office again, in the Rockingham administration, but he was then a spent force. Curiously enough, Pitt, now Earl of Chatham, did not realize this ; he refused to belong to any Cabinet in which the duke was included. Even after the rout of the great Whig families, Chatham still saw in the old man a maleficent influence. It has for this reason been suggested that he indirectly helped George III to establish his personal rule and did a terrible dis-service to the cause of party government. It has been urged that had he co-operated with Newcastle, that cause might have been saved a heavy reverse. Whether this be true or not, it is a mistake to idealize Newcastle and see in him a champion of the noble creed of party government. When he laments the downfall of himself and his friends, he sounds an entirely personal note ; there is not a shadow of a suggestion that he understands that a high principle of popular government is being assailed.

Yet the phenomenon of Newcastle's long ascendancy is most remarkable. In practically every administration, whatever its composition, from 1724 to 1766, his inclusion had been found indispensable. And yet he has nearly always been depicted as a completely ridiculous and contemptible person. He was certainly a very entertaining figure. The unanimous testimony of such different witnesses as Hervey, Horace Walpole, Smollett, Lord Waldegrave, shows that. ' The Duke of Newcastle ', said Lord Wilmington in a famous sentence, ' always loses half an hour in the morning which he is running after the rest of the day without being able to overtake it.' He was generally in a state of alarm, discomposed by the merest trifles, nervous about his health, in horror of damp beds. Horace Walpole describes his conduct at the funeral of George II in Westminster Abbey. ' He fell into a fit of crying at the moment he came into the chapel, and flung himself back in a stall, the Archbishop hovering over him with a smelling-bottle; but in two minutes, his curiosity got the better of his hypocrisy, and he ran about the chapel, with his glass to spy who was or who was not there, spying with one hand and mopping his eyes with the other. Then returned the fear of catching cold: and the Duke of Cumberland, who was sinking with heat, felt himself weighed down, and turning round, found it was the Duke of Newcastle standing upon his train, to avoid the chill of the marble.' He was the most querulous of mortals, always believing himself to be badly and ungratefully treated. His conversation was confused, rambling, contradictory. His speeches in Parliament were incoherent. George II had so poor an opinion of his abilities that he declared him unfit to be chamberlain to a petty German prince.

Nevertheless he was not incapable. He could not possibly have remained in power so long had he been. He had a certain native shrewdness and a grasp of affairs; his methods of business were eccentric, but after his own fashion he was businesslike. His industry was immense; his political experience extraordinary; his skill and assiduity as an electioneer unrivalled. In that capacity he was at his best. The work was one of bribery on a huge scale; but it was a recognized practice, the Duke carried it on with remarkable open-heartedness, genuine kindness, and affability, and it was well and thoroughly done. It was not the work of the utterly incompetent muddler whose portrait Macaulay has made so familiar.

One great proof of his sagacity is that this man, so nervously afraid of a rival, jealous of everybody, never once faltered in his adherence to one of his greatest contemporaries, Philip Yorke, first Earl of Hardwicke. Yorke, the son of a country attorney, owed his early advancement to the Pelhams and he never forgot his indebtedness to his patrons. On the other hand, Newcastle fully recognized the high attainments and mellow political wisdom of the great Lord Chancellor, constantly seeking his advice and as a rule allowing himself to be guided by it. Hardwicke was indeed the oracle of his party, as he was the only real genius in it.

The obvious successor to Somers—to whom he was related by marriage—in the line of our great lawyer-statesmen, Hardwicke was probably an even greater figure. As an equity lawyer, he has been pronounced 'the most consummate judge who ever sat in the Court of Chancery'. He has the distinction of having transformed our equity law from a confused body of haphazard judgements into a coherent system. In the House of Lords he presided for many years with great dignity and his influence on the House was immense.

Yorke owed his early advancement to the patronage of the Lord Chancellor Macclesfield, and to the Pelhams, in whose interest he entered Parliament in 1719 for the borough of Seaford. At the age of thirty he became Solicitor-General; three years later Attorney-General. In that capacity he prosecuted for the Crown the notorious rogues Jonathan Wild and Jack Sheppard and the noted agnostic writer Thomas Woolston. In January 1734 he became Lord Chief Justice and was promoted to the peerage with the title of Baron Hardwicke. His speeches in the King's Bench testify to his conviction of the dangerous lawlessness prevalent in the country and his equally strong assurance that the majesty of the law was the nation's only safeguard alike of social order and individual liberty. We had the best Constitution in the world, he declared, and 'by far the best body of laws that human wisdom can claim'. Early in 1737 he succeeded Lord Chancellor Talbot on the Woolsack.

The inauguration of the Pelham Ministry founded the remarkable partnership in the House of Lords between Hardwicke and Newcastle. From 1742 to 1756 the former was constantly in office; his conciliatory influence was all the time at work, soothing the duke during his frequent perturbations, healing dissensions, providing the reasoned justifications of government policy. During the earlier years he was much occupied with Scottish affairs. To the general ineptitude of Ministers during the Jacobite invasion of 1745 his conduct was an honourable exception. While others minimized the danger and took no measures to meet it, Hardwicke roused the nation to a sense of the situation and worked in practical ways to defend the

The Right Hon.ble Philip. Lord Hardwicke
BARON OF HARDWICKE
Lord High Chancellor of Great Britain.

Sold by Ja.s W.e Ardell at the Golden Head near Southampton Street Covent Garden Price

kingdom. He was mainly responsible for the legislative measures introduced after the suppression of the rebellion for the pacification and settlement of Scotland—those proscribing the wearing of the highland dress, abolishing the clan jurisdictions, incapacitating the non-juring episcopalian clergy, &c. He aimed at establishing a single unitary government control in the Highlands instead of the disintegrating separatist authorities of the chieftains and at opening up that country to more civilized methods of life and industry.

In 1754, on the death of Henry Pelham, it was Hardwicke that was entrusted by the King with the reconstruction of the Cabinet and he was promoted to an earldom. In 1756 he resigned together with Newcastle over the affair of Minorca. He was just as resolute as the duke that Byng should suffer. His enemies pointed out that the head of the Admiralty who had been responsible for the sending out of the expedition was Anson, the earl's brother-in-law. It certainly seems probable that but for Hardwicke's insistence Byng would not have been executed. But, whatever his underlying motives, he certainly had a good case in law and sound principle. The court-martial had unanimously found the admiral guilty of neglect of duty. There had recently been so many cases of naval misconduct being visited with light reprimands, that in 1749 the articles of war had been altered, taking away the discretionary powers of courts martial in the matter of sentence and making the penalty for neglect of duty death. Unless this new rule was to remain a dead letter, Byng had to be sacrificed.

On the failure of the Pitt-Devonshire combination Hardwicke acted the part of intermediary between the former and Newcastle, and so was largely responsible for their joint administration. With Pitt Hardwicke as a rule was on friendly terms, but there were fundamental differences between them. At bottom Pitt was a radical; at bottom Hardwicke was a conservative. The lawyer was always exceedingly critical of new legislation, and on more than one occasion he opposed measures, not because he objected to their main intention, but simply because he did not like the way in which they were drawn up. This was especially

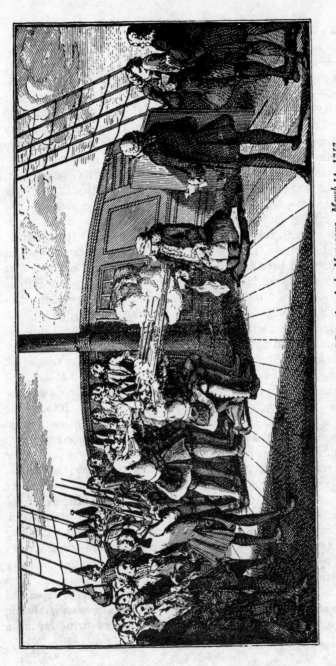

The SHOOTING of Admiral *BYNG*, on board the MONARQUE, *March* 14, 1757

Heading of a Broadside of the time

the case with a Militia Bill of 1756. He objected to this for various reasons ; among others because it had originated in the House of Commons, whereas he believed that all important legislation should be initiated in the Upper House, where the judges were—they always were present in a consultative capacity in those days, ready to give advice and in particular to decide whether any new legislation was really needed at all.

An interesting conflict of opinion between Hardwicke and Pitt, in which the strictly legal point of view of the former gave intense umbrage to ' the great commoner', arose over the case of a man of means who was seized by the press-gang and confined. His friends at once applied for a writ of habeas corpus, only to be told that the writ applied solely to cases in which a crime had been committed, not to such a one as this. Pitt was instantly up in arms. Of what use was the great Habeas Corpus Act of Charles II ; where were the liberties of the subject, if the judges could deny individuals their rights ? With generous and tactless impulsiveness he must needs at once, without consulting Hardwicke or any other legal authority, have a bill framed for compelling the judges to grant the writ at all times. Hardwicke secured the rejection of this measure, not because its object was a bad one, but because it took away the judges' discretionary power. He maintained that although the writ of habeas corpus was a writ of right, the judges must in all cases have the decision whether there was good cause to warrant the issue of the writ. Pitt in this matter was precipitate and misinformed. The fault had lain not with the judges, who were acting according to their rights, but in a defective omission in the Act of 1679 and in the very existence of the impressment system. Hardwicke's view, on the other hand, was too narrow, too purely technical ; and an Act extending the operation of the writ of habeas corpus to non-criminal cases was, as a matter of fact, passed without the slightest difficulty in 1816.

Hardwicke was one of those who sided against Pitt on the issue of declaring war on Spain in 1761 ; but afterwards, refusing overtures from Bute, he went into opposition to the favourite and attacked the Treaty of Paris. The rest of his life he spent in retirement, and he died in 1764.

One of the handsomest men of his time, Hardwicke was undeniably a pompous figure, regarding himself with portentous solemnity and showing ineffable self-satisfaction in the extent of his estates and his success in having entered the exclusive circle of the great land-owning Whig peerage. He had no enthusiasms. For the Constitution he cared much ; for *constitutional progress* very little. The liberty of the press he clearly disliked. Convinced of the innate licence of his age, his preoccupation was with repression. Yet withal, he was a remarkable man and a very great lawyer, and England owed much to one who held aloft the conception of the supremacy of the law and the social necessity of ordered government.

The history of the great Lord Chancellor's family forms a curious epilogue to that of his own career. He had destined them all to play a big part in the state. The eldest, of course, succeeded to the title ; one became a major-general and an ambassador : but they none of them realized their father's expectations, and the story of the most distinguished of them, Charles, ends in tragedy. He followed his father's footsteps at the bar, becoming Solicitor-General in 1756, Attorney in 1762. It was upon his advice—wherein he merely repeated his father's opinions—that the government acted regarding the various legal questions connected with John Wilkes. The family expected that he would one day bring to it the unique distinction of providing the country with a second Lord Chancellor. But on the first earl's death the family went to pieces. ' He died ', wails the eldest son, ' without leaving any *Testament politique* for our future conduct.' Oh that he had left them a book of rules ! Deprived of his judgement, it at once became apparent that they had no judgement of their own.

The career of the second earl is one of utter selfishness and vacillation of purpose; that of Charles Yorke is much the same. He hoped to receive the Woolsack from Chatham in 1766, but Chatham preferred his old friend Chief Justice Pratt, who became Chancellor as Lord Camden. Yorke again had hopes in 1768 when the ministry was reconstituted in the interests of the Bedford faction, and again in vain. Then in 1770 Camden resigned. This time the hoped-for offer was made—by the Duke of Grafton, whose policy was now the very antithesis of Chatham's. Yorke decided on refusal. If political principle and loyalty to party meant anything to him, he had no alternative ; acceptance must mean a breach with all his friends and colleagues. But the temptation was too great for him ; he could not refuse outright. He went backwards and forwards, from one adviser to another, in a hopeless state of vacillation. He decided at last to decline definitely ; had an interview with the King and did so, but was utterly miserable immediately he had taken this honourable course, because the King had made it clear that if he did not take it now, he would never be offered the Woolsack again. Next day there was a levée ; Yorke's wife, knowing him only too well, urged him not to go. But the poor burnt moth could not keep away. He went ; was offered the position one last time and accepted. Then came unutterable remorse. Three days later the unhappy man—his own worst enemy—died, whether a natural death brought on by mental anguish acting on a constitution already enfeebled by over-indulgence in the pleasures of the table, or by his own hand, none can say with certainty.

VII

THE GREAT COMMONER

WILLIAM PITT, Earl of Chatham, was fashioned in a grander mould than any other figure in the eighteenth century. Great as William Pitt, he was great also as Earl of Chatham. Indeed, the last period of his career is perhaps the greatest. Yet he is legitimately known as 'the Great Commoner'. He was the champion of the rights of the people, first against the great Whig party leaders, then against the personal rule of George III. Pitt began his political career as a 'Boy Patriot'; George was nurtured on the doctrines of the *Patriot King*. Both were enemies of the Whig oligarchy and disbelievers in the party system. Yet their ultimate aims were far asunder as the poles. Pitt, by nature intensely deferential to royalty, in the end perceived this and openly defied the King. For the patriotism of Pitt was that of a democrat, of an enthusiast for the cause of Liberty.

Although the grandson of the famous Diamond Pitt, governor of Madras, whose cognomen was due to his possession of a wonderful stone of great value, and although brought up in a lavish household, William had small private means. He was educated at Eton, then at Oxford, at that time as deeply Tory as it was intellectually stagnant, and Pitt felt no affection for his university. He decided to adopt the army as his profession and he obtained a cornetcy in Cobham's Horse. This he owed to the influence of an Etonian friend, George Lyttelton, who became his brother-in-law. This connexion was of the utmost importance in Pitt's early career. For Lyttelton was nephew of Richard Temple, first Viscount Cobham, whose sister married into the Grenville family. When, later on, Pitt married Lady Hester Temple, he became a member of this family group, of which Lord Temple, George Grenville, later of Stamp Act fame, and Lyttelton himself were the chief representatives. The kindly Lord Cobham, a jovial, very coarse-minded soldier, was the nominal leader of this group, and they were generally known as the Cobham Cousinhood or ' Cobham's Cubs '. These formed the nucleus of the ' Boy Patriot ' party. Temple, Pitt's brother-in-law, was a second-rate man, very ambitious and rather disagreeable, and he was to prove Pitt's evil genius ; George Grenville, a disinterested hard worker, exact, punctual, businesslike, was tedious, meticulous, pedantic, totally devoid of imagination and sympathy ; Lyttelton, who at first gave promise of being the most distinguished of the group, a kindly man of the highest principle and of some literary attainments, proved a bad administrator and too wanting in stamina to stand the strain of public life. Pitt easily outstripped them all.

The young cornet, who entered the House of Commons as member for Old Sarum in 1735, early distinguished himself by the vigour of his attacks upon Walpole, and was dismissed his cornetcy. But William Pitt the politician was not to be so easily muzzled as this. He was taken into the household of Frederick, Prince of Wales, patron of the opposition party. He was vehement in denunciation of Walpole's peace policy in connexion with the trade disputes with Spain, and in 1741 zealously supported Sandys's motion for Walpole's removal from the King's counsels for ever.

One cannot be surprised that the young Pitt made himself odious to many. His intense self-confidence, assertiveness, and theatricality seemed very much out of place in a mere novice, in decidedly bad taste. Horatio[1] Walpole once censured his ' furious

[1] First Lord Walpole of Wolterton, Sir Robert's brother, to be distinguished from the better known Horace Walpole, fourth Earl of Orford, who was Sir Robert's youngest son.

declamation' and extravagant gestures. Pitt would neither 'palliate nor deny the atrocious crime of being a young man'. But it was felt that it should be possible to be a young man and yet show a little humility and restraint. Nor was the cause he championed above reproach. The 'Boy Patriots' had no monopoly of patriotism and they had a great deal less political wisdom than the great states-man, whose every act they assailed irrespective of its merits. After Wal-pole's retirement Pitt was just as venomous against his successors. Carteret was ' an exe-crable minister'; the whole policy of the administration during the Austrian Succession War was wrong ; it was the conversion of this 'illustrious kingdom into a mere appendage of a miserable electorate '. The expedient of hiring

WILLIAM PITT
From the painting by Richard Brompton in the National Portrait Gallery

Hanoverian and Hessian troops, and of subsidizing allied states, he assailed with especial bitterness.

When Granville was ousted, Pitt undoubtedly hoped for inclusion in the Pelham's ' broad-bottomed administration '. But his denunciations of the Hanoverian connexion had made him extremely distasteful to George II, and he was excluded. He kept on good terms with the ministry, however, and was even-tually given the very minor post of Vice-Treasurer of Ireland.

Immediately on admission to office he found himself obliged to support the use of Hanoverian troops, which, while in opposition, he had declared inadmissible in any circumstances whatever. There were those that saw in this proof that Pitt was without principle, a man who could be bought with a paltry sum. A doggerel poem by Sir Charles Hanbury Williams put it thus :

> Whilst Balaam was poor, he was full of renown ;
> But now that he's rich, he's the jest of the town.
> Then let all men learn by his present disgrace,
> That honesty's better by far than a place.

It is undeniably true that Pitt was ambitious and that he was not always consistent. But very few politicians have been invariably consistent ; and in any case, Pitt would have agreed that ' consistency is the bugbear of *little* minds '. He was certainly not mercenary, as he soon showed when he was advanced to the office of Paymaster of the Forces. By longstanding custom there went with the stipend extensive perquisites which were far more lucrative. Pitt refused to touch any of these, and showed himself to be a disinterested and vigorous administrator, bent on reforms.

On the death of Pelham in 1754 Pitt was shelved on the not wholly ingenuous pretext of his unpopularity with the King. He was intensely mortified and chagrined, and before long embarked upon a virulent campaign against the duke, which can only be attributed in large measure to personal motives. Thus for a short time he was united with his rival, Henry Fox, in that formidable alliance which annihilated Newcastle's principal lieutenant in the Commons, the useless Sir Thomas Robinson, and reduced to a harrowed silence his far abler colleague, Murray, the future Lord Mansfield and Lord Chief Justice, with whom Pitt was to do battle on many subsequent occasions. When Newcastle capitulated and took Fox into partnership, Pitt never forgave the latter's desertion. His attack on the government became more powerful than ever. On November 13, 1755 he delivered a tremendous onslaught. ' His eloquence,' declared Horace Walpole, ' like a torrent long obstructed, burst forth with commanding impetuosity.' He spoke with withering sarcasm of the Newcastle-Fox coalition. ' I remember at Lyons to have been carried to see the conflux of the Rhone and the Saône ; this a gentle, feeble, languid stream, and, though languid, of no depth—the other a boisterous and overbearing torrent—but they meet at last ; and long may they continue united, to the comfort of each other, and to the glory, honour, and happiness of this nation.' This was but the beginning of a brilliant campaign of oratory, in which one after another Newcastle's henchmen were overthrown in humiliating confusion. He took astounding liberties with the House of Commons ; was histrionic to a degree. ' Did no one laugh ? ' a member was once asked. ' No, sir,' was the reply, ' we were all too much awed to laugh.'

There was more than mere invective in Pitt's attack. There was dangerously powerful argument. The hostilities between French and British in America, which had led to Braddock's disaster in 1755,[1] were but a prelude to that huge struggle which is known as the Seven Years' War and which began in the following year. Pitt saw that the ministry was utterly incapable of carrying on a great war. Its one device was the old one of hiring allies and mercenaries. The nation would achieve nothing, declared Pitt, without self-help. He insisted on the necessity of reviving the militia. ' What an inglorious picture for this country to figure, gentlemen driven by an invasion like a flock of sheep, and forced to send their money abroad to buy courage and defence ! ' Everywhere there were bungling and ineptitude. ' We have provoked before we can defend, we have neglected after provocation, and in every quarter of the world we are inferior to France.' Criticism of this nature in the grave circumstances of the war could not be irresponsible, for it inevitably exposed the critic to the challenge, Could you do any better ? Pitt asked for nothing so much as the chance to show that he

[1] His expedition, directed against Fort Duquesne, the chief of the barrier forts between the Ohio and the St. Lawrence, which connected the French possessions in Canada with those in Louisiana, was ambushed by the French and their Indian allies, and barely a third of the force escaped alive, Braddock himself being killed.

The suspense is just arrived as news of expectation grows every hour into more anxiety. the fate of Louisbourgh and of Olmutz probably decided tho the results unknown. the Enterprise crowns with success on baffled. all this moments an Indications of a second Battle towards the Rhine. Which my life in the

same favouring Providence, that
all will be well ....
the young ones are so delightfully noisy
that I hardly know what P
write. My most affectionate compliments to all

The Congress. Yr ever loving husband
&c &c &c &c Honourable
The Lady Hester Pitt

W. Pitt

'The event unknown.' Pitt writing to his wife from Hayes on Saturday, 1 July 1758

From 'Correspondence of William Pitt, Earl of Chatham', 1838

could. He was absolutely certain of himself. In memorable
words he spoke his confidence. 'I am sure I can save this
country, and nobody else can.' The Minorca disaster gave him
the wished-for opportunity, and, refusing to co-operate with
Newcastle, he took office with the Duke of Devonshire, he
himself acting as one of the two Secretaries of State, the com-
pliant Earl of Holdernesse being the other.

Pitt's first ministry commenced in December 1756, and at
once started to act with vigour. The Hessian mercenaries were
dismissed ; new native regiments were raised, including two
Highland ones ; Pitt's favourite militia scheme was adopted ;
an extensive programme of naval construction was embarked
on, and the naval personnel increased to an unprecedented
figure. Preparations were made for a joint naval and military
attack on the great French fortress of Louisburg, which commanded the estuary of the St. Lawrence. More efficient means
were taken to thwart French movements in European waters,
which had latterly been little checked. Had Pitt been consistent,
there would have been no participation in the continental campaign ; but he was not altogether a free agent in this matter,
as at the beginning of the year an alliance had been concluded
with Frederic of Prussia, which bound us to provide material
aid by land. But in any case Pitt was now, rightly or wrongly,
in favour of participation in the fighting on the Continent,
discerning an infinity of difference between the inconsequent
wanderings across the plains of Germany which had been arranged
by Carteret and Newcastle, in days when British interests were
not directly involved, and provision of the strong support
for our solitary ally, whose destruction could not fail to react very
prejudicially upon our own fortunes in the war. Frederic,
intent upon a descent into Saxony against the Austrians, was
anxious to have his rear on the Rhine protected against French
attack. Frederic hailed the new minister as the man for whom
England had long been waiting. But the man did not hold office
for long. His colleagues were not very loyal ; Newcastle was
on the *qui vive* for a chance to come back ; the King cordially
disliked Pitt. The secretary ', he complained, ' made him long

speeches, which possibly might be very fine, but were greatly
beyond his comprehension.' Pitt's generous advocacy of Byng,
upon whose death the populace were resolved, lost him some of his
popularity. George came to the conclusion that the obnoxious
secretary could be dismissed with impunity. Instantly enthusiasm was kindled once again for the great man. London and
seventeen other towns offered him their freedom; the funds

*This caricature, published at the time of Pitt's accession to office in
1756, depicts his immense superiority to all rivals. From 'A Political
and Satirical History', &c.*

fell; the new ministry could not get on. The result was the
Pitt-Newcastle coalition, whose efficacy was abundantly demonstrated by the triumphant record of the country in the remainder
of the Seven Years' War.

There had been no such consistent brilliance in our war annals
as that of Pitt's second administration. To what extent was he
directly responsible for it? It has been urged that it was his
lieutenants who really did the work; he merely gave encouragement and a general indication of policy. Even were that all,

it is a big all. The encouragement was such as only a great man of magnetic influence could give. He roused the spirit of the whole nation with an infectious enthusiasm and confidence, acting on the principle always that there are no such things as chance and the impossible. In the second place, the ability to grasp, and hold to unswervingly, the broad principles of strategy is so rare that its possession by Pitt in itself entitles him to the reputation of being a superlatively great war-minister. He realized that the theatre of the struggle was the whole world and had imagination big enough to envisage it all as a single thing. Broadly speaking, his conception was to pin the main Bourbon forces on the Continent by helping Frederic—so winning Canada on the plains of Germany ; to maintain command of the sea by blockading the principal French fleets in Brest and Toulon ; to wrest from France her American colonies and West Indian Islands and to oust her from her East Indian possessions and share in the East Indian trade ; to keep her in a state of constant alarm and fear of invasion by frequent descents upon her coasts.

The feature of this scheme most open to criticism is the last. The raids on the French coast were as a whole unsuccessful. Cherbourg was indeed taken in 1758 and its forts and shipping destroyed, but on the approach of a French fleet, the attackers hurriedly departed. Then in 1761 the island of Belleisle was captured. This was all the success achieved by expeditions which absorbed much material and energy, which might have been expended to much greater advantage elsewhere. They were a dissipation of valuable resources. The arguments in their favour are that they served to mystify the enemy as to our real intentions, distracted attention from the Rhine front, were an efficient offensive defence of our own shores. It should be noted that these attacks were undertaken at Frederic the Great's express request.

Such were the main features of Pitt's great strategic design ; that it was consistently carried out was due to his own personal supervision, to his co-ordination of naval, military, and civil authorities, to the fact that his single dominating personality ensured unity of command. But he not only devised general plans, he superintended details, working with indefatigable energy, and keeping all his assistants at the highest pitch of alertness. His dispatches are models, not only of luminous clearness and width of view, but also of minute direction. He kept himself always supremely well informed as to the political situation in Europe and the general military and naval situation.

Black heath Nov. y^{or e} 6th

you did my Dear son the Honour to entrust him with so great and important an affair as the taking of Quebec. which you Sr Plan'd, and he Executed.　　　H: Wolfe.

Mrs. Wolfe to Pitt, 6 November 1759. From ' Correspondence of William Pitt, Earl of Chatham', 1838

He had the great man's gift of picking out men of his own mettle to help him—men like Wolfe and Saunders. Not by any means all the human material he had to use was of good quality, much of it was second or third rate ; but from the men, whatever their merits, who came under his direct influence, he got the very best that it was in them to give.

The *annus mirabilis* of Pitt's military successes was 1759, in which Horace Walpole wrote, ' we are forced to ask every morning what victory there has been for fear of missing one.'

It was the year of the two naval triumphs, of Boscawen at Lagos, of Hawke at Quiberon ; of the taking of Quebec ; of the battle of Minden, in which the British infantry played so sensational a part. The following year was less extraordinary, but also brilliant ; for the taking of Montreal rounded off the conquest of Canada, and Eyre Coote's success at Wandewash was decisive in driving the French out of India. The French West Indian Islands had been taken from them one after another ; their West African possessions, Goree, Senegal, had also gone. Yet Pitt was not satisfied ; nothing less would suffice than the entire destruction of the French navy, the complete humiliation of the Bourbon power. Pitt certainly laid himself open to the charge of desiring to pursue the war to that point of abnormal success which only engenders implacable hostility and the determination to seek revenge. The popularity of the war with the nation as a whole waned after 1760. The financial burden was very heavy. Pitt's demands upon the revenue were as severe as they were imperious. He worried and browbeat the unhappy Chancellor of the Exchequer, Legge, and although acknowledging himself to be no finance expert, attacked and ridiculed his expedients. When objection was raised to the cost of the war, his answer was that we could afford to pay better than France could. Since France was bankrupt, this was small comfort to one who wished to preserve national solvency. His imperious attitude on the finance question was typical ; he bullied his colleagues. He made no attempt to ingratiate himself with them. This made him the easier prey when George III, who disliked Pitt even more thoroughly than George II had ever done, resolved to get rid of him.

He was not at once dismissed on George III's accession, because though the King and Bute were anxious for peace, they wanted it to be a glorious peace, and to secure that had need of the 'organiser of victory' for a season yet. As it happened, even after his resignation the tide of victory continued to flow. Even when the presiding hand was removed, the mechanism it had created still worked efficiently, so well and skilfully had it been devised. Negotiations with a view to peace were seriously opened with France as early as March 1761 as the result of overtures from the Duc de Choiseul, the one great man produced by France during the war. Pitt was not a good negotiator; his methods were blunt, his language dictatorial; he had no talent for bargaining or conciliation. He spoke as victor to the vanquished. Determined to retain all we had won, and to secure adequate safeguards for Frederic, he also wished to exclude France from the Newfoundland fisheries, not only because they were valuable, but because they were a home for the nurture of French seamen. Unsupported by his colleagues in this demand, he withdrew it, but still indulged in ' musts' and ' shalls'. It is true that Pitt at this time knew of the likelihood of the formation of a new compact between France and Spain; it is also true that his intransigent attitude went far to persuade Choiseul finally to enter into this engagement. If Pitt deserves the credit of having foreseen the conflict with Spain, he merits the blame of having helped to hasten it.

Once he knew of the actual conclusion of the Bourbon compact of August 1761 he demanded instant war with Spain. ' France is Spain and Spain is France.' The Spaniards were largely dependent for the sinews of war on their annual treasure fleet; were it arrested or destroyed, the war effort of Spain would not be formidable. Pitt urged that it should never be allowed to reach its destination; but the others in the Cabinet would not hear of Great Britain's being the aggressor, and on this issue Pitt resigned. The King, delighted to be rid of him, graciously said good-bye, when graciousness cost nothing, being but an expression of lightness of heart; but the susceptible Pitt was reduced to tears by the royal condescension and grovelled before the youthful monarch. He accepted a pension for himself and a peerage for his wife. Once more pamphlets appeared, as Bute had hoped, deriding the disinterested commoner who bartered his independence for money and a title. For a time Pitt retired into private life at his country seat at Hayes. His marriage had been a true romance and he was a devoted husband and father, and in nothing did he take greater pleasure than in the education of his son William, who was destined to guide the country in a war even more momentous than that through which the father had just been guiding her.

Pitt soon returned to Parliament, and was once more in opposition, insisting on the necessity of continuing the war in Germany when Bute's ambition was to abandon Prussia ; but it was the preliminary treaty with France and Spain that stung him to fierce indignation ; it was utterly inadequate as a recompense for our efforts. He also made a scathing attack on the cider tax of the incompetent Chancellor of the Exchequer, Dashwood, and poured contemptuous ridicule on George Grenville, when the latter querulously demanded where else to find a new source of revenue. The government was in a bad way. The peace was unpopular ; still more so the cider tax. The injudicious prosecution of those responsible for No. 45 of the *North Briton* was the finishing touch. Though disliking Wilkes personally and feeling the utmost disapprobation of the attacks made in his paper on the King and on the Scots, Pitt powerfully resisted the motion in the House of Commons that privilege of Parliament did not extend to libel. He was practically unsupported. At this time he stood almost alone, completely estranged from the Whigs as well as from the ' King's friends '. This complete breach existed at the time of Grenville's introduction of the Stamp Act in February 1765. Pitt was ill on that date, and in his absence the bill passed almost without opposition. In May and June there were negotiations between George III and Pitt with a view to his formation of a new government. They broke down because Pitt regarded it as essential that Temple should lead for him in the House of Lords, and Temple refused to join the administration.

Thus it was that Grenville was succeeded by Rockingham, not by Pitt. Had the two been able to work together, it would have been a good thing for the country ; but while both were opposed to the taxation of America, they approached the subject from radically different standpoints. Grenville had justified his imposition on the ground that there was no difference in principle between direct and indirect taxation. Logically, therefore, as the colonists did not dispute the right of the mother country to impose the former in the shape of custom duties, they had no case against the latter. Rockingham admitted the justice of this argument, maintained strenuously the government's right to tax,

Bute, as the author of the Peace of Paris, is referred to as Louis XV's friend
('A Political and Satirical History', &c.)

but held it inexpedient to do so. Consequently he accompanied the repeal of the Stamp Act by a Declaratory Act, affirming the right of the mother country to tax. Pitt, on the other hand, was contemptuous of a right which it is not proposed to enforce, and was convinced that there was all the difference in the world between indirect taxation, intended primarily for regulation of trade and direct taxation, intended solely for revenue ; between an unchallenged system of long standing and an innovation strongly objected to. 'No taxation without representation' was to Pitt no mere catchword. It stood for all his dearest convictions, as to popular government and personal liberty. In one of his greatest speeches (January 14, 1766) he triumphantly proclaimed his convictions and rejoiced that America had resisted.

Rockingham was dismissed in July. Again approached by the King, Pitt this time found it possible to form a ministry. Acting on his favourite principle of ' measures not men ', deliberately ignoring party ties, he collected that heterogeneous contingent from divers factions which Burke described as ' a tesselated pavement without cement '. It had a disastrous career. It was weakened at the outset by its leader's acceptance of the earldom of Chatham. He was impelled to take this step partly because he felt that his infirmities needed repose, more particularly because the opposition he most feared, the representatives of the great Whig families, were in the Upper House. While business there was less strenuous than in the Commons, he felt that his opponents among the peers needed closer watching. But the step was most unpopular and robbed the ministry of its greatest asset—its leader's unique command over the Commons—while his declamatory style of oratory was not suited to the Lords.

Still instigated by his persistent fear of the Bourbons, Chatham designed the plan of a Northern Alliance against the hated rival, but it broke down because Frederic the Great, his eyes fixed on Poland and no longer troubling about western Europe, would not give his concurrence. Another object of solicitude was the question of the East India Company and the government of large parts of India. The Company had not shown itself sensible of its new responsibilities ; there had been gross instances of peculation and corruption in Bengal. Chatham wanted to have the whole complicated question thrashed out in a parliamentary inquiry ; but when that inquiry should have opened he was at

Bath, overwhelmed by his terrible malady, the gout, accompanied by other more serious complications, while his own ministry, in which he was already a mere cipher, under the impetus imparted by the volatile Charles Townshend, plunged swiftly into an abyss. So mysterious was the earl's malady, that some refused to believe it genuine. But as a matter of fact it was only too genuine. Chatham's brain was affected ; from April 1767 to April 1769 he was lost in a dreadful mental darkness. His behaviour was extraordinary, his temper violent. He shut himself up, refusing to see any one, even his own wife, for more than a few minutes at a time. It was his misfortune to be tended by Dr. Addington, the fashionable physician of the day, and according to modern medical ideas, his treatment was warranted to kill. Had it not been for the unwearied devotion of Lady Chatham, it looks as though it would have killed. Several months before his recovery, Chatham had announced his irrevocable intention to resign and, despite the protestations of Grafton, the second-in-command in the ministry, and the positive orders of the King, he had carried out his intention.

THE DUKE OF GRAFTON
Caricature by James Sayers

During Chatham's incapacity, his administration had passed from blunder to blunder. The irrepressible Townshend had gratuitously reopened the whole question of American taxation by the imposition of duties on tea and other commodities ; the Wilkes troubles had reached their culmination in the affair of the Middlesex election. Grafton, though nominal leader, counted for nothing ; Shelburne, Chatham's most reliable pupil, had gone ; the controlling influence in the Cabinet was that of the incalculable Bedford.

Suddenly Chatham had a severe attack of gout, which restored his faculties. In January 1770 he reappeared at Westminster a new man ; with eloquence he declaimed against a House of Commons which in twice expelling Wilkes, in declaring him incapable of sitting and his defeated rival duly elected, had converted itself into an arbitrary power, a despotic menace to the people for whose sake it existed. He saw a possible remedy in parliamentary reform, in counteracting the corrupting influence of the rotten boroughs by increasing the representation of the counties. Next to the Middlesex election what most perturbed him was a Spanish attack upon the British settlement in the Falkland Islands, for which not even an apology had as yet been obtained from the Spanish government owing to the Cabinet's tenderness for ' Spanish punctilios '. He returned to the subject of this humiliation again and again, regarding it as a sign of national degeneracy.

He was also much exercised in mind over Lord Mansfield's decision that in trials for libel the question of the criminality of the alleged libel should be determined by the judge, the jury being left to deal only with the jejune question of publication. In this decision Chatham saw the freedom of the press and our whole precious heritage of political liberty placed in jeopardy. His exaggerated devotion to royalty no longer blinded him to the personal responsibility of the King for the ill condition of the

Lord CHATHAM's *Speech, and his Motion, for the* DISSOLUTION *of the present Parliament.*

My LORDS,

IT is not many years since this nation was the envy and terror of its neighbours. Alone and unassisted, it seemed to balance the half of Europe. Nor was the aspect of its affairs abroad more flattering than at home. Concord and unanimity prevailed throughout the whole extent of the British Empire. Whatever heats and animosities might subsist between the grandees, the body of the people was satisfied. No complaints, no murmurs were heard. No petitions, much less remonstrances, for the redress of grievances, were carried up to the throne ; nor were hired mobs necessary to keep the Sovereign in in countenance by their venal fhouts. Nothing was heard, on every fide, but one general burft of acclamation and joy. But how is the profpect darkened! how are the mighty fallen! On public days the Royal ears are faluted with hiffes and hoots; and he fees libels againft his perfon and government written with impunity: Juries folemnly acquitting the publifhers. What greater mortification can befall a Monarch! Yet this facrifice he makes to his Minifters. To their falfe fteps, not to his own he owes his difgrace. By their intrigues the laft inglorious peace, the origin of our evils, was effected and approved by Parliament, though it was loudly condemned by the nation. By their intrigues the laft fhameful convention received the fame fanction. Were this facrifice of our honour and intereft abroad compenfated by the wifdom of our domeftic government, it would be fome comfort. But the fact is, that Great Britain, Ireland, and America, are equally diffatisfied, and have reafon to be diffatisfied with the Miniftry. The impolitic taxes laid upon America, and the Syftem of violence there adopted, have unfortunately foured the minds of the people, and rendered them difaffected to the prefent Parliament, if not to the King. Ireland has various reafons to complain. An enumeration of them would be tedious. You may judge of their number and magnitude by the prefent flame. The meafures taken to carry the Middlefex Election in favour of the Court, the decifion of that Election, the Murders in St. George's Fields, the refufal of the Commons to enquire into thefe Murders, and into the conduct of thofe who advifed his Majefty to beftow thanks and rewards upon the perfons immediately concerned, the payment of the immenfe debt contracted by the Crown without infpecting any account, all thefe circumftances had juftly alarmed the nation, and made them uncommonly attentive to the operations of Parliament. Hence the publication of the Parliamentary Debates. And where was the injury, if the Members acted upon honeft principles? For a public Affembly to be afraid of having their deliberations publifhed, is monftrous, and fpeaks for itfelf. No mortal can conftrue fuch a procedure to their advantage: It, and the practice of locking the doors, are fufficient to open the eyes of the blind; they muft fee that all is not well within. Not fatisfied, however, with fhutting their doors, the Commons would overturn the liberty of the Prefs. The Printers had fpirit, and refifted. The irritated Commons exerted their privilege above the Laws of the Land, and their fervants acted illegally in the execution of their illegal orders. The Magiftrates of London un'ertook the caufe of the Printers, and the protection of the Laws, and of the City's Franchifes. The Commons ftill proceeded with the fame outrageous violence. They called upon the Magiftrates to juftify their conduct, and would not fuffer them to be heard by Counfel. Thofe men, who had allowed the proftitute Electors of Shoreham Counfel to defend a bargain to fell their Borough by auction, would not grant the fame indulgence to the Lord Mayor of London pleading for the Laws of England, and the confcientious difcharge of his duty. Accordingly they committed him to the Tower for not violating his oath. The moft facred obligation of Morality and Religion they voted criminal, when it happened to ftand in competition with their affumed Privileges.—Their next ftep was the Act of a Mob, and not of a Parliament—I mean the erafure of a Recognizance entered at Guild-hall. We have heard of fuch violence committed by the French King: and indeed it feems much better calculated for the latitude of Paris than of London. The people of this kingdom will never fubmit to fuch bafe faced tyranny. They muft fee that it is time to roufe when their own creatures dare to affume a power of ftopping profecutions by their vote, and, confequently, of refolving the Law of the Land into their will and pleafure. The imprudence, and, indeed, the abfolute madnefs of thefe meafures, demonftrates, that they are not the refult of that Affembly's calm, unbiaffed deliberations; but the dictates of weak, uninformed Minifters, influenced by thofe who miflead the Sovereign. It is impoffible that a grave, and once venerable body of men, if left to itfelf, fhould have converted government into a fcuffle with a fingle individual. Were the Commons not abfolute flaves to the man who holds the golden keys of the Treafury, they could never have rendered the very name of Parliament ridiculous by carrying on a conftant war againft Mr. Wilkes. To them it is entirely owing, that he is become a perfon of confequence in the State. They firft made him

From the report in the 'Gentleman's Magazine' of Chatham's speech on his motion for the Dissolution of Parliament, 1 May 1771

kingdom. He hoped that something astonishing and stupendous ' may open his eyes if they are closed and let in upon his mind the distracted and degraded state of his Empire '. Being called to order for this audacity, he became yet more audacious. ' I am misunderstood. I said, *if* they are closed—but now I withdraw the condition and say they *are* closed and must be opened to the state of his Empire, to which he is a stranger.' The lists were opened. To Chatham, George III was ' a stranger in England ' ; to George III Chatham was ' a trumpet of sedition '.

In May 1772 Chatham was espousing the cause of toleration for Dissenters and attacking the episcopate with a barbed irony in a speech of powerful invective, famous for the phrase, ' We have a Calvinistic creed, a Popish liturgy, and an Arminian clergy.' But the great cause in which he did battle in his last days was again that of America. In 1774 and 1775 he attacked the whole policy of the government regarding the colonies, particularly its repressive measures and the Quebec Act. He pressed for the removal of the troops quartered upon Boston, and in February 1775 propounded a scheme for conciliation with America, which was the upshot of a conference with Benjamin Franklin. Clothed in eloquent and magnificent language, this bill asserted the authority of the mother country over her colonies in all matters saving only taxation, annulled all the acts recently passed prejudicial to the Americans, and, thirdly and most important, recognized the American Congress of Philadelphia, which, in the King's view, was an illegal and seditious assemblage. It was the scheme of a great statesman, but it had not the remotest chance of acceptance.

The War of American Independence began. Chatham was horrified at a fratricidal war, which could settle nothing. Soon the successes of the colonists encouraged the Bourbon powers to take counsel together for a war of revenge against Great Britain. It was a most dangerous situation. Chatham on the 20th November 1777 in a speech of passionate eloquence denounced the civil war, especially the method of its prosecution by the government, the use of Hessian troops and Indian auxiliaries. Methods of barbarism tarnished the honour of the army, and success was

PROCLAMATION,

Seiner Excellentz des Herrn General Lieutenant von KNYPHAUSEN, *Commandeur von Seiner Majeſtæt Truppen auf New-York Iſland, Long Iſland, Staten Iſland, und denen davon abhængenden Poſten, &c. &c. &c.*

DENEN Inhabern von Lændereyen und Gærten wird hiedurch alle Aufmunterung und Schutz ertheilet, um einen reichlichen Vorrath von Getraide, Fourage, und Gemueſe anzuziehen.

Wer ſich unterſtehet Vieh oder andere Producte, ſie mœgen Nahmen haben, wie ſie wollen, von Lændereyen oder Gærten wegzunehmen, oder zu ruiniren; an Hæuſern, Gemueſe- oder Obſt-Gærten, und Lændereyen einigen Schaden zu thun; oder ſonſt, auf was Art es ſey, jemandes Eigenthum unrechtmæßiger Weiſe anzugreifen, ſoll, wenn ſolches gegen ihn bewieſen wird, mit der æuſſerſten Strenge beſtraft werden.

Diejenigen, welche von Uebertretern dieſer Proclamation beleidigt zu ſeyn glauben, haben ſich, wenn ſie Einwohner des Diſtricts von New-York ſind, mit ihren Klagen an den Commandanten der Stadt zu wenden; im Fall einer weitern Entfernung aber dem Commandirenden Officier des næchſten Poſtens von Seiner Majeſtæt Truppen davon Anzeige zu thun, damit, wenn ſolche gegruendet, ihnen Gerechtigkeit wiederfahren, und das nœthige remedirt werden mœge.

Gegeben unter meiner Hand im Haupt-Quartier den eilften Mærtz, im Jahr unſers Herrn ein tauſend ſieben hundert und achtzig.

KNYPHAUSEN.

Auf Sr. Excellentæ Befehl
JUSTIN HENRICH MOTZ,
F H. Ober Auditeur.

By his Excellency
Lieutenant General KNYPHAUSEN,
Commanding his Majeſty's Forces, upon
New-York Iſland, Long-Iſland, Staten-Iſland
and Poſts depending, &c. &c. &c.

PROCLAMATION.

ENCOURAGEMENT and Protection is hereby given, to the Poſſeſſors of Farms and Gardens for the Purpoſe of raiſing plentiful Supplies of Grain, Forage, and Vegetables.

Whatever Perſon or Perſons preſume to take away, or to deſtroy Cattle, Stock, or other Produce of any Farm or Garden; to do any damage to Houſes, Gardens, Orchards, or Lands, ; to break down Fences, or otherwiſe to injure private Property, ſhall, upon Proof thereof, be puniſhed with the utmoſt Severity.

Any Perſons who may think themſelves aggrieved, by a Non-Obſervance of this Proclamation, will, "if Inhabitants of New-York Diſtrict," make their Complaints known to the Commandant of the City; if in ſituations more remote, to the Officer commanding the neareſt Poſt of his Majeſty's Troops, in Order, that if well founded, they may obtain proper Redreſs.

Given under my Hand, at Head-Quarters, the Eleventh Day of March, One Thouſand Seven Hundred and Eighty.

KNYPHAUSEN.

By his Excellency's Command,
JUSTIN HENRY MOTZ,
Chief Judge Advocate, Heſſ.

The use of Hessian troops in the War of Independence. A proclamation (in English and German) of Baron Wilhelm von Knyphausen (Commanding Officer of the German Auxiliaries) encouraging the farmers of Upper Manhattan to grow crops and warning the troops not to rob them. From Rivington's 'Royal Gazette'

impossible.　We were but teaching the Americans the art of war, nd they were apt learners.　' My Lords,' he exclaimed, ' if I were an American, as I am an Englishman, while a foreign troop was landed in my country, I never would lay down my arms— never—never—never.'

Nevertheless, when we had been badly worsted, not only on the American continent, but on the sea, he protested vehemently against the recognition of American independence, and when on the 7th April 1778 the Duke of Richmond was to move an address for the removal of our forces in America, he insisted, against the advice of his doctor, on going down to the House.　Swathed in flannel, leaning heavily on his crutches, supported on either side, Chatham entered St. Stephen's for the last time.　He thanked God that though having one foot, more than one foot, in the grave, he had been able to come there to do his duty.　But he was utterly feeble, his words were disjointed, scarcely audible. Occasionally a sentence rang out with the old magic in it, as he protested against the dismemberment of the empire.　' Shall a people that fifteen years ago was the terror of the world now stoop so low as to tell its ancient inveterate enemy, " Take all we have, only give us peace " ? '　And again, ' My Lords, any state is better than despair ; if we must fall, let us fall like men.'　Richmond made a gentle, considerate answer to the speech.　Chatham rose to make a rejoinder, and fell back, struck by the hand of death.　He lingered, however, a few weeks, dying on the 11th May at the age of sixty-nine.　When the vote for a public funeral and monument was carried, George III expressed his surprise at what he regarded as ' rather an offensive measure to me personally '.　But the English people, though on occasion they had turned against him in the past, mourned Chatham as one of the greatest sons of the empire he had done so much to strengthen, to extend, and to exalt.

The greatness of Chatham is not nowadays in dispute.　There are, indeed, types of mind to whom his character makes no appeal.　To the exact thinker it may be unattractive.　Chatham was not an exact thinker.　Nice distinctions, precise technicalities he impatiently brushed aside.　His strong point was neither logic nor theory. There is neither great profundity nor great subtlety in his arguments. He stands firm on one or two general principles, as he understood them—on those maxims of liberty and of government which he discerned in Magna Carta and the Bill of Rights. In the extreme simplicity of his guiding political ideas lay much of his strength, for they had moral grandeur in them. He was a perfervid patriot. The speeches of Shakespeare's John of Gaunt and Henry V are not more instinct with pride in England than are those of Chatham. He loved and venerated his country for its own sake, but still more because it stood, in his estimation, for the great ideal of chartered liberty among the nations.

He was the people's champion. Even granting that his attitude towards the party system was mistaken and disastrous, yet in insisting on broad conceptions of national interest, in his attack on Whig faction and Whig oligarchy, in his appeal to the public outside the unrepresentative House of Commons, in his conception of parliamentary reform, he was a great democratic force. Yet he was no demagogue, no truckler to popular passions. He strongly opposed popular opinion in the cases of Byng and of the American colonies, in each of which the outcry was for condign punishment. He was too proud and too brave to be subservient. ' He has courage of every sort,' wrote Lord Waldegrave, who did not love him, ' cool or impetuous, active or deliberate.'

He was one of the greatest of orators. Gifted with a fine presence, a most commanding mien, he was an accomplished actor. His best speeches were impromptu, for the immediate occasion. They were intended to impress his actual hearers, not to be read afterwards. Thus to judge of the power of his oratory we must go to the accounts of the effect it produced on his audiences. Here there is universal testimony. The effect was extraordinary, amounting even to awe and indeed terror. ' His words', said Lyttelton, ' have sometimes frozen my young blood into stagnation, and sometimes made it pace in such a hurry through my veins that I could scarce support it.' But although they have been for the most part inadequately reported, the fire is still lambent in Chatham's speeches; they abound in phrases which, once known, are not easily forgotten; their fervour, their invective, their sublimity are still alive with the glow of the great personality that produced them. They were grandly conceived, their material being, in the words of Grattan, ' great subjects, great empires, great characters, effulgent ideas.'

Chatham's faults were glaring—his overbearing disposition, his extreme irritability, his ostentation, his lapses from good taste into a style which was stilted and pompous, a histrionic propensity apt to degenerate into a cheap theatricality. There is no need to slur over these foibles; Chatham was so great a man that the complete picture cannot belittle him. If some of the externals were grandiose, the essential figure was grand. A man of action, he had never-failing courage, resolution, and enthusiasm; a prophet, he had the eloquence of lofty and inspiring ideas; a leader of his country, he had the patriot's faith in the fineness of her nature and the splendour of her destiny; a consummate statesman, he had the sovereign discernment of imaginative vision, which is the ruler's greatest attribute.

Fox, Burke, and North

VIII
ROCKINGHAMS AND RADICALS

THE 1770's present us with a most interesting contrast between
the orthodox Whigs and the nascent Radicals. As we have seen,
there was something of the Radical in Chatham, which separated
him from most of the Whig connexions; but in 1769 a quite
new movement of Radical organization, directly due to the
Middlesex election, may be said to have started, the leaders
being outside Parliament and not connected with any of the
Whig elements. At this date the Whigs may be roughly divided
into three groups. There were, first, ' the Bedfords, the Gren-
villes, and other knots, who ', said Burke, ' are combined for no
public purpose, but only as a means of furthering with joint
strength their private and individual advantage '. In the second
place, there was Chatham, with his immediate following—
Grafton, Shelburne, and Camden. In the third place, there were
the lineal descendants of the Whigs of the Revolution—' the *old
Whigs* '—in the line of Walpole and the Pelhams, who since the
retirement of the old Duke of Newcastle, had been led by the
young Marquis of Rockingham, and included among whom were
Edmund Burke, the Duke of Devonshire, the Duke of Richmond,
General Conway. Later on, from 1774, there was numbered
among them the brilliant Charles James Fox, already celebrated
for his powers as a debater, still more so for his gambling, his
extravagance, his debts, who had previously acted as one of the
King's Friends, at Lord North's beck and call.

Rockingham, it is perhaps fair to say, was one of the least talented of British Prime Ministers. His qualifications were those of birth and breeding and high moral character. He had a firm control over his cabinet, his followers being most warmly attached to him. But of parliamentary qualifications he had next to none. He was a bad and nervous speaker. Indeed his nervousness was such that he could hardly prevail upon himself to open his lips in Parliament. With such a leader, the party could hardly prove strong. Besides, they were as a whole young and inexperienced when they first took office in 1765. They were in power just a year. Their second administration started, after our period, in March 1782, and Rockingham died in July, to be followed as Prime Minister by Shelburne, which meant the resignation of those in the ministry who had been most closely attached to their old chief.

Thus the Rockinghams had no luck. In any case they never had much chance owing to the implacable hostility of George III, who hated the aristocratic Whigs and would never employ them if he could possibly avoid it. They could have made themselves strong only by alliance with another group. Negotiations with that purpose were carried on at one time or another, with Bedford and his so-called ' Bloomsbury gang ', and with Pitt, but they were all abortive. There was no reason to regret the failure to coalesce with the Bedfords, who apart from their leader were a disreputable gang, devoid of principle or conviction ; but the inability to gain the support of Pitt was a disaster, not only to the Rockinghams, but to the country.

Although they were in office so short a time, the Rockinghams had a considerable record of accomplishment to their credit in their first administration. They restored military officers who had been deprived of their commissions owing to votes they had given against the government of the day ; very considerably modified the unpopular tax on cider ; arranged a commercial treaty with Russia ; relaxed a number of the commercial restrictions on colonial trade, here following in the path of Walpole ; and lastly, repealed Grenville's Stamp Act. As we have already seen, they accompanied this by a Declaratory Act, affirming the country's *right* to levy taxation. Whether the right did or did not exist was a matter of constitutional or metaphysical argument, on which it was easy to differ, and the Rockinghams and Pitt did differ fundamentally. But, apart from that abstract question, it is probably the case that the repeal of the Stamp Act could never have been carried without the Declaratory Act. The assent of the stubborn or conscientious King could never otherwise have been secured. As it was, there was difficulty enough. It got abroad —by royal inspiration it appeared— that His Majesty did not approve of the repeal. That alone in the existing political conditions would probably have sufficed to wreck what chances of success the measure had. Rockingham took the very necessary course of having a personal interview with the King, who at least agreed that he preferred the repeal of the Stamp Act to its enforcement. With this security, and the Pitt group of course supporting repeal, however little they approved of the accompanying Declaratory Act, the abrogation of the Stamp Act was secured.

Such was the achievement of the Rockinghams in office prior to 1780. But it is perhaps for their conduct in opposition that they are best known, since after all the Rockinghams shone because of the one great luminary among them, Edmund Burke ; and

ROCKINGHAM

Caricature by James Sayers

he was only commencing his political career during the first Rockingham administration, and he was greatest in opposition. He was born in Dublin, probably in 1729. Between 1743 and 1748 he was a student at Trinity College, where Goldsmith was a contemporary. He then proceeded to London, entering the Middle Temple with a view to adopting the barrister's profession. As a matter of fact, he was never even called to the Bar, and forsook law for letters. He nevertheless acquired a sound grasp of legal knowledge, as his political speeches and writings very clearly testify. Yet both at Trinity College and the Temple Burke did not seem to have shown much application, and his reading was of a desultory description. For some years he seems to have lived the life of the needy hack-writer, a member of the Grub Street community, a frequenter of obscure literary coteries and debating societies, a constant theatre-goer, his main occupation being the writing of the *Annual Register*, which he compiled for several years. It was at some date during this period that he married.

His first work was published in 1756, *A Vindication of Natural Society*. This was an imitation of the style, and a satire upon the thought, of Bolingbroke, who had died five years before. Because it succeeded in being a very excellent imitation it failed of being an effective satire. People were taken in ; they hailed the production as a posthumous work of the great stylist. Even such good critics as Lord Chesterfield and Bishop Warburton did so. The truth is that Burke showed in his essay a familiarity with the writings and the thought of Bolingbroke which could only have come from a very close study of him, from one who had been really influenced by him. The fact that he repudiated the doctrines of Bolingbroke was made less plain in this attempted satire than the fact that they had made a strong impression upon him. The most interesting feature in the essay is that at this early stage in his career Burke enunciates one of the cardinal principles of his whole life. He attacks an exaggerated individualism, the idea that the justification of organized society must rest upon ' reasons made clear and demonstrative to every individual '.

For Rhetoric he could not ope
His Mouth but out there flew a Trope

Edmund Burke the orator
Caricature by James Sayers

Burke's second publication was *A Philosophical Inquiry into the Origin of our Ideas of the Sublime and the Beautiful*, of which it is sufficient to say that it was a very early work, possibly written when he was only nineteen, that its sober tone and unexpansive method do not commend it to the modern art critic—it is too purely a piece of strict ratiocination—but that it had a very deep influence on one of the greatest of all art critics, Lessing.

In 1761 Burke took the step which marked the adoption of a life of politics instead of a life of letters. He went back to Ireland as private secretary to William Hamilton, the Chief Secretary to the Lord Lieutenant, and in this capacity he remained two years, until a serious conflict of opinion with Hamilton brought their relations to an abrupt end. It appeared that Hamilton wanted to bind his secretary to him for an indefinite period and for the whole of his time, leaving him no leisure for literary work. This to Burke meant, in his own words, ' annihilating himself for ever '. He gave up his post and returned to London, and here he was living when the Rockingham ministry came into power. Rockingham offered him the post of private secretary, and so the all-important connexion began between Burke and this group of Whig aristocrats, whose policy he was to illuminate with his broad, philosophic vision, whose lasting fame was to be established by him. In December 1765 Burke entered Parliament, as member for Wendover, and a month later he made his maiden speech. He made his mark at once, being complimented on his performance by Pitt and being eulogized by his friend, Dr. Johnson, who wrote that he had ' gained more reputation than perhaps any man at his first appearance ever gained before '.

Henceforward Burke's life was a public one, but a glance may be given at the man apart from Parliament, before we go on to consider his political greatness. When Burke entered Rockingham's service he was a poor man ; yet three or four years later he was able to pay £29,000 for the estate of Beaconsfield in Buckinghamshire. He was able to make the purchase, and to maintain the property as the result, apparently, of successful speculation in stocks. Income derived from an estate in Ireland, which he inherited from his brother, and payment for the literary work he continued to do for Dodsley, the publisher of the *Annual Register*, seem to have been his regular sources of revenue, until he was granted a pension by the King in 1794. Up till then he seems never to have been able to make ends meet, and he was heavily in debt to Rockingham. Burke was

very happy at Beaconsfield, where he did much entertaining, and he was a very eager farmer, earnestly consulting the greater authority, Arthur Young, about cabbages and pigs. But one associates Burke's social life mainly with London and with Dr. Johnson's set, for he was an *habitué* of that wonderful Pump Court circle, with Boswell, Garrick, Goldsmith, Reynolds, Dr. Burney, and Mrs. Thrale. With Sir Joshua his friendship was particularly warm, and he was the lifelong and very devoted friend of Dr.

EDMUND BURKE
From a stipple engraving by J. Jones

Johnson. This intimacy between the staunch Whig and the violent old Tory is one of the most interesting literary phenomena of the century. Each had the deepest affection and highest admiration for the other. Overwhelming as were Johnson's powers as a talker, he, to whom conversation was always an intellectual battle, reckoned Burke's capacity very high. Once when he was ill, Burke's name was mentioned to him. 'That fellow calls forth all my power,' cried Johnson. 'Were I to see Burke now it would kill me.'

The first of Burke's considerable services to the Rockingham party in opposition was his publication in 1769 of an answer to a recent pamphlet by George Grenville which was entitled *The Present State of the Nation*. He made a very close examination, with much statistical illustration, of Grenville's ' projects of economy, of finance, of commerce, and of constitutional improvement', and a vindication of the Rockingham administration in answer to the charges which Grenville had in his pamphlet brought against it. The remarkable point about Burke's essay is that, whereas Grenville of all living statesmen was reported to have the most intimate knowledge of the fiscal facts of the country and the closest grasp of national business, Burke showed himself at least his equal, if not his superior, in these respects.

His next essay was a more important work. *Thoughts on the Cause of the Present Discontents*, published in 1770, had as its theme the agitation which followed upon the Middlesex election when the free institutions of the country had been threatened, not so much by the government's original prosecution of Wilkes, as by the arbitrary proceedings of the majority in the House, which was supposed to represent the nation, by its resolution that privilege did not extend to libel, its expulsion of Wilkes, its refusal to allow him to take his seat when duly elected for Middlesex, its declaration that the defeated candidate was the member for Middlesex. Thereby the whole representative principle was threatened. The situation created by these events was Burke's theme. At the root of the whole evil Burke detected the personal influence of the King, the system of the ' King's Friends ' in Parliament. ' The power of the crown, almost dead and rotten as Prerogative ', he wrote, ' has grown up anew, with much more strength, and far less odium, under the name of Influence.' The remedy lay in freeing the House of Commons from the corruption practised by use of places and pensions conferred by the Crown. Burke did not believe in the popular nostrums of the day—triennial Parliaments and a Place Bill to debar all holders of office from membership of the Lower House. He found the only true remedy in the re-establishment of the unfettered party system ; and the essay ends with a famous eulogy of that system, the greatest justification of it in literature. ' Party is a body of men united for promoting by their joint endeavours the national interest upon some particular principle in which they are all agreed. For my part, I find it impossible to conceive, that any one believes in his own politics, or thinks them to be of any weight, who refuses to adopt the means of having them reduced into practice. It is the business of the speculative philosopher to mark the proper ends of government. It is the business of the politician, who is the philosopher in action, to find out proper means towards those ends, and to employ them with effect. Therefore every honourable connexion will avow it is their first purpose, to pursue every just method to put the men who hold their opinions into such a condition as may enable them to carry their common plans into execution, with all the power and authority of the state.'

In November 1774 Burke was elected one of the members for Bristol, and he continued to represent that city for the next six years, during which the relations between the mother country and her colonies became so critical and developed into disastrous war. This is the greatest period in Burke's career. Not only were his speeches delivered on the American question probably his greatest contributions to literature, but they were perhaps the very greatest speeches ever delivered within the walls of Parliament ; for they are marvellous in their combination of magnificent diction, closeness of reasoning, width and loftiness of view, and the ripest political wisdom. Thus while dealing directly with a particular issue, they are full of doctrine of lasting import. Burke's policy is summed up in the speech delivered on the 19th April 1774 ; and it will be seen that it has much in common with Chatham's ideas on the American question. He agreed that the tea duty, then under discussion, was a small matter—in amount. Yes, but ' would twenty shillings have ruined Mr. Hampden's future ? No, but the payment of half twenty shillings, on the principle it was demanded, would have made him a slave.' It was argued that the dignity of Parliament was involved in insisting on the tax. In that case this dignity was a ' terrible incumbrance, for it has of late been ever at war with your own interest, your equity, and every idea of your policy '. There was only one sound plan, to ' leave

AN ACCOUNT of the Value of all Goods, Wares, and Merchandize; exported from and imported into that Part of Great-Britain called England; from Christmas 1778 to Christmas 1780; distinguishing each Year and each Place.

NAMES OF PLACES.	From Christmas 1778 to Christmas 1779.		From Christmas 1779 to Christmas 1780.	
	Value of Exports. (£ s. d.)	Value of Imports. (£ s. d.)	Value of Exports. (£ s. d.)	Value of Imports. (£ s. d.)
Africa	159217 19 7	33960 16 9	195907 14 0	21689 0 7
Canaries	17494 2 6	2091 15 7	0 0 0	0 0 0
Denmark and Norway	150615 5 4	73171 13 5	17608 19 5	86731 4 4
East Country	50326 0 0	209982 8 0	60285 18 3	299832 4 9
East India	703191 14 4	710323 9 0	1116341 11 4	920726 9 7
Flanders	1041721 1 0	524413 10 7	1535849 4 10	873160 12 11
France	2812 18 0	12972 7 2	5744 4 0	4483 5 8
Germany	1263515 12 4	552604 19 1	1017820 2 0	68110 4 0
Greenland	124 1 0	23620 8 0	165 0 7	38158 17 8
Holland	1359015 13 9	517170 17 4	1111064 14 0	643337 15 3
Ireland	1359415 4 4	1384117 15 4	1888055 10 0	1549587 11 3
Isle of Man	20407 4 3	11252 15 10	20194 8 6	12070 3 6
Italy	507548 17 11	47477 18 7	312600 3 2	80405 3 3
Madeira	18719 2 11	3031 8 10	51907 16 10	2612 5 2
Portugal	647813 19 9	285334 5 3	459673 10 0	523893 18 2
Russia	306072 15 7	120137 14 4	161031 0 5	1150429 12 11
Spain	599765 17 0	220748 5 0		86398 9 0
Gibraltar	4534 1 0	1547 5 0	46836 17 7	1662 19 0
Streights	108403 4 7	252431 12 6	8532 2 3	144180 17 1
Sweden	229 11 0	1474 4 2	49678 10 1	2463 6 6
Turkey			1707 11 7	
Venice	29465 14 11	78532 3 2	28864 10 11	85526 17 7
ISLES.				
Alderney	2401 2 2	8 15 0	3518 11 6	15 15 0
Guernsey	44003 16 7	58878 17 7	54489 3 5	115960 7 10
Jersey	7712 15 4	17912 5 6	12029 15 3	14891 4 5
NORTH AMERICAN COLONIES.				
Canada	521240 6 10	61924 12 7	484692 9 0	3498 3 0
Cape Breton	22 8 0	0 0 0	16 2	0 0 0
Carolina		3732 8 9	236940 16 2	708 4 0
Florida	128811 14 11	23804 19 0	54760 13 8	10486 8 6
Georgia	85 6 0	607 17 5	51888 10 4	2251 4 1
Hudson's Bay	5447 4 0	5111 7 7	3587 11 0	15017 10 4
New England		807 10 0	13 0	32 2 7
Newfoundland	87947 8 11	65725 10 8	1026640 0 6	100257 8 4
New Providence	682 18 1	1256 10 6	0 0 0	400 2 8
New York	349712 7 2	14861 19 8	496602 7 6	15532 9 3
Nova Scotia	227181 10 2	1956 8 2	244158 0 0	777 11 6
Pensylvania	0 0 0			26 10 4

	£	s.	d.	£	s.	d.	£	s.	d.	£	s.	d.
WEST INDIA ISLANDS.												
Antigua	90110	1	0	85957	5	11	106703	19	3	57120	5	8
Barbadoes	140170	12	6	145293	12	6	254847	18	5	120984	1	6
Bermuda	27403	6	8	9292	2	10	1760	7	0	1229	13	10
Curacoa or Curazoa		0	10		0	7		0	6	1556	0	0
Grenades	42268	8	10	31965	0	6				2563	4	7
Jamaica	484365	10	10	1458764	6	6	727659	10	11	541575	14	11
Montferrat	9132	13	2	62204	13	2	11075	3	4	44696	5	2
Nevis	16013	2	3	57922	2	0	17745	4	5	45796	8	8
St. Croix	283	11	3	1813	16	5	152	7	1	7688	0	0
St. Eustatius	14474	2	11	320639	11	9	118249	17	8			
St. Kitt's	118747	6	4	18839	12	1	207562	14	8	323445	13	1
St. Lucia	14410	10	8	103399	8	4	53977	13	6	137200	19	5
St. Vincent	6238	19	8	45562	6	7	27916	11	0	7	4	3
Tobago	10867	8.	6	44879	7	10	25379	4	9	78927	5	4
Tortola	44135	0	6							49023	6	5
SPANISH WEST INDIES.												
Honduras Bay	2066	19	11	10690	1	6	0	0	0	14	1	0
Musquito Shore	1930	18	6	48	12	3	0	0	0	1527	3	0
Falkland Island	0	0	0	3400	0	0	0	0	0			
Northern Fishery	0	0	0	3267	10	0	0	0	0	525	14	9
Southern Fishery	0	0	0							1798	2	6
Total	10437729	1	4	9996740	13	4	1623333	2	5	933839	5	1
Prize Goods	2255700	9	9	1503751	2	2	929721	1	8	828401	2	8
Total of both	1269349	11	1	10660492	5	6	1255254	4	1	1076240	7	9

JOHN TOMKYNS, Assistant Inspector General.

Custom-House, London
February 18, 1783.

British Exports and Imports during the American War of Independence: Significant are the immense exports in 1778–9 to Florida, then practically uninhabited. These must have been smuggled into Carolina and Georgia, which were in control of the U.S. army. British exports to Carolina and Georgia climb from zero and £85 4s. 2d. respectively to £236,940 16s. 2d. and £91,888 4s. 8d. in 1779–80, after the capture of Charleston and Savannah. Florida falls off, as there was no longer any reason for smuggling. Jamaica is alone in the million class.

America, if she has taxable matter in her, to tax herself. I am not here going into the distinctions of rights, nor attempting to mark their boundaries. I do not enter into these metaphysical distinctions ; I hate the very sound of them. Leave the Americans, as they anciently stood, and these distinctions, born of our unhappy contest, will die along with them.'

In his still more famous speech on conciliation with America, delivered on the 22nd March 1775, when the sands were fast running out and war was imminent, his proposition was simply peace. Refined policy, he said, had ever been the parent of confusion ; plain good intention was much more efficacious. ' Genuine simplicity of heart is an healing and cementing principle.' Again he refused to enter into the technicalities of the right to tax. It was a Serbonian bog. ' I do not intend to be overwhelmed in that bog, though in such respectable company. The question with me is not whether you have a right to render your people miserable ; but whether it is not in your interest to make them happy.' He discussed the nature of the ties that essentially bind the mother country and her colonies. They were kindred blood, common privileges, ' light as air, . . . strong as links of iron. Let the colonies always keep the idea of their civil rights associated with your government—they will cling and grapple to you ; and no force under heaven would be of power to tear them from their allegiance.'

These were maxims of policy on which Great Britain acted in later days ; but, impervious to the eloquence and wisdom of Burke, she was moved only by the catastrophe of the loss of her thirteen colonies.

In 1782 the Rockinghams came into power for a second time, Burke in the post of Paymaster of the Forces. His aristocratic friends would have regarded the holding of a higher position by one not belonging to their social standing as indecorous. In February he introduced a Bill for Economical Reform, his object being partly the lightening of taxation, but much more, the cutting off of those means of bribery by which the Crown was able to exert control over the House of Commons. This was Burke's specific in place of the reform of Parliament. In that he did not believe. He was greatly afraid of any measure so drastic. Acknowledging the glaring inequalities in the distribution of seats, he saw no real disadvantage in this ; indeed it 'is perhaps the very thing which prevents us from thinking or acting as members for districts. Cornwall elects as many members as all Scotland. But is Cornwall better taken care of than Scotland ? ' He repudiated the idea of the member of Parliament being merely the delegate of his constituency. He was bound to give its interests his greatest respect and attention, to labour unceasingly to further it, but, as he bluntly told the electors at Bristol, ' his unbiased opinion, his mature judgment, his enlightened conscience, he ought not to sacrifice to you, to any man, or any set of men living . . . and he betrays, instead of serving you, if he sacrifices it to your opinion ' ; and once in Parliament, he stands for the interest, not of one particular locality, but of the whole nation.

But Burke disliked radical plans of reform because he suspected innovation, and because his deference to, and admiration for, the Constitution knew no bounds. It was a sacred thing, not to be tampered with. Political institutions were the gradual work of evolving time and circumstance. They had become adapted to the nation's needs and were an expression of its essential character. Political society was a living organism, not a mere mechanism which could be stopped and restarted, taken to pieces and remodelled all at will. The greatest characteristic of Burke is that he has the historic sense ; he sees in the institutions of the present the potent emblem of the undying past. Possessing that imaginative historic sense, he had a tendency towards conservatism. That which had been evolved out of the changing associations and requirements of successive generations had proved its right to exist by the fact of its existence. To Burke, therefore, all time-honoured institutions were sacred. He was a great defender of the rights of private property ; he believed in the aristocratic principle. The great landowning houses, because of the connexion between their families and the course of English history ' become the public repositories and office of record for the Constitution '. Burke's conservative tendency

grew. It was remarked that in his speeches in the impeachment
of Warren Hastings for his alleged misgovernment in India he
was most of all roused by any hurt done to an ancient dynasty
or ancient religion, pagan though it might be. The climax came
with the outbreak of the French Revolution. His *Reflections*
on that event is his most famous work. When opinion in England
on the Revolution was largely in favour of the revolutionaries,
his superbly eloquent denunciation carried the great majority
of the country with him. He could see no good in the Revolution
whatever. Passion, not reasoned argument, is the key-note of
the book. He made no attempt to appreciate the other side ;
he even became blind to all the evils against which the Revolution
was a just and inevitable protest. He hated the idea of the
Rights of Man. They were merely sophistries. The fundamental error of the revolutionaries in his eyes was that they
regarded political inequalities as moral injustices, thought of
forms of government, not as matters of expediency, but as
matters of equity ; of government as a sort of sacred performance instead of as a piece of business. He repeated the argument
of his *Thoughts on the Present Discontents*. If the individual was
always to be allowed to satisfy his personal feelings about the
desirability or otherwise of every political institution, there
could never be any stability at all, there would always be revolution. Burke would have agreed with Mr. Max Beerbohm when
he says, ' Fallacies and anomalies are the basis of all good government.' In order to serve all the diversified needs of human
society, government cannot be simple and symmetrical, it is
bound to be complex. Simplification, however attractive it may
appear, will only make for inefficiency. Holding such views,
Burke inevitably hated the French Revolution. Because he did,
Burke was welcomed in his latter days with open arms by the
Tories.

The Revolution broke up the Whig party into two very
different groups—those who followed Burke in his conservatism,
on the one hand ; those who allied themselves with the Radicals,
on the other. Among the latter there came to be Fox and
Charles Grey, the future Earl Grey, who carried the great Reform

Bill of 1832, and who later stood definitely for friendship with the French revolutionaries, the cause of Reform and Democracy. It would be unfair to Burke to say that he was not a reformer ; for he spent most of his public life in championing reforms, economical and legal, reforms in our relations with the colonies, Ireland, India : but on the fundamental issue of the reform of Parliament, he was an adamantine opponent. In the principles of Democracy he had never believed. He belonged to the Rockinghams, the old Whigs, the Whigs of the Revolution of 1689. Much of Burke's political philosophy is of import for all time ; but the party to which he belonged was out of date.

CHARLES JAMES FOX

From a stipple engraving by J. Jones

Whence did the new inspiration come into the Whig party ? It came, of course, largely from France, and English Radicalism is mainly a child of the French Revolution. But, though they were less important, there were also earlier antecedents. Sympathy with the cause of the revolting colonies laid some of the Whigs open to part of the democratic doctrines of the Americans. Thus one of the Rockingham leaders, the Duke of Richmond, actually advocated annual parliaments, universal suffrage, equal electoral districts. But it is in the career of the infamous John Wilkes that we must find the main origin of eighteenth-century Radicalism. Whether we like it or not, as Gladstone said, Wilkes must be enrolled among the great champions of English freedom. The life of this singularly objectionable person became inextricably involved with great questions concerning the freedom of the press and our whole parliamentary and representative system. He was an exceedingly coarse, brutal, and dissolute man ; yet he became a popular idol because a great submerged force of public opinion was able to focus itself on him.

Among the supporters of Wilkes was a certain very unclerical kind of clergyman, the Rev. John Horne, better known by the name he assumed later of Horne Tooke ; and largely by his efforts the friends of Wilkes formed an organization. On the 20th February 1769 they met together and founded the Society of the Supporters of the Bill of Rights, as they called it. In 1776 Major John Cartwright started a campaign in the press, advocating drastic changes in our representative system, including the introduction of the ballot and the abolition of plural voting. The same propagandist subsequently played a large part in establishing the so-called Constitutional Society, the Society of the Friends of the People, the Hampden Club—in a word those great Radical societies which aimed at disseminating the doctrines of the French Revolution throughout England.

JOHN WILKES, Esq:
Elected Alderman of London Jan. 2. 1769

According to himself. Frontispiece (? inserted) in the 1769 edition of ' The North Briton '

What is the significance of these facts ? It is that the friends of Wilkes were the first to hit upon the device that eventually forced through parliamentary reform—that of organized agitation outside Parliament altogether, the democratic device of forming associations among those classes who had no adequate say in the government of their own country. The defect in

Burke's reasoning was that he, who laid such emphasis on the recognition of facts rather than theories, ignored the *fact* of a public opinion which was determined on having reform. So long as no one objected to the anomaly of Cornwall returning as many members as the whole of Scotland, the anomaly was harmless ; as soon as people came to regard that anomaly as

According to Hogarth. See p. 361

unendurable, it had to be remedied. As population rapidly increased towards the end of the century and its distribution drastically altered, the old *régime* became intolerable ; the absurdity and injustice of tiny disappearing villages sending two members to Parliament, while big new towns sent none, became too glaring for any intelligent person who suffered from such an anomaly to be indifferent to it. Had the protest of

Radicalism remained almost entirely outside Parliament, a very serious state of things might have ensued. Impatient with Westminster, the organized protesters might have come to the conclusion that instead of reforming it, they might as well sweep it away altogether, and a revolution might have resulted. Revolution and civil war indeed remained an ugly possibility up to the passing of the Reform Act in 1832. That they did not take place was due to the fact that the protest was not entirely outside Parliament, that there was a reform party inside Westminster, the New Whigs. They were not utterly distinct from the Old Whigs; they belonged in many instances to the great aristocratic families. Thus they formed a connecting link between the Old Whigs and the Radicals, supplied continuity between the doctrines of the English Revolution of 1689 and the French Revolution of 1789. There was much that was discordant between those principles. But Whiggism never denoted a consistent cut-and-dried body of theory; whereas it did, on the whole, enshrine a spirit of conciliation and harmony. Because it remained aristocratic, while absorbing a certain element of republicanism in 1688-9, the peaceful revolution settlement was made possible; because it remained aristocratic, while absorbing a certain element of Radicalism in 1789, the peaceful passage of the Great Reform Bill was made possible.

THE PLURALIST

IX

THE DIVINES

THE English Church in the eighteenth century has become a byword for worldliness and lethargy, though the period opened with abundant promise. Two of the most admirable of Anglican societies—the S.P.G. and the S.P.C.K., of which the latter had only been founded in 1699—were both flourishing; the Queen took the keenest and most sincere interest in the Church and gave a valuable practical expression to it by surrendering the Crown's right to first-fruits and tenths. Thus was created the fund, ever since known as Queen Anne's Bounty, for the augmentation of poor livings. The state of the Church of England was so live a political issue throughout the reign that no one could possibly ignore it. Unhappily the High Church contingent—by far the most active at this time—became so closely identified with the Tory party, that when the Tories were discomfited in 1714, they also became discredited. It is with the accession of the Georges and the ascendancy of the Whigs that apathy seems to descend upon the Church. The impression is not wholly justified. There were still plenty of zealous, high-minded, and intellectual clergy; on the other hand there were too many who possessed none of these qualities. The most distinguished bishops and higher dignitaries were often much more interested in the literary and academic world than in the organization of a diocese and the supervision of parochial activities. They were expert controversialists, not inspiring leaders and teachers; were often better witnesses of the 'reasonableness of Christianity' than of its spiritual force. The word 'enthusiasm' was anathema to the well-bred man of Georgian days, cleric as well as layman. It is noteworthy that the pious Lord Lyttelton in his work on St. Paul was at great pains to prove that the apostle was not an enthusiast. It is true that in eighteenth-century parlance the word had a different shade of meaning from that which we give it—being used as a synonym for fanaticism. Nevertheless, it is an ill thing for any society—and most of all a religious society—when it can only detect in divine possession something meretricious.

Pluralism, with its inevitable accompaniment absenteeism, was a crying abuse in the eighteenth century. It was no new phenomenon. Ever since the ecclesiastical disendowments of the sixteenth century a cluster of benefices had sometimes had to be joined together where individually they did not afford a living. It was the inadequacy of the tithes that was at fault, not the incumbent's moral character, when a clergyman had to be presented to more than one so-called living in order to provide him with a moderate competence. Scandal arose whenever a pluralist evinced a cynical disregard of the unfortunate consequences to his different parishes and made no attempt to mitigate them. Bishop Watson was not to blame because the revenues of his see were produced from the tithes of various churches in Shropshire, Leicestershire, Huntingdonshire, &c.; but he was to blame in that he not only took not the slightest interest in these churches beyond providing resident curates for them, but he was scarcely ever in Llandaff or indeed within his diocese,

A JOURNEYMAN PARSON GOING ON DUTY.

A MASTER PARSON RETURNING FROM DUTY.

The contrast between the prosperous and arrogant incumbent and the poor hard-working curate. A caricature by R. Dighton

preferring to live on his private estate in Westmorland.[1] There are far too many instances of such wilful neglect of duty—of the wealthy pluralist doing nothing or next to nothing and leaving his work to be done by a curate who subsisted as best he could on a miserable pittance of £50 a year at most and often as little as £20 or £30. Existence in such indigence was almost bound to be squalid, and the wretches who were prepared to accept it were usually only the spiritless and ill-educated. As bad as the plight of the pauper curate—or possibly worse from the point of view of the reputation of the Church—was that of the domestic chaplain, who was maintained in some opulent eighteenth-century households as part of the equipment of the establishment. He was customarily treated as a mere menial, on an equality with butler and lady's-maid.

It is so fatally easy, from dwelling upon flagrant abuses which strike the eye, to take a jaundiced view of average conditions, that emphasis will be laid in the following pages chiefly upon the nobler and less familiar aspect of the Church's record in the eighteenth century. There are things to charm us as well as to repel in the story. We must not allow the view of Parson Trulliber's pig-sties to blind us to the far more significant presence of Parson Adams with his Aeschylus, or to blot out the pretty picture of the Vicar of Wakefield and his family or the gracious portrait of Sir Roger de Coverley's chaplain. The typical country parson of the period is revealed to us in the diary of the Rev. James Woodforde, and the impression he leaves is a very pleasing one. His was a long and unexciting career. He was a scholar of New College, Oxford, and we get some vivid glimpses of a riotous and hard-drinking junior common room. After holding curacies in Somerset, he returned to the university as a Fellow and a Proctor. The rest of his life was spent as rector of the village of Weston Longeville in Norfolk. All that time,

---

[1] Bishop Watson was also—again largely *in absentia*—Professor of Chemistry at Cambridge, although at the time of his appointment he ' knew nothing at all of chemistry ; had never read a syllable on the subject ; nor seen a single experiment in it '. (*Life of Richard Watson* (1818), vol. i, p. 46.) It should be added that he was a genuinely able and learned man.

Clerical Anticipation

The parson's tithe-pig. A caricature engraved by Cruikshank

The great cause has lately been determined
that peas and beans gathered green, and carried to Market, are a rectorial or great tythe,
and not a vicarial or small one. · This is of
great consequence to the landed estates about
London, where such vast quantities are gathered green for the London markets: They
are always looked upon as great Tythes in the
parishes of Fulham, Chifwick, Ealing, Ifle-
worth, Twickenham, Kingston, &c. &c. &c.

The intricacies of the tithe in kind. A newspaper cutting of the 'nineties

except for occasional visits abroad to Norwich and Oxford, he was content with the simple routine pursuits of a small countryside. He loves out-of-door things, his dogs and his other animals, his riding and shooting. There is no evidence of servile deference to the squire, but he records with satisfaction the occasions when the latter or his family attend a service and when there are carriages at the church door. He lives in comfort and plenty. He and his household must have had colossal appetites. Only a bachelor could have induced a cook to provide such mighty meals. He will sit down to a dinner of two courses, the first consisting of soup, roast pike, roast saddle of mutton, veal collops, the second of eggs, roast fowl, orange pudding, custards and jellies. There is frequent mention of such repasts. No wonder that references to colic are also frequent. In December when he receives payment of his tithes he gives what he calls a ' tithe frolic ', or entertainment to the tithe-payers. There will be about twenty of them who sit down to dinner in the Rectory and are regaled with beef, mutton, plum puddings, wine, punch, and unlimited quantities of ale. Afterwards the company amuses itself with ' droll ' songs, and, the guests having departed, the host retires very tired to bed in the early hours of the morning. The Rector clearly takes a keen interest in all his parishioners and their doings, and particularly in their children whom he christens, and he has money and good advice for the needy and the lame dogs of the neighbourhood. The clergyman fills the place which he is expected to take in the small rural community more than adequately. There is nothing inspiring about this picture, but it is gentle and kindly and fragrant.

In this chapter we shall take a brief glance at a few of the typical divines of the eighteenth century. Four types stand out with clearness. In the earlier part of the period we are confronted with High Churchmen, on the one hand, and Broad Churchmen or Latitudinarians, on the other. In the latter part of the period interest centres in, first, the Mystics, and, second, the Methodists, which term was used to denote both the Wesleyans, who seceded from the Church of England, and the Evangelicals, who remained within it.

The very marked and often embittered division which existed between the High Church and Latitudinarian parties, most obvious in the reigns of William III and Anne, but continuing after the Hanoverian succession, was a grave misfortune for the Church of England, particularly as High Church and Low were very apt to be identified with Tory and Whig, religious questions to be identified with political questions. It was also unfortunate that there came to be a serious divergence between the Upper and Lower Houses of the Convocation, the Upper being preponderantly Latitudinarian, the Lower preponderantly High Church. It was not a salutary state of things that there should be a want of sympathy between the ordinary clergy and the bishops. It was largely due to the fact that some of the most distinguished bishops at the time of the Revolution, even among the famous Seven who had resisted James II, would not take the oaths to the new *régime*. The episcopal appointments made to sees vacated by the non-juring bishops, and indeed throughout William III's reign, went to the Broad Church party—to a number of men who had, as a matter of fact, made great reputations as preachers in the reign of Charles II, which was an age of great preachers.

Over the High Church and Tory clergy we need not linger. They are less notable than the others. Probably the rank and file were not worthy of much attention. The ordinary parish clergy in the latter part of the seventeenth century were very poorly off—many of them miserably so. There were, undoubtedly, poor country vicars who were forced into a position of dependence on their squire, and who found it expedient to follow his politics as they enjoyed his patronage. In the churchmanship of some high Tories there was not a great deal more than a fanatical detestation of Dissenters, as the Sacheverell case is sufficient evidence. The doctor himself was a most unattractive figure—a blustering, violent, illiberal man, whose strength of language was the source of his popularity. He was, says Burnet, ' a bold, insolent man, with a very small measure of religion, virtue, learning, or good sense '. This was the man who by crying up the doctrine of non-resistance and passive obedience was responsible for the downfall of the Whigs. A much more distinguished figure was the celebrated Francis Atterbury, who was one of the driving forces in the Tory party, and the most brilliant of the High Church dignitaries. It is noteworthy that it was he who composed Sacheverell's speech in his defence when he was impeached. In 1713 the Tory government raised him to the bench as Bishop of Rochester. Had Bolingbroke had time to form his intended administration in 1714, the Bishop was to have been his Lord Privy Seal. The well-known story goes that he urged Bolingbroke to proclaim the Pretender, and offered to lead the procession to Charing Cross in full canonicals. That his sympathies were Jacobite there seems no doubt, for he (with one other bishop) deliberately refrained from joining in a general episcopal condemnation

DR. HENRY SACHEVERELL
Philip Overton's engraving after Thomas Gibson

of the rising of 1715, when that rebellion broke out, and in 1722 he was found guilty of Jacobite conspiracy, deprived of his ecclesiastical dignities, and sent into exile. A much more pleasing type of High Churchman was the famous preacher, Robert South, whose name is one of the most illustrious in the history of the Anglican pulpit, a man who was long in doubt whether he could conscientiously take the oaths to the new settlement in 1689, though in the end he decided to do so, but who despite his eminence did not enjoy any high office in the Church. Offered a bishopric in 1713, towards the end of a long life, he sarcastically declined this 'gracious and surprising' offer. We may perhaps add to this list of Tory churchmen the name of the great and terrible Dean of St. Patrick's, Jonathan Swift. The churchmanship of that savage satirist, that embittered misanthrope, will always be a very difficult problem. While possessed of certain high ideals, with a strain of tenderness in his character and private religious beliefs, his inveterate cynicism, his coarseness and flippancy when dealing with divine things, made him a champion of doubtful desirability even against the freethinkers whom he so devoutly loathed. One of his last poems was a blasphemous parody of the Last Judgement.

We may turn to the Latitudinarians, who became so influential with the accession of William of Orange. Two of them became primates during the reign, the second—Tenison, a second-rate person, but the first—Tillotson, a man as lovable as he was learned. A still abler bishop of the same school was Edward Stillingfleet of Worcester, a remarkable preacher, a voluminous writer, in Burnet's opinion 'the learnedest man of the age in all respects'. He died just before the dawn of the new century —in 1699. But certainly the most famous of the Latitudinarian bishops was Gilbert Burnet, Bishop of Salisbury, and as both his character and career are full of interest, we may with advantage linger over his life for a little.

Burnet was a Scotsman, and the first thirty years of his life were spent in his native country. Robert Burnet, his father, was a remarkable man, if only because in days when Presbyterian passion ran very high he stubbornly refused to sign the Solemn League and Covenant. While wishing to remain on good terms with both parties, his own sympathies were episcopalian, and as an episcopalian his son was brought up. He was disciplined with all severity, excessively so, as the future bishop thought. His father, he said, 'humbled me with severe correction', so much so that at times he hated his father. His father also taught him, making him get up for his studies at 4 a.m. 'He perhaps loaded me with too much learning, for I was excessively vain of it,' acknowledges Gilbert. He says he had mastered the Latin tongue by the age of ten. He matriculated at Aberdeen University at the age of nine, and was a Master of Arts before he was fourteen! Despite the frequency of his chastisements, self-conceited the young Burnet undoubtedly was and self-complacent he remained till the end of his days.

He first wished to become a lawyer, but then decided in favour of the Christian ministry. While engaged on his divinity studies, he got to know—obviously to his great satisfaction—some of the most notable Scotsmen of the day—the saintly but irresolute Leighton (at one time a Presbyterian, at another an Episcopalian, who had a great influence over Burnet), and Lauderdale who managed Scotland for Charles II. Burnet also travelled on the Continent, and these early journeys undoubtedly had an important effect upon his theological views. While learning Hebrew in Amsterdam, he became acquainted with Lutherans, Anabaptists, Brownists, Papists, Unitarians, Arminians, and discovered there was so much of good in each of them that he there and then resolved 'never to go in for persecution'. He was especially drawn towards the Arminians; they 'were the men I saw in all Holland of the clearest heads and the best tempers; they had an excellent sense of the practical parts of religion (particularly of love and peace)'. When a few years later Burnet was accused of Arminianism,[1] he repudiated the charge. Free-will doctrines were anathema in Scotland, where Presbyterian and Episcopalian alike were Calvinist. But there is no doubt that already Burnet was feeling his way towards a broader theology.

In December 1664 Burnet became minister of the church of Saltoun, a village fifteen miles south of Edinburgh, and an exceedingly vigorous and earnest minister he at once showed himself to be. He used to preach three sermons a week, which according to the existing Scottish custom were expected to be an hour in length and to be delivered without the aid of notes. Four times a year he examined all his parishioners, old and

---

[1] James Arminius, the Latinized form of Hermanns or Hermannsen, theologian of Leyden, 1560–1609, led a movement in modification of the Calvinist doctrine of Predestination.

young, in the Bible and Shorter Catechism. He saw to it that everybody came to church on Sunday who was physically able to do so, and from time to time had the village searched during the service to ascertain that there were no avoidable absentees. In these days of restored episcopacy in Scotland under Charles II there was not much in the episcopal liturgy to distinguish it from the Presbyterian form. As for the episcopate Burnet was greatly dissatisfied with its conduct and policy. With an extraordinary mixture of self-assurance, courage, and effrontery this village minister, aged twenty-three, wrote a letter to the bishops of Scotland, in which he roundly denounced all their shortcomings and gave them much sound advice! The indictment was merited and the advice was sound; but it

BISHOP BURNET
Engraved by J. Smith from the painting by Riley

inevitably met with reproof, and it deserved to. While minister at Saltoun, Burnet devoured the writings of the mystics and endeavoured for two years to practise a severe asceticism; but, as he had to confess, this suited neither his constitution nor his character: and after he had nearly died of it, he abandoned the attempt.

At the end of 1669 Burnet entered on a wider sphere, becoming Professor of Divinity at Glasgow University, where he remained for the next four and a half years. Here he acquired widespread fame for the eloquence and power of his pulpit oratory, and here he accomplished his first important literary work, the *Memoirs of the Dukes of Hamilton*. But the most important feature of these years was his relation with the Duke of Lauderdale. At first Burnet was much under the fascination of that brutal and imperious minister, and very much in his good graces. The goodwill of Lauderdale secured for him an introduction to, and a very friendly welcome from, the King. He basked in the favour of the great, and at the age of twenty-eight he was offered one of the Scottish bishoprics, which he wisely declined. The attention which the young professor received both from Charles II and from the Duke of York, the future James II, seems to have made Lauderdale jealous. At all events the duke suddenly turned against him, and, becoming a vindictive enemy, easily contrived to turn the royal heart against Burnet. He was struck off the list of royal chaplains, forbidden the court, and advised by the King to go back to Scotland ; but, as he was assured by the Duke of York that if he returned there, unreconciled to Lauderdale, he would most certainly be imprisoned, he decided not to return, and therefore resigned his chair at Glasgow. So ended the Scottish part of his career.

Burnet was now cast adrift, but by the kindness of Sir Harbottle Grimston, the Master of the Rolls, he was made preacher at the Rolls Chapel with a stipend of £100 a year, and in this capacity he obtained fame as a preacher in London as he had previously done in Glasgow. He also obtained a popularity with the Whig or 'country party', owing to his quarrel with Lauderdale, which he found highly embarrassing, as it involved him in an examination before a committee of the House of Commons, which was intent upon obtaining evidence against the duke. A more enviable kind of popularity came to him owing to the appearance shortly after the Popish Plot revelations of the first volume of his great *History of the Reformation*. This event is a landmark in the development of English historical literature ; but its immediate significance in Burnet's career was that he was hailed as a champion of Protestantism at a time when anti-papal fanaticism was at its height. Curiously enough, the Popish Plot

brought him into favour with the court again. His intervention
on behalf of one accused man gave Charles II the impression
that Burnet was after all a moderate man. The two had several
meetings, and encouraged by the King's goodwill, Burnet undertook the gigantic task of endeavouring to reform Charles II's
private life—by letter ! More important by far than the Popish
Plot in its influence on Burnet's life was the episode of the Rye
House Plot and the trial of Sidney and William, Lord Russell.
Burnet was able to appear on behalf of the latter and to show
how flimsy was the evidence against him : nevertheless, Russell
was found guilty of treason and condemned to death. Burnet
was seized by an unworthy fear for his own safety ; but that
mood happily was transient, and he attended Russell during
his last days, endeavouring, together with Tillotson, to induce
the condemned man to abandon his belief in the lawfulness of
resistance to authority, in the hope that his recantation might
win a pardon. In this they failed, and before his death Russell
published a pamphlet justifying his point of view. The authorship of this pamphlet came actually to be ascribed to Burnet,
and Charles believed that he was the true culprit. Thus he was
irretrievably compromised so far as the court was concerned ;
he was dismissed from the preachership at the Rolls Chapel ;
and on the accession of James II he found it expedient to go
into voluntary exile. After wanderings in Italy, France, and
Switzerland, he took up his residence at The Hague and became
the adviser of William and Mary. The erstwhile champion of
the doctrine of non-resistance ere long took part in the expedition which turned James II off the throne of England. His
enemies attributed this to purely personal motives ; but there
is no doubt that the explanation lies principally in the fact of
James II's Romanism and the influence exerted on Burnet's
mind by the heroic episode of Russell's last days.

Burnet imagined himself to be very much in William's confidence. As a matter of fact this was not so. With Mary he was
a *persona grata*, but William did not like him.

With the accession of William and Mary to the English throne,
Burnet became Bishop of Salisbury. Henceforward his time was

divided between his diocesan work and his public duties as a member of the House of Lords. He played a prominent part in Parliament, and a particularly important and honourable part in connexion with the Toleration Act and the attempted reconciliation with the Dissenters, which was tried in a Comprehension Bill of 1689. He was also a member of a committee of Convocation which made a number of recommendations for alterations in the Prayer Book and the rubrics, with the object of conciliating Dissenters. Many very notable suggestions were made, both in the Comprehension Bill and in the committee's report, but both schemes were abortive. Burnet acquired the reputation of being a pronounced party man, and certainly in the latter part of Anne's reign he had become a very zealous Whig, but during William III's days he stood for studious moderation, and he deprecated party divisions altogether.

Conscientious as he was in his parliamentary duties, Burnet from the first made a point of putting his diocesan duties in the forefront. The latitudinarian bishops have often been accused of subordinating their primary episcopal duties to literary and other interests. This was far from being the case with Burnet. No man ever entered an ecclesiastical office with a higher ideal, nobler or more exacting resolutions; no one ever threw himself more completely into the arduous task of performance. He made the most elaborate tours of his whole diocese, getting to know all the parishes, preaching and confirming. He laid great emphasis on confirmation and gave special instructions to all incumbents on the preparation for it. He was most indefatigable in preaching. He was so careful about the training of candidates for orders that he would not delegate their examination to a chaplain, but undertook it all himself. He founded a theological college at Salisbury—the first of its kind. The universities looked on this innovation with such disfavour that ultimately it succumbed to their jealousy; but the design, at all events, was admirable. Burnet paid great attention to the encouragement of clerical societies, the discussion of parochial problems by the clergy, and he kept open house at the palace for their reception. He saw to it that his clergy worked hard. He endeavoured to equalize

the emoluments of livings and to augment those of the small
ones. To Bishop Burnet is due the idea of augmenting poor
livings, not only in his own diocese, but throughout the whole
country from a public fund—a scheme which Queen Mary in
vain tried to carry out during her brief lifetime, but which
reached fruition in the next reign in the shape of Queen Anne's
Bounty.

In Anne's reign he became more engrossed in political matters.
Though still holding to moderation, consorting rather with
Somers and Cowper than Orford and Wharton for example, he

A medal struck to commemorate the foundation of Queen Anne's Bounty

developed more violent views. He was a strong supporter of
the war, while his duties as preceptor of the unhappy little
Duke of Gloucester, Anne's last surviving child, who died in
1700, had brought him into close touch with the Marlboroughs.
But most of all his partisanship was due to the fears of Roman
Catholicism. He was early tortured by an alarming fear of an
attempted Jacobite restoration, and he did his best to convey
his alarms to the Queen. He felt eased in his own mind having
done this, although he saw he had made little impression. He
returned to the charge later on, and drew a blood-curdling
picture of the consequences of ' making peace without Spain '.
In less than three years, he prophesied, the Queen would be
murdered and fires would be again raised in Smithfield. Burnet
did not long survive the real or imaginary terrors of the Tory

administration. He had the satisfaction of witnessing the peaceful accession of George I, but died on the 17th March 1715.

The character of Bishop Burnet is clear-cut. William III once said, not very kindly, he wished he knew everybody as well as he knew the Bishop of Salisbury. He was transparent enough. An extraordinary vigour and vitality is his most outstanding feature. He was a tremendous worker. His literary activities were a life-work in themselves, including his *History of His Own Time*, the *Pastoral Care*, a dissertation on the Thirty-nine Articles, in addition to his *History of the Reformation* and very many smaller productions. He had a vigorous and powerful, though not a profound and certainly not a subtle, intellect. He had plenty of common-sense and broadmindedness, but not a great deal of penetration. He was childishly self-conceited. He was a dreadful busybody, very inquisitive, very talkative and indiscreet, an inveterate gossip. He was utterly lacking in tact. His taste was far from impeccable. But he was essentially humane, kindly, and sympathetic ; he was ardent in the pursuit of his duty and in the advancement of the interests of the Church and the country that he loved so well, for he was a most fervid churchman and as fervid a patriot. And we must not think of the religion of the latitudinarian Bishop Burnet as being merely a matter of morals and the intellect ; it was emotional as well.

The Walpole era was not a happy one for the Church of England. Walpole, as far as possible from being a religious man, regarded the establishment merely as a piece of state mechanism. He was not hostile to the Church, except that he regarded its High Church members as potentially dangerous ; simply he regarded it from an essentially mundane point of view. Convocation, the independence of whose Lower House had made it obnoxious to secular authority in its long controversy with the Bishops since 1701, was allowed to remain in virtual abeyance. It transacted no business between 1712 and 1852. Walpole's adviser in Church affairs was Gibson, Bishop of London, a voluminous writer, an honest and outspoken man, a real power behind the scenes. Also influential was Benjamin Hoadly, successively Bishop of Bangor, Hereford,

Salisbury, and Winchester, and confidant of George II's consort, Queen Caroline, a most able man. He is best known because of the Bangorian controversy, so called because he was Bishop of

BENJAMIN HOADLY, BISHOP OF BANGOR

From the picture by William Hogarth in St. Catharine's College, Cambridge

Bangor when he published the works in which he defended the Erastian position[1] and maintained that Christ ' left behind no

---

[1] Thomas Lieber, or Erastus (1524–83), maintained that the Christian Church had no rights of jurisdiction, no authority to excommunicate, &c. After him, those who believe in the supremacy of the State in ecclesiastical matters are known as Erastians, though Lieber himself never explicitly discussed the problem of the relations between Church and State.

visible, human authority'. The typical higher clergy of this period were like Hoadly in being essentially men of letters and controversialists, taking a very keen interest in intellectual matters, and applying a rationalist and critical spirit to theological and ecclesiastical questions. They were broad-minded men and were as a rule in favour of comprehension, or the inclusion of Protestant dissenters in the communion of the Church of England; but they were inferior to the earlier Latitudinarians in being less earnest and vigorous, less assiduous in the pursuit of their diocesan duties. Hoadly, for example, was negligent in this respect, and indeed was hardly ever seen in Bangor when he was its bishop. While there was a good deal of heterodoxy inside the Anglican Church as well as outside it, Walpole's bishops as a rule were the active opponents of Unitarianism as well as of the popular Deism of the day. There was, for example, Archbishop Wake, as zealous in denunciations of Arianism as he was kindly disposed to the Dissenters and interested in the question of a true Catholic reunion of the dissevered churches.

Some of these clerics took a very pessimistic view of the moral conditions of their own day. Sherlock, successively Bishop of Bangor, Salisbury, and London, is rampant in his diatribes against the ill-living and irreligion of all classes. He took full advantage of a very bad panic caused in London in 1750 by several severe earthquake shocks to bring this lesson home to his own diocese. Archbishop Secker (1693–1768) was equally convinced of the essential evil of the times. There were other bishops, for example, Warburton, Bishop of Gloucester, who were frank optimists, thoroughly contented with the conditions in the Church and society. His watchwords were reasonableness and moderation. The Church of England, he believed, was in a perfectly healthy state so long as she purged herself of all foolish aberrations, extremes, and enthusiasms. He zealously did battle for the establishment, against the Deists and the Non-jurors, but also against the Mystics and the Methodists.

A bishop of a very different type from Gibson, Secker, Warburton, &c., was Joseph Butler, Bishop of Durham (1692–1752), famous as the author of *The Analogy of Religion*, one of the greatest books of the eighteenth century, in which he sought to 'defend the great truths of natural religion, and those of the Christian revelation which follow from them, against all opposers', but which is directed really against the Deists. Butler's dissimilarity from his brethren lay in his reserve, his shrinking from the political world, which they rather courted ; not in the essential character of his controversial work. He, like them, makes his appeal to the reason, eschewing sentiment and enthusiasm.

A number of illustrious names have been mentioned, and they honour the Church to which they belong. At the same time their very eminent virtues were not enough to secure the well-being and influence of the Church, very largely because of the lack of that very enthusiasm which they all so greatly dreaded. In carefully steering between the ritualism of Rome and the austerity of Puritanism, they were adopting a *via media* which had nothing obviously attractive in it save to a small intellectual minority. While the dignitaries were distinguished by intellectual eminence, the mass of the clergy, not possessing that qualification, had little to recommend them. Too often their standard was lamentably low and the performance of their parochial duties perfunctory in the extreme.

The need for a much higher standard of diocesan and parochial work was realized by one Georgian bishop at all events, the saintly Bishop Wilson of Sodor and Man (1663–1755), who laboured with immense zeal and thoroughness and made his diocese a model for all those on the English mainland. But the inspiration of the religious revival of the eighteenth century was to come from a different type of man from Bishop Wilson.

The most effective reply to Hoadly in the Bangorian controversy was written by a clergyman but little known at the time, but who soon after became celebrated as the author of *A Practical Treatise upon Christian Perfection* and *A Serious Call to a Devout and Holy Life*—William Law. Later in life, Law came under the influence of Jacob Boehme, the Moravian peasant, who may be termed the founder of modern mysticism, and after William Blake, Law was certainly the greatest of English eighteenth-century mystics. But his later works had no such influence as the two already mentioned, which exerted an extraordinary effect upon men of the most diverse types. Dr. Johnson confesses that before he went to Oxford he was a lax talker against religion, but then he discovered *A Serious Call* and 'found Law quite an over-match for me ; and this was the first occasion of my thinking in earnest of religion'. Gibbon also was impressed by the power of the same book. Its force lay in the emphasis it laid upon the need of personal holiness, upon the inward spiritual character of religion. As a rule it has been men who have struck this note that have been the great religious reformers. Law did not himself institute a new movement, but, though a High Churchman and one who had serious qualms about taking the oaths, this mystic was, through the Wesleys, the inspirer of the great Evangelical movement.

The figures of John and Charles Wesley and George Whitefield are familiar enough, and no attempt will be made here to retell the well-known story of their lives and of the great movement they initiated. It will be sufficient to note that the two brothers were brought up in ways of piety by their parents in the village parsonage of Epworth in Lincolnshire, amid unhappy surroundings which are described in Sir Arthur Quiller-Couch's novel, *Hetty Wesley* ; that together with twelve others they founded their little society in about 1729 at Oxford, where John was for six years a Tutor at Lincoln ; that they early evinced their zeal for the practical service of their fellow men by visiting the sick and prisoners in the jails, as well as by the strictness and earnestness of their religious views. Then came the mission career in the new colony of Georgia, where John came under the influence of the Moravians. It was at this time that he suddenly ' discovered' the intense importance of the doctrine of Justification by Faith,[1] experienced that metamorphosis of spirit which is termed conversion, and felt an absolute assurance of salvation. After this, much as he had originally been influenced by Law, he reproached him with having kept back the very fundamentals

---

[1] The doctrine that salvation is achieved, not by a man's own works or merit, but by his faith in the redeeming power of Jesus Christ.

GEORGE WHITEFIELD, 1714–70

JOHN WESLEY, 1703–91

of Christianity. Henceforward Wesley emphasized the importance of the missionary spirit, of the preaching of the gospel for the quickening of men's faith and the transformation of their lives ; that is to say, he was what we call an evangelical.

Charles Wesley also worked in Georgia, following his brother's example. But it is a mistake to think of him as merely a pale reflection of John, simply as the hymn-writer of the movement. He was no mere copyist, but a man of great will-power and initiative. The third member of the triumvirate was the most moving preacher of the three : indeed his eloquence was perhaps the most powerful of the century. Where Chatham moved hundreds, Whitefield drove to a very madness of religious fervour many thousands, chiefly of course the less educated members of the community ; but he impressed men of all classes and types, even so sophisticated an auditor as Lord Chesterfield, others as sceptical as Hume and Bolingbroke. He impressed Garrick because of his astonishing histrionic gifts, his great dramatic power, and the startling vividness of the realistic imagery and the homely illustrations that he used. Whitefield was a man of few ideas and distinct narrowness of outlook, his taste was far from perfect, and he could be maudlin and vulgar as well as finely inspiring.

There is no doubt that such revivalist preaching as this produced a great deal of pure hysteria, which was not only of no lasting value, but was positively dangerous. It is also true that John Wesley was an exceedingly superstitious man. He believed wholeheartedly in the reality of witchcraft, demoniacal possession, and other Satanic manifestations, and the influence of Wesleyanism thus tended to foster credulity in what had been essentially an age of reason and critical inquiry. It is also true that the current idea that Wesleyanism at once produced a revival in the English Church is not borne out by the facts. Its results in that respect were not immediate. On the other hand, as to the profound impression created on certain classes of the population by the fervour of the Wesleyan field preachers there is no question—upon the rough miners of Kingswood, Lancashire, and Cornwall, and still more markedly in Wales.

EIGHTY SEVEN YEARS HAVE I SOJOURNED ON THIS EARTH,
ENDEAVOURING *TO DO GOOD.*   *John Wesley.*

ENGRAVED BY H. LONGMAN, LIVERPOOL

1. *James Hamilton M.D.*
2. *Rev.ᵈ John Wesley. M.A.*
3. *Rev.ᵈ Joseph Cole.*

*Drawn as they were seen walking in the Street
at Edinburgh, in the year 1790, by an eminent Artist.*

Indeed the introduction of Methodism is the greatest landmark in the modern history of the principality.

The time came when John Wesley most unwillingly found himself an outcast from the Church of his fathers, and by undertaking the ordination of ministers, created a new religious denomination outside the Church of England. There came, therefore, a breach between Methodism within and Methodism without the establishment. One other body besides the Wesleyans broke off from the Church, i. e. the small but interesting ' Lady Huntingdon's Connexion ', which owed its inception to the remarkable enthusiasm of Selina, Countess of Huntingdon (1707–91), who devoted her whole life to the endeavour to quicken religious consciousness and fervour in the upper classes. But in the 'seventies and 'eighties Evangelicalism was making headway inside the Church. The Wesleys and Whitefield had latterly differed on the subject of the doctrine of predestination. Most of the English Church Evangelicals were in this respect followers of Whitefield. Among the most notable of these early Anglican evangelicals were William Romaine, Henry Venn, and John Newton, who at Olney formed his famous acquaintance with the poet Cowper, much of whose poetry is impregnated with Methodist ideas, and who indeed did more to disseminate evangelical doctrine than Newton and all his *confrères* put together. The Evangelical movement became really powerful subsequent to 1780, in the days of Hannah More, William Wilberforce, Zachary Macaulay, and the other members of the Clapham sect, so called because in 1807 a small community of evangelicals was formed round John Venn, Rector of Clapham. Their influence at the time of the French Revolution and the Napoleonic wars and in the early reform period following 1815 is of vital importance. It has been maintained with much force that the powerful influence of the religious revival in the British Isles strongly counteracted the spread of revolutionary ideas from France and saved the country from serious class antagonism ; while it is certainly true that the motive power behind the crusade for the abolition of the slave-trade, behind the parliamentary movement for other great social reforms, behind the remarkable development of private philanthropy which is so marked a feature of the nineteenth century, was the Evangelical movement.

The history of Wesleyanism completely overshadows that of the older dissenting communities in the eighteenth century. In their annals it was not an epoch of high achievements, being

View of NORTHAMPTON *or* SPA FIELDS CHAPEL, *with the* Countess *of* Huntingdon's House *adjoining*.

Published by Alex^r Hogg, N° 16 Paternoster Row, Sepr 1 1795.

Northampton Chapel, Clerkenwell, acquired by the Countess of Huntingdon and re-opened in her Connexion as Spa Fields Chapel in 1779. Ecclesiastical litigation followed, and Lady Northampton seceded from the Established Church

principally notable for the fight made against the political disabilities imposed after the Restoration, which still survived owing to the incompleteness of the Toleration Act of 1689. Nonconformity was in serious danger from the High Church fanaticism of the Queen Anne Tories. The support of Nottingham for the Whig attack upon the peace settlement of 1711 was only purchased at the price of the Whigs' abandonment of the Dissenters, their acquiescence in the Bill against the practice of Occasional Conformity which had afforded a means of evading the stipulations of the Test Act. In 1714 Bolingbroke delivered his blow against the Dissenters' Academies, but the Schism Act was no sooner passed than it became a dead-letter owing to the Tory *débâcle* on the Queen's death. The accession of the house of Hanover brought speedy relief, the Occasional Conformity and Schism Acts being repealed in 1718. But efforts made at that time and again during Walpole's administration to secure the repeal of the Test and Corporation Acts failed,[1] Walpole himself consistently refusing to support the attempt, as he was convinced it would involve a dangerous national crisis. The Society of Friends obtained a valued privilege when in 1721 they were permitted to substitute for the oath in a court of law a form of solemn affirmation agreeable to their consciences. Atterbury violently opposed this concession, declaring that the Friends hardly deserved to be called Christians at all. A measure introduced in 1736 to soften the hardships of Quakers whose scruples would not permit of their paying tithes to the clergy of the Established Church by making the legal process of recovery as inexpensive as possible, was thrown out in the House of Lords owing largely to the strong opposition of the bishops, who showed a most uncharitable spirit, Gibson and Sherlock being particularly prominent.

In 1732 a special body known as the Nonconformist Deputies was created to look after the political interests of their coreligionists. While totally unsuccessful in their campaign against the Test and Corporation Acts, they were instrumental in bringing about the discontinuance of an odious practice carried on in the City of London, where a by-law was passed in 1742 rendering any one who refused nomination as sheriff liable to a fine of £400, and any one who, being nominated, refused to serve, liable to a fine of £600. After this in the full knowledge that the law of the land prevented Nonconformists from acting as sheriffs, they were constantly nominated expressly because they would be bound to pay the fines. In 1754 the deputies resolved to make a stand against this iniquitous system and they had the satisfaction of hearing it vigorously condemned by Lord Mansfield.

So far as the number of adherents was concerned, the Dissenting

---

[1] But to protect evaders an Indemnity Act was passed annually (from 1727 onwards).

bodies were flourishing when the century opened. Since the Revolution of 1689 there had been a rapid multiplication of meeting-houses. Many of these were simply barns and rooms in private houses; but in 1715 there were upwards of 1,100 Independent and Baptist chapels alone, not reckoning other sects, Middlesex, Essex, Somerset, and Devon being the counties with the largest totals. But there now ensued a period of decline. This was to some extent the result of the spread of Arianism. In 1718 a Presbyterian minister named Peirce was accused of teaching unsound doctrine concerning the Trinity, and an acrimonious controversy arose in the west of England. The matter was referred to the Nonconformist ministers of London and a meeting was arranged to take place in Salter's Hall, Walbrook, to discuss the problem. Over

Iohn the Quaker
Le Trembleur de Londre
Bachetone di Londra

From Tempest's ' Cryes of London ', *1711*

150 attended, but several of the most notable abstained, including

Calamy, the most eminent of Presbyterian divines, and Daniel Neal, the most eminent of the Congregationalists. The suggestion made at the meeting that those present should attest their belief in the Trinity by signing the first of the Thirty-nine Articles was strenuously resisted on the ground that the imposing of a creed in any shape or form was inconsistent with the fundamental principles of Nonconformity. The meeting did no good and the attempt to suppress Peirce merely increased his following in Devonshire. From this time Unitarianism spread with startling rapidity, especially among the Presbyterians, from whose ranks it made so many converts that the denomination, so powerful in England in the seventeenth century, sank into comparative insignificance.

There was a serious defection from Nonconformity during the century in the upper and upper middle classes, largely no doubt owing to the continuance of the political disabilities. The loss of adherents among the well-born and the well-to-do caused distress and anxiety to many of the faithful; but Philip Doddridge, the outstanding Dissenter of his generation, saw in it no cause for perturbation, and deprecated attempts to win back such apostates. In his view the strength of Nonconformity had always lain and always would lie in its hold upon the lower classes, upon the journeyman and the day-labourer. Nevertheless the disappearance of the cultured Puritan squirearchy, of the fine and noble type of country gentleman, of which Hampden and Hutchinson had been examples, was significant of a big break in the history of English Nonconformity. The old Nonconformity, which had played so great a part in the life of the nation under the later Tudors and the Stuarts, which had produced Cromwell and Milton, Baxter and Bunyan, had died out by the middle of the eighteenth century. The losses of Dissent were partly due to a distinct diminution in spiritual force and enthusiasm, for Dissenters were not immune from the lethargy which beset the Church of England. The later years of the era brought a signal revival. The evangelical fervour which Wesleyanism spread broadcast reinspired the older denominations and proved their salvation. Through it a new, virile Nonconformity was created—

All you that are for the Trinity come to
the hall that is subscribed

Four Moderators

A satire on the Nonconformist meeting which (as described in the text) was held in
Salter's Hall, Walbrook, in 1718 to discuss the growth of Arianism

From 'The Scourge', 1720

the widely diffused and influential Nonconformity of the nineteenth century.

At the opening of our period the most prominent among dissenting pastors was Edmund Calamy (1671–1732), a fine example of the old type of Puritan—courtly, scholarly, statesmanlike. But far more familiar to-day are the names of Dr. Watts (1674–1748) and Doddridge (1702–51). Having permanently enriched our hymnology, they are known to thousands who would never otherwise have heard of them, who do not know that Watts had a great reputation in his own day, not only as a most eloquent preacher but also as a philosopher, and that Doddridge was best known to his own generation as a singularly successful teacher. In the later years of the century the most arresting figures are those of two remarkable ministers, better known for their secular than for their theological learning, though they were both notable theologians. These were Richard Price (1723–91) and Joseph Priestley (1733–1804). Both were keen politicians. Together with Doddridge, Price was a stalwart advocate of the cause of the American colonists, and he was a close friend of Benjamin Franklin.[1] Both Price and Priestley welcomed the French Revolution with enthusiasm. It was the former's sermon preached in the Old Jewry chapel on 4th November 1789 in eulogy of the Revolution which provoked Burke's *Reflections* in reply. Priestley was so outspoken in his championship of the movement that on 14th July 1791 an infuriated mob in Birmingham burnt his house and his chapel. So great was his unpopularity that in 1794 he deemed it expedient to emigrate to America, where he remained for the rest of his life. He shared with Tom Paine the distinction of being created a French citizen in recognition of his support of the Revolutionary cause. Price was a distinguished economist, and his theories on the redemption of the National Debt certainly influenced the younger Pitt in the formulation of his Sinking Fund policy, though Pitt

[1] The Nonconformist bodies as a whole were strong supporters of the colonists in their resistance to taxation by the British Parliament. In this, their attitude was in marked contrast to that of John Wesley, who firmly believed in the American policy of Lord North's government.

does not seem to have shared Price's sanguine and erroneous belief that one debt could be advantageously wiped off by raising another. Priestley was a genius, possessed of a wonderfully wide range of knowledge. He was a metaphysician and a really great man of science, the ' discoverer ' of oxygen and one of the founders of modern chemistry. In the ranks of Nonconformity as well as within the Established Church the eighteenth century produced divines of exceptional learning and remarkable intellectual powers.

The lot of the Roman Catholics in the eighteenth century ought not to be passed over in silence. It has been said by Lecky that ' they were virtually outlaws in their own country, doomed to a life of secrecy and retirement, and sometimes obliged to purchase by regular contributions an exemption from prosecution.' By law Popish recusants were forbidden to travel more than five miles from home except by special licence, to come within ten miles of London, to bring an action at law. Any Roman Catholic refusing to take the oaths of allegiance and supremacy if called upon to do so was held to be a recusant. By an act of 1669 a Roman Catholic priest celebrating mass rendered himself liable to perpetual imprisonment, as did any Roman Catholic keeping a school. This statute was virtually a dead-letter, but even a largely inoperative penal code is a latent menace. The English Roman Catholics in the eighteenth century were a small and (as the few available statistics show) a probably diminishing body, yet ignorant popular fears, offspring of an unhappy past, represented them as an increasing menace to the state and rendered possible the clamour against the emancipating policy of 1778 and the ' No Popery ' fanaticism of the Gordon Riots.

Examination of Thomas Bambridge, before a Committee of the House of Commons, in 1729. Bambridge, one of the warders of the Fleet prison, was taken into custody on a charge of cruelty. At a later date he was charged with the murder of one of his prisoners, but was acquitted. Later still, he was for a time a prisoner in the Fleet himself. Hogarth depicts a manacled, almost naked prisoner on the

The ' ex libris ' of the S.P.G.

X

TWO PHILANTHROPISTS
JAMES OGLETHORPE AND JOHN HOWARD

THE idea of social reform by means of parliamentary action
and private philanthropy, so familiar in these days, is of very
recent growth. In the eighteenth century the statesman considered that it was his duty to administer, not to carry through
an elaborate legislative programme. The social legislation of
the Pelhams is quite exceptional. Equally uncommon was the
organization of private benevolence. The reigns of William III
and Anne had been notable for the energy of the great religious
associations, the S.P.G. and the S.P.C.K. and the Societies for
the Reformation of Manners, whose activities mainly took the
shape of securing prosecutions for drunkenness, blasphemy, and
sabbath-breaking. But the great impetus to philanthropy was
the Evangelical movement, which inspired much practical
reform in the later years of the eighteenth century.

The most notable of the philanthropists in the earlier part of
the century was James Oglethorpe, best known as the planter of
the colony of Georgia and familiar to many as a friend of Johnson
and Boswell. The latter must have been a very pertinacious
acquaintance, for he records, ' I was not only invited to make one
in the many respectable companies whom he entertained at his
table, but had a cover
at his hospitable board
every day when I hap-
pened to be disengaged '.
Johnson, while com-
plaining that 'the variety
and vivacity of his con-
versation made it too
desultory ', valued the
animation and learning
of one whom an adven-
turous career had pro-
vided with a great fund
of interesting knowledge
and experience.

General James Oglethorpe
Sketched from life at the sale of Dr. Johnson's books,
18 February 1785

When Johnson knew
him Oglethorpe had
already made a great
reputation. He had
started life as an ensign
in the army and had
served in the final stages
of the War of the Spanish Succession. He then joined the army
of Prince Eugène as a volunteer and fought against the Turks,
being present at the capture of Belgrade in 1717. In 1722 he
entered the House of Commons and gave evidence of a possible
Jacobite tendency by espousing the cause of Bishop Atterbury
when the latter was tried for conspiracy.

The public life of Oglethorpe might henceforth have become
purely parliamentary—and for such he was temperamentally
unsuited—had it not been for his friendship with a man called

REASONS

For Establishing the

COLONY of GEORGIA,

With Regard to the

TRADE of GREAT BRITAIN,

THE

Increase of our People, and the Employment and Support it will afford to great Numbers of our own Poor, as well as foreign persecuted PROTESTANTS.

With some Account of the COUNTRY, and the Design of the TRUSTEES.

By Benjamin Martyn, Esq.

Hoc Natura præscribit, ut homo homini, quicunque sit, ob eam ipsam Causam tamen, quod is homo sit, consultum velit.

CICERO De Officiis, Lib. III.

LONDON.

Printed for W. MEADOWS, at the *Angel* in *Cornhill.* MDCCXXXIII.

On the left, the title-page of a pamphlet expounding Oglethorpe's idealist aims

On the right, an extract from ' The London Magazine' of 1744

From a generous Care and Concern for Mankind, and, a Compassion for the Distressed of every Profession and Clime, he undertook the Settlement of the Colony of *Georgia*, whose Happiness he attended to like a true Patriot, and Thousands, with Justice, bless the Name of their Deliverer. It will not, I hope, be counted a Presumption, if I hint at what might be the Cause of the Ingratitude that many of those Settlers, excited by some bad Persons in a neighbouring Government, have shewn him. The Design of the Settlement was, to provide an Asylum or Place of Refuge for the honest, industrious Poor, and the Unfortunate, with some View to the Relief of the persecuted Protestants in *Germany*. Amongst these unfortunate Persons, it could not be guarded against, that Numbers, unfortunate by their own Vices, or Follies only, intruded themselves amongst the real Objects of Charity. These had no worthy Views, and only sought, in this Country, Means to renew their Riots and Excesses, and to escape the just Punishment Heaven had inflicted upon them. The General was constantly, I suppose, obnoxious to this Crew, as his Manners and Example dictated the utmost Severity of Morals, and Simplicity of Dress and Behaviour.

See page 323

Castell, who was imprisoned in the Fleet as a debtor. Owing to his complete poverty Castell was unable to pay the warder of the prison those fees which would have secured for him fairly decent treatment, and he was consigned to a house where the inmates were down with small-pox ; he caught the disease and died of it. This incident attracted the attention of Oglethorpe to the dreadful conditions prevalent in English prisons generally. He resolved to conduct a private investigation into the whole matter and in 1729 he succeeded in securing a parliamentary inquiry, which revealed many atrocities—such as gross lack of proper provision for the sick, scandalous underfeeding, the barbarous use of heavy manacles and of the thumbscrew. Perhaps the worst feature of all was the existence of a disease peculiar to prison life and known as jail fever, an intensely contagious malady, which was entirely due to insanitary conditions—insufficiency of nourishment, overcrowding, absence of drainage, of open-air exercise for the inmates. Such a state of things was allowed to exist because the national conscience had not yet learnt to concern itself with what happened to the malefactor once he had been found guilty and had passed from the court to the jail.

The case of the debtor Castell opened Oglethorpe's eyes, not only to the state of the prisons, but to the unhappiness of the poor and the problem of pauperism. England had up to this time provided two main remedies—the workhouse, and the foreign plantation or colony. Paupers and wastrels had been sent forth from our shores to be pioneer settlers in our American and West Indian possessions. The latter expedient appealed to Oglethorpe. It was not new in itself, but he proposed a new adaptation of it. He explained his views in an anonymous pamphlet, which appeared about the same time that he obtained a charter for a new colony south of the river Savannah, to be run upon the lines he had indicated. This was in 1732. The settlers were all to be poor people, for whom the mother country seemed to have no place. But Oglethorpe did not intend to start his experiment with mere wastrels and he selected paupers of the better type. The scheme obtained government support and a parliamentary grant because incidentally the colony was to have a semi-military character as a defensive outpost against the Spaniards in Florida. Another distinctive feature of the colony was to be the prohibition of all negro slave labour. But it soon proved that the most significant characteristic of all was the all-importance of the part played by the masterful personality of the Governor, Oglethorpe himself.

In the autumn of 1732 he sailed with 120 pioneer settlers. These were followed by batches of Moravians banished from Austria because of their religious convictions, and of Scottish highlanders. Two towns were started—Savannah, and sixty miles to the south on the sea-coast, Frederica. All was going well when in 1734 Oglethorpe returned to England on a visit. His departure at once revealed the defects of his system. He had already proved himself a man of great enterprise, initiative, and strength of character, a born leader of men. By dint of these qualities he had kept order among his ill-assorted settlers ; but, his strong hand removed, discontents immediately broke out on account of Oglethorpe's rigid prohibition, not only of slaves, but of rum. There was a good deal of turbulence in Georgia during his absence.

On his return the general brought with him the two brothers John and Charles Wesley, the latter as his personal secretary, to supervise the moral and spiritual welfare of the settlement. General and secretary do not appear to have got on well together —the former was too domineering, the latter too independent— and Charles soon returned to England. His place was taken by the third of the great revivalists—George Whitefield. Their experiences in Georgia had a marked influence on the Methodists, especially on John Wesley ; for the budding community, small as it was, contained the most diverse elements, in religion as well as in race and language, and it was perforce tolerant of religious differences. John Wesley was especially impressed by the Moravians who, he found, treated him as the merest novice in religious experience and understanding.

Much of Oglethorpe's time was necessarily devoted to the defence of the colony against the Spaniards. Long before the outbreak of the War of Jenkins's Ear there were threatenings of trouble, and the general made preparations accordingly. He raised a volunteer regiment of 600 in England and concerted alliances with native Indian chiefs. When war actually broke out in 1739, the Spaniards took the initiative, but with practically no result. Oglethorpe retaliated by attacking the Spanish settlement of St. Augustine. He took certain isolated forts, but the capture of the town itself proved beyond his powers, especially when he was abandoned by his Indian allies, who resented his efforts to restrain their savagery. The expedition at any rate saved Georgia from further attack till 1742, when the Spaniards made a formidable attack on Frederica, which Oglethorpe met with great skill and courage. What ultimately saved the colony was a successful game of bluff ; for he disseminated false intelligence to the effect that the colonists were eager for the Spaniards to come on again, as they were sure of victory with the co-operation of a British fleet, which he alleged to be off the coast. Whitefield was so much impressed by the greatness of the colony's danger that he declared that its deliverance could only be paralleled by certain providential deliverances in the Old Testament.

It is typical of the lack of a real colonial policy on the part of the British Government that no public moneys had been allotted to the defence of Georgia, and Oglethorpe was faced with serious financial troubles which necessitated his return to England. He was on the point of embarking once more for America when the Jacobite rebellion of 1745 broke out, and he was attached to the forces of the Duke of Cumberland in the pursuit of the retreating Scots. In a minor engagement at Clifton in Westmorland he was defeated. He was subsequently court martialled, but acquitted, though his former supposed Jacobite inclinations appear to have been brought up against him. Oglethorpe did not again return to America and the remainder of his long life was quite uneventful. He died at an advanced age, variously given as 90 and 104. The intrepid soldier, colonizer, and philanthropist is immortalized in Pope's couplet:

> One, driven by strong benevolence of soul,
> Shall fly like Oglethorpe from pole to pole.

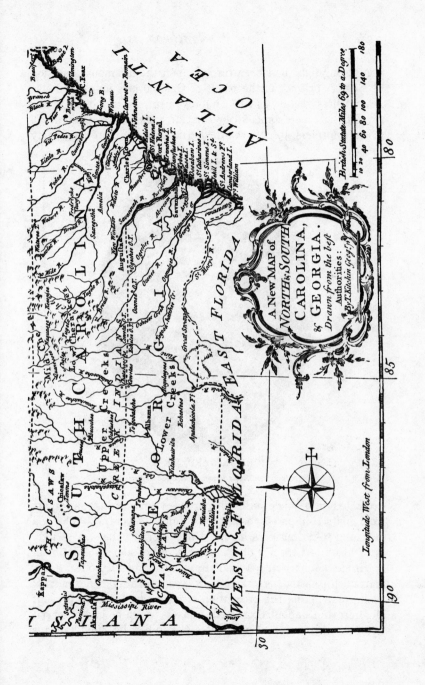

A New Map of
NORTH & SOUTH
CAROLINA,
& GEORGIA.
Drawn from the best
Authorities:
By T. Kitchin Geog.

A strong light had been thrown upon the infamous condition of English prisons as the result of Oglethorpe's investigations ; nevertheless there was little improvement, as is shown by the revelations made some fifty years later by the greatest of all prison reformers, John Howard. No life was ever more completely

JOHN HOWARD, F.R.S.

From the painting by Mather Brown in the National Portrait Gallery

dedicated to a single unselfish purpose than was his, and apart from his self-imposed task it was quite uneventful. The son of a well-to-do business man, a Nonconformist, he was strictly brought up. At the age of twenty-five, out of some odd notion of gratitude, he married his landlady, a widow of fifty-one. Their married life lasted less than three years. In 1758 he married again, first taking the precaution of arranging ' that to prevent all altercations about those little matters which he had observed to be the chief cause of uneasiness in families, he should always

Prison early in the eighteenth century

Reproduced from an original design made for Swift's 'Tale of a Tub' and now in
the possession of Capt. C. A. Fountaine of Narford Hall in Norfolk

decide '. His biographer observes that ' he entertained the most
exalted notions of the authority of the head of a family—notions
derived rather from the scriptural authority of patriarchal times,
than from any of our modern codes of ethics, or systems of
education '.

Prior to his second marriage, in 1756, an experience had
befallen Howard which moulded his future career as the Castell
incident did Oglethorpe's. On his way to Lisbon, the packet on
which he sailed was captured by a French privateer and he, with
the other passengers, was taken prisoner of war. The barbarous
treatment to which they were subjected both on shipboard and
in prison made a permanent impression on Howard and gave him
his life-work. In 1773 he became High Sheriff of Bedfordshire,
and from that date till 1790 he was continuously employed in
prolonged visitations of prisons, not only in the British Isles,
but all over Europe. His great work, *The State of the Prisons*,
was first published in 1777 ; appendices were issued in 1780
and 1784, and the final edition was a great compendium of the
fullest and most detailed knowledge. He had realized that to
make himself master of his subject, he must become acquainted
with conditions on the Continent. Thus he knew the best and
the worst that was being done, the best that could be done.
In other words, he had undertaken unaided the sort of task that
would nowadays be entrusted to a royal commission. He had
borne the entire cost into the bargain, refusing all government aid,
spending £30,000 out of his own resources.

Not content with his exhaustive examination of the prisons
of Europe, in 1785 he started a thorough investigation of the
lazarettos and quarantine stations, with a view to discovering
the best means of preventing plague. From France and Italy
he went on to the Levant, to Malta, Smyrna, and Constantinople.
In order to verify reports he had received by personal experience,
he deliberately boarded a plague-stricken ship at Smyrna,
incidentally had the excitement of being attacked by a Tunisian
corsair while on the voyage, and on arrival at Venice was
quarantined in two lazarettos for forty-two days. In 1789 he
published the results of these later journeys.

A Select and Impartial

ACCOUNT

OF THE

Lives, Behaviour, and Dying
Words, of the most remarkable

CONVICTS,

From the Year 1725, down to the present Time.

CONTAINING

Amongst many Others, the following, *viz.*

Catherine Hayes, for the barbarous Murder of her Husband.

Edward Bunworth, Wm. Blewit, and five more, for the Murder of Mr. *Ball,* in St. *George's-Fields.*

James Cluff, for the Murder of his Fellow Servant, *Mary Green.*

John Gow, alias *Smith,* Captain of the Pyrates, for Pyracy and Murder.

Mr. *Maynee,* one of the Clerks of the Bank of *England,* for cheating the Bank of 4420 l.

Mr. *Woodmarsh,* for the Murder of Mr. *Robert Ormes.*

John Sheppard, who made his Escape out of the Condemn'd-Hole, and likewise out of the Stone-Room in *Newgate.*

Robert Hallam, for the barbarous Murder of his Wife, by throwing her out of Window.

Mr. *Shelton,* the Apothecary, a Highwayman.

Sarah Malcomb, for the barbarous Murder of *Ann Price, Eliz. Harrison,* and *Lydia Duncomb,* in the *Temple.*

John Field, Joseph Rose, Wm. Bush, and *Humphry Walker,* for entering the House of Mr. *Lawrence,* and Mr. *Francis.*

Fælix quem faciunt aliena Pericula cautum.

VOL. II.

LONDON:

Printed by J. Applebee, for J. Hodges, at the *Looking-Glass,* on *London-Bridge*; and sold also by C. Corbett, at *Addison's-Head,* opposite St. *Dunstan's-*Church, in *Fleet-street.* M,DCC,LX.

In the same year he set out upon the last of his travels, and made his way into Russia in order to investigate the truth of reports he had heard of the bad state of military hospitals there. While visiting a Russian army on the Turkish frontier he himself contracted camp fever and died of it in January 1790. It is worthy of note that the first statue admitted into St. Paul's Cathedral was the one erected by public subscription to Howard's memory.

Public recognition had been won long before his death. Ten years earlier Burke had pronounced an eloquent eulogy upon his work. Howard had, he said, travelled, not as others did for pleasure, but ' to remember the forgotten, to attend to the neglected, to visit the forsaken '. His plan had been original, as full of genius as it was of humanity ; ' it was a voyage of discovery ; a circumnavigation of charity '. Burke spoke of the genius of Howard's work ; but what was really most striking in it was its conscientious devotion, its persevering determination. Howard was a man, not of brilliant mind, but of powerful will and untiring purpose. Deeply religious, he was strict in his views, severely simple in his habits—plain in dress, a vegetarian and teetotaller. But he was by no means bigoted or strait-laced ; just as, though one of the greatest of philanthropists, there was no sentimentality about him.

We may now take a glance at some of the details of Howard's work, at the abuses he discovered in the prisons, the remedies he advocated.

First of all, there was often a scandalous insufficiency of food. Magistrates were known sometimes to dismiss the question with the words, ' Let them work or *starve* ', and certainly prisoners were supposed to be able to support themselves by the hard labour to which they had been sentenced ; but as a matter of fact they were not supplied with the necessary tools or materials, and spent their time ' in sloth, profaneness, and debauchery '. The water supply was also insufficient—both for drinking and washing. There was a dreadful lack of fresh air ; what air there was in the prisons was tainted and noxious. So offensive did Howard's clothes become after visiting some of the prisons

TREATISE

ON THE POLICE OF LONDON.

The volume lately published under the above title by one of the Police Magistrates (Mr. Colquhoun, late of Glasgow), may be justly considered as one of the most valuable publications of the present day, containing a mass of information respecting the metropolis, that equally surprises and interests, and suggesting plans for the improvement of its police, which we sincerely hope to see speedily adopted by the Legislature.

The following is the estimate made in the above work, of the persons who are supposed to support themselves, in and near the metropolis, by pursuits either criminal, illegal, or immoral.

1. Professed thieves, burglers, highway robbers, pick-pockets, and river pirates, who are completely proselyted; many of whom have finished their education in the hulks, at Botany Bay—2000.

2. Professed and known receivers of stolen goods, of whom eight or ten are opulent—60.

3. Coiners, colourers, dealers, venders, buyers, and utterers of base money, including counterfeit foreign and East India coin—3000.

4. Thieves, pilferers and embezzlers, who live partly by depredation, and partly by their own occasional labour—8000.

5. River pilferers, viz. fraudulent lumpers, scuffle-hunters, mud-larks, lightermen, riggers, artificers and labourers in the docks and arsenals—2500.

6. Itinerant Jews, wandering from street to street, holding out temptations to pilfer and steal, and Jew boys crying bad shillings, who purchase articles stolen by servants, stable-boys, &c. generally paying in base money—2000.

7. Receivers of stolen goods from petty pilferers at old iron-shops, store-shops, rag and thrum-shops, and shops for second-hand apparel, including some fraudulent hostlers, small butchers, and pawn-brokers—4000.

8. A class of suspicious characters, who live partly by pilfering and passing base money; costard-mongers, ass-drivers, dust-men, chimney-sweepers, rabbit-sellers, fish and fruit sellers, flash coachmen, bear-beaters, dog keepers (but in fact dog-stealers), &c. &c.—1000.

9. Persons in the character of menial servants, journeymen, warehouse porters and under clerks, who are entrusted with property, and who defraud their employers in a little way, under circumstances where they generally elude detection, estimated at about—3500.

10. A class of swindlers, cheats, and low gamblers, composed of idle and dissolute characters, who have abandoned every honest pursuit, and who live chiefly by fraudulent transactions in the lottery, as morocco men, ruffians, bludgeon-men, clerks, and assistants, during the season; who at other times assume the trade of duffers; hawkers and pedlars, horse-dealers, gamblers with E. O. tables at fairs, utterers of base money, horse-stealers, &c. &c.—7440.

11. Various other classes of cheats, not included in the above, viz. persons who set up gaming-houses in different parts of the metropolis, and sharpers who take lottery insurance—1000.

12. Fraudulent and dissolute publicans who are connected with criminal people, and who, to accommodate their companions in iniquity, allow their houses to be the rendezvous for thieves, swindlers, and dealers in base money—1000.

About 1000 public-houses change masters once or twice, and in some instances, three or four times a year in the metropolis, which are generally occupied by such characters.

13. A class of inferior officers belonging to the Customs and Excise, including what are called supernumeraries and glutmen, many of whom connive at pillage as well as frauds committed on the revenue, and share in the plunder to a very considerable extent; principally from their inability to support themselves on the pittance allowed them in the name of salary—1000.

14. A numerous class of persons who keep chandlers' shops for the sale of provisions, tea, and other necessaries for the poor. The total number is estimated at ten thousand in the metropolis; a certain proportion of whom, as well as small butchers and others, are known to cheat their customers (especially those to whom they give a little credit) by false weight, for which, excepting the parish of Mary-le-bonne, there is no proper check—3500.

15. Servants, male and female, porters, hostlers, stable-boys, and post-boys, &c. out of place, principally from ill-behaviour and loss of character, whose means of living must excite suspicion at all times—10,000.

16. Persons called Black Legs, and others proselyted to the passion of gaming, or pursuing it as a trade, who are in the constant habit of frequenting houses opened for the express purpose of play, of which there are at least forty in Westminster, where two banks are kept, or where hazard, rouge et noir &c. are introduced; of these, five are kept in the houses of Ladies of fashion, who are said to receive 30l. each rouf, besides one eighth of the profits; seven are subscription-houses; five have customers particularly attached to them; and thirteen admit foreigners, and every idle and dissolute character, who are either introduced or known to belong to the fraternity of gamblers; where a supper and wines are always provided by the proprietors of the house for the entertainment of their customers.

17. Spendthrifts, rakes, giddy young men, inexperienced, and in the pursuit of criminal pleasures—profligate, loose, and dissolute characters, vitiated themselves, and in the daily practice of seducing others to intemperance, lewdness, debauchery, gambling, and excess; estimated at—3000.

18. Foreigners who live chiefly by gambling—300.

19. Bawds who keep houses of ill fame, brothels, lodging-houses for prostitutes—2000.

20. Unfortunate females of all descriptions who support themselves chiefly or wholly by prostitution—50,000.

21. Strangers out of work, who have wandered up to London, in search of employment, and without recommendation, generally in consequence of some misdemeanour committed in the country—1000.

22. Strolling minstrels, ballad-singers, showmen, tumblers, and gipsies—1500.

23. Grubbers, gin-drinking dissolute women and destitute boys and girls, wandering and prowling about the streets and by-places, after chips, nails, old metals, broken glass, paper, twine, &c. &c. who are constantly on the watch to pillage when an opportunity offers—200.

24. Common beggars, and vagrants asking alms, supposing one to every two streets—3000.

These different descriptions of criminal and irregular people make a total of no less than one hundred and fifteen thousand!!!

From a review of Patrick Colquhoun's 'Treatise on the Police of London', c. 1796

that he could not drive back afterwards in a closed carriage, and the leaves of his memorandum book became so foul that he could not use them till they had been aired for several hours before a fire. How could human beings retain their health while spending fifteen out of the twenty-four hours in close cells or subterranean dungeons, when there was sometimes an inch or two of water on the floor and the straw or bedding was laid in this ? Sometimes there was no bedding of any kind and the prisoners had to lie on the bare floor or rags.

The crime of Catherine Hayes, the murderess, upon which Thackeray based his grim tale ' Catherine '. Having made her husband drunk, Hayes and her accomplice Billings killed him (1726). The head and then the box containing the dismembered body were found in the Thames. Billings was hanged. Hayes, as the slayer of her husband, in accordance with a barbarous law not repealed till 1790, perished at the stake

As bad as any of these evils was the indiscriminate herding together of men and women, old and young, the hardened criminal and the first offender, the sane and the lunatic. The prisons became very schools of vice and crime in such circumstances. ' In some jails ', Howard wrote, ' you see (and who can see it without sorrow ?) boys of twelve or fourteen eagerly listening to the stories told by practised and experienced criminals, of their adventures, successes, stratagems, and escapades.' Thus many who entered jail innocent enough were converted into habitual criminals, their confinement increasing ' the very vices it was designed to suppress '.

Among the bad customs which Howard denounces is that of *footing*, *chummage*, or *garnish*. When a new-comer arrived, the existing inmates of the jail were wont to greet him with the words, 'Pay or strip', which meant that he must either contribute to a common pool, or be divested of most of his garments. The money thus raised was expended on drink and gambling, which resulted in 'riot, brawling, and profaneness', and the scandal of 'debtors gaming away the property of their creditors'.

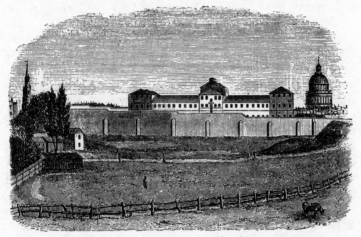

Improvement in prison-construction. The House of Correction in Coldbath Fields, Clerkenwell, built in 1794. From Pink's 'History of Clerkenwell'

Evil customs of another nature were the bringing of the wives and children of debtors into the jails, which led to overcrowding and the corruption of the children's morals ; the fact that some jails were private property and therefore not wholly under the control of the magistrates ; the fact that persons indicted for an offence were liable to be kept in prison pending their trial for a whole year, in an atmosphere of misery and corruption, to be perhaps found *not guilty* in the end.

As the first plank in his reform programme Howard placed the necessity of securing improvement in the siting and the architectural design of prisons. He advocated, in the interests of health, the selection of localities near rivers or running water. He wished to see the construction of arcaded courtyards where the prisoners could take open-air exercise even in bad weather ; the provision of individual cells and the entire separation of the men's and women's wards, of young offenders from hardened criminals ; the provision of effective ventilation, of ovens for the destruction of vermin in clothes and bedding, of chapels, and workshops where prisoners could practise their former trades.

After the advocacy of structural changes comes that of new rules to regulate the conduct of life within the jails. The character of the jailer was of paramount importance. He must be one who could exert the authority of personal example in the restraint of drunkenness and vice. As things were, many jailers ran a tap and had a direct interest in the promotion of drunkenness. To avoid such a temptation jailers should have adequate stipends ; the same applied to turnkeys and all other prison officials. Every prison should be under medical supervision, with a competent surgeon, empowered not merely to recommend, but to enforce. Much greater attention should be paid to cleanliness. Every new inmate of a jail, coming in with dirty clothes, should at once be given a bath, and his clothes should be put into an oven. Howard recommended a distinct prison uniform, regular changes of underclothing, and supplies of clean towels and washing utensils. Food allowances should be reckoned, not by money value, which varied, but by weight. Many magistrates were most remiss in inspecting prisons, being content with an outside view. Inspection must be regular and absolutely thorough. Otherwise no improvement could be permanently maintained.

All these proposals sound to modern ears such obvious common sense that the only surprising thing about them is that it should have needed a Howard to make them. It will be observed that while Howard urged the improvement of the prisons, he had no wish to see them converted into pleasant places ; he believed in rigid discipline and genuine hard labour. Prisons in his eyes were houses of correction and should be deterrents from crime. His argument was that the scandalous conditions prevalent in the jails of his day made them *productive* of crime. While the sensitive were corrupted, the hardened had no objection to conditions of uncleanliness and even delighted in the opportunities afforded for idleness and drink. The reforms which Howard advocated must make prisons more bearable to the young offender, more obnoxious to the really criminal. A strict discipline would take the place of mere chaos.

The reform of the prisons still left many evils in our penal system. It was still barbarous, disfigured by far too lengthy a catalogue of capital offences. It took all the labours of Romilly, Mackintosh, and Peel to convert the code by the middle of the nineteenth century into practically the shape it has to-day ; and even in the prisons there was still left plenty of scope for the devoted work of Elizabeth Fry among female offenders. But the names of Oglethorpe and Howard will always stand foremost among those who first brought the strong light of reason and humanity to bear upon the abuses of our penal system.

Token commemorating Howard

THE DISTREST POET. From an engraving by William Hogarth

Indigence in Grub Street.

XI

GRUB STREET

DANIEL DEFOE—SAMUEL JOHNSON

THE man of letters must be one of the outstanding types in any period which has any intellectual life at all to boast of; but a gossip about the men of letters of the eighteenth century as such would be too diffuse for a short book of this kind. It is better to take some feature of the world of letters which is fairly distinctive of our period. Hence the title of this chapter. The original and actual Grub Street, as distinct from the Grub Street of metaphor, acquired its notoriety in the seventeenth century and is thus described in Johnson's *Dictionary*—' a street near Moorfields in London, much inhabited by writers of small histories, dictionaries, and temporary poems'. Hence the term Grub Street came to be used in reference to the essentially ephemeral productions of the literary hack. That type of writing which is but a running commentary upon current events obtained a very great vogue when partisan spirit ran high in days of Cavalier and Roundhead. The oratory of Parliament was reinforced by the pamphlet and the broadside, the latter being a single sheet, sometimes embellished by a cartoon or other illustration and the letterpress, frequently in the form of doggerel verse,

Londons Gazette here 21.
Nouvelle Gazette
Chi Compra gl' avisi de Londra

From Tempest's ' Cryes of London', 1711.

in satiric style. The earliest English newspaper was probably the *Weekly News* of 1622.[1] In the days of the Long Parliament came various *Mercuries*, the *Mercurius Britannicus*, the *Mercurius Aulicus*, and so on. But under the Commonwealth and Protectorate there was a censorship, particularly strict after 1653. A very important name in the history of English journalism is that of Sir Roger L'Estrange, who in the reign of Charles II edited *The Public Intelligencer* and other periodicals. But L'Estrange was not only an editor ; he was also official licenser of newspapers, when in 1662 the government established a new censorship of the press, which was a severe restraint upon the free expression of public opinion until in 1695 the licensing laws were allowed to lapse. With the press once more free, a great number of periodicals at once rushed into existence, and in the days of Queen Anne journalism was active and important as never before.

[1] Eager interest in the events of the Thirty Years' War created the demand.

Fleet Street in the Eighteenth Century

By the courtesy of the Cambridge University Press

The majority of the contributors to the ephemeral papers of the seventeenth century had been as obscure as their writings. These inhabitants of Grub Street, trying to extract a livelihood out of journalism, were dependent upon the support of a public as yet neither sufficiently large nor sufficiently generous to make it a profitable career. Thus Grub Street was very poor and needy and its inhabitants were usually engaged in a pretty desperate struggle for existence. It was not only the mere hacks who were in this state. Literature of any type was ill-paid unless the writer was so fortunate as to obtain the favour of a wealthy patron. The profitableness of letters, that is to say, depended as yet, to a very large extent, upon the courtier. Literature could only become a democratic force with the wide diffusion of the reading habit among the population. It is not too much to say that what contributed more than anything else to the formation of that habit was the political periodical. It proved to be so attractive that not merely the common literary hucksters, but the greatest writers of the day, found powerful inducement to expend their energies upon it.

The English people have a marked political bent, and it is noteworthy that even Steele and Addison, who in the *Tatler* and *Spectator* deliberately aimed at eschewing party controversy, found this extremely difficult, and both came to be enrolled in the ranks of the party pamphleteer. There was a very powerful new type of patron in the days of Queen Anne, which has existed ever since, in the party caucus, whether in office or out. Harley especially, as we have seen, realized the value of the press to his party ; and in the two succeeding reigns the opposition to Walpole was more dangerous and influential in the press than in Parliament. A great proportion of the political writings of even the greatest authors of this age are now forgotten, save by the professed historian. This is inevitable. Articles written *ad hoc* have seldom a permanent import. On the other hand, some of them are real contributions to literature, such as Arbuthnot's *John Bull*, Steele's *The Crisis*, and in particular the great tracts of Dean Swift, *The Conduct of the Allies* and *The Public Spirit of the Whigs*, the most outstanding of a large number of works of this kind. Swift's genius for satire and invective made him very much at home in this type of literature. Even the apparently quite fictitious *Gulliver's Travels* is full of veiled allusions to contemporary politics.

Swift not only wrote political pamphlets, mainly in the interests of Harley's administration, but he also contributed copiously to an influential periodical, which was started in 1710, named the *Examiner*. Another Tory paper for which Swift wrote articles was the *Post Boy*, edited by a bookseller named Abel Roper, and the rival of the Whig *Flying Post*. These had both been started in the reign of William III, and appeared twice weekly. The first daily paper was the *Daily Courant*, begun in 1702, which, however, confined itself to a bare recital of facts, as did those publications in manuscript which were in fact as in name just *News Letters*. More important was the compendious periodical started by the Whig historian Abel Boyer, which under the title of the *Political State* ran from 1711 to 1729, being issued in monthly parts, two or three at a time. Another kind of journal popular at the beginning of the century was not a chronicle but a critique. Of this type was Defoe's *Review*.

To many people Defoe is known only as the author of *Robinson Crusoe*; to some by his other works of fiction, such as *Captain Singleton* and *Moll Flanders*. But Defoe, who was probably the most prolific writer in our literature, had produced an enormous number of works before he turned his hand to the writing of fiction at all. He was born in 1661; yet the first volume of *Robinson Crusoe*, which was his first novel, did not appear till 1719. Defoe is indeed the great exemplar of the literary Jack of all Trades, and as such he is one of the greatest citizens in the Grub Street republic.

The author of *Robinson Crusoe* came of humble parentage, his father being a butcher in the parish of St. Giles, Cripplegate, named James Foe. Thus the author's name was really Daniel Foe, but in 1706 he started signing himself De Foe or Defoe. He was originally intended for the Dissenting ministry, and he was given a very sound education in a Nonconformist school at Stoke Newington. He soon abandoned the design of becoming a pastor and started business as a hose factor in Cornhill in 1685. Then came adventurous years, for he was one of those who joined Monmouth's ill-fated rebellion, though he fortunately escaped the tender mercies of Judge Jeffreys, and in 1688 he attached himself to the army of William of Orange in its advance upon London. Thereafter Defoe returned to business, foreign trading enterprises taking him abroad to France and Spain ; but his ventures miscarried, and in 1692 he became bankrupt. He very honourably did his utmost to discharge his debts. In 1698 he began his career as a pamphleteer and in 1701 he achieved notoriety by his extremely effective doggerel poem, entitled *The True-born Englishman*. This was a very trenchant and amusing satire upon those who incessantly declaimed against King William and his Dutch friends because they were foreigners, the point being that the Englishman came of a most composite race.

> A True-Born Englishman's a contradiction !
> In speech an irony ! in fact, a fiction !

Again :

> The Pict and painted Britain [*sic*] treacherous Scot ;
> By hunger, theft, and rapine hither brought !
> Norwegian pirates, buccaneering Dane,
> Whose red-haired offspring everywhere remain ;
> Who, joined with Norman French, compound the breed
> From whence your *True-Born Englishmen* proceed !

By this publication Defoe won the personal favour of King William, only a few months before that monarch's death. The accession of Anne brought to the fore religious questions which had an intimate interest for Defoe as a Dissenter, notably the Occasional Conformity bills. He wrote two important pamphlets on this subject, but the memorable one was *The Shortest Way with the Dissenters*, which was a deeply ironical treatment of the theme. Defoe sought to expose the rabid intolerance of the High Church party, which was pressing the bills against the practice of occasional conformity, by suggesting that instead of merely restricting the liberties enjoyed by Dissenters, it would be best to have done with all toleration and extirpate the sects altogether. So faithfully had Defoe as a matter of fact reflected the true sentiments of many of the High Churchmen that they failed to perceive the irony of the pamphlet altogether and hailed it with delight as an exposition of their own views. Correspondingly venomous was their indignation when they discovered the true purport of the pamphlet and that the author was himself a Noncon-

DANIEL DEFOE
The frontispiece of ' Jure Divino ', 1706

formist. For this auda-
cious publication Defoe
was fined and imprisoned
and had to stand in the
pillory three times, while
the House of Commons
ordered the obnoxious
pamphlet to be burnt.
The lot of one condemned
to stand in the pillory was
usually a most unpleasant
one ; he might be the
target for every missile,
contumely and insult : but
the crowd which stood
round Defoe, as he took
his punishment, was
wholly sympathetic, hailed
him as a martyr and drank
his health, so that the punishment was converted into a public triumph. On the first day on which he stood in the pillory he published *A Hymn to the Pillory*, a powerful and caustic attack upon the Government. On the same day there also appeared from his pen *The Shortest Way to Peace and Union*, which was an appeal for reasonableness and common charity.

It was in July 1703 that Defoe underwent the punishment of the pillory ; it was not until August 1704 that he was released from Newgate by the intervention of Harley, who also arranged for the paying of his fine, which he had himself no funds to meet, and procured employment for him. Henceforward out of gratitude Defoe was the devoted friend of Harley. The employment he was given was secret service, the principal sphere of his activity being in Scotland. Defoe got to know the conditions of the northern kingdom very thoroughly, and one of his works is a *History of the Union*. There are extant large numbers of confidential reports and other papers on Scottish affairs, written by Defoe to Harley when the latter became chief minister.

It was while he was still in prison that Defoe started his *Review*. This paper, which ran for a period of over nine years, is a great monument of industry, seeing that it was entirely written by Defoe and amounts in all to some 5,000 printed pages. The record is the more remarkable in that during this same period its author produced eighty other distinct works, making nearly another 5,000 pages. The *Review* was from the first mainly political, though to begin with it also contained lighter matter, some pages under the title of the 'Scandal Club' being devoted to gossip about modes and morals in the manner of the later *Tatler*. The *Review* embraces a great number of different subjects, but the principal themes are foreign affairs, trade, the Scottish Union, and the issue of non-resistance as it was raised by the Sacheverell affair. The burden of his message throughout is eminently sound. He preaches reason and moderation and the assuaging of the fierce fires of party hatreds.

Up to 1710 Defoe's attitude had been unequivocal. He had been a consistent Whig. But with the accession of Harley to power his position became difficult. He felt himself bound by ties of gratitude to the man who, whatever his original plan, speedily became head of a purely Tory government. As he continued to be Harley's paid agent and as he wrote in defence of the administration, he naturally became suspect to his former friends. There is no doubt that Defoe, the Whig martyr, was something of a time-server and not altogether scrupulous. He defended the government's peace policy, although he was not enamoured of the actual provisions of the Treaty of Utrecht ; and on this subject it will now be generally admitted there was as much cause to preach moderation to the Whigs as on certain religious questions there had been reason to preach moderation to the Tories. While there were obvious points in common between Defoe and Harley, between him and the ultra-Tory, the 'high-flier' proper, there could be no sympathy. Some of the most cogent of Defoe's political writings were provoked by the supposed danger to the Hanoverian succession from Jacobite

In the pillory at Charing Cross
From the drawing by Rowlandson

intrigue. Here again he employed his favourite device of irony—in *Reasons against the House of Hanover* and *What if the Queen should die?* Again irony was not understood, and he was represented as advocating the very cause he was in fact denouncing. He was once more committed to trial; once more he owed his salvation to Harley, now Earl of Oxford. But the general result of his literary activities during the Tory administration was that on the accession of George I Defoe was in bad odour. To justify himself, in 1715 he wrote his *Appeal to Honour and Justice*. In 1718, however, he was once more engaged in journalistic work of rather doubtful honesty, being employed by the government in sub-editing Jacobite and High Church papers so as to draw the sting out of them. This meant that he had to pass for a Tory and consort with Tories. Defoe explained that he abhorred his ' bowing low in the House of Rimmon '; nevertheless he was willing to do this work, which certainly no man of a nice sense of honour would have consented to accept.

From now onwards Defoe's centre of interest was not the journal but the novel. In a period of less than twelve years, together with a mass of other miscellaneous writings, appeared *Robinson Crusoe*, the vivid and picturesque *Memoirs of a Cavalier*, *Captain Singleton*, the *History of Colonel Jack*, *Moll Flanders*, and *Roxana*, another essay in the same kind. In these works Defoe may be said to have founded in England the novel of adventure, the historical novel, and the novel of low life. To have made in *Robinson Crusoe* a fresh departure at the age of fifty-nine and to have crowded these works of genius in the last dozen years of a crowded life is an extraordinary feat, eloquent of the amazing industry and vitality of the man. Equally notable is the remarkable range of interests and knowledge revealed in these books, even were we to cut out all the lavish productivity of his first fifty-nine years. There is also a striking modernity of thought, notably in his advocacy of women's education. The moralizing, which is so familiar a feature of *Robinson Crusoe* and many of his other books, is generally of a humdrum and not very exalted order. It is the story-teller not the preacher who lives and will live. As a story-teller Defoe has few rivals. His power of vivid narrative is astonishing and indeed almost unique. In no other author who wrote both, is it so difficult to distinguish between history and fiction. The life-likeness of his *Journal of the Plague Year* has caused many to suppose it the *bona-fide* diary of one who actually lived through London's terrible visitation, although Defoe was only a very small child at the time. No doubt he had a great deal of first-hand information and there is abundance of actual fact in the narrative ; but it is not what it purports to be—a journal. The quality of naturalness, so apparent

Sterne

Sterne touting his own books at Ranelagh

From a print in the British Museum

in this work, is a characteristic of all his fiction. He is a great realist ; his fiction carries instant conviction. The power to convey the impression of actuality is allied with the capacity to impart a vivid interest to even the commonplace. He can make splendid use of statistics and mere catalogues. The inventory of Crusoe's possessions after his shipwreck has the very glamour of romance. This is a great power for the novelist to possess ; it is the greatest that the journalist *can* possess.

In the year of Defoe's death there appeared the first number of a very remarkable periodical, whose editor was the printer Edward Cave. This was the *Gentleman's Magazine*. A rival to it was the *London Magazine*, edited by Astley. A distinguishing feature of both these journals was the reports they gave of debates in Parliament. The publication of any parliamentary proceedings was in those days considered a grave breach of parliamentary privilege. Still the curiosity to know about what passed within the precincts of St. Stephen's was such that the demand produced a supply, parliamentary privilege notwithstanding. The transparent subterfuge adopted by these two periodicals was to print accounts of debates under a fictitious disguise. Thus the *Gentleman's Magazine* narrated the transactions of the Senate of Lilliput and the *London Magazine* those of the Roman Senate ; but the key to the names of the real speakers was perfectly clear. This device did not provide lasting immunity from molestation. Both Houses became angry, and Cave and Astley were both apprehended and brought before the Commons. It became more difficult and hazardous than ever to print reports of debates, and in consequence the records of debates in the forties and fifties of the century are particularly meagre. The sources from which the magazines had derived their information were, first, the materials voluntarily placed at their disposal by speakers who were only too pleased to see their speeches in print, and second, notes taken by hack-writers who made their way within the sacred portals of the two Houses for the express purpose of writing up the speeches. Among these was Samuel Johnson, who from November 1740 to February 1743 wrote the parliamentary debates for Cave.

The Gentleman's Magazine:

Lond Gazette
Londō Jour.
Fog's Journ.
Applebee's ::
Read's ::
Craftsman ::
D. Spectator
Grubstreet J.
W. ly Register
Free-Briton.
Hyp-Doctor
Daily Courāt
Daily-Post.:
Dai. Journal
Dai. Post-boy
D. Advertiser
Evening Post
St James's Ev.
Whitehall Ev.
Londō Evḗng
Flying-Post

ST JOHN'S GATE.

York Journals
Dublin ditto
Edinburgh 2
Norwich two
Exeter two
Worcester 2.:
Northamptō
Gloucester ::
Stamfo2d ::
Nottingham
Bristol News
Bury Journ.
Ipswich do.
Chester ditto
Leeds Merc.
Newcastle C.
Derby Journ.
Reading ditto
Canterbury
Boston : : : b
Jamaica, &c.

Or, MONTHLY INTELLIGENCER.

NUMBER I. for JANUARY, 1731.

CONTAINING,

/more in Quantity, and greater Variety, than any Book of the kind and Price/

I. A View of the Weekly *Essays* and *Controversies*, viz. Of Q. *Elizabeth*; Ministers ;. Treaties ; Liberty of the Press ; Riot Act ; Armies ; Traytors ; Patriots ; Reason ; Criticism ; Versifying ; Ridicule ; Humours ; Love ; Prostitutes ; Music ; Pawn-brokers ; Surgery ; Law.

II. POETRY, *viz.* The *Ode* for the New Year, by *Colly Cibber,* Esq; Remarks upon it ; Imitations of it, by way of *Burlesque* ; Verses on the same Subject ; ingenious Epitaphs and Epigrams.

III. *Domestick* Occurrences,*viz.* Births,

Births, Deaths, Marriages, Preferments, Casualties, Burials and Christenings in *London.*

IV. Melancholy Effects of Credulity in *Witchcraft.*

V. Prices of Goods and Stocks, and a List of Bankrupts.

VI. A correct List of the Sheriffs for the current Year.

VII. Remarkable *Advertisements.*

VIII. *Foreign* Affairs, with an Introduction to this Year's History.

IX. Books and Pamphlets publish'd.

X. Observations on *Gardening,* and a List of Fairs for the Season.

With a *Table* of *Contents.*

By *SYLVANUS URBAN*, Gent.

The FOURTH EDITION.

LONDON, Printed and Sold at *St John's Gate*; by F. *Jefferies* in *Ludgate-street*; and most Booksellers in Town and Country. 1732. (Price 6 d.)

Note, *A few are printed on fine* Royal Paper, *large Margin, for the* Curious.

It must be remembered that Dr. Johnson, who in later life became a literary dictator, so that the age in which he lived is often known as the age of Johnson, began his career as a hack-writer, one of the Grub Street brotherhood. When we think of the bosom friends of his later days—Burke, Reynolds,

SAMUEL JOHNSON

From the mezzotint by James Watson after the painting by Reynolds

Boswell, &c. — let us also remember a bosom friend of his earlier years, the picturesque, essentially Bohemian figure of the young poet, Richard Savage. Before he won fame as the author of the *Dictionary* and the *Rambler*, Johnson was a struggling journalist seeking to make a precarious livelihood by writing up parliamentary debates and doing other miscellaneous work for Cave. He was not at all a good recorder of debates according to our modern standards. It is true that the compilers of Cobbett's *Parliamentary History* included all Johnson's records in that work and made an elaborate defence of their authenticity ; but this cannot be maintained. There is intrinsic evidence of their unauthenticity in the reports themselves, because all the speakers speak alike, they all use Johnsonese ; neither in diction nor in mode of argument is there anything to distinguish one speaker from another. In addition to this there is Johnson's own confession that he virtually composed the speeches in his reports—no doubt in many cases incorporating the substance of arguments actually used—but by

S I R,

YOU will, we hope, pardon the liberty we take the following LIST *of* NEWS-PAPERS, *which is composed of all that are [in] London. We have distinguished them by name, time of publication, and politics, [and] we can afford to send them, free of Postage, (if paid half-yearly in London) to any par[t] Scotland, and Ireland, at per annum. You may depend on the utmost punctuality, wh[ich] very low charge, is our best recommendation to public favor and patronage. The studie[s] of this plan for universal accommodation, has given it a decided superiority over all oth[er] corrected the disappointments so generally complained of by Country Gentlemen, that of their News-Papers in due course from the time they are printed. It will be our chief [care] your favor and recommendation.—You will be pleased to observe, that in this List we ha[ve] the Tax put on by the Printer, on account of the rise of paper, to our former cheap pri[ce].*

We have the honor to be, with respect, S I R, Your most humble Servants,

WILLIAM TURNER a

LONDON NEWS-PAPERS.

NAMES.	WHEN PUBLISHED.	POLITICS.	CHAN IN
Daily Advertiser	Every Morning	Neutral	4 17
Morning Post and World	Ditto	Anti-Ministerial	
Morning Chronicle	Ditto	Ditto	6 4
Gazetteer	Ditto	Ditto	
Public Ledger	Ditto	Ministerial	5 11
Morning Herald	Ditto	Anti-Ministerial	
Times	Ditto	Ministerial	
Oracle and Public Advertiser	Ditto	Anti-Ministerial	
True Briton	Ditto	Ministerial	6
Star	Every Evening	Anti-Ministerial	
Sun	Ditto	Ministerial	
Courier	Ditto	Anti-Ministerial	
London Evening Post		Ministerial	
London Chronicle		Anti Ministerial	
English Chronicle		Neutral	
General Evening Post	Every Tues. Thurs. & Sat.	Ditto	
Whitehall Evening Post		Anti-Ministerial	
St. James's Chronicle		Ditto	3 2
Evening Chronicle		Ditto	
Evening Mail		Ministerial	
London Packet	Every Mon. Wed. and Fri.	Neutral	
Lloyd's Evening Post		Ditto	
Courier de Londres	Every Tuesday and Friday	Ditto	3 3
London Gazette	Every Tuesday & Saturday	Ministerial	0 0
Sunday's Review		Ditto	
Sunday's Gazette		Neutral	
Sunday's Monitor	Every Sunday	Ditto	
Sunday's Recorder		Anti-Ministerial	
Observer		Neutral	
County Chronicle	Every Monday	Ditto	1 1
Ayre's Craftsman		Ditto	
Say's Craftsman		Anti-Ministerial	
Westminster Journal	Every Friday Evening	Neutral	
Old British Spy		Ditto	
Baldwin's Journal		Anti-Ministerial	
Lloyd's List	Tuesday and Friday		1 0
Price Current	Friday		2 0
List of Exports and Imports	Every Day		2 12
Stock List			1 1
Sound List			3 13
Course of Exchange			1 1

* *A newsvendor's circular letter of the 'nineties*

A strip has been torn away to the right, destroying the pence column of the subscription rates

his own admission taking care 'that the Whig dogs should not have the best of it'.

Johnson was a high old Tory, and it is a great tribute to the exceptional charm of John Wilkes's conversation that he, the arch-demagogue of his day, prevailed over the natural strong prejudice against him existing in the bosom of the arch-Tory. Their political views were diametrically opposed. Johnson stood for the old deferential ways ; Wilkes for the new and self-confident ways of a new democracy. We have already seen that the career of Wilkes was incidentally connected with the freedom of the press, that at a time when members of Parliament were particularly sensitive to publicity, when many of them were supporting inside Parliament, in connexion with Wilkes himself, a course of action which was profoundly distasteful to the London populace, they found themselves powerless to maintain their conception of parliamentary privilege, to withstand the demand for the publication of parliamentary transactions. The press was a greater power than ever before, in the days of the *North Briton* and the *Letters of Junius*.

While in the sphere of politics Johnson stands as the representative of the old order, in one respect he stands for a new order. When the great *Dictionary* was on the point of publication, the Earl of Chesterfield went out of his way to indicate that he would welcome the dedication of that work to himself. Not even Wilkes was more antipathetic to the Doctor than the brilliant and cynical Chesterfield, and their dislike was mutual. ' I thought ', once said Johnson, 'that this man had been a Lord among wits ; but I find he is only a wit among Lords.' To Chesterfield, the great authority on deportment, Johnson must have appeared a barbarian. The Doctor possessed great natural courtesy, but his methods of showing it were unconventional, while his table-manners—he was a great trencherman as well as a phenomenal tea-drinker—were somewhat wolfish. But if the Doctor's uncouth manners disgusted the immaculate Chesterfield, the latter's moral outlook was anathema to Johnson. Now that he had by his own labours made a name, he was not going to gratify the vanity of a dilettante peer, who had made no attempt to

Johnson and Boswell walking together (caricature by Rowlandson)

Johnson under Boswell's roof (caricature by Rowlandson)

'*My Wife had Tea ready for him which it is well known he delighted to drink at all hours, particularly when sitting up late. He shewed much complasency that the Mistress of the House was so attentive to his singular habit, and as no man could be more polite when he chose to be so, his address to her was most Courteous and engaging, and his conversation soon charmed her into a forgetfulness of his external appearance.*'—*Vide 'Journal', p. 14*

help him in his days of stress, by ministering to his glorification.
He wrote to the Earl, therefore, the famous letter in which he
defined a patron as ' one who looks with unconcern on a man
struggling for life in the water, and when he has reached the
ground encumbers him with help '.   While the characteristic
feature of Johnson's prose is its grandiloquence, certain passages

Circulating-Libraries, Bath.

THE PROPRIETORS *of the* CIRCULAT-
ING LIBRARIES *in* BATH, *respect-*
fully inform their Friends and the Public, that
on account of the present very great and the in-
creasing expence of new Publications, and of
Books in general, they will be under the neces-
sity (after the expiration of the present Month)
of altering the Terms of Subscription to

          L. S. D. .
          0   2   6 a Week.
          0   5   0 a Month.
          0   7   6 for Two Months.
          0 10   6 for Three Months.
          1   1   0 per Year.
              JOSEPH BARRATT,
              JOHN BULL,
              WM. MEYLER,
              S. HAZARD,
              JAMES MARSHALL,
              JOHN BALLY,
              THOMAS GIBBONS.

Advertisement showing the growth of the circulating library at the end of the century

in his published writings, his conversation as a whole, and some
of his correspondence show that he could be master of the most
crisp and terse expression.   This letter is a striking example.
It was, says Carlyle, ' the far-famed blast of doom proclaiming
into the ear of Lord Chesterfield and through him, of the listening
world, that patronage should be no more.'

The letter is indeed Grub Street's fulmination against sycophancy, its victorious assertion of independence—independence
of life, of judgement, of thought.   Sycophancy is incompatible
with intellectual integrity.   Johnson was no innovator in matters

of belief, religious or political ; yet just as much as any proclaimer
of a new and unpopular creed, he stands for the principle of
honest thinking. ' Clear your mind of cant ' was one of his
characteristic exhortations. Many of Johnson's opinions—
especially his criticisms of poetry—seem nowadays hopelessly
bad and wrong-headed. But they are always deserving of
respectful study, because they are absolutely sincere. Johnson
never praised anything merely because it had the sanction of
a great name or because it was the fashionable thing to do. His
opinions are invariably the deliberate judgements of a powerful
intellect. It is not to be denied that Johnson had limitations ;
he was insensible to certain types of poetical effect which happen
to be popular in our days. But the prejudice against the matter-
of-factness of Johnson is foolish and unfortunate if it blinds one
to the sterling wisdom of his judgements on men and things ;
just as mistaken as a prejudice against the grandiosity of his
literary style if it prevents us from appreciating its real grandeur
when, as for example in many passages of *Rasselas*, thought and
expression are in close harmony.

Yet after all the man was far greater than his works, the
Johnson of Boswell's biography more important than the
Johnson of *Rasselas*. Most of us know him best through his
devoted biographer ; and in getting to know the extraordinary
personality there revealed, of the ugly, slovenly, dictatorial
Doctor we come into close contact with a great deal of all that
was best as well as most characteristic of the eighteenth century,
of much that has been best and most characteristic of England
in all her history.

ADVERTISEMENTS.

I shatge the Round of *Publishing.* I. Phyficians, Chyrurgeons and Gardiners. II. Attorneys and Painters. III. Schools Publick Notaries, and Woodmongers IV Brokers, Coaches, Carriers, and fuch like; and then Phyficians, and fo round agin if defired: And if any would fee the Lifts not here, 'tis but looking One, Two, or Three Numbers back, and they may have their defire. And any in England, if it be reputable for me, for fmall charge may be thus inferted.

PAINTERS.		
BATTLE.		
Mr. Wych, Mortlack.		
FLOWER.		
Mr. Bogdan, St. Martin's Lane.		
Mr. Simon Verelft, Weftminfter.		
FLOWER and FRUIT.		
Mr. Van Loon, Long-Acre.		
HISTORY.		
Mr. Cook, Long-Acre.		
Mr. Verrои. Burleigh, Lincolnſh.		

LANDSCAPE.
Mr. Edema, Savoy.
Mr. Griffier, Salisbury-Court,

LIFE.	
Mr. Caufabon,	
Mr. Clofterman,	Covent-Garden
Sir G. Kneller,	
Mr. Vande-Vart,	
Mr. Conner, Gerard-freet.	
Mr. Hawker, Gerard-freet.	
Mr. Duboys,	Great Queen-ftr.
Mr. Moreland,	
Mr. Richardfon,	

Mr. Dahl, Leicefter-fields	
Mr. Lely, Leicefter-fields.	
Mr. Claret,	
Mr. Tillon,	Linc-Inn-fields.
Mr. Herm. Verelft,	
Mr. Walton,	
Mr. Cock Long-Acre.	
Mr. Jarvis, Long-Acre.	
Mr. Seeks, Ludgate-hill.	
Mr. Cummins, Norfolk-freet	
Mr. Mury, Norfolk-freet.	
Mrs Beale, Pall-Mall.	
Mr. Hill, York-buildings	
Mr. Schalker, York-buildings,	

LIMNERS.	
Mr. Bryan, Brownlow-freet.	
	Drury-Lane.
Mr. Crofs, Henrietta-ftr Cov Gard.	
Mr. Gibfon. New-ftr. Cov. Garden.	
Mr. Hoskins, Long-Acre,	
Mr. Dixon, St. Martin's-Lane.	

SE A.
Mr. Vande Velde, Pickadilly.

STILL-LIFE.
Mr. Roeftrate, King-ftr Co. Garden

An advertisement in Houghton's 'Collection' of 29 March 1695. The lift of painters is interesting both for the number of Dutch and other foreign names which it contains (see p. 358), and for the claffification which it adopts

XII

THE ARTISTS

THE twentieth century, unlike the Victorian era, which tended
to be in reaction (like any other age) against its immediate predecessor, finds much in the eighteenth century to cherish and
admire. The pre-eminence of its greatest portrait-painters,
Reynolds, Gainsborough, and Romney, has always been unquestioned ; that of its great landscape-painter, Wilson, who was
neglected in his own day, is now fully recognized. The thraldom
of the Victorian Gothic revival having passed away, there are
many who find more pleasure in the simple yet stately lines of
Georgian architecture than in the greater elaboration of the
Gothic and Jacobean styles. The present popularity of the lesser
arts of the eighteenth century is no less marked. The ware of
Wedgwood, the furniture of Chippendale and Sheraton are far
more highly valued than in their own period. The very term
' Georgian ' as applied to art has come to connote something
chaste, severe, unpretentious, essentially in good taste. Thus
it has come about that it is the best in Georgian art that is thought

of as characteristic of it. Yet it is obvious that in no century can there be complete uniformity of type, and the more thoroughly its art is studied the more clearly will diversity be discovered. The eighteenth century, like all others, had its aberrations ; it produced work which was florid and meretricious as well as work which was refined and genuine. It is always dangerous for a mode, however good it may be in itself, to become fashionable. Fashion in art as well as in costume means monotonous uniformity in the mass and exaggeration outside it. Eighteenth-century enthusiasm for things Italian led sometimes to a slavish and unimaginative imitation—for example of the Palladian style in architecture—and zeal for classical models and devices introduced them where they were quite inappropriate to the outrage of the essential spirit of the classics. In every age some of its greatest minds will be found rebels from the prevailing tendency of their time. Hogarth went out of his way to assert in the most combative fashion his dislike of Italian masters whom it was heresy to decry, even perversely affecting to belittle Raphael and Titian, because he revolted against the canting admiration simply of what it was the convention to admire, and against the contemporary habit of introducing classical or Italian conceits into wholly incongruous surroundings. Blake in his queer gibing squibs at the expense of art patrons and the Royal Academy, suggested that a great deal of contemporary connoisseurship was simply affectation. Dissimilar as they were in most other respects, Hogarth in the earlier and Blake in the later years of the century were alike in their detestation of shams and conventions, in their intense sincerity and their complete originality.

William Hogarth (1697–1764), the son of an unsuccessful schoolmaster and hack-writer, early showed artistic talents, and he was apprenticed to a silver-plate engraver. After his apprenticeship was over he supported himself by designing plates for booksellers and print-sellers. It is by his prints that Hogarth is best known, but he was a painter as well as an engraver. Some of his portraits are excellent. That of Garrick and his wife is charming ; those of himself with his dog, and of Captain Coram, the founder of the Foundlings' Hospital, show his re-

markable power of characterization; while in those of Simon,
Lord Lovat, the malignant old Jacobite executed in 1747 for
his complicity in the Forty Five, whose repulsive countenance
still leers out at the world so realistically in Hogarth's picture, and

Hogarth at his easel. A portrait painted by himself

of Wilkes, in which the demagogue's squint and the less amiable
side of his character are emphasized,[1] there is apparent the artist's
sardonic humour. But more familiar than these portraits are the
series of pictorial moral tales, the *Harlot's Progress* (1732), the
Rake's Progress (1735), and *Marriage à la Mode* (1745). Here

[1] At one time Hogarth did work for Government, and in this way he fell
foul of Wilkes, who attacked him violently in the *North Briton*.

Hogarth is revealed as a great satirist, imparting to the fantastic, the ridiculous, and even the humdrum an element of the terrible, unmasking the current tendencies of society, and revealing the unholy realities which underlie the conventional happenings of its everyday existence.

In his lectures on the *English Humourists* Thackeray bracketed Hogarth with Fielding and Smollett. The grouping together of the artist with two novelists is not merely fanciful, it is eminently appropriate. For Hogarth is essentially a humourist, if often a grim one, and still more essentially a dramatist. In the great didactic series, and equally in such other pictures as the ironical set entitled *The Election* and the dreadful *Gin Lane*, he gives us a representation of scenes of contemporary social life at least as vivid and powerful as anything in the pages of the novelists. As Thackeray says, he is invaluable to the historian, for he gives ' the most complete and truthful picture of the manners, and even the thoughts ' of his century. Probably the criticism which the average man most readily makes of Hogarth's works is that nearly all his figures are ugly, and the criticism is not merely superficial. While it is not true that there is no beauty in his pictures—he has left quite sufficient evidence of his capacity to depict beauty when he wished to—that element is certainly not prominent. There is a good deal of crudity in his work and there is no prettiness whatsoever. Caricature is perhaps its most marked feature, and indeed it is as a caricaturist that Hogarth has most influenced English art ; he is the progenitor of Gillray and Cruikshank.

William Blake (1757–1828) was the son of a hosier, who appears to have been a Swedenborgian, so that the atmosphere of mysticism was familiar to him from his earliest days. His father had the sense to perceive that the boy was quite unfitted for any ordinary trade, and so, like Hogarth, he was early apprenticed to an engraver. This was a well-known and expert craftsman Basire, who taught Blake the elements of his art very soundly and sent him to make drawings from the monuments in Westminster Abbey, and to dream strange dreams in those Gothic surroundings. A subsequent art master tried to win Blake's attention

From 'The Rake's Progress'

from the 'unfinished works of art' of Michelangelo and Raphael, in which he was absorbed, to those of Rubens and Charles Lebrun. Blake snorted his contempt for painters who by their devotion to what he regarded as the merest accessories of art showed that they had never begun to learn what art really meant. In 1780 he exhibited his first picture in the Royal Academy. Two years later he married Catherine Bouchier, who proved a perfect wife for him in her patient understanding of her husband even in his most eccentric moods. Shortly afterwards he published his first poems—*Poetical Sketches*; in 1790 the *Songs of Innocence*. The *Book of Thel* and the *Marriage of Heaven and Hell*, though not published till later, belong to the same period in authorship. The outbreak of the French Revolution had a profound effect upon Blake, who made the acquaintance of two of the most notable of its champions in England—Tom Paine and Mary Wollstonecraft. Blake was inspired to write *The French Revolution, A Song of Liberty*, and *America : A Prophecy*. These were followed in 1794 by *Europe : a Prophecy* and *The Book of Urizen*. In these and the subsequent prophetic books, *The Song of Los, Jerusalem*, and *Milton* he reveals himself in his threefold character. They are poems ; they are prophecies ; and they are, with their author's own illustrations, works of art.

In Blake the mystic, the poet, and the artist are so inextricably blended that they cannot well be considered apart. According to his own theory the artist was essentially both seer and prophet. For it was the artist who by aid of his imaginative vision was able to discern the eternal world, which is the only real world, the world unlimited by time and space and unshrouded by the illusory phantoms of our earthly experience—to discern it with eyes undimmed by the reason, which recognizes only temporal things, by the senses which see in beauty (an earnest of immortality) only its mundane and voluptuous aspect, by the so-called moral judgement, which separates by a crude dichotomy of good and evil a universe which is essentially one, to the detriment of spiritual liberty and progress. Blake's characteristic pictures are all other-worldly. As a small boy Blake was beaten by his parents because he said he saw angels, because he saw Ezekiel

The second scene of ' Marriage à la Mode '

sitting under a tree. All through his life he had these visions ; what he saw he delineated in his pictures and described in his poems. He lived in a realm of personified ideas, and his work is therefore intellectual, not sensuous. He possessed, therefore, in a supreme degree the capacity to concentrate in his pictures upon what was essential to his conception, eschewing mere elaboration of detail and meretricious display. For this reason, though his paintings and engravings are nearly all of small dimensions, they convey the impression of bigness and sublimity, and despite the obvious disparity in size suggest an affinity to Michelangelo, whom of all the great painters Blake most revered. For this reason also Blake is a master of design.

He was as original in his methods as in his ideas. The text of his *Songs of Innocence,* as it appeared in 1789, was hand-printed and the plates were engraved on copper by a process which has been described as etching reversed, that is to say the eating away by the acid of the remainder of the plate left the outline of the letters and the design raised up as in stereotype. The outlines of the design were then coloured by hand. For his paintings Blake used not oils, of which he disapproved, but tempera—and tempera of an unusual kind, for he mixed his pigments not with yolk of egg but with a solution of glue. He also invented a process of what has been called colour-printing, by which design and colour were both stamped upon paper from a thick mill-board to which they had been first applied.[1]

Most of Blake's pictures are illustrations of poems. He illustrated his own lyrics and prophetic books. He produced marginal illustrations for Young's *Night Thoughts,* the most striking of which—for example, that of Time Hastening Away—reveal the

---

[1] *Cf.* Darrell Figgis, *The Paintings of William Blake* (1925), p. 25. 'Every emotion, every quality of imaginative daring, is searched in this series of Colour-printed Drawings, almost invariably with the effortless ease of mastery. . . . Those that remain form a series that would place their maker among the greatest artists, even if no other of his works had survived. They would do more than this. They would put him among the few creators whose works haunt the memory because they throw light into strange places of elemental being, troubling unsuspected depths and unfolding half-forgotten powers of urgent majesty, beauty, and strength.'

ELEGY

WRITTEN IN A

COUNTRY CHURCH-YARD.

THE Curfew tolls the knell of parting day,
  The lowing herd wind slowly o'er the lea,
The plowman homeward plods his weary way,
  And leaves the world to darkness, and to me.
Now fades the glimmering landscape on the sight,
  And all the air a solemn stillness holds,
Save where the beetle wheels his droning flight,
  And drowsy tinklings lull the distant folds:
                                          Save

A water-colour by Blake illustrating the first page of Gray's Elegy. From the unique copy belonging to His Grace the Duke of Hamilton

extraordinary contrast between the splendid imagination of the artist and the mild and somewhat turgid eloquence of the verse. An even more obvious contrast is that between the commonplace lines of a now forgotten writer named Blair entitled *The Grave* and the powerful designs with which Blake embellished them, using them as a vehicle for expressing his own profound imaginings on Death. He found a much more fitting inspiration in the Book of Job, in Dante's *Divine Comedy* and, most of all, in Milton's *Paradise Lost*.[1] Nothing that Blake ever did was finer than his delineations of the Ancient of Days, the frontispiece of *Europe : a Prophecy*, yet inspired by Milton's lines :

> He took the golden Compasses, prepar'd
> In God's eternal store, to circumscribe
> This Universe . . .

Elohim creating Adam, Satan calling up his Legions, Satan exulting over Eve. No one can fail to perceive the magnificence of conception, the powerful imagination of works such as these. Nor can any one help feeling the weird terror which is in the very essence of such pictures as those of the Lazar House, Los Howling, Bromion and Oothoon bound back to back in the cave of Theotomoron, and the Ghost of a Flea. Such spectres may have been conceived in madness, but it was the madness of genius.

When Blake was a young man he was once recommended by the recognized *doyen* of the artist's profession in England, Sir Joshua Reynolds, to ' work with less extravagance . . . and to correct his drawing '. Blake might with advantage have taken Reynolds' technical advice in good part, but the two men were temperamentally poles apart, and Blake abhorred Reynolds and all he represented in art. Certainly to turn from Blake (or Hogarth for that matter) to the great fashionable portrait-painters of the eighteenth century is to pass into an utterly different world. It is to pass from the bustling rough and tumble of the City streets (in Hogarth's case), from heights and depths of elemental being (in Blake's), into the placid comfort and ele-

[1] Blake also illustrated *Paradise Regained, Comus*, the *Ode to the Nativity*, *L'Allegro*, and *Il Penseroso*, but here the inspiration was, as a rule, less congenial.

gant repose of the nobleman's drawing-room. One is conscious that though the portrait-painter's craftsmanship may be of a higher order, one has descended to a lower imaginative plane ; and to some eyes the often crude and unfinished figures of Blake may appear to have a rarer beauty than the rich and exquisite accomplishment of Reynolds' or Romney's art.

The eighteenth century is obviously a great epoch in the history of English portraiture if only because the painters were Englishmen. In the previous century many fine portraits had hung upon the panelled walls of England's palaces and her country houses, but they had been the canvases of Holbein, Van Dyck, and Lely, all of them foreigners, though they did so much of their work in England. At the opening of the eighteenth century the premier portrait-painter in the country was the German Sir Godfrey Kneller, who had settled in England in

Sir Joshua Reynolds, by himself

1674 and in 1688 became court-painter in succession to Wissing. He lived till 1723. We owe to him many fine and attractive portraits, even if they are not of the first order, of the great figures in the reigns of William III, Anne, and George I. By the middle of the century the complete domination of the foreign artist was a thing of the past, and a great native school of portraiture was flourishing. In 1723 Allan Ramsay, subsequently court-painter to George III, was born; in 1723, Reynolds; in 1727, Gainsborough; in 1734, Romney.

Sir Joshua Reynolds (1723–92) is one of the most familiar figures of the century, not only as a painter, but as a social personage. The son of a schoolmaster, he proved a very idle and indifferent scholar, but the pen-and-ink sketches with which he

Boydel sum delin

A View of the Royal Exhibition
at Somerset House

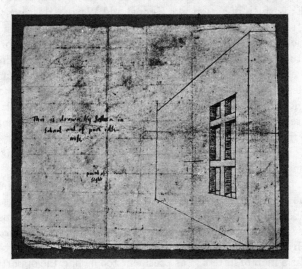

(1) *Reynolds's engagement-book and diary, open at April 1769, the month in which knighthood was bestowed upon him, and giving the names of distinguished sitters*

(2) *A perspective drawing made by Reynolds as a boy, on which his father has written, 'This is drawn by Joshua in school out of pure idleness'*

By permission of the Editor of 'The Times'

lavishly decorated his exercise books showed the bent of his mind and the nature of his gifts. But his father for some time hesitated between the safe and the venturesome, between making his son an apothecary or an artist, before he took the decision by apprenticing him to a portrait-painter named Hudson. In 1749 Reynolds made a voyage with Keppel in the *Centurion* to the Mediterranean, after which he spent two or three years studying the works of the great masters, and incidentally catching in the cold Venetian galleries the chill which rendered him permanently deaf in one ear. He settled down in London in 1752, and speedily became the most fashionable portrait-painter of the day. In the course of the next fifteen years many of the most distinguished people of his time sat to him—beauties like Lady Sarah Lennox, the Countess Waldegrave, and Elizabeth Gunning, Duchess of Hamilton ; statesmen like Hardwicke, Rockingham, Burke, and Conway ; men of action like Keppel and Warren Hastings ; men of letters, such as Johnson and Gibbon ; the stars of the stage— Garrick and Mrs. Siddons. After 1770 the volume of his portrait-painting diminished and he turned his attention to imaginative subjects, as in his picture of Ugolino in Dante, and to fanciful studies of children, beggars, &c.[1] But it is as a portrait-painter that Reynolds is best remembered, and rightly so. With classical and religious themes he revealed his limitations, for the sublime and the spiritual, the worlds of the hero and the saint, were alike foreign to the temperament and the genius of this consummate portrayer of an eighteenth-century aristocracy.

Reynolds' name is intimately associated with the beginnings of the Royal Academy. He was its first president, and its early success and its early traditions owed much to his zeal and inspiration. As president he delivered a series of lectures or *Discourses* which have given their author a permanent place as an art-critic and as a man of letters ; as president too he had the opportunity of evincing those remarkable social gifts, to which his deafness

---

[1] It is worthy of record that Reynolds had a scheme for the decoration of the interior of St. Paul's by fresco, which it has been left for a much later generation to carry out. The Dean of that day refused to sanction such pagan ornamentation.

THE STRAWBERRY GIRL, by REYNOLDS

First exhibited at the Royal Academy in 1773, now in the Wallace collection

proved no impediment. Whether as an entertainer in his own house or in the clubs which he founded—notably the Turk's Head Tavern, of which Burke and Goldsmith were also members —he revealed the tact, courtesy, and tolerance of the perfect host, not a little of the diplomatic gifts of the courtier, and those remarkable conversational powers which made him the only man besides Burke who could vie with Johnson. There is no doubt that he thoroughly enjoyed the position in the fashionable world which his unusual combination of artistic and social gifts had won for him, and that he sometimes tried to compete in outward display with those who were its members by birth. Thus, when he moved into a fine new house in Lincoln's Inn Fields in 1760 he had a truly marvellous coach constructed (for his sister's use), richly carved and gilded and ornamented with resplendent panels illustrative of the seasons.[1] No doubt too he thoroughly appreciated the virtual dictatorship which he wielded in the Academy circle, and he is said to have been jealous of some of his great contemporaries, of Wilson, whom he under-estimated, of Romney, whose success in later days rivalled his own.[2] Such a description may seem to suggest a small man; but fundamentally Reynolds was large-hearted, and as an artist he is one of the great figures not only of England but of the world. His superiority to his predecessors and to such lesser contemporaries as Ramsay lay in his ability to depict individuality, to catch the distinctive expression or gesture which was indicative of character, and not simply to paint a type, making one Georgian cavalier much like any other Georgian cavalier, and one Georgian duchess much like another Georgian duchess. Ruskin referred to Reynolds as one of ' the utmost masters ', and ranked him as a colourist with Titian, Tintoretto, Paul Veronese, and Turner.

Gainsborough (1727–88) was probably an even more accomplished artist than Reynolds—certainly he had a greater range, being at least as great a painter of landscapes as of portraits.

[1] See W. H. Beechey's prefatory memoir to Reynolds' *Literary Works* (2 vols. 1852), vol. i, pp. 139–40.

[2] On the other hand Reynolds warmly admired Gainsborough's work, and their quarrel, healed before the latter's death, was certainly due to Gainsborough.

From earliest boyhood he showed the keenest love of the countryside and he used to play truant from school in order to indulge it,
so that opinion was divided as to whether Tom would grow up to
be hanged or to be renowned. He started upon his career as an
artist at a very early age, but it was so unremunerative that his
marriage when still a mere boy seemed most improvident, though

THOMAS GAINSBOROUGH
Painted by himself. From the engraving by Bartolozzi

his wife had a moderate competence. Gainsborough had none of
Reynolds' social gifts or social ambitions, and he was quite
content with his retired domesticity in Ipswich in the company
of his wife, to whom he was devoted, his violin, and his sketch-
book. But it was not till his migration to Bath in 1760 that his
success as a portrait-painter began. When the Academy was
inaugurated in 1768 he was elected a member. Six years later
he settled in London with a clientele almost as distinguished as
that of Reynolds himself.

His best known portraits are those of the younger Pitt, the Miss Linleys, Mrs. Siddons, and ' A Young Gentleman ', the last being the picture commonly known as the ' Blue Boy '. Reynolds in one of his *Discourses* contended that the central man of colour in a picture should always be red, yellow, gold, or brown—never blue. Whether or not Gainsborough's canvas was painted in answer to this argument, as has been suggested, it certainly demonstrated that a very beautiful effect could be produced with the central mass of colour a monotone of vivid royal blue.

Gainsborough is one of the greatest of English landscape-painters. Entirely free from the hypnotism of Poussin, Salvator Rosa and the Italian mannerisms which were the bane of some of his contemporaries, he was influenced by the Dutch School, by Ruysdael and Hobbema, the atmosphere of whose country was so much more akin to England's than that of any southern land. But most of all he drew his inspiration from nature itself—from the English scenery which he had known and understood since boyhood. He loved to depict the typical cloudy skies of England and undulating leafy country enriched with the moist freshness of recent rain.

The third of the great trio of portrait-painters, George Romney (1734–1802), never quite succeeded in acquiring the tastes and characteristics of a really educated man, and though he achieved at the zenith of his career a professional success comparable with that of Reynolds, his life was one of very chequered happiness and it had a tragic close. In early manhood he made an ill-considered match with an ignorant simple-minded servant girl in Kendal. When he became prosperous and famous, husband and wife lived apart, not apparently through any estrangement but because Mrs. Romney was afraid of the gay and sophisticated life of London. As he grew older Romney became irritable and morose. Obsessed with the idea of mere size, he spent his time devising grandiose schemes—which never came to anything—for colossal pictures on subjects taken from Milton. Eventually his mind gave way, and the unhappy man returned to Kendal, to become utterly dependent upon the ministrations of his neglected yet devoted wife for his remaining years.

COTTAGE CHILDREN

Engraved in mezzotint by Henry Birche after Gainsborough

At the outset of his career Romney owed much to the kindness of Richard Cumberland, the pompously conceited poet and dramatist who, whatever his failings, proved a good friend to the young artist and sang his praises in verbose panegyrics and obtained many patrons for him, and later on to Lord Thurlow, who, dubbing Reynolds ' a great scoundrel and a bad painter ', because he was a Whig, was a great champion of his brilliant young rival. Romney at one time made the acquaintance of Emma, Lady Hamilton, and, being captivated by her beauty, painted many portraits of her in all manner of poses and guises, though not quite so many as has sometimes been imagined, since some of his supposed pictures of her were actually painted before he had ever met her. Romney's portraits have not perhaps the same depth and dignity as those of Reynolds and Gainsborough, but they are exceedingly attractive, especially his studies of female beauty and of handsome boyhood—for instance, the delightful portrait of Charles Grey, afterwards of Reform Bill fame, before he left Eton. Pictures of such freshness and charm will never cease to delight, and the reputation of Romney tends to grow.

GEORGE ROMNEY

Drawn from an original picture by himself by J. Jackson, R.A.

Art in the eighteenth century was largely conditioned by the requirements of its patrons, and what the patrons usually wanted was portraits of themselves, their wives, and their families. If landscapes appealed to them at all, they were the landscapes of their own houses and estates that they wanted to possess. The more faithful the reproduction of the original the better it pleased, so that the imaginative treatment of nature was not encouraged. Consequently a number of the landscape-painters of the century

—and this applies particularly to the early water-colour artists—
are essentially topographers. Of the two supreme landscape-
painters one, Gainsborough, has already been dealt with. The other,

LADY HAMILTON, by ROMNEY

Richard Wilson (1714–82), cared so little about fashion and was
so poorly patronized that he died almost in penury. He and
Gainsborough present an interesting contrast, for the latter
represents a Dutch influence and the former an Italian influence.
Wilson has been termed 'the father of British landscape-painting',
and rightly, since he was producing some of his finest work at

a time when Gainsborough was still living in the obscurity of Ipswich.

Little is known with any degree of certainty about Wilson's life. He began as a portrait-painter, and some of his portraits—notably those of himself, of a brother-artist J. H. Mortimer, and of Peg Woffington are of outstanding merit. His decision to devote himself mainly to landscape is popularly attributed to the influence of Francis Zuccarelli, whom he met in Venice, but Wilson had painted good landscapes before he ever saw Zuccarelli, who was a much inferior artist to himself. Zuccarelli later on migrated to England, where he became a very influential member of the Royal Academy, and far more successful in selling his landscapes than Wilson ever was. While the work he had done during his six or seven years' sojourn in Italy secured for Wilson the admiration of Vernet and other artists on the Continent, he obtained little recognition or profit among his fellow countrymen. Indeed, his fortunes tended to decline, and at one time towards the end of his life his only dependable source of income was a paltry £50 a year which he received as Librarian of the Royal Academy. The greatest of his pictures had indeed been painted from nature in Italy ; into a number of his later English and Welsh landscapes he introduced an Italian atmosphere to their detriment. While his method of composition derives from Claude Lorraine, his beautiful skies and finely luminous colouring are individual. Wilson created a real school of landscape in England, his most prominent pupil being Joseph Farington, whose *Diary* is nowadays better known than his pictures.

Of the painters of landscape in water-colour the earliest important figure is that of Paul Sandby [1] (1725–1809), who has been described as the 'father of British water-colour art'. Sandby belongs to the category of topographers ; he was not a big enough man to break away completely from convention. On the other hand, he put a good deal of fancy and of individuality into his drawings.

[1] His elder brother Thomas was an architect of note. He was at one time private secretary and draughtsman to the Duke of Cumberland. He was present at Dettingen and also accompanied the Duke on his Flemish and Scottish campaigns. He subsequently became Deputy Ranger of Windsor Park, and he planned Virginia Water and the landscape scenery round it.

Drawing of Godalming by Girtin

By permission of the Governors of the Whitworth Art Gallery, Manchester

Another of the more original of the topographers was Michael Angelo Rutter, who did charming work. But the two great artists who raised water-colour landscape to a higher level than mere topography were J. R. Cozens (1752–99)[1] and Thomas Girtin (1775–1802). The former, with remarkable economy of means and using little variety of colour, produced finely imaginative work. While Cozens made much use of the pencil, his pictures being really tinted drawings, Girtin with greater technical accomplishment relied mainly on the brush. Girtin and Turner were born in the same year; the latter had a very long life, Girtin a very short one, for he died at the age of twenty-seven. Yet in that brief career he produced work worthy to be compared with Turner's finest water-colours.

Of the engravers who worked in England during the century one of the most famous is a foreigner, Francesco Bartolozzi (1730–1813), who resided in the country between 1764 and 1802. A man of great versatility, he was etcher, line engraver, stipple engraver, and painter. His very numerous works in all these media were proof of an equally remarkable industry. His engravings are never mere copies of the original paintings— usually Italian—from which they are taken, but are individual works of art. Of English line engravers the chief were Sir Robert Strange, a jealous rival of Bartolozzi, who specialized in historical subjects, and William Woollett, who specialized in landscape. Paul Sandby, who also did many landscape engravings, is important as the originator of the process of aquatint, which he developed from a similar method used by a French engraver named Le Prince. William Wynne Ryland, who learnt the system of stippling in France, was the first to introduce it into England, where it became extremely popular. The art of mezzotint, revived about the middle of the century by James McArdell, was practised by a number of able workers in this medium—Valentine Green, James and Thomas Watson, John Raphael Smith, and Richard Earlom.

[1] His father, Alexander Cozens, was also a water-colour painter. He did work of a similar kind to his son's, but not as fine, though it was more highly esteemed by contemporaries.

Blenheim Palace, designed and built for the Duke of Marlborough by Vanbrugh in 1715

The architecture of the eighteenth century is practically all of the classical or Renaissance style, but it is not all of the same character. Broadly speaking, the architects of the period belong to one or other of two different camps. On the one hand, Wren and his followers, studying not only Italian but French models, and of the Italians Bernini as much as Palladio created a monumental style in the baroque taste. The other party, led by Lord Burlington, selected from Italian architecture Palladio for their master, and cried up Inigo Jones as his prophet.

When Sir John Vanbrugh (1666–1726) and Nicholas Hawksmoor (1661–1736) were associated with Wren at the Office of Works in 1702, the rooting of baroque in England seemed assured. The former, who had already made his fame as a dramatist before he turned his attention to architecture, succeeded Wren as surveyor of Greenwich Hospital in 1716. Lacking his master's sureness of taste and consummate skill, he was really a brilliant amateur, gifted with a grandiose imagination, to whom the baroque style and the accidents of patronage afforded superb opportunity. His most famous works are Castle Howard and Blenheim Palace, both of them florid and gigantic. In each case the monumental character of the exterior is impressive, the interior being much less imposing, with a multitude of comparatively small and undistinguished rooms quite out of keeping with the magnitude of the building. The entirely comfortless character of Blenheim inspired Pope's lines :

> 'Thanks, sir' ; cried I, ' 'tis very fine,
> But where d'ye sleep or where d'ye dine ?
> I find by all that you've been telling,
> "That 'tis a house, but not a dwelling." ' [1]

In the smaller houses which he subsequently planned—Eastbury, Seaton Delaval, and Grimsthorpe—Vanbrugh's style became

---

[1] See, however, the defence of Vanbrugh's boast that his houses were the most convenient ever planned, in G. Webb's introduction to vol. iv of the *Complete Works of Sir John Vanbrugh* (Nonesuch Press, 1928), pp. xvi-xviii, where it is argued that his design was eminently suitable for the great nobleman's mansion, and that he aimed at providing a number of self-contained suites, so that not only the owners but their illustrious guests could live and hold their levees independently.

simpler and quieter. A thoroughly catholic taste may include a liking for his pretentious exercises in the grand manner, but most people will feel that to be really impressive grandeur of design must be inspired by sublimity of thought and nobility of purpose, and will sympathize with the spurious epitaph on Vanbrugh :

> Lie heavy on him, earth, for he
> Laid many a heavy weight on thee.

Nicholas Hawksmoor derived his technique from Wren, his ideas from Vanbrugh. He designed several of the fifty new City churches built by order of Queen Anne, of which the finest is Christ Church, Spitalfields, but his best known work was done in Oxford, where he was the author of the Clarendon Building (in collaboration with Vanbrugh), of the main quadrangle of Queen's, and of the northern quadrangle of All Souls, together with the two weak Gothic towers by which this master of baroque perversely and inconsequentially chose to embellish it.

The leader in the other camp of Georgian architects, the great champion of the Palladian style in England,[1] was Richard Boyle, third Earl of Burlington. It is likely that not a great deal of the work usually attributed to him was actually done by him ; nevertheless he is important as a noble patron of fine taste and great talent, who fostered the reaction against the massive ponderousness of Vanbrugh. Much the most distinguished of Burlington's protégés, though some of his work really belongs to the Wren tradition, was James Gibbs (1682–1784), the author of the churches of St. Mary-le-Strand and St. Martin-in-the-Fields in London, of the Senate House in Cambridge, and of the Radcliffe Camera in Oxford. The most faithful of Burlington's men were Colin Campbell, who designed Houghton for Sir Robert Walpole, and William Kent. The latter was an astonishing jack-of-all-trades, who became adviser-in-chief in all matters artistic to the fashionable world and designed gardens, furniture, clothes, and ornaments as well as buildings. That he was a very accomplished,

---

[1] G. Webb, *op. cit.*, p. xxxiii. ' . . . The Palladianist School is before all things the school of men who have studied in Italy. It is the architecture of the Grand Tour.'

though not an inspired, architect is seen in his work in the great house of Holkham in Norfolk and in the Horse Guards, a fine example of the Palladian style. While his architectural designs were generally good, his others were almost always bad. In the second scene in *Marriage à la Mode* Hogarth has depicted the inelegant heaviness of a room furnished and decorated in the Kent manner.

ROBERT ADAM

In the later years of the century the chief representative of the older tradition was Sir William Chambers, whose masterpiece was Somerset House, an extraordinarily successful building, in which splendid use is made of the river frontage. His was the most powerful influence in the Academy after Reynolds' day, and he founded a school of architects, of whom the most noteworthy is James Gandon, who designed the Customs House and the Four Courts in Dublin.

The work of the brothers Robert and James Adam, of whom the former (1728–92) was the more important, is related to that of the Burlington clique, inasmuch as it was inspired by the study of classical models abroad. The elder was particularly impressed by the great ruin of Diocletian's palace at Spalato, of which he made a minute examination in 1750. It is their work as decorators that is most familiar—their oval and elliptical designs for their ceilings, their doorways flanked with fluted Doric columns and surmounted by fanlights, their characteristic mantelpieces and sideboards, their painted furniture covered with elaborate ornamental designs

The brothers Adam as Architects

A section of Kedleston from 'Vitruv. Brit. iv. 51'

of fans, wreaths, honeysuckle. But the Adams were fine architects and not merely decorators, as they showed in their re-modelling of Sion House, in Adelphi Terrace, and in their native

'Fan' inlay on a slab-table designed in 1775

Adam slab-table designed in 1775

Adam drawings reproduced by the courtesy of the Editor of 'The Connoisseur'

city of Edinburgh in the houses in Charlotte Square. Robert Adam, who was not a modest man, boasted that he had revolutionized domestic architecture in England. Standing for the principle that the architect should also be the decorator in order

The methods of Kent and 'Capability' Brown as parodied by R. Payne Knight in 'The Landscape, a Didactic Poem' (1794). The upper of the two engravings shows the 'Nature' of the Improvers with its shaven lawns, its 'nude waters', its monotonous 'clumps', and its serpentine walks. The lower shows the return to Nature advocated by Knight, and other champions of the Picturesque school.

to secure harmony between the design of a house and its furnishings, the brothers Adam certainly succeeded in combining dignity with comfort and in bringing plenty of light and air into their interiors by the characteristic device of vistas of rooms opening one into another.

Though the predominance of Renaissance architecture in the eighteenth century was never seriously challenged, there did exist after about 1750 a small Gothic movement, with which Horace Walpole and his strange Gothic villa at Twickenham will always be associated, but it did not attain important dimensions until the opening of the next century and the advent of Wyatt. The battle of the styles and the evolution of public taste can be traced in the history of the eighteenth-century garden. There was an early reaction against the trim formalism of the Dutch gardens of the period of William III and Anne with their straight avenues, neatly clipped shrubs, and symmetrical yew-borders. To the classical craze is due the Greek temples, arches, and statues of Stowe. Later on an oriental fashion brought with it Chinese grottoes and pagodas such as the one which still exists at Kew. The romantic influence, exemplified by Bridgeman and Launcelot or ' Capability ' Brown, is seen in the attempt to transform the garden into a luxuriant wilderness. Brown went up and down the country grubbing up beautiful old world pleasaunces, of which their owners had grown tired, and substituting the most artificially contrived of wild ' natural ' landscapes. The most absurd extravagance of this craze for nature was the planting of occasional dead trees to give an air of verisimilitude.

For its sculpture Georgian England depended very largely upon the foreigner, most of the great sculptors being either foreigners or of foreign extraction. Such were Peter Scheemakers, a native of Antwerp, who was responsible for the monuments erected to the memory of Sir John Barnard and Clive and others of the great Englishmen of his time, and John Michael Rysbrack, born in Brussels, who executed the monuments (designed by Kent) to Isaac Newton and Earl Stanhope in Westminster Abbey, and who was wholly responsible for the monuments in the Abbey to Kneller and the Duke of Newcastle, and (in the Poets' Corner) to Ben

Roubiliac's terra-cotta model for a bust of Hogarth
National Portrait Gallery

(Left) Wedgwood 'granite ware' with gilt handles and festoons, (Centre) deep blue and white, (Right) crystalline agate imitating natural stone

A pair of ewers, emblematical of wine (Satyr, goat's head, and vine leaves) and water (Triton, dolphin's head, and seaweed), designed by Flaxman. The ground is of light blue and the figures, &c., in white jasper

Wedgwood ware in the Art Gallery, Bury, Lancashire. Reproduced by the courtesy of the Editor of 'The Connoisseur'

OF China-Ware I fee but little imported in the Year 1694, I prefume by reafon of the War and our bad luck at Sea. There came only from Spain certain, and from India Certain twice. 'Tis a curious Manufacture, and deferves to be encourag'd here, which without Doubt Money would do; and Mr. Dwoit at Fullham has done it, and can again in any thing that is flat: But the Difficulty is, that if a hollow Difh be made, it muft be burnt fo much, that the Heat of the Fire will make the Sides fall. He tells me that our Clay will very well do it; the main Skill is in managing the Fire. By my Confent, the Man that would bring it to Perfection, fhould have for his Encouragement 1000 l. from the Publick, tho' I help'd to pay a Tax towards it.

Of Tea-pots, there came but 10, and thofe from Holland. To our Credit be it fpoken, we have about Faux-Hall (as I have been informed) made a great many, and I cannot gainfay, but they are as good as any came from abroad.

The next are Tobacco-pipes, of which came from Holland, Grofs 110, Chefts 4. I have feen fome very long ones, and alfo fmall from thence, that truly are very fine. If there comes no more, they'll do us no great hurt. I think they muft be permitted to be Patterns to fet our People on Work, and if our Smoakers would ufe none but fine ones, I queftion not but we fhould make as fine as any body.

NOW for Tobacco-pipe Clay; a good Sort whereof is gotten at or nigh Pool, a Port Town in Dorfetfhire, and there dug in fquare Pieces, of the bignefs of about half a Hundred Weight each; from thence 'tis brought to London, and fold in peaceable Times at about eighteen Shillings a Ton, but now in this time of War is worth about three and twenty Shillings.

The Ordinary Pipes are fold for Eighteen Pence the Grofs, and the Glafed ones for Two or Three Shillings.

Extracts from leading articles in Houghton's 'Collection' of March 13, 1695/6, and Jan. 12, 1693/4. The taste for china was greatly encouraged by the Dutch East India Company, which imported large quantities of Chinese porcelain into Europe in the latter half of the century. Before its close the potters of Delft were busily engaged in imitating the blue and white of Nankin. The liking for Chinese models is also found in England in the reign of William III. The white enamelled ware which the Delft workers made in their imitation of the genuine oriental porcelain was being manufactured in England, mostly by Dutchmen, in the reign of Charles II. Lambeth was the centre of the industry. Dr. John Dwight of Fulham, referred to above, was in 1671 granted a patent for his discovery of 'the mystery of transparent earthenware, commonly known by the names of porcelain or china'; but it is not now believed that he ever produced anything which could be strictly described as porcelain

The second extract—January 12, 1693/4—shows us the Dorset clay, in later years used locally by the Poole pottery industry, being sent up to the London potters

Jonson, Milton, Prior, and Gay. On a higher plane is Joseph
Nollekens (1737–1823), who also came of a Flemish family—a
most eccentric man, uncouth in appearance and manner, miserly,
far from cleanly, and very ignorant outside his own profession.
Most of his works are portrait busts, but his most distinctive and
his greatest achievements are of an imaginative kind, such as his

JOSIAH WEDGWOOD
From a plaque made in his own factory

Venus chiding Cupid and Venus anointing her Hair. Louis Fran-
çois Roubiliac (d. 1762) was the greatest sculptor of the century
in England. Seven of the monuments in Westminster Abbey are
by him—the finest being that of the Duke of Argyll, the figure
representing Eloquence in which was pronounced by Canova to
be the finest piece of modern art in the country. Another of his
great works is the statue of Shakespeare in the British Museum,
originally done for Garrick.

Of the native sculptors the most outstanding were Thomas
Banks (1735–1805), John Bacon (1740–99), and John Flaxman

Chelsea statuette of Wilkes

Wilkes holds a scroll inscribed 'Magna Charta' and 'Bill of Rights'. A book at his feet is
'Lock on Govt.'. A cupid holds a cap of liberty

(1755–1826). Banks, whose early work created so favourable an impression that he was sent to study in Italy at the expense of the Royal Academy, was an artist of real intellectual power and the first Englishman to produce classical sculpture in the grand manner. His best known work is the large monument to Eyre Coote which stands in the north transept of Westminster Abbey.

Chippendale chair with interlaced back and cabriole legs, design from the 'Director', third edition, 1762

Bacon's most familiar works are the Chatham monument in the Abbey and the statues of Howard and Dr. Johnson, the latter represented in inadequate and incongruous classical garb, which were the first two monuments admitted into St. Paul's Cathedral. Flaxman's principal achievements belong to the nineteenth century. His career, however, began, after he had by sheer self-confidence and determination triumphed over the disadvantages of an unhappy and delicate childhood, in the pottery works of Josiah Wedgwood, who employed him to make wax models taken from classical friezes and vases. By 1787 he had earned enough money to be able to make the pilgrimage to Rome, then regarded as the indispensable novitiate to an artist's career, and it was then that his career as a sculptor began.

Wedgwood, the greatest figure in the history of the ceramic art in England, established a small factory at Stoke in 1754; a larger one at Burslem six years later, and in partnership with Thomas Bentley of Liverpool the famous Etruria factory near Hanley in 1769. The defect of seventeenth-century earthenware has been that only a thin white coating disguised the crude red or buff-coloured clay of which it was made. The discovery that it was possible by mixing a carefully selected white burning clay with finely ground flints to produce a ware which was white throughout

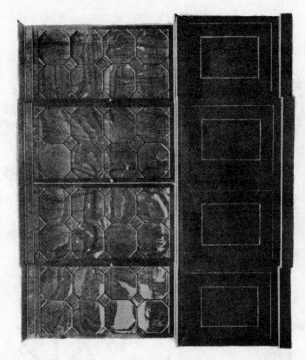

Mahogany Chippendale bookcase of about 1780

Satinwood china cabinet or bookcase in Sheraton style, of about 1790

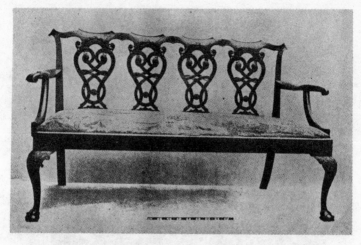

The 'Bury' (Chippendale) four-backed settee, date 1745–50.

Chippendale chair, about 1755. Carved back. Cabriole legs ending in claw-and-ball feet.

Adam mahogany wheel-back arm-chair of about 1780.

Sheraton Furniture. The two drawing-room chairs are designs from the appendix to Sheraton's own 'Drawing-book'

Below, an inlaid sideboard with pedestals, knife-vases, and cellaret (height of the pedestals over all 6 ft. 2 in., and total length 9 ft.).

led to the much improved pottery of Turner and Warburton in the first half of the eighteenth century. But Wedgwood, a man of genuine intellectual keenness, many-sided interests, and inventive genius, produced earthenware greatly superior to anything hitherto seen in England, and his business enterprise being equal to his craftsman's skill, his tea-pots, coffee-pots, and jugs were soon to be seen on every kitchen-dresser, his scent bottles and buckles on every lady's toilet-table, his cameos, bas-reliefs, and plaques in every drawing-room in the country, while he developed the export trade in his wares so extensively that within his own lifetime it became five times as large as the domestic trade.

The great porcelain works of Chelsea, Bow, Worcester, and Derby were all established within the middle years of the century. The most remarkable of the porcelain manufacturers was William Duesbury, the founder of the Derby works, who also acquired those of Chelsea and Bow. About 1773 the celebrated crown first made its appearance, together with the letter D as the firm's trade-mark, by permission of George III, who gave Duesbury his patronage. Early crown Derby was pre-eminent by reason of its freedom from the influence of Dresden or Sèvres, which had completely dominated English models hitherto, and by the wonderfully rich blue which Duesbury discovered and combined very effectively with fine gilding. Dr. John Wall, the founder of the Worcester factory, was, like Duesbury, a man of genuine originality. He specialized in the reproduction of oriental models, especially those of Nankin. While good work was also done at Bristol, Lowestoft, and Coalport, these factories are not associated with men of the same calibre as Duesbury and Wall.

In the first half of the eighteenth century English furniture was of a very heterogeneous character, but the outstanding influence was that of William Kent. Chippendale's work is a development from Kent's, but it marks a very clear and important advance, the advent of the new development being heralded by the publication in 1754 of his book entitled *The Gentleman and Cabinet Maker's Directory*, the most important treatise on furniture design which had ever appeared in England. Chippendale was essentially eclectic, so that there is not one single Chippendale style. He was equally interested in Gothic, French, and bizarre Chinese designs. What was characteristic of him was good craftsmanship in a variety of different styles, the combination of lightness and delicacy with solidity, in which respect his work was a great improvement on Kent's. But the essential problem of furniture construction in the century being how to secure the utmost delicacy of carving in mahogany without sacrificing durability and practical usefulness, the singular gracefulness of Hepplewhite's furniture, which gives the appearance of fragility while being really quite strong, indicates a still further advance. Thomas Sheraton designed furniture on similar severe but charming lines; but, on the other hand, it was not all of the same chaste character, for coming latterly under the influence of the French styles of the Consulate and Empire periods he tended to abandon his former austere manner and to introduce elaborate embellishments of doubtful taste, including the effigies of strange beasts, sphinxes, and other fantastic adornments. Sheraton was of a vain, self-assertive, dogmatic and angular character, and suffered from the damaging effects of threadbare poverty and a hard and bigoted religious creed. He published treatises on baptismal regeneration as well as his *Cabinet-maker's and Upholsterer's Drawing-book*, a chaotic work containing many otiose irrelevances by which he blandly conceived that he had put Chippendale and all his other predecessors completely out of date. He was a man of cross-grained temper, but he certainly possessed artistic genius.

HACKNEY COACH FARES *from different Parts of the Town to various Places of Pleasure.*

Drury-Lane Theatre, Covent-Garden Theatre, Colman's Theatre, and Ranelagh.

	Dr. L. P. Ho.		C. G. P. Ho.		Colm. P. Ho.		Ran.	
	s.	d.	s.	d.	s.	d.	s.	d.
Aldersgate street - - -	1	6	1	6	2	0	3	0
St. Ann's-church, Soho - -	1	0	1	0	2	0	2	0
Bishopsgate-street within - -	1	6	1	6	2	0	4	0
———— without - -	2	0	2	0	2	6	4	0
Blackman-street, over London-bridge	2	0	2	0	3	0	4	6
————, over Blackfriars -	2	0	2	6	3	0	4	6
————, over Westminster	2	6	2	6	1	6	3	0
Bloomsbury-square - -	1	0	1	0	1	0	3	0
Buckingham-gate - -	1	6	1	6	1	0	1	0
Charing-cross - - -	1	0	1	0	1	0	2	0
Foster-lane end, Cheapside -	1	6	1	6	1	6	3	6
Cheapside, end of King-street -	1	6	1	6	1	6	4	0
Chelsea-college - -	3	0	2	6	2	6	1	0
Cornhill, Freeman's-court -	1	6	1	6	2	0	4	0
Fenchurch-street - -	1	6	2	0	2	0	4	6
Fleet-street, Obelisk - -	1	0	1	0	1	0	3	6
Gracechurch-street - -	1	6	1	6	2	0	4	6
Hackney-church - -	4	6	4	6	5	0	6	6
Holborn, end of Leather-lane -	1	0	1	0	1	6	3	6
Hyde Park Corner - -	1	6	1	6	1	0	1	6
St. James's Palace-gate -	1	0	1	0	1	0	2	6
Islington - - -	2	0	2	0	2	6	4	6
Knightsbridge - -	2	0	2	0	1	6	1	6
Marybone - - -	1	6	1	6	1	6	3	0
Mile-end turnpike - -	2	6	3	0	3	6	6	0
Minories - - -	2	0	2	6	2	6	5	0
Moorfields - - -	1	6	1	6	2	0	4	6
Oxford-street, Pantheon -	1	6	1	6	1	0	2	6
———— end of Orchard-street	1	6	1	6	1	0	2	0
Palace-yard and St. Margaret's-church	1	0	1	0	1	0	2	0
St. Paul's Church-yard -	1	0	1	6	1	6	3	6
Ratcliffe-cross - -	3	6	3	6	4	6	6	6
Shoreditch-church - -	2	6	2	6	3	0	5	0
Smithfield - - -	1	6	1	6	1	6	3	0
Temple-bar - - -	1	0	1	0	1	0	3	0
Tottenham-co. road, end of Goodge-str.	1	0	1	0	1	0	3	0
Tower-gate - - -	2	0	2	0	2	6	4	6
Union-street end, Borough -	2	0	2	0	2	6	5	0
Whitechapel-bars - -	2	0	2	0	2	6	5	0

George Colman the elder, the popular dramatist (1733–94), after having managed Covent Garden Theatre for a time, purchased the Haymarket Theatre, which is called by his name in this guide to hackney carriage fares. Date, end of century

Profiles of Garrick and Hogarth

XIII

DRAMA, STAGE, AND MUSIC

AT the opening of the reign of Queen Anne the drama was still 'Restoration drama', that of Congreve, Vanbrugh, and Farquhar. The plots of the plays were still as a rule indelicate and their language outspoken, so that ladies were wont, if they visited the theatre at all, to wear vizard masks—a practice which was forbidden by royal edict in 1704. There were other causes which made the theatre, even half a century later, a doubtful place of resort for gentlewomen. Although it improved as time went on, the behaviour of eighteenth-century playgoers was apt to be rough and unmannerly, and any disapprobation of a performance was shown emphatically and forcibly. Lord Mansfield once laid down the law of hissing. 'Every man', he declared, 'that is at the playhouse has a right to express his approbation or disapprobation instantaneously, according as he likes either the acting or the piece ; that is a right due to the theatre, an unalterable right.' But audiences in Mansfield's day were not content with merely hissing ; their resentment might lead to dangerous violence. It was a sure sign that a scene of uproar was intended or anticipated when the ladies in the house were hurriedly led out by their cavaliers. On one occasion when a certain popular French dancer failed to appear, a terrible riot ensued. The cry ' Fire the house ' was raised by a noble marquess, the stage was stormed, swords were drawn, the scenery, the musical instruments, and the furniture of the theatre were all destroyed. Another serious disturbance took place when the time-honoured custom of admitting footmen and lackeys into the upper gallery free of charge was suspended by a certain manager. This privilege was not universally abolished till 1780.

Audiences became more decorous as the intimacy of the theatre decreased, as the auditorium grew longer, the distance between stage and spectators greater. In the days of Garrick the apron stage, thrust out into the auditorium, disappeared, and footlights were introduced, so that the mimic world behind them became remote as it had never been before. Until 1762 it had been customary to accommodate privileged patrons on the stage itself. For the theatre-goer of small means there was the upper gallery, the price of admission to which was usually one shilling, or the centre gallery, for which you paid two shillings. The more fashionable parts of the house were the pit and the lower boxes or gallery, for which five shillings was charged. But when the celebrated actor-manager, John Rich, moved from humbler surroundings into his fine new theatre in Covent Garden in 1733, he definitely recognized the stage as forming part of the ordinary sitting-accommodation of the house and charged half a guinea for its superior attractiveness. To the young gallant who was an *habitué* of the theatre, half its charm lay in being on or behind the stage, among the actors and actresses all the time, and the cynosure of envious eyes in pit and boxes. Sometimes so great was the crush on the stage that the players had difficulty in making their entrances and exits through the throng. The practical inconvenience of this custom, and its great inappropriateness from a dramatic point of view, were so obvious that more than one attempt was made to suppress it. But financial considerations could not be ignored,

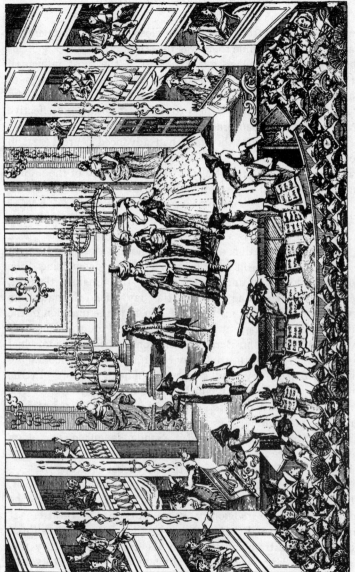

The eighteenth-century Theatre and Stage. The engraving commemorates a riot in Covent Garden Theatre, 1763

and managers were reluctant to close a very remunerative part of the house, while there was the still more serious argument that valuable patronage might be lost if the most influential of their clients were dislodged from their favourite coign of vantage. It needed a man of Garrick's force of character and strong sense of dramatic fitness to make a resolute and effective stand against this bad practice.

By this date, 1762, the stage had advanced a great deal in general respectability. Even before the accession of Anne there had been a famous protest against the immorality of the drama. In 1698 there had appeared Jeremy Collier's famous invective, *A Short View of the Immorality and Profaneness of the English Stage*, and this attack was followed by others less well known. In 1711 the two Houses of Convocation addressed to the Queen a strong condemnation of the contemporary drama. In 1719 a certain chaplain in a nobleman's house, denouncing ' the horrid blasphemies and impieties' of the English theatres, demonstrated that the plays of the day offended against no fewer than 1,400 texts in the Bible. In 1735 the question of the influence of the stage was brought forward in the House of Commons by Sir John Barnard, who complained of the mischief done by the London theatres, ' by corrupting youth, encouraging vice and debauchery, and greatly prejudicing trade '. In the middle of the century William Law, the mystic, wrote a treatise *On the Absolute Unlawfulness of the Stage*, in which he maintained that ' the playhouse . . . is as certainly the house of the devil as the church is the house of God '. Similar language is common in the later decades of the century, when latent Puritanism was reinforced by the new energy of the Methodist revival.

Diatribes against the drama do not necessarily influence it. They simply indicate that there is a hostile element in the population, which religiously keeps outside the theatre. It must be remembered that even among the leisured and cultured classes the theatre-going public in the eighteenth century was never a very large one. Apart altogether from those to whose piety the theatre appeared an essentially depraved place, there were many who, while having no moral scruples, were not attracted by this particular kind of entertainment, who in a domestic age enjoyed only the domestic amusements of the tea-table, the card-table, and one may add the writing-table—for it is by no mere accident that so many eighteenth-century novels are

Theatre Ticket designed by Hogarth

Fielding's 'The Mock Doctor', adapted from Molière's 'Le Médicin malgré Lui', was first produced in 1732 at Drury Lane

written in epistolary form ; there is no doubt that people in those days thoroughly enjoyed writing very long letters to one another.

But there is evidence that some of the attacks did have a direct influence upon the theatre. Collier's did serious damage to the regular drama, and for a time attracted managerial attention away from it to the variety show. It also suggested to some authors the question whether the standpoint of the playwright need necessarily be, if not immoral, non-moral, whether the drama might not be moralized. Let the comedy continue to cater for its old public by harping on the same theme, that of illicit love and intrigue, but let the critics be propitiated by making virtue clearly triumphant in the end. Both Addison and Steele, who in all their writings zealously avoided indelicacy of subject and coarseness of language, contributed to the dramatic literature of their day. Perhaps the greatest theatrical event of the reign of Queen Anne was the production in 1713 of Addison's *Cato*. Hopelessly turgid and undramatic it appears to us now, but it had a great success in its own day, partly because of the topical political allusions which each party contrived to read into it to its own satisfaction, but partly because of its apostrophes of virtue, of liberty, and of patriotism. Steele wrote a number of comedies ' on the side of the angels ', which were regarded by contemporaries as somewhat tame in consequence, and yet have not impressed posterity as high examples of moral elevation. Hazlitt, for example, wrote : ' Nothing can be better meant, or more ineffective. It is almost a misnomer to call them comedies ; they are rather homilies in dialogue, in which a number of pretty ladies and gentlemen discuss the fashionable topics of gaming, of duelling, of seduction, of scandal, &c., with a sickly sensibility, that shows as little hearty aversion to vice as sincere attachment to virtue. . . . The sting is indeed taken out of what is bad, but what is good at the same time loses its manhood and nobility.' Another playwright who wrote in the same vein was Colley Cibber (1671–1757), whose comedies are now as dead as dead can be, but who still lives in his own *Apology* for himself, and who still is notorious as an adapter of Shakespeare because of the numerous outrages which he committed in the adapting process. Cibber claimed that he had always the interests of virtue at heart when he wrote his plays, and he was no doubt quite sincere in his moral aim, but this only proves that his moral standard was by no means exalted.

After the temporary set-back sustained by the drama as the

result of Collier's diatribes there came another, also temporary, but also serious, in 1737, when the Licensing Act was instituted by Walpole. This measure was not a complete innovation. The King's Master of the Revels had for generations had authority over stage-players ; by the fiat of the Lord Chamberlain *Polly*, the successor to *The Beggar's Opera*, had been suppressed. But the right of superintendence over the stage had been undefined and spasmodic. It now became systematized, and it exists to this day. For a long time past the object of the censorship has been understood to be the safeguarding of the stage from indecency and profaneness, but this was not the aim of Walpole's legislation. He was thinking, not of the protection of the public against immorality, but of the protection of politicians against abuse. The stage had proved one of the most effective vehicles for the ventilation of anti-ministerial criticism. Not all the wit of Pulteney and Bolingbroke in the *Craftsman* had been as useful a weapon against Walpole as *The Beggar's Opera* ; and some of Fielding's comedies, such as *Pasquin*, had been exceedingly outspoken. It is worth noting that Barnard, who had uttered so strong a protest against the evil influence of London theatres, was strongly opposed to the idea of a stage censorship, and had objected to the Lord Chamberlain's action in prohibiting the production of *Polly*. But the great attack upon the licensing system came from Lord Chesterfield, when the Bill came before the House of Lords. The press and the stage were, he maintained, society's ' two out-sentries ', and the powers now to be wielded by the Lord Chamberlain amounted to the placing of a tax upon wit.

The drama during the reigns of the first two Georges was at best third-rate, and except to the antiquarian it has little interest. So far as the ordinary reader is concerned, it has been decently buried, and there is no occasion for its resurrection. This period produced the most execrable travesties of Shakespeare—the worst perhaps being Lord Lansdowne's conversion of *The Merchant of Venice* into *The Jew of Venice*, in which Shylock became a low comedy figure. Tragedy of a sort continued to be written—so stilted and bombastic in character that it is only memorable because it provoked the satire of Fielding and Sheridan, being exquisitely ridiculed in *The Tragedy of Tragedies or The Life and Death of Tom Thumb the Great*, and in *The Critic*. But one of the eighteenth-century tragedians has a permanent niche in the history of English literature—not because he is read to-day (he is not), but because he had considerable influence abroad as well as in England as the reviver of the type of domestic tragedy which flourished in Elizabethan and Jacobean days, of which *Arden of Feversham* and *The Yorkshire Tragedy* are examples. This was George Lillo, whose best-known work is *The London Merchant, or the History of George Barnwell*.[1] Lillo went not to palace or council-chamber for his themes, but to the shop and counting-house, and his dialogue, however heavy and unnatural it may appear to us, was intended to be homely and colloquial. Lillo, like Steele, had an ethical purpose, and *George Barnwell* was for many years regularly acted at holiday seasons for the moral benefit of London apprentices. Another practitioner of this form of art was Edward Moore, whose plays *The Foundling* and *The Gamester* had a great vogue in their day.

The popularity of the legitimate drama in the first half of the eighteenth century was far eclipsed by that of the variety stage. The ballet, the masquerade, tight-rope dancing, made a much stronger appeal to the general populace of London. The king of all variety entertainers in the century was Rich, himself a very admirable mimic, but most successful as a producer. He ministered lavishly to the average man's love of the spectacular, provided elaborate scenery, real water, real animals, and he was once only dissuaded from bringing an elephant upon the stage because it was proved to him that the hole in the wall of the theatre which would have to be driven to admit the entrance of the beast would be so large as to imperil the stability of the building. Above all, Rich was the purveyor, or rather indeed the creator, of English pantomime. Rich's entertainments commonly consisted of two parts. The *pièce de résistance* would be of a more or less serious nature, a play culled from Ovid's

[1] Lillo was preceded in this genre by the less well-known Aaron Hill. See A. Nicoll, *Early XVIIIth Century Drama*, p. 119.

At *LEE* and *HARPER's* Great Theatrical Booth,

ON the *Bowling-Green*, behind the *Queen's-Arm* Tavern, near the *Marshalsea-Gate*, during the Time of Southwark Fair, will be perform'd, The True and Antien History of

WHITTINGTON.

Shewing how he came to London to seek his Fortune, having been advis'd to it by a Cunning Woman; his Money being spent, he sat down to condole himself at a Merchant's Door, who took him into his Family to be a Scullion The Merchant sending a Ship to the Kingdom of Morocco, call'd his Servants, according to Custom, to send their Ventures; among which Whittington appear'd, and having nothing but a Cat he sent her. The Ship arriving at Morocco, which Kingdom being much infested with Rats and Mice, the Emperor return'd for the Cat, a great Quantity of Gold Dust and several precious Jewels. While the Ship was on her Voyage, poor Whittington was so cruelly treated by Madge, a Cook-maid, that he resolved to return into the Country; being got two Miles from London, and hearing the Bells ring fancy'd they spoke to him to return, and that he should be Lord-Mayor of London, which induc'd him to go again to the Merchant's, where he had not long been before the Arrival of his Treasure, half of which he bestow'd for the City's Use; whereon he was unanimously elected Lord-Mayor in all the Pomp and Pageantry us'd in those Days.

The Part of Whittington, by Mr. Morgan.

With Variety of Singing and Dancing by the best Masters. Particularly, The Song of Mad Tom of Bedlam, by Mr Plat. Thames and Augusta, by Mr. Plat and Mr. Papilion.

The Cloaths and Scenes are all entirely New

At *LEE* and *HARPER's* Great Theatrical Booth,

BEHIND the *Marshalsea-Gate*, leading to the *Bowling-Green*, during the Time of Southwark-Fair, will be presented, A new Opera, never perform'd here before, call'd,

The DEVIL *to* PAY: Or, *The* WIVES Metamorphos'd
Intermix'd with above Thirty New Songs, made to old Ballad Tunes, and Country Dances.

The Part of Sir John Loverule, by Mr Mullart.
Ranger, by Mr Taylor; Doctor, Mr. Ayres; Butle, Mr. Rosco; Cook, Mr. Eaton. Lady Loverule, Mrs. Mullart; Noll Jobson, Miss Tollet; Lettice, Mrs. Coker; Lucy, Mrs. Hulitt: And the Part of Jobson, the Cobler, by Mr. Hulett.

And the better to entertain the Gentry, M S. *Lee* has engag'd a Company of Tumblers, lately arrived in London, who perform several surprizing Tricks; particularly, one throws himself off a Scaffold twelve Foot high; another throws himself over 12 Men's Heads; He likewise leaps over 6 Boys, sitting on 12 Men's Shoulders; another tumbles over 16 Swords, as high as Men can hold them; and several other diverting Things too tedious to mention

With variety of Singing and Dancing by the best Masters.

The Cloaths and Scenes are all entirely New.

We shall continue Playing from Ten in the Morning, 'till Nine at Night.

N. B. The right Book of the Droll is Sold in the Booth, and is Printed and Sold by G. LEE, in *Blue-Maid Alley, Southwark*; and all others (not Printed by him) are false.

Advertisements of pantomime and variety entertainments for Southwark Fair in 'The Grub-Street Journal' of Sept. 9. 1731.

G. Lee was a well-known holder of booths. 'The Devil to Pay' was an early ballad-opera, first produced at Drury Lane in 1731.
A farce aimed at the Nonconformists, it was one of the most popular light pieces of its day

STAG HUNT and FOX CHASE.

ROYAL CIRCUS,

The Company at the CIRCUS beg leave to acquaint the
Nobility, Gentry, and Public, that
Young CROSSMAN will appear

THIS and every EVENING next Week,
on HORSEBACK, and challenge all the Horsemen
in Europe.

FRICASSEE DANCING, VAULTING, TIGHT-ROPE
DANCING, PYRAMIDS, GROUND and LOFTY
TUMBLING, &c. &c. &c.

The Performance will commence with a Grand Entry of
Horses, mounted by the Troop.

Young CROSSMAN's unparalleled Peasant Hornpipe, and
Flag-Dance, not to be equalled by any Horseman in this
Kingdom.

LE GRAND SAUT DE TRAMPOLINE, by Mr POR-
TER, (Clown) who will jump over a Garter 15 Feet
from the Ground, and fire off two Pistols.

THE MUSICAL CHILD, (Only Nine Years of Age) will
go through his wonderful Performance.

Mr. SMITH will go through a Variety of Performances
on a Single Horse.

THE HUMOURS OF THE SACK,

Or, The CLOWN deceived by a Woman;
FRICASSEE DANCE,
By Mr. CROSSMAN and Mr. PORTER.

Mr. INGHAM (from Dublin) will throw an innumer-
able Row of Flipflaps.

Mr. CROSSMAN will vault over the Horse backwards
and forwards, with his Legs Tied, in a manner not to be
equalled by any Performer in this Kingdom.

GROUND and LOFTY TUMBLING, by the whole
Troop.

The AFRICAN will go through his astonishing Stage and
Equestrian Performances.

LA FORCE DE HERCULES;
Or, The RUINS OF TROY.

Mr. PORTER will perform on a single Horse, in a ludi-
crous manner.

Young CROSSMAN will leap from a single Horse over
Two Garters, 12 feet high, and alight again on the Saddle, and Play the Violin in various Attitudes.

The TAYLOR's DISASTER,
Or, his Wonderful Journey to BRENTFORD,
By Mr. PORTER

To conclude with a REAL FOX and STAG CHASE,
by twelve couple of Hounds, and two real FOXES, and
a real STAG HUNT, as performed before their Majesties.

Breaking and Teaching as usual.

A Newspaper advertisement of the end of the century

A Female Wire Dancer, at Sadler's Wells

Metamorphoses or some classical fable, in which would appear gods and goddesses, nymphs and naiads, scenery, dresses, and dances being of an elaborate type. Between the acts of this legendary drama there would be interwoven comic episodes from the eternal comedy of Harlequin and Columbine, the most amazing tricks being produced by the wand of Harlequin—huts being transformed into palaces, men into wheelbarrows, sausage-shops into Indian encampments. The transformation scene as an adjunct of pantomime is one of the gifts of John Rich to the English theatre.

While pantomime was the delight of the ordinary rag-tag and bob-tail, the cultured tended more and more to give their suffrage to the sentimental comedy of which Steele had set the type. An extreme fastidiousness came to be the characteristic of the fashionable audiences in the later decades of the century. Critics of the beau-monde shuddered at the horseplay, the blood-thirstiness, the sensationalism which had appealed forcibly to Elizabethan audiences, and demanded a nice decorum—not necessarily of subject and situation, but certainly of language and diction, a careful avoidance of extremes, of the highly coloured, the emotional, the obstreperous. Playgoers like Chesterfield and Horace Walpole did not want to be harrowed or thrilled or to be made to laugh outright. They wished to be kept mildly amused, pleasantly interested, by a stage reflection of the good manners of their own mannered circle. Their requirements were met by such dramatists as Richard Cumberland, who, however, introduced some variety in drawing the contrast between artificial civilization and the crudity of outlaw life, notably *The Brothers*; George Colman the elder, who, however, could sometimes laugh at the foolishness of the extreme sentimentalists; and Hugh Kelly, who produced unadulterated sentimentality of the most mawkish kind, evidently to the complete satisfaction of his patrons.

In 1768 Garrick produced Kelly's masterpiece, *False Delicacy*. No play of the century was a more triumphant success. While it was running at Drury Lane there was presented at Covent Garden Goldsmith's play *The Good-Natur'd Man*. It is an interesting commentary on the taste of the time that the latter was a failure. Contemporaries condemned it precisely on account of its possessing the quality which to the modern mind appears to give it incontestable superiority over its rival—spontaneity. There is unforced humour in Goldsmith's scenes and characters. There lay the trouble—they were too funny, unbecomingly so. The most amusing scene in the play was hissed at the first performance and was subsequently omitted in deference to public feeling. But in his second play, *She Stoops to Conquer*, Goldsmith conquered. Even the most sophisticated proved unable to resist the assault of Tony Lumpkin.

Goldsmith invented no new dramatic form or method ; but he introduced into the comedy of manners a new vivacity, a genuine humanity, such as had given to the first part of *The Vicar of Wakefield* its abiding freshness and charm, putting into his work for the stage something of the warmth and attractiveness of a personality which was essentially whimsical and lovable. This dunce at school, who passed through three universities without learning anything, this would-be medical practitioner, who remained hopelessly ignorant of medicine and incompetent to practise, this amateur flute-player, who started his career by a continental Odyssey with nothing but his little instrument between himself and starvation, this would-be historian of England who could not be bothered to consult any authorities—just because of his queerness and his humanity gave to the English drama, as he did to the English novel and to English poetry, something precious and imperishable.

Goldsmith was surpassed by Sheridan, who had greater dramatic skill, and was indeed the greatest dramatic genius of the century with the exception of Congreve. Sheridan's versatility was such that he had three distinct careers—the first that of a knight-errant, the second that of a playwright, the third that of a statesman and orator. Before he was of age he had become notorious by escorting to France a certain fair lady, Miss Linley, whose heart was set upon entering a nunnery in defiance of her parent's wishes, going through at any rate the form of marriage with her at Calais, and fighting two duels as a consequence of this scatter-brained escapade. A year or so later, parental opposition having been withdrawn, he settled down to peaceful married life with his *inamorata*, and the following year blossomed forth as a great dramatist with the appearance of *The Rivals*. That delightful play was, like *The Good-Natur'd Man*, at first a failure, but, when revived in January 1777, it became an immense success, and it firmly established Sheridan's reputation. In 1777 there appeared *A Trip to Scarborough*, a very clever adaptation of Vanbrugh's *The Relapse*, in which Lord Foppington, rather less amusing than in the original, becomes more a figure of flesh and blood, and in which the whole action becomes dramatically stronger. In the same year came the masterpiece, *The School for Scandal*, and in 1779 that delectable burlesque *The Critic*. In 1780 Sheridan entered Parliament, and his career as a playwright closed. While he wrote other pieces—the farce *St. Patrick's Day*, the operetta *The Duenna*, the tragedy *Pizarro*—Sheridan's fame as a dramatist rests upon *The Rivals*, *The School for Scandal*, and *The Critic*. In these three plays there is revealed much of Congreve's brilliance together with a jollity and exuberance which have kept them permanently on the English stage, while Congreve's piercing wit is almost entirely relegated to the library.

Had it not been for the figures of Congreve at the one end of the century and Sheridan at the other, it would have been legitimate to argue that the eighteenth-century stage in England was much more remarkable for its actors than for its dramatists. In this period the personality of the player came to count, very often, for much more than the play, and people went to the theatre, not because they were attracted by the piece, but because Garrick or Mrs. Siddons was in the cast. The great actor of the Restoration drama was Betterton, who died at the age of seventy-five in 1710. In the next generation the stars were Colley Cibber, James Quin, and Charles Macklin. Cibber's début as an actor was unfortunate. He had to take a message to the character whom the great Betterton was portraying. As he approached the doyen of the stage the novice was seized with such panic that he completely forgot his part. Betterton

The *THIRD DAY*.

For the Benefit of the R E V I V E R.

By HIS MAJESTY's Company of Comedians,

AT THE

THEATRE ROYAL

In D R U R Y - L A N E,

This present *Tuesday*, being the 7th of *March*, will be
presented a New Moral MASQUE, call'd

C O M U S.

Alter'd from *Milton's* MASQUE at *Ludlow Castle*,
and now Adapted to the Stage.

The Principal Characters by

Mr. *Quin*,	Mr. *Mills*,
Mr. *Milward*,	Mr. *Hill*, and
Mr. *Cibber*,	Mrs. *Cibber*,

The MUSICK compos'd by Mr. *ARNE*.

The Vocal Parts by

Mr. *Beard*, Mrs. *Clive*, Mrs. *Arne*, and Others.

The Dances by

Monsieur *Denoyer*, Monsieur *Muilment*, Mrs. *Walter*,
Mrs. *Thompson*, and Others.

Boxes 5 s. Pit 3 s. First Gallery 2 s. Upper Gallery 1 s.

N. B. To prevent any Interruption in the Musick, Dancing, Machinery, or
other Parts of the Performance, Side Boxes only will be form'd on the Stage.
For the Accommodation of the Ladies, and (by Desire) Five Rows of the Pit
will be Rail'd in at the Price of the Boxes, where Servants will be admitted
to keep Places, and the Ladies are desir'd to send them by 3 o' Clock.

To begin exactly at Six o'Clock.　　　　　　　*Vivat Rex.*

Books of the Masque will be Sold in the Theatre, at One Shilling each.

---

*A BILL in the Gabrielle Enthoven collection, announcing the third performance
of an operatic version of 'Comus' at Drury Lane on March 7, 1738, by 'His
Majesty's Company of Comedians . . . To begin exactly at Six o'Clock'*
By permission of 'The Times'

was furious at the contretemps brought about by a bungler, whose name he did not even know. ' Forfeit him ! ' he exclaimed. It was explained that that was impossible, as this beginner had no salary. Determined to penalize him in some way, Betterton then ordered, ' Put him down ten shillings a week, and forfeit five ! ' Cibber was not happily endowed by nature, being very short, corpulent, with a broad face, thin legs, and large feet, while his voice was shrill and apt to crack when raised in passion. Despite these disabilities it was Cibber's ambition to excel as *jeune premier* and in tragic parts ; he actually made his name by his excellence in characters for which his physical peculiarities were an advantage—in those of grave coxcombs, such as Lord Foppington—for it has to be remembered, that the beau of the early eighteenth century, unlike his successor of the macaroni period, had the solemn, majestic strut of the peacock, was not neat, lithe, and dapper.

Quin, like Colley, fancied himself in tragedy, but was really best in comedy, his great part being Falstaff. He was in private life a singularly disagreeable personage—a glutton and a heavy drinker, foul-mouthed, irascible, and infinitely self-important, and his one saving grace was a gift of lively repartee. On the stage he was the superlative of gorgeousness and the grand manner. Splendidly apparelled in brocades and embroideries, lace and ruffles, Quin, with very little variety of intonation but in a majestic bass, would mouth his heroic polysyllables with an air of superb self-complacency and complete detachment from the audience. Macklin, Quin's great rival, also an unpleasant and bad-tempered individual, excelled in Shylock, and he is noteworthy as having given the death-blow to the low-comedy conception of the Jew, his own rendering being a great piece of tragic acting. Macklin's methods appear to have been less stagy and ostentatious than Quin's. At all events the latter used to complain that Macklin's presence on the stage with him was disturbing, being antipathetic to the grand manner.

These were the gods of the theatre when the young David Garrick took the world by storm. Of a Huguenot family, Garrick started life as a wine-merchant, but trade did not prosper, and his innate love of acting led to his first appearance on the stage, under an assumed name, at Ipswich. It was, however, on the 19th October 1741, when taking the part of Shakespeare's Richard III at a little theatre in Goodman's Fields, that he

A Copy of the PLAY BILL *that announced the first appearance of* Mr. GARRICK.

October 19th, 1741.

GOODMAN'S FIELDS.

At the late Theatre in Goodman's Fields, this Day will be performed,

A Concert of Vocal and Instrumental Music,
DIVIDED INTO TWO PARTS.

TICKETS AT THREE, TWO, AND ONE SHILLING.

Places for the Boxes to be taken at the Fleece Tavern, near the Theatre.

N. B. Between the Two Parts of the Concert will be presented an Historical Play, called the

LIFE AND DEATH OF
King Richard the Third.

CONTAINING THE DISTRESSES OF K. HENRY VI.
The artful acquisition of the Crown by King Richard,
The Murder of Young King Edward V. and his Brother in the Tower,
THE LANDING OF THE EARL OF RICHMOND,
And the Death of King Richard in the memorable Battle of Bosworth Field, being the last that was fought between the Houses of York and Lancaster, with many other true Historical Passages.

The Part of King Richard by A GENTLEMAN,
(Who never appeared on any Stage).

King Henry, by Mr. GIFFARD,   Richmond, Mr. MARSHALL,
Prince Edward, by Miss HIPPISLEY,   Duke of York, Miss NAYLOR,
Duke of Buckingham, Mr. PATERSON,   Duke of Norfolk, Mr. BLAKES,   Lord Stanley, Mr. PAGETT
Oxford, Mr. VAUGHAN,   Tressel, Mr. W. GIFFARD,   Catesby, Mr. MARR,   Ratcliff, Mr. CROFTS,
Blunt, Mr. NAYLOR,   Tyrrel, Mr. PUTTENHAM,   Lord Mayor, Mr. DUNSTALL.

The Queen, Mrs. STEEL,   Duchess of York, Mrs. YATES,
And the Part of Lady Anne, by Mrs GIFFARD

WITH

Entertainments of Dancing,

By Mons FROMET,   Madame DUVALT,   and the Two Masters and Miss GRANIER

To which will be added a Ballad Opera, of One Act, called

The Virgin Unmask'd.

The Part of Lucy, by Miss HIPPISLEY

Both of which will be performed Gratis, by Persons for their Diversion

The Concert will begin exactly at Six o'Clock.

A copy of the play-bill announcing the first appearance of Garrick as Richard III

suddenly leapt into fame, and gained the enthusiastic praise of Cobham, Lyttelton, and Pitt. In the following year he appeared at Drury Lane and Covent Garden and in Dublin. Although his success was instantaneous, and once having made his name he never looked back, Garrick for a time had to struggle hard against the jealous animosity of the actors of the old school.

His methods were as different as possible from Quin's. As that veteran put it, ' If the young fellow is right, I and the rest of the players have all been wrong '.

> Poor Quin, who damns all churches but his own,
> Complains that heresy corrupts the town,
> That Whitefield Garrick has misled the age,
> And taints the sound religion of the stage.

DAVID GARRICK

From a painting by Pompeo Battoni

But as the writer of these lines adds :

> When doctrines meet with general approbation,
> It is not heresy, but reformation.

The most dangerous of Garrick's enemies was Samuel Foote, who wrote a number of satirical farces, which had a great vogue at the time for the same reason that they have had no vogue at all since—that they were essentially topical. Foote was also a very able comedian, a wonderful and a very cruel mimic, a bit of an epicure, rather eccentric, and very much a snob.

But Garrick triumphed over all hostility, for he brought to the stage something novel and tonic. He did not merely declaim in the grand manner of Quin. His methods were natural, his style was quietly realist. Quin's stage costume was either a fantastic garb intended to be classical or ornate contemporary dress ; Garrick chose clothes such as would indicate the character

Reynolds's picture of Garrick being solicited by the Muses of Tragedy and Comedy

he was portraying but not distract attention from the acting. Thus, in *Macbeth* he did not wear a kilt to show that the hero was a Scot or antique armour to show that the period of the play was the eleventh century, but he wore a scarlet and gold military uniform, whose anachronism would have seemed incongruous to our eyes, but which was perhaps truer to the mind of Shakespeare than the meticulous historical accuracy which the taste of a later day demanded. On his return from a prolonged continental tour Garrick introduced into the English theatre for the first time the use of footlights—hitherto the stage, like the auditorium, had been lighted by chandeliers. These new lighting effects made the stage-scene more of a picture, while a concentration of light upon the actor's face gave far more importance to facial expression as an element in the actor's art. Garrick excelled in depicting subtle changes of thought or mood in this way, so that it was said that his face was a language in itself. He was able to individualize the parts he played as his contemporaries could not. It was said of his chief rival in popular favour, Barry, that in *King Lear* he was ' every inch a King ', but of Garrick it was said that he was ' every inch King Lear'. Dr. Johnson spoke of his ' universality '. We should call it versatility. It was noted of Cibber, the great exponent of the coxcomb, that he was always a coxcomb, even in such parts as Iago and Wolsey ; of Booth, who had taken the title *rôle* in Addison's *Cato*, that, whatever the part, he was always a philosopher. Garrick himself once said that no actor could be a great tragedian unless he was also a good comedian, and Reynolds's famous picture of Garrick torn between the tragic muse and the comic muse reminds us that he at all events was great both in tragedy and comedy. The service which Garrick rendered to the Shakespearean revival has often been misstated. He certainly did not initiate it ; the great Shakespearean *rôles* figured in every star actor's repertoire before Garrick's day ; nor did he sound the death-knell of Shakespearean travesty. His own adaptations of *A Midsummer Night's Dream* and *The Tempest* were deplorable. Garrick's service to Shakespeare was in his acting, in the fact that he made the great characters stand out, not as stock conventional figures, but as live human beings.

Goldsmith in the on the whole rather ill-natured lines devoted to Garrick in *Retaliation*, describes him as ' an abridgement of all that was pleasant in man ', and ' As a wit, if not first, in the very first line ' ; and Johnson, who assumed quite a proprietary air towards Garrick—they were educated in the same school in Lichfield—spoke of him as ' the first man in the world for sprightly conversation '. Garrick was not only a great actor, but a member of the Johnson circle, and of other distinguished

Mrs. Abington as Scrub in Farquhar's 'The Beaux' Stratagem'

Cartoon by James Sayers

circles as well—in other words a great public figure. No other man ever did as much to raise the social standing of the actor's calling.

Of Garrick's contemporaries most are forgotten—save for Peg Woffington, famous for her beauty, for her skill in such different parts as those of noble ladies, homely gossips, and dashing minxes, for her immense, rather hoydenish good nature, and her constant infidelities. But Garrick's other leading ladies, such as Mrs. Clive and Mrs. Abington, are now no more than names deciphered on the facsimiles of ancient play-bills, and the same may be said of those sterling actors Mr. King and Mr. Dodd, and ' Gentleman Smith ', the original Charles Surface, debonair, perfect as the man about town, and Barry, who looked so fascinating as Romeo that all the young ladies in the audience fell in love with him and vowed he was much superior to Mr. Garrick.

Although he continued in management for some time afterwards, Garrick virtually retired from the stage in 1766 ; the next great star of the eighteenth-century theatre, Mrs. Siddons, did not establish her position till 1782. Sarah Kemble, one of the numerous children of an itinerant player, was born in the Shoulder of Mutton Inn at Brecon in 1755. Her father did not want her to adopt his profession, and she took service as a lady's maid, but soon she was reciting Shakespeare and Milton in the servants' hall, and a little later before the quality in the drawing-room. In 1773 she married William Siddons, a rather down-at-the-heel actor of an obsequious and even cringing disposition. The husband and wife acted in very inferior theatrical companies in the west of England. In these early days the immortal Sarah was of fragile appearance, very timid and nervous ; yet she moved an audience of intending scoffers to tears at the little spa of Cheltenham, then just on the threshold of its fame as a watering-place, by her performance in Otway's *Venice Preserved*. Garrick heard of her and sent an emissary to report upon her. A second report came from a clergyman, who saw her at Worcester, and informed Garrick that she had an excellent figure and would do particularly well in ' breeches

*Costume on the stage at the end of the century.   Miss Farren and Mr. King as ‘Lady
Emily Gaxville’ and ‘Sir Clement Flint’*

*From an engraving by J. Jones after J. Downman.   Lent by the courtesy of the Editor
of ‘ The Connoisseur’*

parts '. It was arranged that Mrs. Siddons should come up to London for trial. The servile husband was very anxious to be included in the bargain, but it does not appear that he got his way. In any case this first essay in the metropolis was not a success, and when Sheridan succeeded to the management of Drury Lane he did not re-engage Mrs. Siddons, on the ground

MRS. SIDDONS

By John Donaldson, in the Collection of the late J. Pierpont Morgan, Esq.

that Garrick had not regarded her as a first-rate actress. She returned to the provinces and, touring up and down the country, gained a great deal more experience and a great deal more confidence. From 1778 and 1782 she was in Bath, and her successes there were a prelude to a second venture in London. On the 10th October 1782 she appeared at Drury Lane in Southerne's *The Fatal Marriage,* and achieved a success as sensational as Garrick's had been. For some time she continued to act almost exclusively the parts of tender and gentle heroines, but her performance in February 1785 as Lady Macbeth revealed her as a great tragic actress. Prior to this the great Lady Macbeth of the century had been Mrs. Pritchard, an immense favourite with the theatre-going public. Mrs. Pritchard had always used a candle in the sleep-walking scene ; Mrs. Siddons

The CRITIC or TRAGEDYREHEARS'D.

Published Feb.y 24th 1786 by S. W. Fores, at the Caricature Warehouse, N.o 3 Piccadilly

Mr. Puff and Tilburina

Published Feb. 24th, 1786, by S. W. Fores, at the Caricature Warehouse, No. 3 Piccadilly

did not propose to do this. So susceptible were eighteenth-century audiences that the Drury Lane management were apprehensive of trouble as the result of this departure from tradition, but so intense was Mrs. Siddons's acting that no one even noticed the omission of the candle. Lady Macbeth remained her greatest part ; but she also excelled as Katharine in *Henry VIII*. Nowadays we think of her as a great tragedienne, because we know her best by her picture as the Tragic Muse. A beautiful woman as well as a great actress, she was the delight of portrait-painters.

Particularly in the first half of the eighteenth century the drama had a serious rival in opera. There were two distinct types of opera. There was, first, what is known as ' ballad-opera ', in which the music was usually English, derived either from folk-song melodies or from popular tunes of the day. Such operas were essentially simple and popular, but they were musically sometimes of a higher and sincerer type than their more pretentious rivals. By far the best-known work of this nature was *The Beggar's Opera* (produced in 1728), whose popularity in its own generation was as phenomenal as that which it achieved when it was revived in the twentieth century. The cast and the promoters of the entertainment were doubtful whether it would succeed, and were nervous at the first perform-ance, but well before the end of the first act they were reassured by hearing the Duke of Argyll in one of the boxes exclaim, ' It will do—it must do—I see it in the eyes of them '. The original success of the play was due largely to the story and to the political allusions, often at the expense of Walpole, which gave such umbrage in the royal circle that two of its chief patrons, the Duke and Duchess of Queensberry, were forbidden the Court. But *The Beggar's Opera* also held its audiences because it was musically attractive, because its songs were catchy and charming.

Incidentally *The Beggar's Opera* was an excellent burlesque of the absurdities of the sentimental drama and of the second type of eighteenth-century opera—the Italian, which Dr. Johnson defined as ' an exotic and irrational entertainment '. That may have been the point of view of the people who rejoiced in Gay's masterpiece, but there was a large section of the musical public in eighteenth-century England, as there has been of other times, who appreciated any kind of music other than its own. At the opening of the century there was a strong per-suasion that the only good music in the world was Italian music. In truth the Italian operas which were in vogue at that date were of a very low order of artistic merit, being totally undramatic and consisting of endless arias written specially to suit the individual requirements of the Italian *virtuosi* who sang in them.

In many cases their sole *raison d'être* was that they should afford an opportunity for vocal gymnastics : it was vocal gymnastics that the audiences went to hear. Sometimes, in the earliest years of the century, only the leading *rôles* were taken by Italians singing in their own language, all the minor parts being sung by

Concert-ticket designed by Hogarth

From Ireland's 'Graphic Illustrations of Hogarth', 1799

natives in English. But similar linguistic confusion has been known on the boards of Covent Garden in the twentieth century.

While Italian opera was popular in a certain set in the first decade of the eighteenth century, it did not gain widespread support at first, because the general prejudice against Papists and foreigners had to be overcome. More widely diffused popularity followed upon the appearance of Handel in England in 1710. Handel had made a reputation as a composer in his native country before he was twenty-one, but since then he had studied in Italy and become saturated with the Italian influence, so that it was an Italian, and not a German style, that he brought with him to England. It is as an English musician that he is now, quite rightly, counted : for he was only in his twenty-sixth year when he arrived, and he spent the remainder of his long life, with one short interval, in England, becoming naturalized in 1726. He became even in his own lifetime a great national institution. His opera *Rinaldo*, produced in 1711, was a signal success ; its successor was the same ; and after he had written a *Te Deum* in celebration of the Treaty of Utrecht he was granted a life-pension by Queen Anne. At the Georgian Court subsequently he basked in royal favour, while he was a protégé of the Duke of Chandos and of other nobles.

But the sun did not shine constantly. For a short period after his accession George I was hostile—Handel had been *Kapellmeister* at the Court of Hanover, and he had deserted for the larger world of London. But George I did not long remain unforgiving. More serious was the rivalry of another composer of Italian opera, who also settled down in England and gained an important following—Giovanni Buononcini—so that all musical London was divided between the two. A popular catch ran—

> Some say compared to Buononcini
> That Mynher Handel 's but a ninny ;
> Others aver that he to Handel,
> Is scarcely fit to hold a candle.
> Strange all this difference should be,
> 'Twixt Tweedledum and Tweedledee.

The verdict of posterity is at strange variance with the conclusion arrived at in this rhyme ! Handel's early popularity suffered something of an eclipse after the arrival of his competitor. In 1729 he went into joint management with a competent Swiss impresario named Heidegger, and his fortunes revived, but an unfortunate quarrel with an Italian singer some years later led to the estrangement of many of his best patrons, and a rival opera was established in Lincoln's Inn Fields in 1733. Thither

A Concert at Montagu House, 1736

From a drawing by Marcellus Laroon in the British Museum

went the Prince of Wales and many of the aristocracy, and Lord Hervey tells us how George II and his Queen used to sit shivering in the empty Haymarket Theatre, where one of Handel's operas was being performed, while all the rest of the world followed the Prince. In 1737, as the result of his ill-fortune, Handel went bankrupt.

Ere this Handel had turned his attention to a new type of composition. Until he was well on in middle life he was known

G. F. HANDEL

almost exclusively as a writer of operas. He wrote thirty-six of these. They are now almost entirely forgotten, though expert opinion holds that, embedded in a vast deal that is dull and conventional, there are a number of fine airs, as good as any in his better-known works. But in the history of opera Handel cannot take a high place, for he brought nothing new to its development. He was quite content with existing banalities, and made scarcely any attempt at characterization or the dramatically appropriate. His lasting greatness is based almost entirely upon his oratorios. To Handel and his contemporaries the word did not mean at all what it means nowadays. It meant to them simply any kind of choral music performed in the concert room, and was just as much an ordinary entertainment as the opera was. It was not necessarily sacred music, either by subject or in feeling. There was indeed very little that was religious in Handel's music or his temperament, and he simply took to the writing of oratorios because he found that people were getting tired of his operas, and that the oratorios paid better. He was a very

SUSANNA

an

ORATORIO

Set to Musick by

M͚ HANDEL

London. *Printed for: I. Walsh, in Catharine Street, in the Strand, of whom may be had, The Works of M͚ Handel, Geminiani, Corelli, and all the most Eminent Authors of Musick.*

Engraved title-page (reduced) of 'Susanna', one of Handel's later works

practically minded man, who believed in giving the public what it wants. Besides, the production of oratorios was much less expensive !

Handel had written the oratorio *Esther* before 1720 ; it was the discovery that a revival of it in 1732 pleased the public that determined him to devote himself for the future primarily to this form of composition. But it was some time before he achieved a really great success with it. Both *Israel in Egypt*, produced in 1738, and *Saul*, produced in 1740, were coldly received, and there is a well-known story of Lord Chesterfield leaving an auditorium practically empty save for the ever-faithful royal patrons at one of these performances because he thought it indecorous to intrude on his sovereign's privacy. Lack of support in London induced Handel to give the first performance of his one religiously conceived oratorio, *The Messiah*, in Dublin, where it achieved an immense success. When his masterpiece was performed in London there was little enthusiasm, and although Handel wrote *Samson* and a number of other similar works in the meantime, he was again a bankrupt in 1745. His first genuine success with an oratorio in London came next year, when *Judas Maccabaeus* was first sung. This marked the turn of the tide, and, although his numerous other works were not all received with equal favour, his general popularity remained unabated. His reputation was secure, and the remainder of his days were untroubled, save by the terrible affliction of blindness, till his death in 1759.

Despite the fact that his extraordinarily copious output contains a very high proportion of inferior work, quite unworthy of his renown, Handel's name is the most famous in the whole history of music in England. On the other hand, there is no doubt that the immense authority which he exercised during his lifetime, and the still greater influence which he exerted after his death, was a great misfortune from the point of view of the development of national English music. Very many of his contemporaries and successors were content to be merely imitators of Handel, and he remained the predominant, all-pervading power over music in these islands until the vogue of Mendelssohn

This is to give Notice
To all Shopkeepers and Others,

THAT at the Printing-House in Bow Church Yard, Cheapside London, all manner of Business in Printing, either at the Letter-Press or Rolling press, continues to be carried on by THOMAS COBB, who married the Widow of the late Mr. JOHN CLUER, who kept the said Printing-House

Where Shopkeepers Bills, and Bills of Parcels are curiously engraved on Copper: Also Marks for Tobacconists, Haberdashers of Hats, &c. are engraved on Wood or Copper.

Labels for Surgeons Chests, Apothecaries, Grocers, &c. may be had there, painted or plain.

Also Blank Receipts for Taxes, &c. Titles for Hungary-Water, Directions for Daffey's Elixir, and Spirits of Scurvey-Grass.

Likewise Club-Orders and Funeral Tickets.

All Sorts of Pictures painted or plain, Lottery Pictures for Children, Copy-Book Covers, and a new Round-Hand Copy-Book with the Copies set on the Top of every Leaf for Learners to write underneath.

⁎ At the abovesaid Printing-Office may be had all Sorts of Paper for Writing Musick, sold cheaper than at any other Place.

Likewise Mr. Handel's Opera's, and many other Books of Musick, are there Engraved, Printed and Sold.

N.B. The Wholesale and Retale Warehouse for Dispensing Dr. Bateman's Pectoral Drops, by Letters Patent under the Great Seal of Great Britain, is still continued to be kept there.

Note also, That for those Persons who employ the said THOMAS COBB's Rolling-Press, he repairs their Copper-Plates, when necessary, gratis.

A printer's advertisement in 'The Grub-street Journal' of March 9, 1731

'Mr. Handel's Opera's ... are there Engraved, Printed and Sold'

brought yet another foreign influence into our midst. After all, Handel was a German by birth and an Italian by musical choice and training, and he never attempted to put anything of England into his works. It is indeed to be regretted that the greatest of English composers, Purcell, had not raised up a school of composers in his succession before he died in 1695. The Handel influence distracted attention from national sources of inspiration, and this country, the home of the madrigal, which had in Elizabethan and Jacobean days led the world in song, came to be regarded on the Continent before the closing of the eighteenth century as a distinctly unmusical country.

Eighteenth-century England herself was quite self-complacent, if we are to judge from the writings of that fashionable teacher of music, best known to posterity because he had the distinction of being father to Madame d'Arblay, viz. Dr. Charles Burney, who wrote several dissertations on the state of contemporary music in the principal countries of Europe and a great History of Music, which is of permanent interest as an indication of the taste and judgement of a cultured English musician of the period.

By far the best known of the native-born composers of the eighteenth century—as he was also the most popular in his own day—was Dr. Thomas Arne (1710–78). He has a very long series of compositions to his credit: a setting of Addison's *Rosamund*; a burlesque entitled *The Opera of Operas*, based on Fielding's *The Tragedy of Tragedies*; a setting of *Comus*; a comedietta, very popular at the time, called *Love in a Village*; various operas in the Italian manner; and a number of oratorios just as secularly minded as the operas. But while all these are forgotten, its patriotic sentiment has preserved *Rule, Britannia!* and the great charm of their fluent melody keeps in perennial life his settings of Shakespeare's lyrics, *Where the bee sucks; Blow, blow, thou winter wind*; and other lovely songs, such as *When daisies pied*.

The other notable composers of the century wrote mainly church music. Such were William Croft (1678–1727), who was organist at Westminster Abbey, the author of some of the finest of our hymn tunes; Maurice Greene (1695–1755), a great anthem writer; William Boyce (1710–79), another distinguished anthem writer; Thomas Attwood (1765–1838); and the greatest of all, Samuel Wesley (1766–1837), the son of Charles Wesley, who in his admiration for Bach escaped from the prevailing Handelian

CHARLES BURNEY

From the portrait by Sir Joshua Reynolds, by permission of the Curators of the Examination Schools, Oxford

infection, but whose works belong mainly to the nineteenth century.

A number of the organist-composers wrote glees as well as anthems, and the development of glee singing, a form of music as characteristically English as the earlier madrigal, is a distinctive feature of the eighteenth century. Although a Madrigal Society was founded in 1741, the madrigal had as a popular form of part-singing died out well before the end of the previous

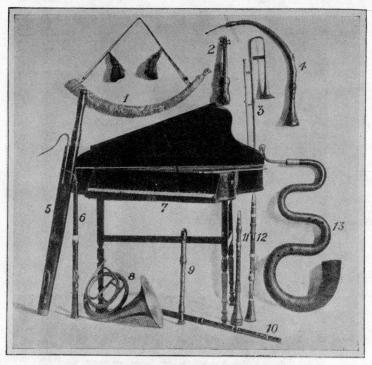

Musical Instruments of the Eighteenth Century

(*1*) *Horn of carved ivory* (*2*) *kit or pocket violin* (*3*) *trombone or sackbut* (*4*) *cor anglais*
(*5*) *bassoon* (*6*) *hautboy* (*7*) *spinet* (*8*) *horn* (*9*) *English flute or recorder* (*10*) *German flute*
(*11 and 12*) *clarionets* (*13*) *serpent, the predecessor of the ophicleide*

By permission of the Rev. F. W. Galpin, M.A.

century. The glee—not necessarily a gleeful piece of music— although a lower form of art, was more obviously melodious than the madrigal. Samuel Webbe (1740–1816) was the most distinguished of the glee composers. Others were the brothers Stephen and William Paxton, Stevens, Callcott, and Horsley.

An eighteenth-century family orchestra.

Granville Sharp, the philanthropist, with his brothers and sisters and other members of the family, on board their barge the 'Apollo'. Many of the instruments in the picture are the same, or very similar, to those reproduced on the opposite page. From a picture by Zoffany.

THe Territories from whence came moſt Ships to *London* laſt Year next to *Germany*, were the *Engliſh Plantations* in the *Weſt Indies*, and from thence came 138. What, not two Thirds of the Number of what came from the little Country of the *United Provinces.* Surely their Prudence and Induſtry are much to be commended and immitated ; and whether 'tis our Idleneſs, Fearfulneſs, Loſſes, or other Employments of our Men and Ships, by reaſon of the War, I won't determine , but one would think that from *Hudſon's Bay, New-England, New-York, New Jerſey, Penſylvania, Maryland, Virginia* and *Carolina* ; on the Main, *Bermudos, Barbados, Nevis, Jamaica* and our other Iſlands in the Ocean ſhould employ ; more eſpecially, conſidering that Mr. *Roberts* in his Map of Commerce, ſays that 201 Ships have been loaded at *Barbadoes* in one Year, 1660. and theſe were upwards of 15505 Tuns, which were about 80 Tuns apiece one with another. And this Iſland is but 28 *Engliſh* Miles long, and half as broad, which being meaſured, is 126000 Acres. Were the reſt of the Plantations huſbandried agreeable to this, our Trade might be vaſt indeed , but a great many of them yield more bulky Commodities, and ſo might ſurely (if we would) employ many more Ships ; altho' I am not unſenſible of many Ships coming from the *Weſt-Indies* to divers others of our Ports than *LONDON*, but how many, I know not, altho' the general Cuſtoms of *London*, are as eleven to fifteen of the whole Kingdom. I am ſenſible alſo that divers Ships with Tabacco, &c. do unlade in ſome of our Out Ports, and pay the Duty, then relade, and ſo for *Holland.*

The ſame Mr. *Roberts* ſays, there are about 40 Sail a Year laded from *Virginia*, and 10 from *Maryland* of three or four hundred Tuns each ; and I preſume by theſe he means not the *Weſt Indians* Trading, one with another ; and doubtleſs the Trade has been far greater ſince then Mr *Roberts* ſpeaks of.

In order to improve this *Weſt-Indian* Trade, I believe it would be well worth while to have it ſome body's Buſineſs to make a good Natural Hiſtory as well as can be, and to ſtudy how every thing therere may be improved, and what uſeful known matters grow in other Countries, that in Probability might grow there, and alſo to ſettle the *Guinea-Trade* for *Blacks*, which are the uſefulleſt Merchandize can be carried thither, except *White-Men* : For according to their Plenty is the Product: But if the keeping our *African-Company* in Suſpence, they ſhall exclude others, or not be of uſe to us, will belong to another Argument.

On *November* 24. 1681, in Number 3 of my firſt *Quarto Volume,* I publiſhed my Thoughts to prove that the Plantations did not depopulate, but rather encreaſe or improve our People ; and I have alſo proved it ſo that none will gain-ſay me, that the more People we ſend to our Plantations, the more we muſt have at home, ſo long as ever it can be imagined that People will love their Intereſt, but thither I refer my Reader ; and on *Friday* next expect more from.

Yours

John Houghton, F. R. S.

From the *Golden Fleece* in *Grace-Church Street* and Corner of *Little Eaſt-Cheap, London.*

Imperial ideas. A leading article reproduced from Houghton's 'Collection' of Dec. 20, 1695

XIV

EMPIRE-BUILDERS

No selection of representative men in the eighteenth century would be complete which did not include the empire-builders. The British Empire both contracted and expanded during the period. On the one hand, there was the loss of the thirteen colonies as the result of the War of American Independence; on the other hand, there was the acquisition of Canada and India mainly as the result of the Seven Years War. It is not with wars and conquests that we are now concerned, and among the empire-builders we do not here include Wolfe, because he captured Quebec, or Eyre Coote, because he won the battle of Wandewash over our French competitors in India; and if we do include Clive, it is not because he was the victor of Plassey. The building of the British Empire has consisted not merely in the gaining of new territories, but (more important) in the development of new conceptions of the relations between these islands and their dependencies. The loss of the American colonies taught a salutary lesson. By discrediting the old colonial theory that the colonies existed primarily for the mercantile benefit of the mother-country, it led to the working out of those fundamentally different ideas of empire of which the modern phase, the British Commonwealth of Nations, is evidence. This process, however, has belonged mainly to the period since 1839, the date of Lord Durham's famous *Report* on Canada, which marks the most important turning-point in British imperial history : for the immediate effect of the loss of the colonies was disillusion, the sorrowful conviction on the part of many that the problem of maintaining amicable relations between parent and daughter communities was insoluble, that sooner or later every colony must be expected to assert its complete independence.

Nevertheless, Great Britain in the eighteenth century has valuable achievements to its credit in the realm of imperial government. The conquests both of Canada and of India presented the difficult problem of the proper treatment of subjects of alien race. A few words ought to be said about the Canadian question. Here was a conquered French population. Was it simply to be brought straight away under the ordinary British system of government, or was it to be allowed to develop along its own lines, retaining its peculiar law and custom ? At first, while the Catholics enjoyed freedom of worship, English was made the official language, and while in the meantime Canada remained under military governorship, the intention was to introduce a purely British political system : for what greater blessing in the world could there be than the bestowal of the benefits of the incomparable British constitution ? But it at once appeared that the Canadians had no appreciation of such advantages—neither understood nor wanted them—and the very wise and statesmanlike governor, Sir Guy Carleton, prevailed upon the home government not to insist upon the maintenance of exclusively British political institutions, despite the vociferous demand for this made by the minute minority of English-speaking settlers.

In 1774 the much-abused administration of Lord North passed the Quebec Act, which safeguarded the Roman Catholic religion in Canada together with French law and custom in all civil matters, while it introduced English law and the jury system in criminal cases. The New England colonies strongly disapproved of this Act, which they regarded as tantamount to the establishment of Popery, and undoubtedly its adoption helped to embitter the feeling between the home government and the American colonists. On the other hand, it is equally certain that it was the means of preserving Canada to us in the war which followed : for the Canadians refused to make common cause with the New Englanders who had denounced their religion against a government which had granted them religious freedom.

After the war there was a large immigration of dispossessed loyalists from the United States into Canada. The majority of these ' United Empire Loyalists ', as they were termed, settled in the maritime province of Nova Scotia. So great were their numbers, indeed, that a separate colony was made of the part where they had congregated, and it was named New Brunswick. But another big contingent made its way into what was then a wilderness, the great district, now Ontario, west of Quebec, north of the Great Lakes. Thus there grew up side by side two very different communities—the western entirely British ; the eastern, despite a considerable British immigration, still predominantly French. The younger Pitt decided that these two settlements, so different by race and tradition, should be politically separate, and his Canada Act of 1791 divided the country into two distinct provinces, Upper and Lower Canada. The wisdom of this proceeding was questioned at the time, and it was roundly denounced afterwards by Lord Durham ; but its significance, for our present purpose, lies in the fact that Pitt refused to assent to the petitions of the English minority, who would have liked to see the French institutions swept away. The fairest method seemed to be, so far as was practicable, to separate the British and the French populations, allowing each to develop in its own way. French Canada was given its own elected legislative assembly and nominated legislative council, just as Upper Canada was given them. The type of self-government thus bestowed was severely criticized as inadequate in the Durham Report ; but the measure of autonomy granted to the French-speaking people was such as they had never enjoyed when their own countrymen held Canada.

The story of the creation of an efficient system of government in British India is still more striking. In the history of the British in India during the century there are two different processes. There is, first, the process of war against the rival trading company of France and against native states, which culminates in the battles of Plassey, fought against the Nawab of Bengal in 1757, and of Wandewash, fought against the French in 1760. The great hero in this process is Clive. There is, secondly, the process of consolidation, of the evolution of a system of government, involving the solution of the problem of the relations between the British and the natives. The great hero of this second process is Warren Hastings.

It is necessary to grasp the conditions of native India during the struggles between the rival European trading companies. While there was a general uniformity of social and economic custom over the whole vast country, it was in every other way disunited—by multifarious differences of race and language, by the bitter religious feud of Hindu and Mussulman, by the social cleavages produced by a rigid system of caste. While the Mohammedans formed only a small minority of the population, politically they had up to 1707 been predominant, as the rule of the great Mogul Empire had been effective over the whole of northern India and, latterly, over a considerable part of southern India as well. But with the death of the great Aurungzib in that year the Mogul Empire fell to pieces. Feudatory princes, such as the Nawabs of Bengal and Oudh, made themselves virtually independent, and the famous Hyder Ali began to make himself master of Mysore. More important was the aggrandizement of the warlike, predatory Hindu tribesmen, the Mahrattas, whose raiders were now to be seen in every part of the country and who became predominant over the whole of central India. They were solely a disturbing and destructive force, having neither culture nor capacity for organization. While for a time the chieftains of Poona, known as the Peishwas, were able to maintain a general supremacy, their power was soon challenged by other Mahratta rulers, such as the Bhonsla of Nagpur, the Sindhia of Gwalior, the Holkar of Malwa. To disruption within the country there was added incursion from without. Afghan

A Proposal for the Sale of several Rech Indian Goods, by way of Ticket or Lot, to the Value of 1500 l. consisting of fine Cabinets and Skreens, Tables, Stands and Glasses, Tea-Tables and Stands ; Chests, Trunks, &c. and several other sorts of Japan: *Several Sets of fine* China *Jarrs ; also all sorts of* China, *fine* Indian *wrought Beds and Quilts, Rich* Indian *Silks, viz.* Atlasses, Cuttanees, *and several other sorts of* Indian *Silks, fine* Indian *Fanns, Muslins and Callicoes ; and several others too long to incert.*

AT the *Indian* Ware-house, at the Sign of the *Black Bell* in *Bedford-street Covent Garden*, by *Joseph Rose*, and *Elix. Madox*, will be delivered out 12000 *Tickets*, at 2 s. 6 d. each, and there shall be also 12000 *Blank Tickets* prepared, 240 whereof shall be made *Benefits* ; which said *Benefits* shall contain in Goods to the Value above mentioned.

The first Ticket drawn shall have 20 l. Value if not *Benefited*, but if *Benefite* 20 l. Value above its *Benefit.*

The *Benefits* are to be

1		150 l.
1		100
1		80
1		60
2 each	30 l.	60
4 each	20	80
10 each	14	140
20 each	8	160
30 each	5	150
40 each	4	160
60 each	3	180
70 each	2	140

240 *Tickets.*　　　　　　1460 l.

First *Ticket* 20
Last *Ticket* 20

1500 l.

Advertisement of a sale by lottery of Indian goods
From Houghton's 'Collection', *January 5, 1693/4*

warriors penetrated the mountain passes with a view to spoil rather than conquest. In 1761 there took place a great battle at Panipat between them and the Mahrattas, in which the latter were thoroughly defeated. Had the Afghan victor, Ahmed Shah, so wished, he might have used this success to establish his rule over northern India. The significance of the battle is that, while it meant a definite set-back to the Mahrattas, the Afghans took no real advantage of it. This state of things afforded an opportunity for political aggrandizement to the British traders.

But the directors of the British East India Company had no desire for political aggrandizement. Quite the contrary. They wished to keep free of all political entanglements as far as possible, being intent solely upon the development of their trade monopolies. The commerce carried on by the Company consisted of two kinds. First and most important, there was the exchange of Indian wares—cotton, silk, muslin, embroideries, spices, &c.—for British woollens, hardware, metals, &c. But there was also a valuable trade eastwards to China and Japan in Indian opium and grain. The servants of the Company were paid very small salaries. The emoluments were not so absurdly small as is sometimes supposed, for to the salary we have to add subsistence and other allowances. Still the rate of pay was certainly low and the stipend of juniors little more than nominal. It was an understood thing that the Company's servants supplemented their salaries by the proceeds of private trade, and indeed it was this opportunity for independent trading, under the Company's special privileges, that formed the real inducement to enter the Company's service. In the principal western trade private enterprise was not permitted, but it was sanctioned in the east-going trade. Here the Company's staff were at liberty to make their own fortunes without let or hindrance. But there existed another kind of trade which offered powerful attractions. This was the internal trade of India itself, which stood altogether outside the Company's charter. Neither the corporation nor its officials as individuals had any right to take part in this, the preserve of the native merchant. But the attraction proved irresistible, and after 1757 the Company's servants entered

CARGOE of Dutch East-India Ships.

2855924 lb Pepper
33553 lb. ditto white.
322417 lb Nutmegs.
105528 lb. Mace.
8000 lb. Cinnamon.
8301 lb. Seed Cloves.
1653000 lb. Saltpetre.
364133 lb. Sapanwood.
3945 lb. Ebony of Amboina.
14710 lb. ditto of Ceylon.
256250 lb Copper of Japan in Staves
199845 lb. Tin.
55316 lb. Green Ginger.
10020 preferved Nutmegs.
13 Pots preferved Cloves.
1092 lb Oyl of Nutmegs in Cakes.
14161 lb. Cardamom.
27660 lb. Benjamin.
65 Bezoar Stones.
4200 Reals black Ambergris.
132 lb. Sanguis Draconis.
352 lb. Borax
5393 lb. Radix China

1740 lb. Gallingal.
136 lb. Birds-Nefts.
50 Canafters Tea.
11550 lb. Coffee.
428 lb. Cowries.
250 lb. Sugar.
33984 Canes of one Joint.
1400 Bamboo Canes.
70879 ps Several forts of China Ware
78047 lb. Bengal Silk.
11838 lb Floretta Yarn.
12903 lb. Cotton Yarn.
6697 lb. Carmenia Wool.
11132 ps. Taffatas,
747 ps. Silk Allejaes.
119 ps. Bengal Silks.
300 ps. Atlafles.
980 ps. Soosjes.
1317,2 ps. Neckcloths.
293 ps. painted Chints of the Coa.
6845 ps. painted Handkerchiefs.
5498 ps. Morees.
21800 ps and 15 packs Salampores
700 ps. Betillees Seftergantine.
900 ps. Betillees Otizael or R 25.

1200 ps. Betilles d'Ornael.
500 ps. Betillees Allejae.
853 ps. Betillees Camman.
2624 ps. Mulmuls.
2777 ps. Coffaes.
696 ps. Doras.
206 ps. Terindains.
3031 ps. Humhums.
200 ps. Curtobanees,
822 ps. Alibanees.
9440 ps. and 1 Pack Parcullaes.
3600 ps. Gurrahs.
2000 ps. Cambays
525 ps Milmils.
110 ps. Bedticking.
2000 ps Patena Chints.
8578 ps. Romals,
5193 ps. Caetjaes of several forts.
20320 ps. Photas,
792 ps. Ginghams.
4000 ps. Dungarees.
3200 ps. and 3 Packs Bafts.
21770 ps. and 61 Packs Long Cloths.
4962 ps Sail Cloth.

Typical merchandise from the Dutch East Indies

A cargo advertised in Houghton's 'Collection' of Friday, August 3, 1694

extensively into this traffic and soon came to have a predominating share in it. Possessing the *dustuk* or pass which exempted the Company's goods from the payment of dues to the native rulers, and conducting their business through their native agents or *banyans*, they were able to undersell the native merchants. This was an undoubted abuse, and the higher authorities tried to keep it in check, with small success. But while the servants of the Company were under some sort of discipline, the free merchants were not. These, unattached to the Company, though enjoying the use of the Company's licence, had originally been confined to the ports ; but penetrating into the interior they also began to meddle in the domestic trade, and there was none to restrain them.

The turning-point in the history of the East India Company came when the young Nawab of Bengal, Suraj-ud-daulah, jealous of British influence, attacked and seized Calcutta, an event followed by the crime of the ' Black Hole ', which Clive avenged at Plassey. In place of Suraj-ud-daulah the British set up his treasurer, Mir Jafar, as Nawab. The new ruler was the nominee of the Company, which, king-maker by the force of its arms, proved itself to be the controlling force in Bengal. When conspiracies broke out against the Nawab they were suppressed by the Company's troops. Powerless apart from his European protectors, Mir Jafar proved most ineffective. For one thing he dared not deal with the irregularities of which the Company's servants were guilty, and it is during this period, 1757–60, that they made good their control over the internal trade. Mir Jafar proved so nerveless that the Company grew tired of him and deposed him in favour of Mir Kassim Ali ; but the latter proving too independent, Mir Jafar was restored in 1764. The conditions in Bengal grew worse and worse. The native government could not govern, while the Company's employees, quite naturally keen to make fortunes quickly while such excellent opportunities offered, resented any efforts, on the part either of officers of the Company or of native authority, to put a restraint upon their activities. Vansittart, an honourable and well-meaning man, who had succeeded Clive as President of Bengal in 1760, could make no headway against the abuses which characterized the next five years.

The directors at home, who had at first been ignorant of the

THE OLD EAST INDIA HOUSE IN LEADENHALL STREET 1648 TO 1726

FROM A PAINTING IN THE POSSESSION OF Mr PULHAM OF THE INDIA HOUSE 12 INCHES BY 8

ill use their staff were making of their privileged position in India, entirely disapproved of the intervention in the domestic trade, and in 1765, disturbed at the ill-repute which was coming upon the Company as the result of this misconduct, they sent back Clive to Bengal to effect a thorough reformation. In 1759 Clive had made a remarkable suggestion to Pitt, viz. that the Company should take over the actual sovereignty of Bengal, which should afterwards be transferred to the Crown. This was the right line of advance. The source of all the evils from which Bengal had been suffering was the fact that the controlling power there was the East India Company, yet it refrained from accepting any responsibility for the good government of the country. Power divorced from responsibility is always a great evil. It meant in this case that the native rule, having no prestige whatever of its own, was rendered impotent. Either the Company must clear out of Bengal altogether and leave the native authority free to exert itself or it must unequivocally take up the administration itself. But the Company's directors were determined to do neither. They knew that to leave Bengal would not mean native independence ; it would simply mean opening the door to their competitors, French, Dutch, or Portuguese, to come in and take the place they vacated. They were simply a commercial body. They were intent on the development of their valuable monopoly. They had no authorization to undertake the rule of great Indian territories. When its servants were attacked by native princes the Company must defend itself. They could not hope to remain entirely free from political entanglements, but they must keep as clear of them as circumstances permitted. Clive, therefore, who had had his own vision of a better way at an earlier date, was in 1765 expected to reform the existing system, but certainly not to substitute another.

Clive's task involved dealings both with the Company's men and with the native authorities. On the part of the former he encountered a hostile spirit. He was resolved to put down the pernicious practice of accepting presents from natives— a thoroughly oriental method of greasing the wheels of business, known as *nuzzerana* or *teep*, which European traders had adopted with alacrity. Again, officers in the Company's army had been accustomed to receive a gratuity from the Nawab of Bengal. When Clive declared that this must cease, the officers thought to frustrate him by resigning *en masse*. But Clive was not the sort of man to be thus intimidated. He accepted the resignations, and filled the vacant places from the Madras army or by giving commissions to the Company's clerks. With regard to the internal trade, Clive's solution was that the profits of the salt monopoly should be divided among the Company's servants

LORD CLIVE

Engraving by Bartolozzi after a picture by Nathaniel Dance

as an increment to salaries, so as to reduce the temptation to indulge in irregular private commerce; but the directors refused to accept this suggestion.

With regard to the question of the relationship between the Company and native powers, the essential feature of Clive's plan was a close understanding with the Mogul. That potentate happened to be quite helpless and a fugitive from his capital, Delhi. Nevertheless, Clive chose to regard him as wielding the paramount authority in India. A treaty was concluded whereby, on the one hand, the Mogul handed over to the Company the *diwani* or right of collecting the revenue of the provinces of Bengal, Behar, and Orissa, while, on the other hand, the Company agreed to pay the Mogul an annual tribute of £260,000 a year. At the same time, with the Company's help, the Mogul was set up in a new capital, Allahabad. Clive also made a specially close alliance with Oudh, which he proposed to maintain as a buffer-state against the Mahrattas.

Macaulay has bestowed the highest praise on these transactions of Clive. ' He remained in India about a year and a half, and in that short time he effected one of the most extensive, difficult, and salutary reforms that ever was accomplished by any statesman.' The encomium is pitched much too high. Clive secured an improvement in conditions during his own residence in the country by the mere force of his own personality, but he had not succeeded in improving what was an inherently evil system ; as events proved, he had made it worse. He left a dual control by native and European.

The feature of his scheme which appealed most forcibly to the minds of the directors and to the public imagination at home was the grant of the *diwani*. It was confidently expected that after the expenses of the country's government had been met and the annual tribute to the Mogul been paid, there would remain a handsome annual surplus to go into the coffers of the Company. So rosy did prospects appear that the proprietors of the Company began to demand a higher dividend and Parliament to consider the possibility of securing a share of the spoil for the national exchequer. Chatham, at this time in power, was of opinion that the whole position of the East India Company, and especially its territorial rights, called for a parliamentary investigation. But when Chatham's health broke down and he withdrew entirely from the control of his administration, this scheme was abandoned, and the facile Chancellor of the Exchequer, Townshend, made of the matter nothing more than a simple financial deal, whereby the directors were promised that there should be no inquiry, and they agreed to pay £400,000 a year to the Treasury. This arrangement was concluded in 1767.

The hopes founded upon Clive's proceedings all proved vain. The years 1766–72 were even worse than their predecessors ; they were the blackest in all the history of British India. In the first place the proceeds of the *diwani* were most disappointing. The Company did not actually collect the revenue themselves ; the collecting was arranged by native officials, called *zemindars*, on behalf of the Company. Although the yield of the *diwani* was surprisingly small, there was evidence that there was much oppression on the part of the tax-gatherers. The Company therefore appointed supervisors from their own numbers to see that the money was actually paid in by the collectors and also to protect the *ryots* or small peasant proprietors, who were seldom much above the level of mere subsistence, from irregular and excessive demands. The truth was that Bengal was a rich country, but its inhabitants were poor. But the supervisorships did not work well, for the new officials were still allowed to indulge in private trade, which remained their main concern. Indeed the abuses of private trade reached their climax in these years. The source of mischief still remained the same. The Company was still seeking to enjoy the advantages of power, while evading its responsibilities. The *diwani* which Clive had obtained from the Mogul was not a privilege, it was a function of government ; in Indian practice it included not only the collection of the revenue but also the duties of civil administration. All the functions of government belonged, in Indian parlance, either to the *diwani* or the *nizamut*, the latter consisting of police and military jurisdiction. The Company had not taken over the *nizamut*, but in practice they had a good deal to do with it, for, their army being the most efficient force in the country, they were really in supreme military control.

The culmination of this grievous period came in 1769, when Hyder Ali made his first onset of devastating violence upon the plains of the Carnatic, and in the following year when an unparalleled famine swept off a third of the population of India. The Mahrattas, securing control of Delhi and desirous of having the titular lord of India in their care and keeping, invited the Mogul to return to his own capital, and the invitation was accepted. The Mogul abandoned Allahabad and his English friends. What now remained of Clive's handiwork ? Tribute paid to the Mogul was tribute paid to the Mahrattas ; the *diwani*, for which that tribute was the price, was now worthless, because, stricken by terrible drought and consequent famine, the wretched population died, it could not pay. So severe were the effects of these calamities upon the East India Company's position that, far from being able to contribute its £400,000 to the government, in 1772 it had to obtain a loan of a million from the government in order to stave off bankruptcy, and its shares fell with a slump. If the Company was to be saved at all, drastic measures must be taken. The man whom the directors this time selected to retrieve a desperate situation was Warren Hastings.

Of all the great proconsuls whom this country has produced Hastings was perhaps the most remarkable : yet the recompense for his services was not honours, but an impeachment which lasted upwards of seven years, and upon which before his eventual acquittal in 1795 he had to spend over £70,000, the whole of his fortune. Over men of this type there will always be controversy. Entrusted with a task of the utmost difficulty, frequently called upon to make decisions in extreme emergency, unfaltering in judgement, resolute and forceful in action, his methods were sometimes high-handed and they gave great umbrage to tender consciences. The hostile view, brought forward in masterly orations by Burke and Sheridan, who were chief managers for the impeachment, has been enshrined in Macaulay's famous essay, in which, while the praise is never more than grudging, the denunciations are full-blooded—and many readers owe their first, sometimes their only acquaintance, with Hastings to this essay.

After an education at Westminster School, Hastings had at the age of eighteen secured a writership in the East India Company, and in 1750 he had started work in Calcutta. From the first he showed himself to be an Indian merchant quite out of the ordinary, by his interest in native customs and in oriental

Churchill, Oxfordshire. The nearest house on the right was the birthplace of Warren Hastings

Photograph by Mr. Percy Simms

languages and learning, and by his diplomatic skill as a negotiator with Mir Jafar and Mir Kassim. Whereas his colleagues were making great fortunes very rapidly, when Hastings retired, accompanying Vansittart to England in 1764, he was by no means a rich man. It is interesting to note that one of the few things known of his sojourn in England is that he tried to interest Dr. Johnson in a scheme for the study of Persian learning, probably at Oxford University.

His career after his return to Bengal in 1772[1] divides itself into three clearly distinct periods—the first, perhaps the most important, running from 1772 to 1774. This is the period of his constructive work. It is essential to remember, if the barest justice is to be done to Hastings, that he was sent out, not to reform India, but to make the East India Company once more prosperous. What the directors expected him to produce was money. Hastings had the sagacity to perceive that the Company could not become prosperous again so long as it remained indifferent to the welfare of the ordinary native. The whole situation hinged, to a very large extent, upon the lot of the miserable *ryot*, prey as he was to drought, extortion, and oppression. He must be freed from the fear of irregular and excessive demands. There must be a new and equitable assessment of the land, from the taxes upon which the revenue was mainly derived. Hastings saw to it that the use as tax-gatherers of lawless and undisciplined native troops, who had merely plundered and terrified, was abolished.

As regards the private trade, Hastings was not able to accomplish all he wanted, but he introduced one great reform in the abolition of the use of the *dustuk* for private trade, so that the merchandise of all, of British and native traders, paid uniform dues. It had been expected that Hastings would be active in the punishment of offenders, but, as he informed the directors, his opinion was that, whatever the conduct of individuals might have been, the blame was attaching not to persons but to the system. On this question of the system he would not compromise as Clive had compromised. He unhesitatingly took the

[1] He was in Madras from 1769 to 1772.

view that the authority of the Company and the sovereignty of Great Britain must be implanted in the constitution of Bengal, that the Company must govern and assume responsibility for the natives, ' people whom as our subjects we are bound to protect '. With a zealous eye to their well-being, he gave great attention to judicial reform. He set up two high courts at Calcutta, one for criminal and one for civil cases, to administer Indian law. He established similar provincial courts for all the districts of Bengal. Judges received no more perquisites as of yore, but were paid fixed salaries. It was typical of Hastings's sense of reality that, while he showed great concern for the maintenance of Hindu law for the Hindu, he reserved the right of interference to himself and his advisers in exceptional cases where the fact of a much less serious view of the heinousness of an offence being taken by a native than

WARREN HASTINGS

As a young man. Mezzotint by T. Watson after a portrait by Reynolds

would be possible to a European seemed to endanger the maintenance of peace and order.

As regards relations with native potentates, Hastings in one instance reversed, in another extended, the arrangements made by Clive. First, he declined to continue the payment of the tribute to the Mogul, holding that the Company had never received any equivalent for this, and that in present circumstances it would simply go into the hands of the Mahrattas. At a stroke, therefore, he saved the Company more than a quarter of a million a year. On the other hand, by what is known as the Treaty of Benares he drew still closer the bonds between the Company and Oudh, which became virtually a vassal state of the Company. It was in connexion with Oudh that Hastings's questionable proceedings started. He lent a brigade of the Company's army to the Nawab for use against the Rohillas, an Afghan tribe who had not long since descended upon the Hindu population of Rohilcund. Much eloquence has been expended in denunciation of this transaction. By Hastings's contemporary enemies and by Macaulay since their day, the Rohillas were represented as an innocent and guileless race, remarkable for their peaceful dispositions and their advanced culture, ' the finest population in India '—the truth being that they were turbulent and predatory invaders of the country who did not belong to India at all. On the other hand, the war which the Nawab was encouraged to wage against his unwelcome neighbours was undoubtedly terrible and the triumphant prince's methods barbarous, and the propriety of hiring the Company's troops in such a way, even for the purpose of increasing the security of the frontier against Mahratta and Afghan inroads, is, to say the least of it, very doubtful.

The second period of Hastings's great work in India is ushered in by Lord North's Regulating Act of 1773—a notable measure, because it was the first attempt to bring the activities of the East India Company under Government control. While it left the directors free to transact their financial business just as before and kept them in possession of their political power in India, it made the important proviso that all dispatches relating to political questions must be submitted to Government inspection. The Act also set up a Governor-General of Bengal with a council of four, and gave them authority—this unfortunately was not clearly defined—over the Bombay and Madras presidencies. Again, the Act established a Court of Judicature at Calcutta to administer English law. It was to be entirely independent of the Company, so that it might judge impartially any charge brought against the Company's servants. It should be noted that Burke and the Rockingham party strongly assailed North's

"The Skirmish"

An Advanced Gun playing

The Company's Troops

From a drawing in the United Services Museum

measure as an infringement of the sacred rights of property, because it impinged upon the Company's charter.

The Act was thoroughly praiseworthy in intention, and as the first legislation which showed recognition by the British government of the responsibilities imposed upon the country by its hold upon India, it has first-class importance. The British Crown became sovereign of the territories controlled by the East India Company, although as yet the British government did not directly intervene in Indian affairs. Yet the Act had several serious defects, as events speedily showed. It restricted the powers of the Governor-General by leaving him at the mercy of a hostile council, and it left uncertain the relations between the new Court of Judicature and the Governor-General and Council, also between it and the native courts. Had the expert advice of the man on the spot, Hastings, been sought and taken, the measure would have been different in several respects.

Warren Hastings, first Governor-General under the terms of the Act, had abundant reason to curse it between 1774 and 1776. One member of the new council, Barwell, had previous experience of Indian affairs, and although no great friend to Hastings, usually voted with him. The other three members had no experience of India whatever, and they were invincibly hostile to Hastings. They were Philip Francis (almost certainly the author of the *Letters of Junius*), Monson, and Clavering. Francis was the only one of this trio that counted. An acrid, ambitious man, he was persuaded before his departure from England that Bengal was a land of iniquity and that Hastings was the source of all its sins, and it is clear that he aimed at forcing the Governor-General from his office and securing the position for himself. There is no occasion here to go into the details of the long and unedifying story of the contest which ensued. Hastings, in a perpetual minority at his own council-board, was thwarted at every turn ; he could only look on exasperated, as the dominant trio endeavoured to reverse his policy at every opportunity, and in so doing committed blunder after blunder. Thus when the Nawab of Oudh died, they made his successor cede Benares to the Company and hand over nearly all the contents of his treasury to the late Nawab's widow and his mother, the famous Begums or princesses of Oudh. The resources of the native government were thus impoverished and its utility as a buffer-state greatly diminished. They gave power to a certain Mohammed Reza Khan, who had been very influential in the old days of the vicious Dual System, made him deputy-Nawab, and seemed intent on a partial restoration of that system. They encouraged accusations against Hastings. An informer came forward named Nuncomar, who had a grudge against the Governor-General. While he was launching his charges, he was himself brought before the four judges of the Supreme Court on a charge of forgery which had been preferred against him before the arrival of the new council in India. He was unanimously found guilty by the judges, was condemned to death, and hanged. The disappearance of Nuncomar from the scene was certainly opportune for Hastings. Francis subsequently alleged that there had been collusion between Hastings and the Chief Justice, Sir Elijah Impey, who was an old school-fellow of the Governor-General. There was no evidence behind this suggestion, and the simple facts of the case are that the charge against Nuncomar had been made long before the latter turned informer against Hastings, that all four judges agreed as to his guilt, and that the death sentence was in accordance with English law.

The death of Monson in 1776 was a great relief to Hastings, because the reduction of the numbers in the council gave the Governor-General a casting vote. But just at this time his Governor-Generalship was nearly brought to an end. The government had been disturbed by the news of the Rohilla war—into the causes of which Francis and his coadjutors had soon after their arrival in India started an inquiry—and Lord North would certainly have liked to see Hastings removed. By eleven votes to ten the directors decided that removed he should be ; but the court of proprietors voted to the contrary effect. Then an agent in England, with whom Hastings had lodged a conditional resignation, thought the feeling against his principal so strong that the resignation ought to be presented. Presented it was, and the directors chose one of their number named

Wheler as Governor-General in Hastings's place. When Wheler arrived in Calcutta, however, he found him in no mood to resign. He repudiated the agent's action. The appearance of Wheler did not even have the effect of restoring the balance against Hastings on the council : for it so happened that Clavering had died shortly before the newcomer's arrival. While the Governor-General thus remained supreme in the council, the relations between him and Francis grew worse and worse until there was an open breach, followed by a duel. Soon after this, in 1780, Francis left India, to pour his venom into the sympathetic ears of Burke.

Up to 1776 Hastings had been reduced almost to impotence, but since then he had accomplished more good work, especially in connexion with the judicature. When he had first heard of the intention to create courts in India administering English law, he had in the spring of 1774 written to Lord Mansfield in strong defence of the maintenance of Hindu laws, whose codification and translation into English he had started. He wrote : ' It would be a grievance to deprive the people of the protection of their own laws, but it would be a wanton tyranny to require their obedience to others of which they are ignorant.' The Mohammedan law, which was in force in about a quarter of Bengal, he declared to be as comprehensive and as well defined as that of most European States. When the English courts were established under the Regulating Act a conflict inevitably arose between them and the native courts, and the Supreme Court aimed at overriding the native courts. In resistance to this proposal the council were united, but the struggle went on till 1780, when Hastings found a solution in the suggestion that Impey should be not only Chief Justice of the Supreme Court, but also Chief Judge of the chief native Civil Court. Impey, who was qualified for his new office by a knowledge of Persian and Hindu law, was thus won over to the support of the native courts, which were given a new prestige and validity by this arrangement.

While the final period of Hastings's career in India (1780–5) is notable for a number of administrative reforms, for his encouragement of Indian learning and education, it is chiefly memorable because in these years when the British Empire was fighting for its life, not only in America but all over the world, he preserved our possessions in India from destruction. Encouraged by hopes of French assistance, the Mahrattas and Hyder Ali of Mysore entered into a league to drive the British into the sea ; and it seems probable that, had it not been for Hastings's wonderful vigour and determination, the presidencies of Bombay and Madras must have succumbed. He sent one army down to Madras, another across India to the relief of Bombay. The war was taken into the enemy's country. The great Mahratta stronghold of Gwalior was seized by Popham by a brilliant feat of arms in 1780, and next year Eyre Coote administered a sound defeat to Hyder Ali at Porto Novo. He met the ruler of Mysore in the field often again before his own death in April 1783, but never with quite the same degree of success. The arrival of French naval forces under the brilliant Admiral Suffren and of a small land force under Bussy prolonged the war, but the Mahrattas were forced to make peace in the summer of 1782, and the French were hampered by the lack of bases, Hastings having seized all the French Indian stations before the arrival of Suffren. While great credit was due to the commanders in the field, the master-hand was Hastings's, and it was primarily owing to his indomitable spirit, his quickness of decision, his diplomatic skill (in dealing with the Mahrattas), that British India was saved.

Inevitably the defence of India was expensive ; Hastings could not look for financial help from home, and he had recourse to some desperate expedients. Thus, he instructed the Nawab of Oudh to recover the treasure which had been handed over to those noble ladies, the Begums. Again, he called upon Cheyte Singh, rajah of Benares, a vassal of the Company, to provide £50,000 and troops for his suzerain. The rajah refused ; thereupon Hastings imposed the huge fine of £500,000, and, taking a mere handful of men with him, he went in person to Benares to collect the money himself and to put the recalcitrant ruler under arrest. Cheyte Singh, however, slew Hastings's men, and the Governor-General had to flee from the city, which with the surrounding country was now in a state of revolt. Unperturbed, he at once planned the suppression of the rebellion, which was brought about by the redoubtable Popham. It is worth noticing that it was Pitt's vote against Warren Hastings in the House of Commons on the question of the treatment of Cheyte Singh, when he had remained neutral on the apparently much more serious question of the Rohilla war, that led to the adoption by the House in the spring of 1787 of the resolution to impeach Hastings, who had left India in February 1785.

The fervour of Burke's zeal against Hastings is interesting in more than one way. He was sincerely persuaded that the late Governor-General was an arch-criminal ; his powerful imagination pictured horrid scenes of terrible cruelty and oppression, and once he had been stirred to a *saeva indignatio* he showed himself in this instance—as again in the case of the French Revolution—quite incapable of seeing more than one side of the question. But his state of mind has a greater significance than this. Though he was the protagonist, and his was the eloquence which clothed the sentiment in glowing and resplendent colours, Burke did not stand alone in feeling strong resentment against the supposed misdeeds of Hastings. The impeachment proved that British feeling could be deeply stirred by the allegations of cruelty and injustice done to native India.

Indignation had stirred the Whigs to action prior to Warren Hastings's retirement from India. In the Coalition Ministry of Fox and North two India Bills had been produced, with the assistance of Burke, with the object of effecting a complete change in the government of India. Whigs who had vehemently protested against the Regulating Bill of 1773 as a wicked interference with the rights of property now proposed a much more drastic measure, defending it on the ground that the Company's wrongdoing had now justified the violation of their charter. They were satisfied that the legislation of 1773 had been ineffective, and in this conclusion Hastings would have entirely concurred. The new proposal was that the commercial side of the East India Company's business should be controlled by

The Political Banditti assailing the Saviour of India

From a satirical print of 1786, issued during the impeachment of Hastings. The three banditti
represent Burke, North, and Fox

BLOOD on THUNDER fording the RED SEA.

Gillray's caricature of 1788. Lord Thurlow is shown as Hastings's supporter.

WARREN HASTINGS

a board whose members were chosen by Parliament from among the proprietors, while its political authority should be in the hands of seven commissioners, whose names were included in the Bill ; after four years their successors were to be nominated by the Crown. The commissioners were to have complete control of the Company's patronage. The commissioners named in the Bill were all supporters of the ministry, and it was easy to represent to George III that the motive of the measure was not anxiety for the welfare of India but a desire to aggrandize the Coalition. The King had no hesitation in using his personal influence to have the Bill thrown out in the House of Lords. This led to the fall of the Coalition and the accession of the young Pitt to power.

In 1784 he introduced his own measure for the better government of India. Conceived on the same lines as that of Fox, it did not go quite so far in restricting the Company's powers. It left the patronage in the hands of the directors, except that of the appointments to the governor-generalship and the governorships of Bombay. Madras was placed in the hands of the Crown. Political authority was not entirely taken away from the directors, who retained their full commercial superintendence, but they were subjected to the supervision of a Board of Control, consisting of one of the secretaries of state, the Chancellor of the Exchequer, and other privy councillors selected by the Crown. While the Board was to consult with the directors, it had the final word in all questions of policy. The reduction in the membership of the three councils in India from the Governor and four others to the Governor and three others showed that Pitt had been impressed by the unworkableness of the former system. This was a justification of Hastings ; on the other hand, the stipulation that wars of aggression must cease and that there must be no pacts or alliances with native rulers was an obvious censure upon one of the cardinal features of the late Governor-General's policy.

Hastings's successors loyally endeavoured to abide by this ruling, but their uniform inability to do so was strong testimony to the impracticability of the ordinance. Wars of defence proved

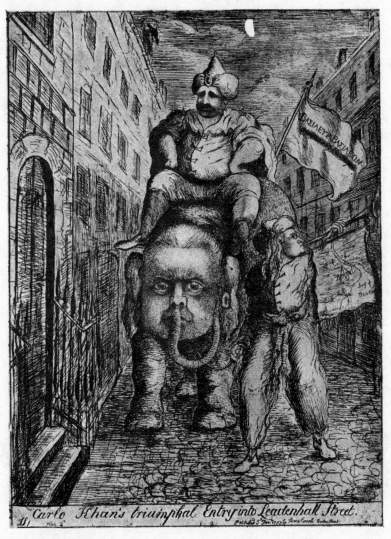

Carlo Khan's triumphal Entry into Leadenhall Street.

A Satire upon Fox's East India Company Bill

Fox, King of Kings, makes his triumphal entry, heralded by Burke's trumpetings

to have a knack of leading to increase of territory just as much as wars of aggression did. The British power in India could decline or it could go forward. The one thing it seemed incapable of doing was standing still in accordance with the ideals of Pitt's Act, by which India was governed till after the Indian Mutiny— in fact for the remainder of the East India Company's existence.

The Act of 1784 is important, but not so important as the work of Warren Hastings, of which it was in part a tacit repudiation. For it was Hastings that established the permanent principles of British rule in India. It was he that converted the haphazard and occasional interference of a trading company with the affairs of an alien people into a systematic and responsible government, accepting the task of maintaining peace and order as a trust on behalf of the native population, whose laws and customs were preserved, while the State was strengthened by the infusion of something which as yet the native had not developed —political capacity, the art of organization and efficient administration. Hastings possessed both the sense of responsibility and the sense of reality. He had high ideals for the British rule in India. There is no doubt about them, because they are constantly repeated in his correspondence and his memoranda. But he was also always alive to the needs of the moment, resolute to deal with problems, as they arose, instantly and forcibly. Because when under pressure of a great emergency his methods were sometimes drastic and even high-handed, his enemies refused to believe in the sincerity of his ideals. Thus, the man who did more for the natives of India than any other Englishman of the eighteenth century was represented as a tyrant and a monster of cruelty. A truer view was forthcoming from the Indians themselves. As the inhabitants of Murshedabad wrote, ' thousands reaping the benefits' of his rule, ' offer up their prayers for the prosperity of England, and for the success of the Company '.

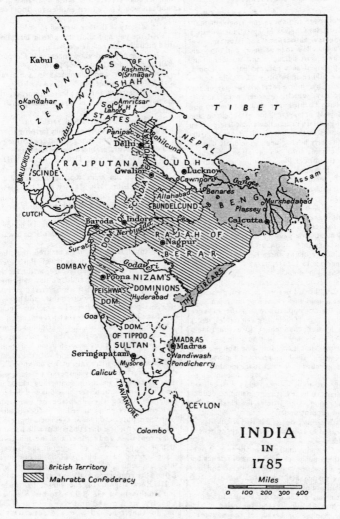

India at the time of Warren Hastings' retirement in 1785.

GENERAL ORDERS,

FOR THE INFANTRY OF THE LINE, THE MILITIA, AND FENCIBLE INFANTRY.

Adjutant-General's Office.

Whereas, over and above the provision made for cloathing, for Chelsea Hospital, for lodgings, and for medical assistance; and likewise, over and above the allowance of beer, and other articles, provided in barracks and quarters; and of bread provided at a reduced rate in Camp, the private soldier of infantry of the line, serving at home, heretofore received the pay of six-pence per day, which, together with the sum of two-pence farthing per day granted to him by his Majesty's warrant, for establishing and conciliating certain other allowances lately given him, amounts to the sum of eight-pence farthing; his Majesty having been graciously pleased to take the same into consideration, is pleased to direct, that under the following regulations, there shall, from the 25th of this present month of May, be paid to each private soldier of infantry, in addition to the said sum of eight-pence farthing, the farther sum of three-pence three farthings, making in the whole the sum of one shilling daily —out of this advance of pay the soldier is to pay the extra price of bread and meat now paid by the Public, which at present amounts, upon an average, to the daily sum of one penny three farthings ; so that the nett increase in future, to each soldier, will be two-pence per diem.

With respect to the disbursement of this shilling per day, his Majesty has been pleased to order, that a sum not exceeding four shillings per week, shall be applied towards the expence of the soldiers mess (including vegetables, &c.) unless he himself shall chuse to appropriate a further part of his pay to that purpose :—

That a sum, not exceeding one shilling and sixpence a week, shall be retained for necessaries, to be accounted for as usual, monthly.

That the remainder of his pay, amounting to one shilling and sixpence per week, shall be paid to the soldier, subject to the accustomed deduction for washing, and articles for cleaning his clothes and appointments.

And his Majesty, out of his Royal bounty, is further pleased to order and direct, for the benefit of the soldier—

That in Camp he shall receive the sum of five-pence farthing per week, being the difference between the allowance and value of bread and beer in quarters for barracks, and the ordinary (increased) supply of bread in camp.

That if meat, of the quality proper to be provided for him, should exceed the price of sixpence per pound, or bread, of the household quality, the price of one penny halfpenny per pound, such extra price shall be allowed by the Public, upon a quantity not exceeding three quarters of a pound of meat, and one pound of bread per day, for each man.

That when any soldier shall, with the approbation of his Commanding Officer, provide himself with lodgings, and the several articles of small beer, &c. to which his billet would entitle him, he shall receive the same allowance as the publican would have been entitled to, under such billet.

His Majesty is further pleased to order,

That the pay and allowances to a Drummer, shall be daily thirteen-pence farthing ;

That the pay and allowances to a Corporal, shall be daily fourteen-pence farthing ;

That the pay and allowances to a Serjeant, shall be daily eighteen-pence three farthings.

His Majesty is further pleased to order, that the pay and allowance of the invalids, shall be daily,

To a Private. eleven pence farthing ;

To a Drummer, thirteen pence farthing ;

To a Corporal, thirteen pence three farthings ;

To a Serjeant, eighteen pence farthing ;

And that the Serjeants, Drummers, and private men of the Militia and Fencible infantry, shall be placed on the same footing respectively as those of the Line. His Majesty is further pleased to order, that the like nett addition of two-pence per diem, shall be made to all his Soldiers serving out of Great Britain.

Field Marshal the Duke of York is happy to announce the King's gracious intentions towards the whole of his army.

His Royal Highness rests assured, that these new instances of the liberality of Parliament, and of his Majesty's paternal care, will rivet that affection for their King and Country which has ever been the pride of British Soldiers, and that a continuance in steady discipline, and honourable conduct, will merit those gracious favours that have been repeatedly shewn them.

On this occasion, his Royal Highness cannot but add, that however incredible it may appear, that there should exist a wretch, so lost to honour and humanity, as to league with the enemy, and to aim at the utter ruin of his Country, yet there are certainly many desperate persons, who have persevered in cherizing Treachery and Sedition ; and who, under specious and delusive pretences, taking the advantage of unguarded moments, have endeavoured to seduce Soldiers from their duty, and render them accomplices in their Treasons, the direct object of which is universal confusion and rapine, and the overthrow of that happy system of Religion and Government secured to us by the blood of our ancestors ; and which, for so many ages, has rendered Britain the admiration and envy of the world !

His Royal Highness is convinced, that the love and attachment of the Soldier to his King and Country, are firm and unshaken ; and that, holding in abhorrence all base and scandalous attempts to shake his loyalty and true affection, every good Soldier will repel with indignation the instigators of such wickedness, and glory in any opportunity of exposing them to the exemplary justice of their insulted Country.

By Command of Field Marshal his Royal Highness the Duke of York.

WILLIAM FAWCETT,
Adjutant-General

The institution of the famous shilling a day as the private soldier's pay dates from 1797 during the wars of the French Revolution

XV

THE SOLDIERS

THE period covered by this volume contains four wars of great magnitude—those of the Spanish and Austrian Successions, the Seven Years War, and the War of American Independence ; yet it does not include many figures of outstanding military capacity. To make up for this, there belongs to it the man whom the Duke of Wellington termed the greatest who ever appeared at the head of a British army. The only possible rival for that position is the Iron Duke himself, and while it can hardly be shown that there were respects in which Wellington outshone Marlborough as a commander, there are, on the other hand, respects in which Marlborough was clearly superior to Wellington. Whatever may be thought of Churchill's private character and of his conduct as a politician, there is no question at all of his transcendent military genius. Yet he was fifty before he began his great career as a commander in the field.

We know plenty about his faults, for he had many detractors who pursued him with an inveterate malignity, and among them was Swift, whose pen was as powerful as it was virulent. That he was guilty of base ingratitude to James II, who first raised him into prominence from the humble obscurity in which he began life ; that while serving Queen Anne he was in correspondence with the Jacobites ; that he favoured the prolongation of a war which brought him such prestige ; that he had great ambitions ; that he was mean and avaricious with regard to money—all this may be true. Yet it can legitimately be urged in extenuation that he lived in an age of low political morality, that he was no worse than his compeers in his Jacobite correspondence, which was certainly not genuine, but simply a form of life insurance in case the dispossessed line came to its own again, that this avaricious man refused an offer of £60,000 a year rather than risk the trouble which its acceptance seemed likely to cause among the allies, that his ambition and zest for war have undoubtedly been greatly exaggerated by his political enemies, who stopped at no slander or falsehood in their anxiety to undermine the influence of the man who raised the country to a pitch of military glory which she had not known since the far-off days of the Black Prince and Henry V.

What were the qualities of Marlborough's military genius ? In the first place—and most important of all—he possessed imagination, a gift which has not been given to many soldiers, and this enabled him to envisage a great campaign, fought in a wide area in different countries, as a single whole, to fathom the plans of his adversaries, and to concoct schemes to outwit them. He was one of the most resourceful of men, and his greatest successes owed much to his extraordinary ingenuity. Possessed of width and penetration of view, he was a born strategist, having begun his career in the school of Turenne, that great master of the art of war, who by his brilliantly executed campaigns had done so much to give the French armies under Louis XIV the reputation for invincibility, which was only shattered by his great English pupil on the battlefield of Blenheim. Besides resembling Turenne in his capacity to plan an elaborate strategic scheme, Marlborough was like him in his fighting instinct, his inclination for the offensive and for quick, powerful, and decisive action. Military operations in the seventeenth century had as a general rule, save under such captains as Gustavus Adolphus and Turenne himself, been leisurely and ponderous, consisting of much marching and countermarching and long-drawn-out sieges, but of comparatively few sharp and determined engagements. Professional troops were regarded as so precious that pitched

PORTRAIT-BUST OF MARLBOROUGH

From the portrait by John Michael Rysbrack

battles were avoided. Marlborough always sought such battles, invariably fought to win by destroying the enemy's field armies.

In the next place, Marlborough possessed one of the highest qualities of the statesman—and a soldier, if he is to attain greatness, needs such qualities in addition to those which are specifically military—the gift of an almost inexhaustible patience. His control of his own temper was wellnigh perfect, and no one ever had his temper tried more persistently. He was scarcely ever allowed a free hand. He was the victim of persistent jealousy. There was plenty of interference and carping criticism at home, but very much worse were the obstructionist tactics constantly followed by his allies, both German and Dutch, but especially the latter. Two of the principal Dutch generals, at different times perforce Marlborough's colleagues, named Opdam and Schlangenberg, seemed to make it their one object in life to oppose and thwart him. Worse still was the Dutch system of field-deputies, i. e. of attaching civilian representatives to the army, who, totally devoid of military experience and knowledge as they were, yet had the opportunity of creating disastrous delays by their deliberations and the authority to enforce their inexpert opinions on the first captain of the age. It is impossible to exaggerate the intense irritation which this atrocious system inflicted upon Marlborough or the extent to which it frustrated his plans. Some of his most brilliant enterprises were not brought to fruition, or could not even be embarked upon at all, owing to this exasperating interference. Yet with all this intense provocation Marlborough refrained from quarrelling with his allies, using his extraordinary diplomatic gifts to cajole and persuade the men with whom he perforce had to work into co-operation with him. Had there been no such obstruction to overcome, Marlborough might have brought the war to a victorious conclusion long before it actually finished, and in a much more glorious fashion ; but had he not been a superb diplomatist, the most self-commanding, most infinitely tactful of soldier-statesmen, that obstruction would have prevented the war from ever being won at all.

Again, Marlborough was essentially a leader of men. Clear-sighted and resolute, with a well-grounded faith in his own judgement and in the valour of his troops, he inevitably inspired implicit confidence in them. Moreover, he was good to look upon—a fine, handsome figure, a soldier in mien and in stature as well as in intellect. He was a strict disciplinarian ; but at the same time he cared zealously for his men's comfort and well-being, and there was no cold aloofness about him. Herein there is a well-marked distinction between Marlborough and Wellington. The men who served with the one in Flanders, with the other in the Peninsula, were in both cases to a large extent the scum of the earth, but whereas Wellington was either abusive or disdainful of the scum, Marlborough's more sympathetic nature warmed to the scum. And his men were attached to him, as their nickname for him—'Corporal John'—is witness. That is to say, the personal magnetism of Marlborough conveyed itself to the rank and file, though, it should be remembered, the majority were foreigners—Dutch, Hanoverian, &c. Whatever their lives may have been before they joined the forces—and many of them were jail-birds—they endured the severe hardships of his campaigns with extraordinary cheerfulness and answered with alacrity the exacting demands he often made upon their endurance and devotion. The moral level of Marlborough's armies was an exceptionally high one. He would not suffer either brutality or looting, though the latter had from the days of the Thirty Years War onwards been regarded as the natural and pleasant accompaniment of every campaign.

Marlborough's great battles are household words—Blenheim, Ramillies, Oudenarde, Malplaquet—but to understand his skill one must follow the broad conceptions of his campaigns, even more than the tactics of his pitched battles. For the battles were but necessary incidents in the working out of a great strategic scheme. Not that Marlborough was a strategist simply and solely. He was great on the field of battle also, great because of his dauntless, unfaltering leadership, and great also as a tactician. There were times when he personally superintended the placing of his batteries ; times when he himself led his cavalry, of which he made great use for close hand-to-hand fighting, for he was essentially a believer in shock tactics. No one had a keener eye for the weaknesses in an opponent's position ; no one was more alert to take immediate advantage of any such opportunity. It was thus that Blenheim was won—by the detection of the weakness of the French centre, although it was to all appearances sufficiently protected by the marshy land in front of it.

Still, the big strategic plans are the most interesting and the most important things to follow in the career of Marlborough. The problem most often before him between the years 1702 and 1711 was that of breaking through the successive line of fortresses which protected the north-eastern frontier of France. Owing to the fact that Spain was in alliance with France there lay all the Spanish Netherlands between France and Holland, and the great fortresses of the Scheldt and the Meuse had to be forced before those of French Flanders could even be approached. To begin with, indeed, the line held by the French was farther north than the line of the Scheldt, and ran across Dutch Brabant, just south of the Dutch strongholds of Grave and Nimeguen and the river Waal. This line in 1702 Marlborough succeeded in turning, by the capture of Venloo and Ruremonde, and he drove the French right flank back on Liége, which he also captured. This was a brilliant achievement, but had he had his way, he would have attempted something more ambitious, would have sought out the enemy's field armies in open battle instead of contenting himself with the siege of fortresses.

The following year the next of the great fortresses of the Meuse—Huy—was captured, and some further progress westward was achieved ; but this was much less than Marlborough had designed : for he had contemplated a converging movement by Dutch and English on the French positions in the Low Countries, but the Dutch spoilt everything by a rash and precipitate attack, undertaken in disobedience to orders.

In 1704 Marlborough executed his brilliant march from the lower Rhine to the upper Danube and those operations which culminated in the triumphs of Schellenberg and Blenheim. Vienna was in imminent danger, from the rebel Hungarians in the east under Racoczy, from the Elector of Bavaria, and from the French armies of Tallard and Villars. To meet this menace there were the imperialist forces under Marlborough's great compeer, Prince Eugene of Savoy, but reinforcements were badly needed, and Marlborough saw that no one but himself could provide them. He was determined to do so. But he knew that the consent of the Dutch for so bold a scheme, one which would take him and his men far from the Dutch border, would never be forthcoming. He therefore decided to hoodwink them, as well as the enemy. He took elaborate means to make it generally known that he intended a campaign on the Moselle, which would have as its object the turning of the French position in the

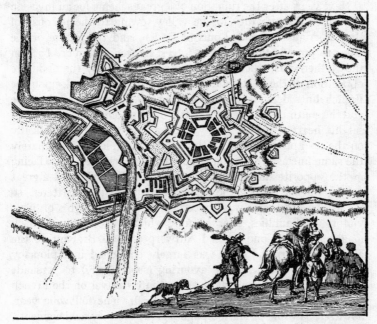

An engraved plan of Charleroi, one of the French frontier fortresses built by the great French military architect Vauban

Spanish Netherlands, and he obtained the assent of the United Provinces to this scheme. At first his movements in the neighbourhood of Bonn and Coblentz seemed to prove that operations in that neighbourhood were about to commence; but, acting with great rapidity, Marlborough moved into Mainz, thereby giving the French the impression that he contemplated activities in Alsace. Then suddenly he swept right away from the Rhine valley, across the Main and the Necker, met Prince Eugene, struck the Danube in the neighbourhood of Ulm, and before either Dutch or French had at all realized what was afoot, was in a position to co-operate in those brilliant operations which saved Vienna and the House of Austria, and at a blow shattered the French reputation for invincibility.

Next year, after the ruination of a great scheme for an invasion of France through the Moselle valley, owing to the jealousy of the imperialist general, Louis of Baden, and the failure of the allies to provide the necessary forces, he was once more back in the Netherlands, where he was only prevented by the obdurate opposition of the field-deputies from making an attack upon the French lines defending Brussels from the direction of Genappe and the south-east. Had the battle upon which Marlborough had set his heart taken place, it would have been fought practically on the field of Waterloo, for the English occupied approximately the same line as Wellington adopted 105 years later, only facing in the opposite direction. In 1706 Louis XIV planned a great general offensive along the whole front, but it was shattered, so far as the north-east was concerned, by Marlborough's brilliant victory of Ramillies, near Namur, which forced Villeroy back in absolute rout and opened Antwerp and all Brabant to the allies. In 1707 the duke was largely employed in diplomacy instead of in the field, endeavouring (successfully) to persuade Charles XII of Sweden, whose advent into the war on the French side seemed imminent, to remain neutral. The following year, however, saw one of Marlborough's great military achievements. Though considerably inferior to the joint opposing armies of Vendôme and the English Jacobite, Berwick, he won so over-whelming a victory at Oudenarde that, though he was one never given to boasting, he claimed that, given another hour of daylight, he would have brought the war to a victorious conclusion there and then. His wish for an immediate invasion of France was overborne, and he had to be content with the successful siege of the great French frontier fortress of Lille and the fall of Bruges and Ghent. In 1709 Marlborough was faced by a much worthier adversary than Villeroy in Marshal Villars, the ablest of the French marshals, and after the taking of the elaborate mined defences of Tournay he met Villars in the terrible battle of Malplaquet, and gained a great victory at a terrible price, the British casualties being more than double those of the French, and the solitary gain from the victory being only the fall of Mons, while the French *moral* was actually improved as the result of the battle, so splendidly had they contested its issue.

In 1710 Marlborough captured Douai, Aire, and St. Venant, and made himself master of the low plain of the Lys, but he acted

BLENHEIM HOUSE

'Erected at the Publick Expense in Commemoration of the Victory at Blenheim, and settled on the Great Duke of Marlborough and his Descendants for ever'

with caution, Villars having a great numerical superiority and having prepared a defensive line of great natural strength, along the valleys of the Canche, the Scarpe, and the Sensée, which he boasted would prove his great adversary's '*non plus ultra*'. This obstacle it became Marlborough's task to break through in 1711, and the campaign of that year is perhaps the greatest of all his great achievements. By a veritable masterpiece of ingenious manoeuvre Villars was completely befogged. At one moment it appeared that the Duke was intent on the capture of a single important position ; next he seemed intensely chagrined that having taken it he had been forced out of it--seemed indeed to have thrown up the sponge and gone off altogether ; then it appeared he intended a frontal attack on Villars's formidable entrenchments. Villars's whole attention became concentrated on the scene of the anticipated assault : whereupon Marlborough made a great forced march by night to another part of the line altogether, and penetrated the redoubtable *non plus ultra* entirely without loss. He then proceeded to invest and to take, in the face of a numerically stronger enemy, the important fortress of Bouchain, near Cambrai. In his plans for the future lay the capture of Maubeuge and Le Quesnoy, the sole remaining fortresses between him and Paris, and then the dictation of a triumphant peace in the French capital. But these things were not to be. Harley and St. John were intent on peace by negotiation, not by the prowess of the Whigs' hero-general. Marlborough's campaigning days were over.

In comparison with Marlborough contemporary British generals were unimportant. Ormonde, who succeeded him, the handsome Tory idol, had small military capacity ; Cutts, whose valour had much to do with the capture of Venloo in 1702, and who was third in command at Blenheim, was a fighter rather than a general, his extraordinary courage and contempt for danger gaining him the sobriquet of ' the Salamander ', while Swift unkindly called him ' as brave and brainless as the sword he wears ' ; Webb, who greatly distinguished himself at Oudenarde, was best known for his victory over the French in 1708 at Wynendael, when he successfully protected a British convoy *en route* from Ostend to the main forces beleaguering Lille, an important service which Marlborough generously acknowledged, but not in his first dispatch, so that Webb had a grievance against the Duke, who was accused of seeking to keep all the glory for himself; Cadogan, Marlborough's right-hand man, to whose skilful arrangements as Quartermaster-General, the success of the Blenheim campaign was largely due, a most admirable staff-officer, a most efficient military administrator.

During the War of the Austrian Succession perhaps our best general was the Earl of Stair, who commanded at Dettingen. Had he been left to carry out his own policy he would have acted with vigour and decision, but George II—a keen soldier himself, undoubtedly, as his father had been before him—would never leave him alone. After Stair came the mild and mediocre Marshal Wade, whose reputation rests upon his roadmaking in Scotland, and then the Duke of Cumberland, the ' butcher ' of Culloden. But Cumberland was an able man and a good soldier, and it is unjust that he should be best remembered for his severity in dealing with the rebel clansmen at the conclusion of the '45. Horace Walpole, when making a list of the great men he had known, included together with those of his own father, Carteret, Pitt, and Mansfield, the name of Cumberland. He became Commander-in-Chief at the early age of twenty-four, at a difficult time when our military prestige had sadly fallen, and, although beaten at Fontenoy,[1] won golden opinions by the vigour of his movements in the campaign and his personal bravery on the field of battle. Colonel Joseph Yorke wrote : ' I never saw or heard of such behaviour as the Duke's : he rode everywhere, he encouraged the wavering, he compli-

Prince William, afterwards Duke of Cumberland, aged four, as the first Knight of the revived Order of the Garter, 1725

mented the bold, he threatened the cowards. . . . Had the nation seen him they would have adored him.' Cumberland was also defeated at Lauffeld in 1747 and at Hastenbeck in 1757. He was an unlucky commander and far from a brilliant one. On the other hand, he was determined to stubbornness. Owing to the amount of attention which has been directed to the harshness, indeed brutality, displayed in his suppression of the rebel clansmen after Culloden, less than justice has been done to his military achievement in defeating the Pretender's forces. He restored the *moral* of the English troops, which had fallen to pieces utterly as the result of the Canter of Coltbrigg and Prestonpans, where Sir John Cope's forces had gone to pieces in the first encounters with the rebels ; and when

[1] See note on p. 489.

it was anticipated that he would wait till summer before following Charles Edward into the Highlands, he preferred to face the rigours and obstacles of a winter campaign in difficult country and bring the rebellion to an end at the earliest possible moment. But Cumberland's chief title to fame is as a reformer. He was a sound administrator and a very severe disciplinarian. He changed the whole character of the War Office and subordinated the civil authority of the Secretary-at-War to that of the Commander-in-Chief. His ideas of discipline were rather of the martinet type, stiff and exceedingly meticulous after the Prussian manner ; but there was much need of severity in the army in Cumberland's day, especially among the officers, who were inclined to treat army life as a glorified holiday and to ignore most of its duties.

In the Seven Years War, as we have already seen, Pitt at first had to work with rather mediocre material. Of the generals on the American continent Loudoun and Abercromby were incompetent. Three other men stand out in fine contrast—Howe, Amherst, and Wolfe. Brigadier-General Howe, the eldest of three brothers, of whom one was the famous admiral, the other the British Commander-in-Chief during part of the War of American Independence, was killed at the early age of thirty-three at Ticonderoga in 1758. In his brief military career he had shown extraordinary promise, and he is noteworthy for having realized that the Cumberland type of discipline and the methods of Frederic the Great, however well suited they might be for Europe, were worse than useless in the New World. The art of American warfare must be learnt, not from the military text-book, but from the American Indians. As keen on his profession as Wolfe, who greatly admired him and regarded him as the best officer in the British army, he was beloved by his men, whose every hardship he bore with them. Pitt had him appointed second-in-command to Abercromby, to counteract the latter's inefficiency, and it has been said of the Brigadier's death that ' in Lord Howe the soul of General Abercromby's army seemed to expire '.

Of the same school as Howe, but of course far better known

55

GLORIA · MUNDI

3441   Dec 1756

The popular view of Cumberland

Caricature of 1756

than he, was James Wolfe. They were alike in being able to combine strict discipline with humanity and friendliness with their men, as generals of the Cumberland school could not—such, for example, as Hawley, whom Charles Edward defeated at Falkirk, and the gallant Braddock, who paid the penalty for the

GENERAL JAMES WOLFE
From the painting by Gainsborough

rigidity of the system, when he perished in his disastrous engagement with a mixed force of French and Indians in 1755, from inability to adapt himself to the novel requirements of Indian warfare. Wolfe obtained his commission at the age of fourteen, Such child officers were not infrequent at the opening of the eighteenth century. We read of one aged twelve campaigning in Flanders and ' behaving with more courage and conduct than could have been expected from one of his years '. Wolfe was a major at twenty ; a lieutenant-colonel at twenty-three. He was only thirty-two when he died. Red-haired, tall and lanky, extremely delicate, he was not much of a soldier to look at, though not so completely ill-favoured, so lacking in chin, as the best-known portrait of him suggests, for that portrait is almost

Licking the raw recruit into shape. Satirical sketch by Bunbury, 1780

certainly not authentic. His ill-health was persistent, and what with the ravages of rheumatism whenever he was in the field and of incessant sea-sickness whenever he was at sea (which was very often) he lived a miserable life. But he was, notwithstanding, full of enthusiasm for soldiering, confident of his powers, and wholesomely ambitious. Pitt had marked him out as the only officer in the unsuccessful Rochefort expedition who showed any ardour. He had served with distinction in the capture of Louis-burg. But he was still a comparatively unknown man when Pitt selected him for the enterprise against Quebec. A few months later, in the hour of death, he had won an immortal fame on the Heights of Abraham.

It is possible to criticize his conduct of the operations, to point out that he spent a long time in unsuccessful enterprises, whose failure reduced him to the depths of despair ; that he took a long time to recognize that it was from the west that Quebec was really vulnerable ; that had he realized this sooner the heroic effort of the scaling of the Abraham Heights, which might easily have proved a disaster, would not have been necessary ; that much of the credit for the capture of Quebec belongs to Wolfe's naval coadjutors, Saunders and Holmes, without whose intrepid co-operation the whole enterprise must inevitably have mis-carried. But it is ungenerous to cavil, and the instinct which demanded a public funeral for the fallen hero and which has cherished the memory of the battle of the Heights of Abraham as one of the most heroic episodes in the history of British arms is a just one.

A much less romantic figure than that of Wolfe is that of Amherst, the captor of Louisburg in 1758, of Ticonderoga in 1759. Undemonstrative, cautious, and slow, Amherst was also safe and sure. It has been declared by a great authority[1] that he, not Wolfe, was the true conqueror of Canada, and that as a military administrator he had no equal between the days of Marlborough and Wellington, so fine was the laborious, unspectacular work of organizing the gradual conquest of a wide and for the most part trackless country.

There is one other soldier-figure in the Seven Years War period as brilliant as Wolfe's, and a much greater one—that of Robert Clive, the unknown East India Company's clerk, who suddenly at Arcot revealed himself as a soldier of innate genius, and who was to prove himself to be not only (to use Pitt's phrase) a ' heaven-born general ', but a great empire-builder. While he had extraordinary skill and an intuition for perceiving

[1] The Hon. Sir J. Fortescue.

the right moment for action, Clive's greatness lay chiefly in his
dauntless will and inexhaustible courage. He knew the military
capacity of native troops, but it took an iron nerve to face, with

Prefent State of the Land Forces of Great Britain, as made up to the 1ft of May, 1796:

Life Guards	2 Regiments.
Horfe Guards (Blues)	1
Dragoon Guards	7
Dragoons (Heavy)	9
Ditto (Light)	26
Foot Guards	3
Infantry	90
Ditto (Corps not numbered)	16

Making in all 154 Regiments,
and forming an effective force of 16,500 Cavalry,
and upwards of 88,000 Infantry, which, with four
Battalions of Artillery, brings the total to near
110,000 regular troops; exclufive of Fencible Cavalry, Infantry, and Militia.

The Foreign Subfidiaries amount to about 17,000.

Hanoverians 12,000   Heffians 5000

The following is an account of the Generals and Field Officers up to the prefent day:

Field Marfhals	3
Generals	31
Lieutenant Generals	55
Major Generals	151
Colonels	122
Lieutenant Colonels	565
Majors	701
Total	1628

Shows the strength of the army near the end of the century, under the special stress of the Revolutionary Wars. At the opening of the Georgian era there was a strong prejudice against the existence of more than a skeleton standing army, and in session after session motions were brought forward in Parliament for a reduction of the forces. Thus, for example, even in 1738 when the Opposition were pressing for a declaration of war against Spain, Carteret moved that the numbers should be reduced from 18,000 (the existing small figure) to 12,000. This attitude was of course primarily due to persuasion that army officers, like all other paid servants of the State, were liable to become minions of Walpole

a mere handful of three thousand men, the onslaught of fifty
thousand, as Clive did at Plassey.

The War of American Independence is one of the most disastrous in our annals, and the generals who took part in it have
inevitably been under a cloud. Yet, as a whole, they were
not incompetent men by any means, and it has to be remembered

that in nearly every field engagement in the long conflict the colonists were beaten. Gage, the first commander-in-chief, was certainly not very capable, but his two successors, Howe and Clinton, were both able soldiers, as were also Burgoyne, who was forced to surrender at Saratoga, and Cornwallis, who after some brilliant successes in the Carolinas and Virginia, which seemed to be restoring the fortunes of the war, had to surrender at Yorktown. Howe was certainly indolent and latterly indifferent, and there was a most unfortunate lack of concord between Clinton and Cornwallis. But the British failure in the American War was not due to its generals, but to circumstances over which they, for the most part, had no control—to the mere fact of operating in a hostile country thousands of miles from home in days when it took weeks to cross the Atlantic ; to the fact that the authorities at home never grasped the simplest elements of the

BURGOYNE
Caricature by James Sayers

problem and completely underestimated its difficulties ; to the impossible and mischievous attempt to direct the operations of the war from Whitehall ; to the fact that the man who made that attempt, the Secretary of State for the Colonies, was Lord George Germaine,[1] the notorious officer who either through cowardice or jealousy of his commander-in-chief, Prince Ferdinand of Brunswick, had neglected to obey orders at the battle of Minden in the

[1] Better known as Lord G. Sackville. He took the name Germaine in 1770. He was raised to the peerage as Viscount Sackville in 1783.

Seven Years War, and so had failed to convert the astonishing
advantages won by the British infantry into an overwhelming
victory, and who in this American War by his gross carelessness
and ineptitude and insolent conduct towards the general on the
spot destroyed whatever chance of success there was ; most of
all to the fact that when France and Spain intervened on behalf

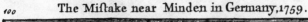

100 The Miſtake near Minden in Germany,1759.

Caricature satirizing Sackville's conduct at the battle of Minden

of the colonists we were unable to maintain the command of the
sea, which was absolutely vital to the very existence, let alone
the victory, of our armies in America.

It is a melancholy story ; but there were relieving episodes in
it, and one of the greatest is the defence of Gibraltar against
a Spanish siege which lasted three years seven months and twelve
days. It could never have held out so long had it not been twice
provisioned, once by Rodney, once by Howe ; but the great hero
of the defence is General Eliott, afterwards Lord Heathfield, whose
fine rugged face has been made familiar to all frequenters of

the National Gallery by Reynolds's portrait. By his invincible intrepidity, his calm endurance of privations, his peculiarly humorous methods of maintaining discipline, he sustained the spirit of the garrison unfaltering. Once when a soldier was

LORD HEATHFIELD
From the portrait by Reynolds

charged with having expressed a wish to join the Spaniards, Eliott asserted that madness could be the only explanation, and ordered him to be bled, put into a strait-waistcoat, fed on bread and water, and prayed for in church. His own diet was simple enough, for he was a teetotaller and a vegetarian, with, however, a fondness for suet puddings.

Note to p. 479.

The successful withdrawal of the Allied troops after the defeat of Fontenoy was due to the skill of the Commander-in-Chief of the British infantry, the veteran John Ligonier, who as a Huguenot refugee had served in the British army in Marlborough's great campaigns. His long record of active service in the field brought him the reward of an earldom and a field-marshal's baton in 1766. Latterly looked upon by the younger men as very old fashioned, he had a great reputation abroad as well as at home for his personal courage and chivalry and for the magnificent discipline which he had always maintained among the men under his command.

THE Gazette of *April* 23, 96. fays, that Capt. *Richard Walfh*, Commander of a *French* Privateer, who was found guilty of High-Treafon, was executed at *Dublin*. That *Robert Lowick*, *Ambrofe Rookwood*, and *Charles Cranburn* were found guilty of High-Treafon, and condemned accordingly. That feveral Affociations were prefented and received very gracioufly, and Mr. *Charles Marley* was Knighted. Of *April* 27, That the *Anglefea*, Captain *Callwell* brought into *Plymouth* a Privateer of St. *Malo*'s of 18 Guns and 120 Men. That a *French* Privateer of 16 Guns, 6 Patereroes and 160 Men took fome Ships; but foon after the Privateer rnn upon a Sand and was loft; but the Men efcaped by help of the Prizes. That the *Portland* took a *French* Ship who liad 46 Guns, and alfo a Dogger of 110 Tuns both laden with Wine and Brandy, and a third fhe put a fhoar. That Sir *George Rook* arrived the 25th Inftant in the *Downs* with his Majefty's Ships, and a great Fleet of Merchantmen, in all 190. That on the 24th Inftant was launched at *Shoreham* a new Fifth-Rate Ship named the *Lion*, carrying 12 Guns and 135 men, built by Mr. *Tho. Ellis*. That feveral Affociations have been prefented and received very gracioufly.

News of Sir George Rooke. From Houghton's 'Collection' of May 2, 1696

The following are the Ships which are to go under the command of the Hon. Sir Charles Wager, viz.

Ships names.	Captains	Guns	Men
Namur	Edward Falkingham	90	680
Princefs Amelia	Edward Reddifh	80	520
Cornwall	Rt Hon. Lord Forbes	80	520
Norfolk	Roberts	80	520
Berwick	Coningfby Norbury	70	440
Buckingham	Charles Brown	70	440
Edinburgh	Sir Challoner Ogle	70	440
Grafton	Nicholas Haddock	70	440
Hampton Court	Rt Hon. Ld. Vere Beauclerc	70	440
Kent	Chriftopher Obrian	70	440
Canterbury	Edward Hook	60	365
Dreadnought	Alexander Gaddes	60	365
Exeter	Durrell	60	365
Sunderland	Mann	60	365
Advice	Martain	50	280
Portland	Rowzer	50	280
Romney	Medley	50	280
Diamond	Anfon	40	200

Sir Charles Wager hoifts his flag on board the Namur, and Admiral Balchen hoifts his flag on board the Princefs Amelia. P.

A group of notable naval commanders of the early eighteenth century. From the 'Grub-street Journal' of July 8, 1731

XVI

THE ADMIRALS

ALTHOUGH the Revolution of 1689 led to a considerable increase in the size of the Royal Navy, there was in some respects a deterioration in efficiency. The Stuarts, whatever their faults, had at least been zealous for the navy, and James II, as Duke of York, assisted by the invaluable Mr. Samuel Pepys, had been an excellent administrator at the Admiralty. In Robert Blake the Commonwealth period had produced a great naval genius whose like was not to be seen till Nelson. The conditions of life in the navy in the eighteenth century, especially in the first half of it, were deplorable. The ships were constantly falling into a foul and unseaworthy condition, and scurvy was rife owing to their insanitary state. The rate of mortality was terribly high, deaths from sickness being much more numerous than casualties in battle. If Marryat's description of naval life at the end of the century seems brutal enough, what can we say of the appalling picture drawn by Smollett in *Roderick Random* of the conditions in 1741, when he served as surgeon's mate in the ill-starred expedition of Admiral Vernon against Cartagena ?

The eighteenth century produced many of the most famous naval captains in our history, but it also produced a large number of mediocre admirals, especially in the earlier half. The record of the navy during the great War of the Spanish Succession is no way comparable with that of the army. The Tories tried hard to bracket Rooke with Marlborough, but the attempt was rather too obviously absurd. Rooke showed commendable dash and determination in 1700 in forcing his way into Vigo harbour and destroying or capturing all the vessels there, but he was very unenterprising after this. Though a brave man, he was inordinately weighed down by a sense of his responsibilities. The successful attack upon Gibraltar, with which his name is most commonly associated, was only undertaken under positive orders after a period of indecision and inactivity on his part; the garrison of the fortress was exceedingly weak; and the credit of the naval part of the enterprise in any case belongs rather to Rear-Admiral Byng, afterwards Viscount Torrington, the victor of the battle of Cape Passaro, and the father of the Admiral Byng shot for neglect of duty. The capture of Gibraltar was followed by a general action with the French fleet off Malaga. It was a drawn fight, in which not a single vessel was taken on either side. The indecisive character of this engagement was due to the tactics employed by the Anglo-Dutch fleet. The Admiralty Instructions at this time prescribed it as the correct method of attack that the fleet should preserve an intact line, each vessel bearing down so as to engage its opposite in the enemy fleet. This manoeuvre was difficult of accomplishment and rendered a thorough victory unlikely save in the event of greatly superior gunnery. Slavish obedience to the letter of these instructions often hampered the success of our naval operations in the eighteenth century and was in marked contrast to the aggressive, determined methods of Blake in earlier and of Nelson in later days.

Sir Clowdisley Shovell, often associated with Rooke, but unlike his colleague a Whig, who began life as a cabin boy, had a distinguished career in the Mediterranean and contributed largely to the success of the enterprise against Barcelona in 1705, but his career was tragically cut short in 1706, his flagship, homeward bound, striking in fog the sinister reefs of the Bishop and Clerk among the Scilly Islands, and all on board perishing.[1] Another

---

[1] Shovell's body, only just living, was washed ashore. It appears that a woman, who coveted his emerald ring, was the actual cause of his death.

Sir Cloudesly Shovel, in the Association, with the Eagle, Rumny, and the Firebrand, Lost on the Rocks of Scilly, October, 22. 1707

brave and accomplished admiral was Sir John Leake, whose
achievements, also in the Mediterranean, are too little known.

The period 1714–57 is far from glorious in our naval annals.
It contains, indeed, one of the most thorough of victories in the
battle of Cape Passaro (1718), when a Spanish fleet was destroyed,
though we were not at war with Spain ; but for the most part the
navy was not in at all a satisfactory condition. It is notorious
that when war broke out with Spain in 1739 it found the fleet in
a very ill-prepared state ; and perhaps even more discreditable
was the lack of fellow-feeling and of proper discipline among

A medal struck in 1739 exalting Vernon and his Portobello enterprise

senior officers. When Admiral Vernon at the outset of the war
started off on his mission to destroy the Spanish settlements and
to distress their shipping, his initial enterprise against Portobello
was successful, but the more ambitious undertaking against
Cartagena failed lamentably owing partly to the appalling
mortality due to the insanitary condition of his ships, partly to
the hostility between Vernon and his partner in this joint military
and naval operation, General Wentworth. Both were much to
blame. The assistance given by the troops was inadequate ; on
the other hand, Vernon demanded the impossible, and his conduct
was that of a truculent and overbearing bully.

Perhaps the worst instance of naval insubordination in the
eighteenth century is that of old Admiral Benbow's last battle,
fought in the West Indies in 1702, in which he was mortally
wounded. The French fleet on that occasion escaped destruc-

tion solely because several of the English captains failed to take any part in the action at all. When he lay dying, a message was sent him by the French commander: 'Yesterday morning I had no hope but I should have supped in your cabin. As for those cowardly captains of yours, hang them up, for by God! they deserve it.' But another very bad instance of misconduct occurred on the 11th February 1744, when Admiral Mathews attacked a combined French and Spanish fleet off Toulon. In his anxiety to engage the enemy Mathews did not wait till his leading ship was abreast of the enemy's van, but

Blakeney was Deputy-Governor of Minorca when it was besieged by the French under the Duke of Richelieu in 1756, and, owing to supposed cowardice or treachery on the part of Admiral Byng in failing to relieve it, was obliged to surrender. On the medal B stands for Byng

bore down at once, to bring his own flagship into immediate action with the largest hostile vessel, thus breaking his line. His rear vessels, under the command of Admiral Lestock, were considerably behind when the battle opened, but they failed entirely to take any part in it because Lestock did not bear down upon the enemy at all, but remained strictly in line. It was notorious that he was on bad terms with his chief, and it was suspected that he had deliberately kept out of the battle in order to embarrass him, knowing that he could shelter himself under the technicality of the Admiralty Instructions. The indecisive character of the battle of Toulon raised a clamour at home and it rained courts-martial, charges being brought against Mathews and Lestock, and eleven out of the twenty-nine captains present at the battle. It has often been stated that Mathews was court-martialled because he had broken the line, but this is not the case.

Great as was the public dissatisfaction awakened by the battle of Toulon, it paled into insignificance in comparison with the fury of indignation aroused by the failure of Admiral John Byng at Minorca in 1756. Most of the public execration fell on the unhappy admiral himself ; others seeking to exculpate him placed the odium upon the Board of Admiralty, the presiding genius at which was the great Lord Anson. He enjoyed a great reputation, but some now averred that ' nature had not endowed him with those extraordinary abilities which had been so liberally granted him by the whole nation '. As a matter of fact, whatever the extent of his responsibility for the Minorca failure, Anson was one of the great naval reformers of the century, a fine administrator, who introduced many improvements in the conditions of seamen in the navy and issued a new set of Admiralty Instructions superseding the old. He presided at the Admiralty during the Seven Years War, that is to say in the days not only of Byng, but of Hawke and Boscawen, days marked as a whole not by failures, but by brilliant successes. Nevertheless, he will always be best known for what he accomplished in his earlier days, when as Commodore Anson he sailed round the world in the *Centurion*.

' Memorable', says Carlyle, ' among the sea-heroisms of the world,' this voyage gave proof that ' real captains, taciturn sons of Anak, are still born in England,' and over the Spanish War, ' that otherwise altogether hideous puddle of mismanagement, platitude, and disaster,' he sheds ' some tincture of heroic beauty '. The design of the expedition was that it should sail round the Horn and carry destruction along the Pacific coast, raiding the Spaniard's Peruvian settlements, and should capture the great Acapulco galleon on its way homeward laden with the gold of Mexico. In fine, with his small squadron Anson was to emulate the buccaneering exploits of Davis, Coxon, and Swan, in those same seas some fifty years earlier. It was intended to send together with the seamen a contingent of infantry. In the end the infantry were not forthcoming, and 500 Chelsea pensioners were detailed to take their place ! Of these, all that had strength enough to do so deserted, most wisely, at Portsmouth. The remaining 259, a collection of invalids and cripples, among whom septuagenarians were numbered, went on the expedition. Not a single one of them survived to tell the tale of their adventures.

The squadron consisted of the *Centurion* of 60 guns, the *Gloucester* and *Severn* of 50, the *Wager* of 28 guns, a converted East India merchantman, and a small sloop. They enjoyed good weather as far as Madeira, but even as early as this scurvy had broken out and was taking toll of the miserable crews. By the

One of the causes of Byng's inactivity was his being hypnotized by the letter of Admiralty Instructions and by fear of getting into trouble as Mathews had done

time they were approaching the Horn every second man was down with it. The terrible weather for which that formidable cape is famous was never more awful. Through gales of ice, growing ever fiercer, they battered their way for more than fifty days. The great seas sweeping over the vessels broke upon decks and rigging frozen to ice. In the frightful cold and exposure the ravages of scurvy made dreadful havoc and over two hundred died of the horrible disease. It was with difficulty that any men at all could be mustered for the ordinary duties of the watch. In these appalling buffetings the vessels of the squadron were separated, and two of them never reappeared, having been driven back on the Brazilian coast. One of these, the *Wager*, when off the shores of Terra del Fuego, was badly damaged, and eventually wrecked. The annals of seafaring contain no more terrible tale than that of this disaster, of the sufferings and adventures of the survivors, among whom was a midshipman, by name Byron, who afterwards became an admiral and was the grandfather of the poet. Thus at the age of seventeen he started a career whose voyages were notorious for such consistency of violent weather as to earn for him the nickname of ' Foul-weather Jack '.

At last, after a final most terrific hurricane of all, the *Centurion* succeeded in making the island of Juan Fernandez. Next day arrived the tiny sloop ; later there hove in sight the *Gloucester* ; but her mortality had been so high that she could hardly be navigated, and for weeks she appeared, disappeared, and re-appeared on the horizon in her attempt to make the island. When at length she succeeded in doing so, out of her original crew of 300 less than 80 remained.

After a stay of three months to recuperate, Anson started off again with his three vessels. Having taken several prizes, he made a descent under cover of darkness on the small fortress of Paita, captured it with only three casualties, burnt the town, and made off with its treasure. He now decided to lie in wait for the Acapulco galleon ; but his ships were seen, and the galleon was detained in port to wait till the following year ! He next proposed to intercept the Manila galleon, but heavy weather again upset his plans. The *Gloucester* became waterlogged and had to be abandoned, the remnant of her crew being transferred to the *Centurion*. Aboard the flagship the men were dying like flies ; the commodore, therefore, made one of the Ladrone Islands to obtain the fresh food and water which were essential to save the survivors from the ravages of the scurvy. By this time Anson himself had succumbed to the malady. While he and the other sick were convalescing ashore, the *Centurion* was caught by a terrific gale and driven from her anchorage. Days passed and she made no appearance. Anson was preparing for the heroic enterprise of

The MANILLA GALEON taken by ADMIRAL ANSON

crossing the Pacific to Macao on the coast of China in a small boat of fifteen tons, which he had captured, when, after an absence of eighteen days, the *Centurion* at last hove in sight.

In the *Centurion* Anson reached Macao, and after refitting once more set sail in search of the treasure ships. He had left Spithead on the 18th September 1740 ; it was now the 19th April 1743. This year, owing to the detention of last year's galleon in Acapulco, there would be two possible prizes. With his single ludicrously undermanned ship the heroic commodore proposed to capture both. He made for the Philippines and there lay in wait. At last, on the 20th June, one of the treasure ships was sighted. Fully anticipating that a consort would soon be visible on the horizon, Anson bore down, prepared to fight both, though he was so short-handed that he could not properly man his guns, and while keeping men at each gun to load it he had to detail a detachment to run from gun to gun and fire them as rapidly as possible. But even with this serious disadvantage his broadside did terrific execution. The Spaniard's decks were swept repeatedly, while the *Centurion* sustained little damage, the enemy's casualties were five times as numerous as Anson's, and the great galleon was taken. There were nearly 500 prisoners to be guarded as well as an additional ship to be navigated. There was but little sleep for the Englishmen ; nevertheless Anson reached Canton without mishap, and on the 15th June, 1744, the *Centurion* reached home at last. There is no more inspiring tale of indomitable courage and persistence in the face of interminable discouragements, difficulties, and calamities.

It is no wonder that the generation of sailors brought up under Anson's guidance proved men of stern mettle, brave and resolute fighters. Among these was Saunders, who co-operated with Wolfe in the operations against Quebec. He won Pitt's heart because, when, on his way home, his task accomplished, and at the mouth of the Channel, he heard that Hawke was engaged with the Brest fleet, he instantly deflected his course in order to take part in the fray. He was not in time to share in the glory of Quiberon, but the will to seek out the enemy at all times and occasions, wherein is the spirit of victory, was there.

H.M.S. Centurion, 60 Guns, 1743

From the model in the United Services Museum

The battle of Quiberon Bay was the greatest of many great services rendered his country by 'the great Lord Hawke'. His first important command had been the *Berwick*, which, manned with pressed men and ' very little, weakly, puny fellows, that have never been to sea', took part in Mathews's engagement off Toulon, where Hawke first proved his fighting quality. In September 1746 he was given command of a squadron with orders to cruise between Ushant and Finisterre. On the 12th October he sighted a French fleet, consisting of 9 men-of-war and 300 merchantmen. Hawke had the numerical superiority, but the French had four ships more heavily armed than any of the British. The French commander sought to avoid an engagement, but Hawke, giving the signal for a general chase, prevented this, and succeeded in taking six of the nine French warships—a brilliant piece of work.

In 1748 Hawke was promoted Vice-Admiral of the Blue, but for the next eight years his work was almost entirely at home and mainly administrative, in connexion with Anson's reforms. In June 1756, on the news of Byng's failure at Port Mahon, he was at once dispatched to the Mediterranean, but Port Mahon had fallen long before his arrival and nothing could be done. In 1757, Hawke, now Admiral, was chosen to conduct the naval operations connected with the Rochefort expedition. Its failure was in no way due to the admiral, but something of a cloud was cast upon all who had participated in it. Next year he was given the task of preventing the departure of a French convoy of troops destined for America. He succeeded in forcing the ships to seek safety in shallow waters, but was unable to destroy them owing to a lack of fire-ships and bomb-ships, of which he had complained to the Admiralty, with whom his relations were at this time very strained. Being of an autocratic temper and entirely without fear of responsibility, he took no pains to be on good terms with Whitehall, and especially with regard to the provisioning and the medical services of his ships took matters with a high hand.

In 1759 it was known that the French were preparing an invasion of England. Flat-bottomed boats for the conveyance of troops were ready in Havre ; it needed but the junction of the

EDYSTONE LIGHT HOUSE

This Lighthouse, as it appears above, was begun in July 1706 and finished in 1709. It is erected on the Edystone Rock, 3 Leagues S.E. and N.W. of Ramhead and 4 Leagues from Plymouth. The Rock is harder than Marble, therefore in order to fasten the foundation of the Building, there are 36 Holes cut into the Rock, from 20 to 30 Inches deep, & 6 Inches Square at Top but at the depth of 6 Inches, they are no more than 5 Inches Square, and thence narrowing they are, at bottom 3 Inches wide and 9 Inches broad, into those Holes Iron-Rods are fixed which serve to tye and Cramp the Solid Parts of the Building to the Rock. The Diameter of the Foundation of this Building is 24 feet, the height of it near 100 feet. In the Year 1696 the famous Henry Winstanly began to erect a Light-House on this Rock, which, after 4 Years Labour he finished, yet a curious manner, but in the Dreadfull Storm 27 Nov. 1703, it was Destroyed, and the Ingenious Projector perisht with it A. is part of Cornwall. B. part of Devonshire.

The safety of the seas. The second Eddystone lighthouse, finished in 1709

Brest and Toulon fleets to conduct them across the Channel for the attempt. The attempt was never made. Rodney demolished the flat-bottomed boats at Havre, Boscawen destroyed the Toulon fleet, and Hawke the fleet of Brest, after a most remarkable blockade of that great arsenal. The task of maintaining a continuous blockade on so exposed a coast was in the days of the sailing ship one of the utmost difficulty. Yet Hawke kept it up not only through the summer months, but also into November, weathering heavy seas in the open, and only when this was utterly impossible in the severest south-westerly gales running into Torbay for shelter. Luckily a gale severe enough to necessitate this could usually be relied upon to keep Conflans, the French admiral, storm-stayed in harbour, and immediately the conditions began to moderate Hawke would hurry back to his post. The weather at the commencement of November was very bad, and returning on the 16th, after an enforced sojourn in Torbay, Hawke had news that the Brest fleet was at sea, making southward. Against a powerful breeze from the south-east he made after them, and on the 20th, when he was off Belle Isle, sighted his quarry. Hawke made no attempt to form an orthodox line, but ordered his leading ships to go off in hottest pursuit. They were too fast for Conflans. But though he could not outsail him, the French commander still hoped to balk his enemy. With the sea rising under a squally and stiffening north-west wind dangerous to the unwary on that coast, Conflans ran inshore into the mouth of the river Vilaine, not expecting that the English would dare follow him on to a lee shore, amid reefs and shoals to them unknown. Hawke had no pilot and no chart ; yet he did not hesitate. Where the enemy could go he could go. He followed Conflans into Quiberon Bay, and the battle opened.

Hawke himself made for the French flagship, round which the shallow water was boiling and hissing. The risk of approaching was pointed out to the admiral by his navigating officer. 'You have done your duty in warning me,' was his answer, 'now lay us alongside the French Commander-in-Chief.' Another French vessel thrust herself between Hawke and his predestined victim. Two single devastating broadsides and she sank.

Other enemy ships sank or struck their colours. The engagement had not started till 2 p.m. ; it was now dark. In Hawke's simple yet graphic words, 'Night was now come, and being on a part of the coast among islands and shoals, of which we were totally ignorant, without a pilot, as was the greatest part of the squadron, and blowing hard on a lee shore, I made the signal to anchor'. Next morning the French flagship ran ashore and was burnt ; seven other vessels, jettisoning their guns and stores, ran up the Vilaine, where they went to pieces. Six had already been captured or sunk ; eight only succeeded in escaping. The Brest fleet as a unit had ceased to be. Not even the defeat of the Armada or the battles of Camperdown, Aboukir Bay, or Trafalgar were more complete or more effective victories, and Hawke, because of it, takes his place among the great sea-captains of all time.

The victory of Lagos, which was the complement of Quiberon Bay, though less important and much less sensational, was no less complete. Boscawen had tried to induce De la Clue to come out from Toulon by sending in three of his own ships to attack. They had been driven off by the fire of the shore batteries, and as these ships needed repairs and the whole squadron refurbishing, Boscawen put into Gibraltar. Several of his ships were still refitting when the admiral got news that De la Clue was out. With characteristic energy Boscawen immediately put to sea. During the night five of the enemy ships became separated from the rest ; Boscawen engaged the remaining seven and an obstinate fight ensued, but De la Clue, with five ships, succeeded in running into the neutral waters of Lagos Bay and esteemed himself safe ; but Boscawen, undeterred by the fear of violating Portuguese neutrality, boldly and unscrupulously entered the bay. Two of the French ships were run ashore and burnt ; two others surrendered. The remnant of the Toulon fleet was driven upon Cadiz.

Boscawen is a picturesque figure. From his habit of carrying his head on one side he got the nickname of 'wry-necked Dick' ; but his men, who loved him, more often spoke of him as 'old Dreadnought'. This was the name of a ship he commanded in his early days, and a story is told in explanation of this title which may be apocryphal, yet well indicates the sort of reputation he enjoyed. It is related that one night when the *Dreadnought* was cruising alone, the officer of the watch wakened Boscawen with the intelligence that two large vessels, apparently Frenchmen, were bearing down upon them, and asked him what it was best to do. 'Do!' exclaimed Boscawen, preparing to go out on deck clad only in his night-shirt, 'Damn 'em, fight 'em!' Boscawen was a very strict disciplinarian, but like Hawke he was sincerely concerned for the welfare of his men, and he paid greater attention to matters of health, and especially to ventilation, than was usual in his day.

Rodney, the third of the three distinguished seamen who helped to frustrate the French design of invasion in 1759, had a very picturesque career. A man of remarkably handsome appearance both in early and later life, as his portraits show, 'his person was more elegant', it was said, 'than seemed to fit his rough profession; there was something that approached to delicacy and effeminacy in his figure'. Rodney was connected with some of the most distinguished families in England, but he was bred to the sea from boyhood. Still he had all the failings of the man of pleasure, lived a disorderly sort of life, was an inveterate gambler, and as a consequence was perpetually in debt. Financial difficulties, indeed, nearly brought his career to an untimely end, when he had reached the rank of rear-admiral; for he was in such desperate straits that to escape from the dunning of his creditors he went and lived in Paris. The quixotic kindness of the Marshal de Biron, who helped him to meet his liabilities, enabled him to return to England and his profession. He thereby did an exceedingly ill turn to France, as events were to prove.

At the end of December 1779 Rodney started off on the very important double mission of relieving Gibraltar, then closely invested by Spain, and of proceeding to take up the Leeward Islands station. On the 16th January, in heavy weather, a Spanish squadron was sighted off Cape St. Vincent making its way to Cadiz. Rodney enjoyed a great numerical superiority, but the enemy were far ahead and might easily have escaped. Rodney at once set his course so as to cut in between the Spaniards and the land, and he thus forced an action which took place at night and in a fierce gale. Only two of the nine Spanish ships succeeded in escaping. This victory was followed by the relief of Gibraltar,

ADMIRAL EDWARD BOSCAWEN

From the portrait by Sir Joshua Reynolds, in the National Portrait Gallery

and at a bound Rodney established his position in popular esteem as a great naval leader.

He now proceeded to take up his command in the West Indies, and on the 17th April he was in action with de Guichen, who had just succeeded to the French command in those waters. The battle might have been as decisive as his last achievement had his intentions been properly understood by his subordinates.

He had beforehand explained that he proposed to concentrate his entire strength against a certain part, not the whole, of the French line. On the day of battle he decided to attack the enemy's rear. But his orders to this effect were misunderstood by Sir Hyde Parker, commanding the British van, and, owing to contradictory orders from Rodney and Parker, some confusion resulted, and an indecisive engagement was the consequence.

Rodney's most memorable battle took place at one of the most dangerous crises in English history. In 1781 had taken place the surrender of Cornwallis at Yorktown, that decisive event which secured the independence of the United States. The French and Dutch made a resolute attack upon our West Indian Islands, and it was doubtful if we should succeed in retaining Jamaica, Barbados, &c. Not even on our natural element, the sea, did it appear that we could hold our own. It seemed that Great Britain had already sunk to the rank of a second-class power ; and then, a blaze of sunshine in a gloomy sky, came the battle of the Saintes.

The Saintes are a small archipelago lying between the islands of Guadeloupe and Dominica. The French intended a descent upon Jamaica, and for this purpose De Grasse, with a fleet of 35 warships and 150 merchantmen, conveying 5,000 troops, had arrived in West Indian waters, prepared to co-operate with a Spanish fleet and military contingent of 8,000 men. On the 19th February 1782, Rodney effected a junction with Admiral Samuel Hood, who in some complicated manoeuvring with De Grasse a fortnight before, off Nevis and St. Kitts, had shown himself a commander of brilliant resource. On the morning of the 12th April Rodney was wakened with the joyful intelligence that ' God had given him his enemy on the lee bow '. The distinguishing feature of the action which followed was the breaking of Rodney's line. The leading British ships, with the admiral's full approval, when they made contact with the French fleet turned off and ran parallel until they were ranged against the corresponding vessels in the opposite line. When, however, Rodney himself in the *Formidable* bore down he did not follow suit, but struck boldly through the French line, where a large gap

GEORGE BRYDGES RODNEY, FIRST BARON RODNEY

From the portrait by Sir Joshua Reynolds, in St. James's Palace. Reproduced by the gracious permission of His Majesty the King

had been made by one French vessel, the *Glorieux*, being knocked right out of the line by a hurricane broadside fired by one of the British van as she passed. The next four British ships followed the *Formidable*. Meanwhile, farther to the French rear, another gap had been created by the fierceness of the British fire, and through this passed the whole of Hood's squadron. Thus the entire French fleet had been broken up into disunited atoms, its line of battle pulverized. There was heavy fighting all day, but about 6 p.m. De Grasse on the largest and most powerful man-of-war afloat, the *Ville de Paris*, hauled down his flag. To Hood's intense disgust no effort was made to follow up this splendid victory by a vigorous pursuit of the fleeing fragments of the beaten fleet. Instead, Rodney signalled to lie to. The reason of his inactivity seems to be that at the age of sixty-four he was prematurely old, and that he was physically exhausted by the strain of twelve hours' continuous fighting. He was content with what he had done. He had saved Jamaica and restored British naval prestige.

The question where lies the credit for the successful manoeuvre whereby the battle of the Saintes was won has been highly controversial; but expert opinion now seems to award it to Sir Charles Douglas, Rodney's captain of the fleet, who urged the manoeuvre upon the admiral. The latter petulantly retorted that he would not break his line, but the golden opportunity was so obvious that he almost immediately afterwards allowed himself to be overborne. Douglas and Affleck, a captain who spontaneously carried out the same manoeuvre farther ahead, belonged to the same school—that of the great and heroic Kempenfelt, who is popularly known because of his tragic end and Cowper's familiar poem, *The Loss of the Royal George*, but who deserves rather to be known as the inventor of a sound system of signalling[1] and as one of the chief inaugurators of

---

[1] It has been said of his Signal Book, that it ' bridges the chasm that separates the old navy from the navy of Nelson, and constitutes a revolution which (for far-reaching effects) will challenge comparison with the adoption by the navy of heavy artillery in the age of Drake '.—G. Callender, *The Naval Side of British History*, p. 176.

NAVY OFFICE

This is a neat pretty Building, made very Commodious for Business; the Office where the Commissioners meet and the several Clerks keep their Books, being placed in the midst of a large Court, apart from the rest of the Buildings, as it appears in this Draught; It is so Built for the safety of their Books in the Case of Fire: the rest of the Court is set apart for the Residence of the Commissioners and other Officers. The Commissioners of this Office, see to the building of his Majesty's Ships, and to the keeping them and the Docks in good Repair, &c.

Exclusive of the HIRED ARMED VESSELS, which are chiefly employed in protecting the Coasting Trade of GREAT BRITAIN.

	Line	50 s	Frig	Sps.	Tot
In Port and fitting - - -	7	2	28	87	124
Guard-ships - - -	4	2	2	0	8
In the English and Irish Channels - -	42	0	35	52	129
On the Downs and North Sea stations -	14	3	31	76	124
On the Baltic Service - -	0	0	0	0	0
At the West India Islands and on the Passage	1	0	12	30	43
On the Jamaica station	3	1	23	9	36
American & Newfoundland stations -	0	0	8	6	14
C. of G. Hope, E. Ind. and on the Passage	9	7	8	13	37
Africa and on Sec. Exp.	0	1	6	5	12
On the Lisbon Station - -	0	0	0	0	0
Spain and Portugal without the Straits -	11	0	6	3	20
In the Mediterranean -	31	4	56	36	126
Hospital and Prison Ships	22	3	4	0	29
Total in Commission	144	23	219	317	703
Receiving Ships -	7	3	11	0	21
Serviceable and repairing for Service -	9	1	2	2	14
In ordinary - -	14	0	14	23	51
Building - -	23	2	5	0	31
Total	197	29	252	342	820

STATE OF THE ORDINARY AT EACH PORT.

	Line.	50's	Frig	Sps	Tot.
Portsmouth - -	11	0	9	16	36
Plymouth - -	12	0	6	4	22
Chatham - -	5	1	0	0	6
Sheerness - -	2	1	6	2	11
River - -	0	2	6	3	11
Total	30	4	27	25	86

The strength of the Navy increased greatly during the century both as regards the number and tonnage of the vessels. Thus in 1702 the number of ships in the Navy, exclusive of sloops and smaller vessels, was 175, representing over 140,000 tons : in 1760 there were 270 such ships, representing almost exactly double that tonnage. In 1793, at the commencement of the war of the Revolution, there were 309 of these ships (tonnage 373,000 odd). In 1801 the number had risen to 407 (tonnage 518,000)

the practice of those bold tactical methods which, as used by Jervis, Nelson, and Saumarez, made the epoch of the Revolutionary and Napoleonic Wars the most justly famous in our naval annals.

With the name of Kempenfelt in this connexion there should be bracketed that of Lord Howe, 'Black Dick', as his men called him, whose greatest exploits, however, belong to that later period. There was another advocate of bold and unorthodox tactics, who was not a sailor at all, but a fussy, studious Scots laird, who was Scott's original for the character of Monkbarns in *The Antiquary*, named Clerk of Eldin. In 1780 Clerk published a work on naval tactics, in which he condemned the existing school of naval thought and urged the tactic of breaking line. There was courage and to spare in the British navy—so ran his thesis—but a stereotyped tactical system robbed it of its effectiveness. An open mind, freshness of outlook, more direct methods, were needed to secure results commensurate with our maritime tradition. Clerk, the lay theorist, Howe and Kempenfelt, the practical demonstrators of his theories, pointed the way to Nelson.

SELECT LIST OF AUTHORITIES

CHAPTER II

THE principal Manuscript authorities for the political history of England, 1702–83, are to be found in the Public Record Office and in the British Museum. Few Calendars of State Papers relating to the eighteenth century have been printed. There are, however, a *Calendar (Domestic) for 1702–4* (2 vols.) and Calendars of *Home Office Papers for 1760–75* (4 vols.), of *Treasury Books and Papers* (up to 1745), *America and W. Indies, 1700–14* (10 vols.), and *Acts of the Privy Council* (Colonial Series) for the whole period. Of the manuscripts in the British Museum among the most valuable are the voluminous *Newcastle Papers* and *Hardwicke Papers* and the *Chatham Papers* (part of which have been published as the *Chatham Correspondence*, 4 vols., 1858). Many of the Historical Manuscripts Commission publications are relevant to this period, as for example the following: The MSS. of the Duke of Portland, vols. ii, iv–viii for the *Harley Papers*; the Stuart MSS. for the history of Jacobitism; the MSS. of the Earl of Mar and Kellie and of the Earl of Marchmont for the Union with Scotland; the MSS. of the Earl of Carlisle for Parliamentary proceedings under George II; the Charlemont MSS. for Irish affairs; the Dartmouth MSS., vol. ii, and the MSS. of Mrs. Stopford-Sackville for the American Question and the American War.

The eighteenth century is famous for its wealth of memoirs, diaries, and correspondence. The most important are Lord Hervey's *Memoirs of George II*; Horace Walpole's *Memoirs of George II*, his *Memoirs of George III* and the so-called *Last Journals* (ed. Dr. Doran, 1859), and, even more useful, his *Letters* (ed. Mrs. Paget .Toynbee, 16 vols., 1903–5); the *Historical Memoirs of Sir Nathaniel Wraxall*; the *Autobiography of the Duke of Grafton* (ed. Sir W. R. Anson, 1898); the *Correspondence of the fourth Duke of Bedford* (3 vols., 1842); the *Grenville Correspondence* (4 vols., 1853); the *Correspondence of George III, 1760–83* (6 vols.), recently edited by the Hon. Sir J. Fortescue.

The outstanding secondary authority is Lecky, but Stanhope's histories of Queen Anne and of the period 1713–83 are still worth reading. The best modern surveys are by I. S. Leadam (1702–60), and W. Hunt (1760–1801) in Longman's *Political History of England*, and by Sir C. Grant Robertson in *England under the Hanoverians* (Methuen).

For constitutional history there are the first two volumes of Erskine May's *Constitutional History of England* (3 vols., 1912), but this only begins at 1760, and for the earlier period there is nothing more modern than Hallam. Sir W. R. Anson's *Law and Custom of the Constitution* should be consulted. The second volume of Professor E. R. Turner's *The Privy Council of England in the Seventeenth and Eighteenth Centuries* is, and his promised history of the Cabinet for the same period will be, valuable. In the meantime it is necessary to consult articles on the Cabinet in the *English Historical Review*, by H. W. V. Temperley in vols. xxvii and xxxi and by Sir W. R. Anson in vol. xxix.

Parliamentary history must be studied in the *Journals* of the two Houses, in the *Manuscripts of the House of Lords* printed so far only for the years

1702–10, the *Complete Protests of the Lords* (ed. J. E. Thorold Rogers, 3 vols., 1875), and for reports of debates Cobbett's *Parliamentary History* (vols. vi to xxiii), which can be supplemented by the reports in the *Annual Register* (from 1758). Secondary authorities for the Lower House are E. and A. Porritt's *The Unreformed House of Commons* (2 vols., 1909), and G. S. Veitch's *The Genesis of Parliamentary Reform* (1913), and for the Upper House the present writer's *The House of Lords in the Eighteenth Century* (1927).

For Foreign Policy, G. F. and C. de Martens' *Recueil des principaux traités depuis 1761* (Gottingue, 1807–35), vols. i–iii, and C. G. de Koch, *Histoire abrégée des traités de Paix* (15 vols., Paris, 1817–18), are useful ; also four volumes of *Diplomatic Instructions* published by the Camden Society, for Sweden, 1689–1727, Denmark, 1689–1789, France, 1689–1729 (2 vols.). Among notable treatises dealing with particular aspects of foreign policy are E. Bourgeois, *La Diplomatie secrète au XVIIIᵉ Siècle* ; E. Armstrong, *Elisabeth Farnese* (1892) ; A. W. Ward, *Great Britain and Hanover* (1899) ; G. F. Chance, *George I and the Northern War* (1909) ; W. Coxe, *Memoirs of Horatio. Lord Walpole* ; P. Vaucher, *Robert Walpole et la Politique de Fleury* (Paris 1924) ; R. Waddington, *Louis XV et le renversement des Alliances* : *Préliminaires de la Guerre de Sept Ans* (Paris, 1896), and *La Guerre de Sept Ans* (4 vols., 1899–1907). Reference may also be made to Seeley's *The Expansion of England* and to the introductory chapter in the *Cambridge History of British Foreign Policy*.

The relations between England and Scotland may be studied in the standard histories of Scotland, by J. Hill Burton (vol. viii), P. Hume Brown (vol. iii), and Andrew Lang (vol. iv), and these may be supplemented by Defoe's contemporary *History of the Union* ; Hume Brown's *The Legislative Union between England and Scotland* (1914) ; A. V. Dicey and R. S. Rait's *Thoughts on the Union between England and Scotland* (1920) ; W. C. Mathieson's *Scotland and the Union, 1695–1747* (1905) ; J. Mackinnon, *The Union of England and Scotland* (1896) ; and G. W. T. Omond's *The Lord Advocates of Scotland* (2 vols., 1883).

The best guide to Irish affairs is Lecky's *History of Ireland in the Eighteenth Century*, originally forming an integral part of his *History of England*, subsequently published separately in 5 vols. R. Dunlop's chapter in vol. vi of the *Cambridge Modern History*, and his *Life of Grattan* (1889), and T. D. Ingram's *A Critical Examination of Irish History* (2 vols., 1900), should also be noted.

For Colonial history and the American Revolution J. A. Doyle, *The Colonies under the House of Hanover* (5 vols., 1882–1907) ; G. L. Beer, *British Colonial Policy, 1754–1765* (New York, 1907) ; H. E. Egerton, *Short History of British Colonial Policy* (6th ed., 1910) ; J. Fiske, *The American Revolution* (2 vols., 1891) ; Sir G. O. Trevelyan, *The American Revolution* (3 vols., 1905).

For the history of India, Sir A. Lyall, *The Rise and Expansion of the British Dominion in India* (5th ed., 1910) ; V. A. Smith, *The Oxford History of India* (1923) ; Ramsay Muir, *The Making of British India, 1756–1858*, extracts from documents with connecting narrative.

CHAPTER III

(a) *Original authorities.*

A number of these have been mentioned in the text—the novels of Fielding, Smollett, and Fanny Burney, and memoirs, diaries, and correspondence, in particular the Letters of Lady Mary Wortley Montagu, Henrietta, Countess of Suffolk, Lord Chesterfield, and Horace Walpole, the *Diary of Bubb Dodington*, Gibbon's *Autobiography*, Fanny Burney's *Diary and Letters*, the *Life and Letters of Lady Sarah Lennox* (edited by the Countess of Ilchester and Lord Stavordale, 2 vols., 1902).

Accounts of travels through the country are very useful, such, for example, as Celia Fiennes's *Through England on a Side-Saddle in the time of William and Mary* (1888) ; Defoe's *Tour through the whole island of Great Britain* (3 vols., 1724–7, new ed., 1927); C. de Saussure's *A Foreign View of England in the reigns of George I and George II* ; Voltaire's *Lettres sur les Anglais* ; Le Blanc, *Letters on the English and French Nations* (Eng. trans., 2 vols., 1747) ; P. J. Grosley, *A Tour to London, or New Observations on England* (1772, trs. T. Nugent) ; C. Moritz, *Travels through various parts of England in 1782*, in vol. ii of Pinkerton's *Collection of . . . Voyages and Travels* (17 vols., 1808–14) ; Arthur Young's *Tour through the Southern Counties* (1768), *Tour through the North of England* (1770) ; *Tour through the East of England* (1771); T. Pennant's *Journey from Chester to London*, in Pinkerton, vol. iii.

Much variegated information as to social and economic conditions may be gleaned from the *State Papers* (*Domestic*) and the *Home Office Papers*. The extensive use which can be made of such sources as Sessions Records, Population Returns, and Parliamentary Papers is admirably illustrated by Mrs. George's book on *London Life in the Eighteenth Century* (see *infra*). For the condition of the rural population see also F. M. Eden, *The State of the Poor* (1797), Cowper's *The Task*, iv.

For the watering-places, Christopher Anstey's *The New Bath Guide* (1767), and Goldsmith's *Life of Richard Nash of Bath* (1762).

For the seamen, Cook's *Voyages* ; Fielding's *Journal of a Voyage to Lisbon* ; Smollett's *Roderick Random* and *Peregrine Pickle*.

(b) *Secondary authorities.*

On the subject generally, *Social England* (ed. H. D. Traill), vol. v ; chapters v and xxi in Lecky's *History of England* ; W. C. Sydney's *England and the English in the Eighteenth Century* (2 vols., 1891) ; Thackeray's *Four Georges* ; Austin Dobson's *Eighteenth Century Vignettes* (three series, 1892–6).

For the Wits, the Salons, and the Watering Places, J. H. Jesse, *George Selwyn and his Contemporaries* (4 vols., 1882) ; S. P. Kerr, *George Selwyn and the Wits* (1909) ; E. J. Climenson, *Elizabeth Montagu, the queen of the blue-stockings*, containing her correspondence (2 vols., 1906) ; R. Huchon, *Mrs. Montagu* (1907) ; A. Barbeau, *Life and Letters at Bath in the Eighteenth Century* (1904) ; Lewis Melville, *Society at Tunbridge Wells* (1912).

For rural life, Lord Ernle, *English Farming Past and Present* (4th ed. 1927), chs. vii–x ; A. Johnson, *The Disappearance of the Small Landowner* (1909) ; J. L. and B. Hammond, *The Village Labourer* (4th ed., 1927) ;

W. Hasbach, *The English Agricultural Labourer* (1908); E. Davies, article on ' The Small Landowner ' in *Economic History Review*, 1927. For town life Defoe's *The Complete English Tradesman* ; J. L. and B. Hammond, *The Town Labourer* (1925) ; M. D. George, *London Life in the Eighteenth Century* (1925) ; Dorothy Marshall, *The English Poor in the Eighteenth Century* (1926).

For the beginnings of the Industrial Revolution, P. Mantoux, *La Révolution industrielle* (Paris, 1906) ; A. Toynbee, *The Industrial Revolution of the Eighteenth Century in England* ; Louis Moffit, *England on the Eve of the Industrial Revolution* (1925); S. Smiles, *The Early Engineers*, i.e. Brindley, Watt, &c. (3 vols., 1861–2).

CHAPTER IV

(a) *Original authorities.*

Bishop Burnet, *History of My Own Times.* (Best edition. 6 vols., 1833.)

Dean Swift, *The Conduct of the Allies* ; *History of the Four last Years of the Queen* ; *The Behaviour of the Queen's Last Ministry* ; *Journal to Stella* ; *Correspondence.*

Bolingbroke, *Letters and Correspondence* ; *Letter to Sir William Windham. The Wentworth Papers* (1883).

Historical MSS. Commission publications—*Buccleuch MSS.*, vol. ii (for correspondence of Duke of Shrewsbury); *Portland MSS.*, vols. iv and v (for Harley Correspondence) ; *Bath MSS.*, vol. i (for correspondence of Godolphin, Marlborough, &c.).

(b) *Secondary authorities.*

John, Lord Campbell, *Lives of the Lord Chancellors*, vol. iv (for Somers).

E. S. Roscoe, *Robert Harley, Earl of Oxford* (1902). Hardly an adequate biography.

W. Sichel, *Bolingbroke and his Times* (2 vols., 1901, 1902).

W. Bagehot, *Biographical Studies.* Contains an excellent essay on Bolingbroke.

K. Feiling, *History of the Tory Party* (1924), chapters xiii–xvi.

Theresa Merz, *The Whig Junto* (1907).

There are no adequate lives of Wharton, Orford, or Halifax. There are histories of the reign of Queen Anne by T. Somerville, Earl Stanhope, W. D. Wyon, and Herbert Paul, but nothing is better than the opening chapter in Lecky and the relevant portion of Leadam (*supra*, chapter ii).

CHAPTER V

(a) *Original authorities.*

For the general history of the period, the *Memoirs* of Hervey and of Horace Walpole and the *Letters* of Chesterfield : and in the H. M. C. publications the *Onslow, Townshend,* and *Carlisle MSS.* ; the *Diary of Lord Chancellor Cowper* (1833), and of *Mary, Countess Cowper* (1864).

Coxe's *Memoirs of Sir Robert Walpole* (3 vols.) contains a large selection from his correspondence.

(b) *Secondary authorities.*

Lord Morley, *Walpole* (Twelve English Statesmen Series).
P. Vaucher, *Robert Walpole et la Politique de Fleury* (Paris, 1924).
W. Ernst, *Life of Chesterfield* (1906).

CHAPTER VI

(a) *Original authorities.*
The *Newcastle* and *Hardwicke Papers* in the Brit. Mus. ; H. Walpole's
Memoirs and *Letters.*

(b) *Secondary authorities.*

W. Coxe. *Memoirs of the Pelham Administration* (2 vols., 1829).
G. Harris, *Life of Lord Chancellor Hardwicke* (3 vols., 1847).
P. C. Yorke, *Life of Lord Chancellor Hardwicke* (3 vols., 1913). This is a
     most important work, containing copious transcripts from the *New-
     castle* and *Hardwicke MSS.*
Basil Williams, ' The Eclipse of the Yorkes ' in *Roy. Hist. Soc. Transactions,*
     Third Series, vol. ii.
There is no biography of Newcastle. No one has had the courage to
tackle the 800 folio volumes of his correspondence, which form only a part
of the lavish materials available.

CHAPTER VII

There is a full bibliography of the sources for the life of Pitt in Basil
Williams's standard *Life of William Pitt* (2 vols., 1915). Chatham's papers
are in the Record Office ; a selection from them in the *Chatham Correspondence* (4 vols., 1839). J. Almon's *Anecdotes of Lord Chatham* is based on
contemporary information and is useful for Pitt's speeches. W. D. Green's
biography in the Heroes of the Nations series has been superseded by Basil
Williams's larger work; A. von Ruville's biography (English trans., 3 vols.,
1907) is based on valuable research, but is characterized by a rather perverse
hostility to Pitt. Lord Rosebery deals attractively with Pitt's younger
days in his *Chatham, his Early Life and Connections* (1910). For Pitt's war
policy, J. S. Corbett. *England in the Seven Years War* (2 vols., 1907). For
Pitt's attitude to parties see D. A. Winstanley, *Personal and Party Government* (1910), and his *Lord Chatham and the Whig Opposition* (1912).

CHAPTER VIII

The Earl of Albemarle's *Memoirs of the Marquis of Rockingham* contains
some original correspondence, but is not very satisfactory otherwise. For
Burke, his collected *Works* (8 vols., 1901–6), and his *Correspondence, 1744–97*
(4 vols., 1910). The brief life by Lord Morley in the English Men of Letters
series is admirable. For Fox the *Memorials and Correspondence of C. J.
Fox*, edited by Lord John Russell (4 vols., 1853); the brilliant short study by
Sir G. O. Trevelyan, *The Early History of C. J. Fox* (1880), and his *George III*

and Charles Fox ; and J. L. Hammond, *C. J. Fox : a political study* (1903). For Wilkes, the *Correspondence of John Wilkes*, with a memoir by John Almon (5 vols., 1805) ; and a *Life* by H. Bleackley (1917). The early history of the parliamentary reform movement may be studied in the numerous pamphlets of Major John Cartwright and his *Life and Correspondence*, edited by F. D. Cartwright (2 vols., 1826) ; in the *Political Papers* of Christopher Wyvill (6 vols., 1794–1802) ; and in the standard secondary authority on the subject, G. S. Veitch, *The Genesis of the Parliamentary Reform* (1913).

CHAPTER IX

General histories of the English Church for this period are vols. v and vi in Hunt and Stephens's *History of the English Church* (by W. H. Hutton and G. Overton and Relton, respectively) ; Abbey and Overton's *The English Church in the Eighteenth Century* (1896), and J. Wickham Legg's *English Church Life from the Restoration to the Tractarian Movement* (1914). See also J. Beresford, *The Diary of a Country Parson : the Rev. J. Woodforde* (3 vols., 1924–7). For the history of the Dissenters, H. S. Skeats, *History of the Free Churches of England, 1688–1851* (1868), and W. H. Clark's *History of English Nonconformity*, vol. ii. For the Roman Catholics, H. Butler's *Memorials of the English Catholics* (4 vols., 1819–21), vol. ii ; G. Oliver's *Collections illustrating the History of the Catholic Religion in Cornwall, Devon, Dorset, Somerset, Wilts., Gloucestershire* (1857).

The Convocation controversy at the opening of the century evoked a considerable pamphlet literature, e.g. Atterbury's *The Rights, Powers, and Privileges of an English Convocation vindicated* (1700) ; White Kennet's *Ecclesiastical Synods and Parliamentary Convocations* (1701) ; Gibson's *Synodus Anglicana* (1702).

For Atterbury see his *Epistolary Correspondence, Speeches, &c.* (5 vols., 1783–96) ; many of his letters in *Stuart Papers* (H. M. C.) ; and H. C. Beeching's *Francis Atterbury* (1909). For Burnet his *History of His Own Times* and T. S. Clarke and H. C. Foxcroft, *Life of Bishop Burnet* (1907). For Gibson the biography by N. Sykes (1926). Hoadly's *Works* (3 vols.) were published in 1783 ; there is no biography. For Secker his *Works*, with life by Beilby Porteus (6 vols., 1811). There is a collected edition of Warburton's *Works* with a prefatory biographical note (12 vols., 1811). There are several editions of Joseph Butler's *Works*, one edited by W. E. Gladstone (2 vols., 1896), one by J. H. Bernard (2 vols., 1900), and a biography by W. A. Spooner (1901). There is more than one edition, also, of the *Works* of Thomas Wilson. That of 1847–63 in 7 volumes includes a Life by Keble. For Law, his *Works* (9 vols., 1892–3), and J. H. Overton, *William Law, Nonjuror and Mystic* (1881).

There are several editions of John Wesley's *Works*, the third in 14 vols., 1829–31 ; also of his *Journal*, the standard edition being that of 1909–16, in 8 vols. There are numerous books about Wesley and the Wesleyan movement, of which the following may be cited—R. Southey, *Life of Wesley* (3rd ed., 1846) ; L. Tyerman, *Life and Times of John Wesley* (1870–1) ; Julia Wedgwood, *John Wesley and the Evangelical Reaction of the Eighteenth*

Century (1870) ; J. H. Overton, *John Wesley* (1891). See also Tyerman's *The Oxford Methodists* (1873), and Overton's *The Evangelical Revival in the Eighteenth Century* (new ed. 1900).

Watts's *Works* were published in 1812–13 (9 vols.) ; Doddridge's (with memoir) in 1802–5, in 10 vols., and his *Correspondence and Diary* in 5 vols., in 1829–31. Price published numerous works, the principal being a *Review of the principal Questions and Difficulties in Morals* (1756) ; *Observations on the Importance of the American Revolution* ; and *The State of Public Debts and Finances*. There is no collected edition. A collection of Priestley's *Theological and Miscellaneous Works* (26 vols., 1817–32) was edited by J. T. Rutt, the author of *The Life and Correspondence of Joseph Priestley* (2 vols., 1831–2), but there is no collected edition of the scientific works.

CHAPTER X

For Oglethorpe, *Brief account of the establishment of the Colony of Georgia under General James Oglethorpe* (1735) ; R. Knight, *Memoirs of Oglethorpe* (1867) ; Austin Dobson, *A Paladin of Philanthropy* (1899) ; and the references in Boswell's *Life of Johnson*.

For Howard his own *State of the Prisons in England and Wales* (1777), and his *Account of the principal Lazarettos in Europe* (2nd ed., 1791) ; and J. B. Brown's *Memoirs of Howard* (2nd ed., 1823).

CHAPTER XI

(a) *The history of the Press.*

J. B. Williams, *History of English Journalism to the foundation of the Gazette* (1908). For the early history.

H. R. Fox Bourne, *English Newspapers* (2 vols., 1887).

Nathan Drake, *Essays illustrative of the Tatler, Spectator, and Guardian* (3 vols., 1805).

Essays illustrative of the Rambler, Adventurer, and Idler (2 vols., 1809–10).

Catalogue of Periodicals in Hope Collection in the Bodleian.

Crave and Kaye's *List of Periodicals* (Press of Univ. of California).

(b) *Defoe.*

There is no complete edition of Defoe's Works ; indeed such are the difficulties in identifying all his contributions to the Press that there probably never will be one. There is a collection of *Novels and Miscellaneous Works* (20 vols., 1840–1), and another with the same title in Bohn's Library (7 vols., 1887–93). There is a new edition of Defoe's *Works* now in course of publication by Blackwell.

See also :

Later Stuart Tracts (ed. G. A. Aitkin, 1903), for some of Defoe's most famous pamphlets.

W. Lee, *Life of Defoe* (1869).

(c) *Johnson.*

There are numerous editions of his *Works* ; those of 1801–10 (12 vols.) and 1825 (6 vols.) contain A. Murphy's *Essay on the Life and Genius of Samuel Johnson* (1792), useful on Johnson's methods as a reporter of debates. The best edition of Boswell's *Life* is that edited by G. Birkbeck Hill (6 vols., 1887).

See also :

Birkbeck Hill, *Johnson : his friends and critics* (1878).
Leslie Stephen, *Johnson* (English Men of Letters Series).
Sir W. Raleigh, *Six Essays on Johnson* (1910).
A. Lyell Reade, *Johnsonian Gleanings*, Parts III, IV, V.

CHAPTER XII

Allan Cunningham, *Lives of Eminent British Painters, Sculptors, Architects* (revd. ed., 3 vols., 1879–80).
C. R. Grundy, *English Art in the Eighteenth Century* (1928).

(a) *Painting and Engraving.*

R. and S. Redgrave, *A Century of Painters of the English School* (2nd ed., 1890).
Austin Dobson, *William Hogarth* (1907 ed.).
Thackeray, *The English Humorists of the Eighteenth Century* (on Hogarth).
Anecdotes of Hogarth by himself, with essays by Walpole, Lamb, &c. (1833).
Laurence Binyon, *The Drawings and Engravings of William Blake* (1922).
Darrell Figgis, *The Paintings of William Blake* (1922).
Irene Langridge, *William Blake* (1904).
Sir Joshua Reynolds, *Literary Works* (Bohn, 2 vols., 1890, 1896).
—— *Discourses delivered to Students of the Royal Academy* (with introd. by Roger Fry, 1905).
Sir W. Armstrong, *Reynolds* (1900).
—— *Gainsborough and his Place in English Art* (1894, 1904).
Sir Herbert Maxwell, *George Romney* (1902).
T. E. Ward and W. Roberts, *Romney : a biographical and critical essay* (1904).
T. Wright, *Life of Richard Wilson* (1824).
Frank Rutter, *Wilson and Farington* (1923).
A. W. Tuer, *Bartolozzi and his Works* (2nd ed., 1885).
W. Sandby, *Thomas and Paul Sandby* (1892).
C. E. Hughes, *Early English Watercolour* (1913).
G. Goodwin, *McArdell* (1903).
M. C. Salaman, *The Old Engravers of England* (1906).
W. T. Whitley, *Artists and their Friends in England, 1700–99* (1928).

(b) *Architecture.*

R. Blomfield, *History of Renaissance Architecture in England* (2 vols., 1897).
G. Webb, Introduction to vol. iv of the *Complete Works of Sir John Vanbrugh* (Nonesuch Press, 1928).

G. A. Gotch, *The English Home, Charles I—George IV* (1918).
H. Field and M. Bunney, *English Domestic Architecture of the Seventeenth and Eighteenth Centuries* (new ed., 1928).
Sir William Chambers, *Treatise on . . . Civil Architecture* (1791).
Works on Architecture of R. and J. Adam (3 vols. reproduced, 1901–2).

(c) *Sculpture.*

Mrs. Esdaile, *English Monumental Sculpture since the Renaissance* (1927).
J. T. Smith, *Nollekens and his Times* (ed. G. W. Whitten, 2 vols., 1920).

(d) *Ceramics and Porcelain.*

A. H. Church, *English Earthenware* (1884).
—— *English Porcelain* (1885).
W. Burton, *History and Description of English Pottery* (1904).
—— *History and Description of English Porcelain* (1902).
B. Rackham and H. Read, *English Pottery* (1924).
S. Smiles, *Josiah Wedgwood : his personal history* (1894).
> Lady Farrer has edited Wedgwood's *Correspondence* (2 vols., 1903 ; 1 vol., 1906).

(e) *Furniture.*

Percy Macquoid, *History of English Furniture* (4 vols., 1904–8).
Herbert Ceszinsky, *English Furniture of the Eighteenth Century* (3 vols., 1911).
J. M. Bell, *Chippendale, Sheraton, and Hepplewhite Designs reproduced* (1900).

CHAPTER XIII

(a) *Drama.*

A. W. Ward, *History of English Dramatic Literature to the death of Anne* (new ed., 3 vols., 1899).
Allardyce Nicoll, *History of Early Seventeenth Century Drama, 1700–50* (1925).
Dr. John Doran, *Their Majesties' Servants ; Annals of the English Stage from Betterton to Kean* (ed. R. W. Lowe, 3 vols., 1888).
P. Fitzgerald, *New History of the English Stage from the Restoration to the Liberty of the Theatres* (2 vols., 1882).
An Apology for the Life of Mr. Colley Cibber . . . written by himself (new ed., 2 vols., 1889).
Memoirs of Richard Cumberland, by himself (2 vols., 1807).
Private Correspondence of Garrick with celebrated Persons (2 vols., 1831–2).
W. L. Cross, *The History of Henry Fielding* (1910).
Austin Dobson, *Life of Goldsmith* (1888).
Ll. C. Sanders, *Life of Sheridan* (1890).
W. Sichel, *Life of Sheridan* (2 vols., 1909).
A. Murphy, *Life of Garrick* (1801).
P. Fitzgerald, *Life of Garrick* (1868).

Mrs. C. Parsons, *Life of Garrick* (1906).
—— *The Incomparable Siddons* (1909).

(b) *Music*.

Ernest Walker, *History of Music in England* (2nd ed., 1924).
Fanny Burney, *Memoirs of Dr. Burney* (3 vols., 1832).
Dr. C. Burney, *History of Music* (4 vols., 1782–9).
—— *The State of Music in France and Italy* (2 vols., 1773).

CHAPTER XIV

In addition to the works on Colonial history cited in the General Bibliography, the following are useful for the Canadian problem discussed in this chapter : A. G. Bradley, *Lord Dorchester*—i.e. Sir Guy Carleton (1907) ; R. Coupland, *The Quebec Act* (1927) ; H. E. Egerton and W. L. Grant, *Canadian Constitutional Development : Shcwn by Speeches and Dispatches* (1907).

For India in addition to works already cited in General Bibliography : *Clive MSS.* in H. M. C. rept. vi, appendix ; Sir G. Forrest, *Life of Lord Clive* (2 vols., 1918) ; H. Dodwell, *Dupleix and Clive* (1920) ; *Selections from Letters, Despatches, etc., in the Foreign Department of the Government of India, 1772–85* (edited by Sir G. Forrest, 3 vols., Calcutta, 1890) ; *Selections from the State Papers of the Governors-General of India,* also edited by Forrest (2 vols., 1910) ; Burke's speeches on the impeachment of Warren Hastings in his *Works,* vol. vii ; M. Monckton Jones, *Warren Hastings in Bengal, 1772–4* (1918).

CHAPTER XV

For the military history of the period generally, the Hon. Sir J. Fortescue's *History of the British Army,* vol. i. For Marlborough, his *Letters and Dispatches* (ed. Sir J. Murray, 5 vols., 1845) ; W. Coxe, *Memoirs of Marlborough,* with his original correspondence (3 vols., Bohn) ; and T. Lediard's contemporary biography (3 vols., 1736). The French version of the wars of Marlborough may be found in De Quincy's *Histoire Militaire du règne de Louis le Grand* (1726), and the *Mémoires de Villars* (vol. lxix in the Petitot collection, also 6 vols., 1884–1904). Of recent studies on Marlborough the best are by F. Taylor, *The Wars of Marlborough, 1702–9* (2 vols., 1921), and C. T. Atkinson's biography (new ed., 1924). For the second Earl of Stair, who commanded at Dettingen, *The Stair Annals* (2 vols., 1875), vol. ii ; for the Duke of Cumberland, two volumes by the Hon. Evan Charteris, one (1913) dealing with the period 1721–48, the other (n. d.) with the Seven Years War. For Wolfe, A. Doughty's *The Siege of Quebec and the Battle of the Plains of Abraham* (6 vols., Quebec, 1901), and A. G. Bradley's *Wolfe* (1895). For the American War and its generals, C. Stedman, *History of the American War* (2 vols., 1794)—the author served under Howe, Clinton, and Cornwallis ; Gen. J. Burgoyne's *A State of the Expedition from Canada* (1779) ; and *The Clinton-Cornwallis Controversy* (ed. B. F. Stevens, 2 vols., 1888).

CHAPTER XVI

(a) *Original authorities.*

Navy Records Society :
Vol. iii. *Letters of Sir S. H. Hood*, 1781–3 (1895).
Vol. ix. *Journal of Sir George Rooke*, 1700–2 (1896).
Vol. xxix. *Fighting Instructions*, 1530–1816, edited by J. S. Corbett (1905).
Vol. xxxv. *Signals and Instructions*, 1776–94, edited by J. S. Corbett (1908).
Vol. xlii. *Papers relating to the loss of Minorca*, edited by Admiral H. W. Richmond (1913).
Vol. lii, liii. *Life of Sir John Leake* (1920).
Richard Walter, *Anson's Voyage round the World* (15th ed., 1780).
John Clerk of Eldin, *An Essay on Naval Tactics* (1797).

(b) *Secondary authorities.*

Laird Clowes, *History of the Royal Navy* (1897–1902), vols. ii and iii.
John Campbell, *Lives of the Admirals* (8 vols., 1818), vols. iii–vi.
A. T. Mahan, *Influence of Sea Power on History*, 1660–1783 (8th ed., 1889).
—— *Types of Naval Officers*, i.e. Hawke, Rodney, Howe, &c. (1902).
Sir J. K. Laughton and others, *From Howard to Nelson* (12 biographies, 1899).
Sir J. Barrow, *Life of George, Lord Anson* (1839).
—— *The Mutiny of the Bounty* (n. d.).
M. Burrows, *Life of Admiral Lord Hawke* (1896).
Maj.-General Mundy, *Life and Correspondence of Admiral Rodney* (1830).
D. Hannay, *Rodney* (1891).
Sir J. S. Corbett, *England in the Mediterranean* (1904).
—— *England in the Seven Years War* (1907).
Rear-Admiral H. W. Richmond, *The Navy in the War of 1739–48* (1920).
B. Tunstall, *Admiral Byng and the Loss of Minorca* (1928).

INDEX